Making History

Years of Change

1700 to the present

BRITISH SOCIAL AND ECONOMIC HISTORY

John Patrick

Formerly Lecturer in History
Aberdeen College of Education

Mollie Packham

Formerly Head of History
Falmer School, Brighton

John Murray

Making History

Already published in this series

The Age of Invasions:
    Britain 55 BC – AD 1200
Struggles for Power: Britain 1300–1700
The Age of Empire:
    The British Overseas 1700–1900

In preparation

The Twentieth-Century World

Cover
top left: Chartists' procession to Kennington Common, 1848
bottom left: London miners' wives' demonstration, 1984
top right: the funeral of the Suffragette, Emily Davison, 1913
bottom right: the Jarrow Crusade, 1936

© Mollie Packham and John Patrick 1989

First published 1989
by John Murray (Publishers) Ltd,
50 Albemarle Street, London W1X 4BD

Typeset by Phoenix Photosetting, Chatham
Printed and bound in Hong Kong by
Colorcraft Ltd.

British Library Cataloguing in Publication Data
Packham, Mollie
  Years of change: British social and economic history, 1700 to the
  present day.
  1. Great Britain, 1714–
  I. Title   II. Patrick, John, *1931–*
  941.07

ISBN 0–7195–4357–6

Contents

Acknowledgements

The maps were drawn by Anne Craig, and all other pieces of artwork by Ian Foulis Associates.

Thanks are due to the following for permission to reproduce copyright photographs: p. 149, Aerofilm; p. 97, T & R Annan and Sons; p. 156 (top right), Atomic Energy Authority; pp. 193, 194, Austin Rover; pp. 11, 15, 38, 89 (bottom), 109, 110 (bottom right), 118 (right), 137, 230, 232 (left), 248, cover (top and bottom right), BBC Hulton Picture Library; p. 243, Barnardo Film Library; p. 189 (right), B.T. Batsford Ltd; p. 214, Birmingham Museum and Art Gallery; pp. 204 (right; top and bottom), 257, 258, 259, Birmingham Reference Libraries; pp. 75, 85, Bristol Museum; p. 253, Bristol United Press Ltd; pp. 197, 198, British Airways; pp. 169, 170, British Coal; p. 67 (bottom), British Museum, Trustees of; pp. 177, 178, British Steel; p. 59, Cambridge University Library; p. 255, Centre for the study of Cartoons and Caricature, Canterbury; p. 223, The Cork Examiner; p. 45, Neil Cossens, *BP Book of Industrial Archeology* (Peter Stoddart), published by David and Charles; p. 186, Courtaulds PLC; p. 210, Cumbernauld Development Corporation; p. 221, The Cutty Sark Society; p. 154, (top left), Electricity Council; cover (top left), Mary Evans Picture Library; cover (bottom left), Format (Jenny Matthews); pp. 23, 103, 113, Fotomas; p. 174, Lewis C Grant Ltd and Dundee University Library; pp. 218, 240, Guildhall Library Museum; p. 61, Hamilton Public Library; p. 190, ICI; pp. 81, 128 (left), 141, Illustrated London News; pp. 148, 159, 216, 225 (both), Imperial War Museum; p. 217, Intercity; p. 134. International Planned Parenthood Federation; pp. 37, 48, Ironbridge Gorge Museum Trust; p. 5, Isleham, Vicar of; p. 123, Islington Libraries; p. 157, F. Krupp Historisches Archiv; p. 250 (both), Labour Party; pp. 154 (left), 205 (left), Leeds City Libraries; p. 143 (bottom), Leicestershire Museums Service; p. 122 Arthur Lockwood; p. 247 (right), London Museum; p. 220, London Transport Museum; p. 195, Lucas Industries plc; pp. 51, 106 (bottom), *The Age of Turnpikes* published by Luton Museum; pp. 155, 236, Purcell's *History of the Twentieth Century* published by Macdonald; pp. 52, 199 (both), Chris E Makepeace; pp. 29, 33, 35 (both), 86, 88, 89 (top), 114, 115, 116, 118 (left) 173 (right), 179, 232 (right), The Mansell Collection; p. 233, The Marconi Company; p. 89 (bottom), Museum of Mankind; p. 229 (all), National Motor Museum, Beaulieu; p. 51, National Museum of Wales; pp. 9, 74, National Portrait Gallery; p. 211 Newcastle-upon-Tyne, City Engineer; pp. 106 (top), 143 (top), Norfolk Museums; p. 226, Pakistan International Airlines (PIA); pp. 20, 28, 40, John Patrick; p. 181, Photo Source; p. 156 (bottom left), Planet Earth Pictures; pp. 6, 26, Public Records Office; p. 17 (both), Rothamsted Experimental Station; p. 140, Royal Institute of British Architects; pp. 43, 67 (top right and left), 73, 77 (bottom), 80, 83, 173 (left), 187, 213, 222 (left), 235 (top left), Science Museum; p. 180, Strathclyde Regional Archives; pp. 147, 167, 168, 182 (both), 200, 222 (right), 224, 237 (both), 251, Topham Picture Library; p. 60, Trinity College, Cambridge; p. 91, University of Reading Institute of Agricultural History; p. 50 *The Industrial Revolution* by M E Beggs Humphreys, Hugh Gregor, Darlow Humphries, published by Unwin Hyman; p. 127, Victoria and Albert Museum; p. 247 (top left), Wayland Press; p. 72, Wedgwood Museum, Trustees of; p. 235 (bottom left) Wiener Library; p. 104, Wellcome Institute Library; p. 156 (top left), Welsh Development Agency; p. 205 (right), Alan Wilson; p. 108, Wisbech and Fenland Museum.

The authors and publishers are also grateful to the following for permission to reproduce copyright material: p. 181, R J Unstead, *Britain in the 20th Century*, A & C Black (Publishers) Ltd; p. 168 Patrick Renshaw, *The General Strike*, Curtis Brown Ltd; p. 181 Ronald Blythe, *The Age of Illusion*, Hamish Hamilton Ltd; p. 154, R J Unstead, *The Incredible Century*, Macdonald; p. 137, John Prebble, *The Highland Clearances*, Martin Secker & Warburg Ltd; p. 172 Times Newspapers, 'Last Gasp of the Big Spenders'; p. 138, Times Educational Supplement; p. 225, K Poolman, *Zeppelins over England*, Unwin Hyman Ltd.

We are also grateful to: BBC Enterprises, for permission to quote interview material from P. Pagnamanta and R. Overy, *All Our Working Lives* (1984); Century Hutchinson for permission to quote material from Leslie Baly, *Scrapbook 1900–1914*; and *The Guardian* for permission to quote the extracts on pp. 150 and 200.

Introduction

Aim

In *Years of Change* our aim is to study the rise and decline of Britain as an industrial power since 1700, and in particular to explore how the lives of people in Britain have changed as a result.

Coverage

We have not aimed to provide an all-inclusive social and economic history of Britain since 1700. Instead we cover enough key topics to enable readers to tackle any of the published British Social and Economic History GCSE syllabuses. By selecting such key topics we can tackle each one in some depth, and provide a wide range of studies to help users practise all the relevant historical skills required by the GCSE.

Studies

Each study is carefully designed to develop particular historical skills or concepts within the domains defined by the History Working Party of the Secondary Examinations Council.

To help you select a range of studies which cope with all the varied requirements of the GCSE each study is marked with one or more of the following symbols. These indicate which particular skills or concepts the study seeks to develop.

K The skills needed to recall, select and deploy historical knowledge or frame an inquiry.

Ev The skills needed to assess and interpret historical sources.

Em The ability to empathise: to see events from the perspective of people of the past.

Ca The concepts of cause and consequence.

Ch The concepts of continuity and change.

S The concepts of similarity and difference.

Since many of the categories overlap however, a study may well develop more skills and concepts than the symbols indicate.

Other study helps

At the end of each chapter there is a set of *Recall* questions, including written work and discussions, which look back over the content of that chapter. In addition a computer disc of multiple choice questions based on material in this book is available from Akadimias, University of Wales, Bangor. It should prove useful to students whose exams include multiple choice questions, or to teachers who find such questions a useful way to test factual recall and conceptual thinking.

Course work

You can use the studies in the book as a basis for course work in a variety of ways. For example, short studies developing empathy, or dealing with historical evidence can be combined to form a course-work unit. Alternatively, longer studies such as the Lancashire Riots (page 34) or the field study (page 257) might form a complete unit in themselves.

1
Britain from 1700 to 1851: Introduction

Part One
Defoe's Britain

DEFOE AND HIS TRAVELS

At the beginning of the eighteenth century, Daniel Defoe, a famous English journalist and novelist, went on several long journeys around Britain. Defoe travelled on horseback. It was easier than walking, but not much quicker because the roads were so bad. In 1724 he published an account of his travels.

The three largest towns

Defoe set out from London, the biggest city in the world with about 750,000 inhabitants. It had already swallowed up several places such as Deptford and Islington which had once been separate villages. Defoe noticed that London was still growing, with 'new squares and new streets rising up every day'.

London was at least ten times as large as any other town in Britain. It had grown so big because it had good harbours, several markets, many industries and was also the capital city. Bristol and Norwich, the next largest towns, were also ports.

The countryside

When he left London, Defoe travelled mostly through the countryside, out of sight of any town. Some areas were wild and uncultivated. In Kent, Sussex and Hampshire he rode through miles of woodland. In the north of England he toiled over 'barren and frightful' moorland. The south and Midlands were the most densely populated areas. Here he passed through numerous small villages, many surrounded by open fields, looking much as they had in the Middle Ages. Often his travels took him past large country houses. These were the homes of the aristocracy, and they were increasing in size and number as the country grew richer.

Defoe took farming and the countryside for granted, and rarely wrote much about them. He was more interested in industry and trade. Yet the vast majority of British people lived in the countryside, and got their living from farming.

Market towns

The countryside was dotted with towns. Most of them, such as Cleaveland in Yorkshire (Illustration 1) consisted of a market place and a few streets of half-timbered or, in some areas, stone-built houses. (In half-timbered houses the wooden framework is exposed.) Every town had at least one church and

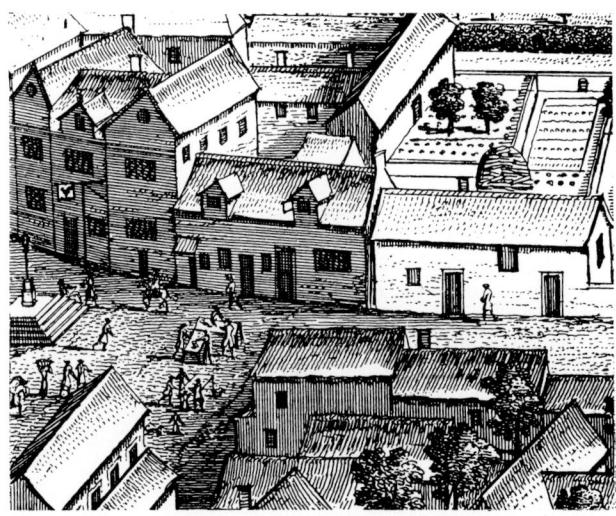

Illustration 1 An engraving made in 1720 of the centre of Cleaveland, a small market town in Yorkshire.

several inns. Many still had the remains of their medieval walls.

Defoe visited many market towns. He noticed that the goods on sale varied from place to place, depending on what the local people produced. For instance, the people in the valleys surrounding Leeds in West Yorkshire kept sheep and made cloth

from their wool. So twice a week a market was held in Leeds where the clothiers (people who make or sell cloth) sold their produce.

When they had sold their cloth, the clothiers went to the provision market to buy food. Defoe noticed that they grew hardly any corn and produced very little beef or mutton (mutton is the meat from

Study

1 Copy the map and the key.
2 Label: London; Norwich.
3 Using the symbols in the key, mark in regions where Defoe travelled *i* through woodland; *ii* across moorland.
4 Write 'open fields' in the region where this system of farming was still carried on.

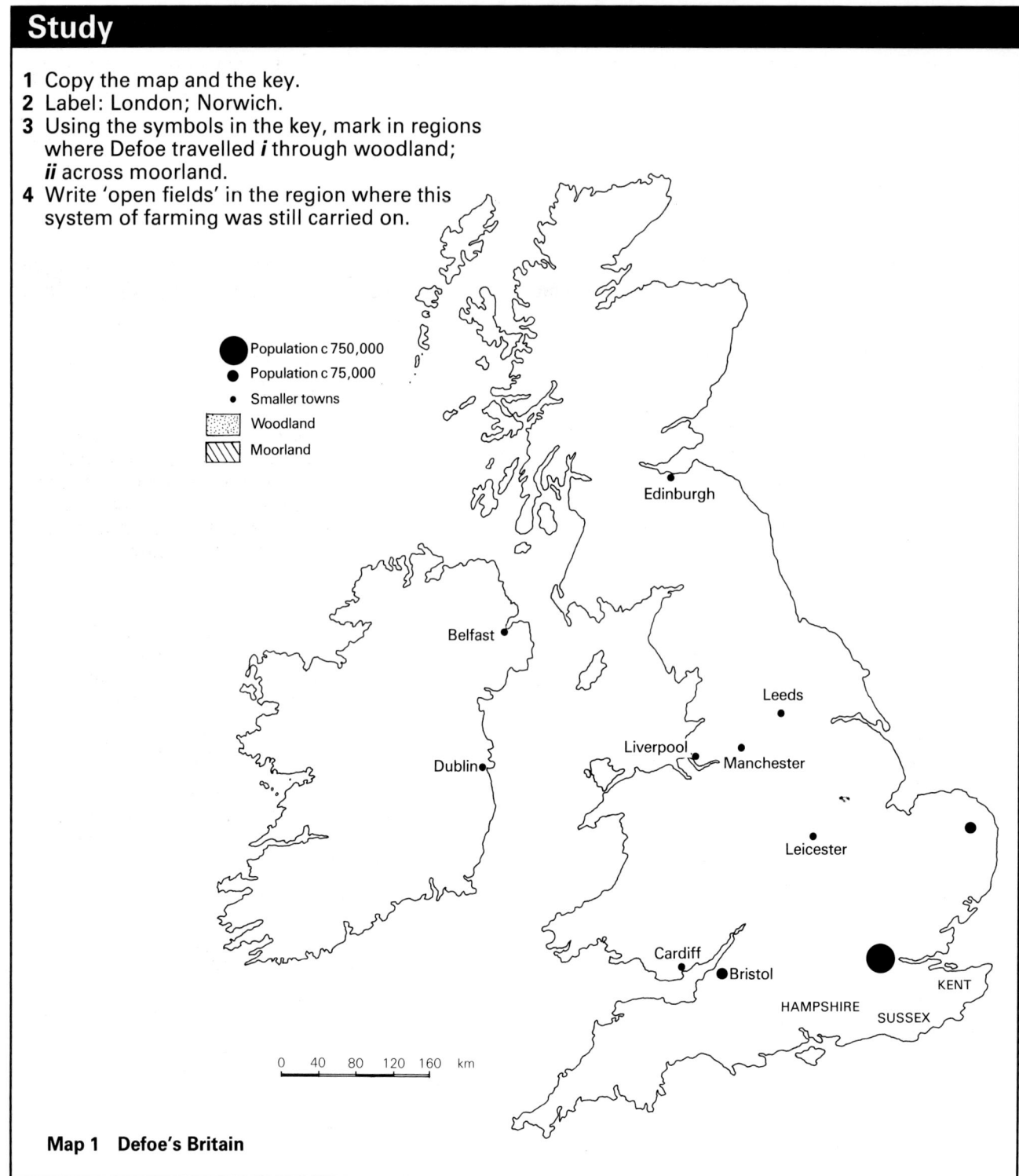

Population c 750,000
Population c 75,000
• Smaller towns
Woodland
Moorland

Edinburgh

Belfast

Leeds

Liverpool
Manchester

Dublin

Leicester

Cardiff
Bristol

KENT

HAMPSHIRE
SUSSEX

0   40   80   120 160   km

Map 1   Defoe's Britain

sheep). So they had to buy corn grown in Lincolnshire, Nottinghamshire and East Yorkshire; sheep, cattle and butter from North and East Yorkshire and cheese from Cheshire. In this way, farmers over a wide area benefited from the West Yorkshire cloth trade.

Manufacturing towns

Some English towns were manufacturing centres, using raw materials from close at hand. In Leicester, Defoe found 'multitudes of people' using wool from local sheep to weave stockings. In Nottingham, in addition to stocking weavers, there were potters using local clay to produce mugs and pots.

The manufacturing town that impressed Defoe most was Manchester. Its chief industry was making cloth out of raw cotton imported from India. Manchester was growing fast and with 10,000 inhabitants was among the biggest towns in England. But, because it had grown up recently, it had no mayor or corporation, and sent no members to Parliament. Defoe described it as 'the greatest mere village in England'.

Changing Britain 1700–1851

Defoe realised that Britain was changing. He noticed that he had to keep adding to his description to keep it up to date. But he can never have imagined the changes which were to take place in the next 150 years.

The first section of this book shows how and why these changes took place and how they affected the people of Britain.

Study

In this study you will:
Ev assess some primary and secondary sources and consider how we use them as evidence.

Sources

A source is a starting point for an investigation into life in the past. The sources in this book contain information about life in Britain since 1700. This information can be used as evidence of what Britain was like during those years. Read the source below.

Source 1A

Bideford is a pleasant, clean, well-built town; the more ancient street which lies next the river, is very pleasant, where is the bridge, a very noble quay, and the customs-house. But beside this, there is a new spacious street . . . well built . . . and . . . inhabited with . . . wealthy merchants, who trade to most parts of the trading world.

Daniel Defoe, *A Tour through the Whole Island of Great Britain* (1727).

1 Which of these statements about Bideford in the eighteenth century *i* can, *ii* cannot be supported by evidence from the source?
—Bideford was a port.
—The town was prosperous.
—The buildings were made of stone.
Give reasons for your answers.

Primary sources

Daniel Defoe wrote his *Tour* between 1724 and 1727. His book is a source of information about Britain at the beginning of the eighteenth century. Because Defoe lived at the time he was writing about and had travelled through much of Britain, his book is a *primary* or first-hand source.

Secondary sources

John Patrick, one of the authors of this book, used information from Defoe's book when he was preparing the section on Defoe's Britain that you have just read. This account is a *secondary* source of information on the eighteenth century. The author has no first-hand knowledge of what life was like at that time, so he based his ideas on what he read in Defoe and other sources for that period. Some parts of the chapter are printed in inverted commas to show that they are copied directly from Defoe.

2 Look through the section of Defoe's Britain and give an example of:
  a an extract from a primary source;
  b three or four sentences from a secondary source.
3 If you find that a primary and secondary source about Bideford in the 1720s contradict each other, would this prove that:
  a the primary source was unreliable;
  b the secondary source was unreliable?
Give reasons for your answer.
4 How might you decide which was the case?

Part Two
Britain in 1851

Study

In some ways, Britain in 1851 was a very different place from the country that Defoe had travelled round in the 1720s. Use the information in Britain 1700–1851 and the maps below to work out some of the ways in which Britain:

Ch had changed between 1720 and 1851;
remained the same.

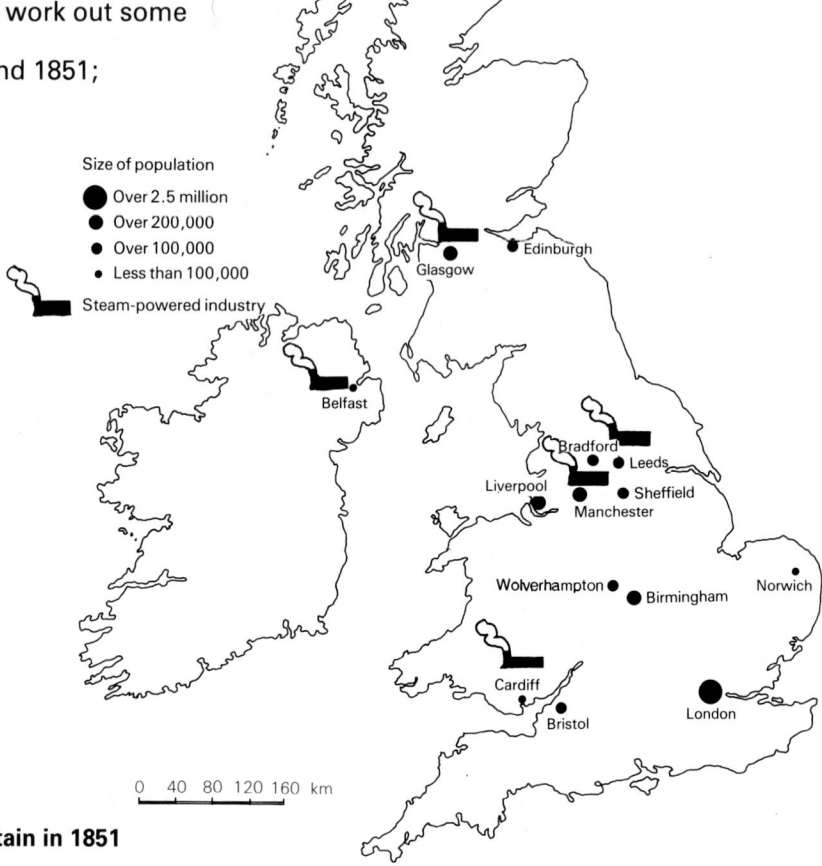

Size of population

● Over 2.5 million
● Over 200,000
● Over 100,000
• Less than 100,000

Steam-powered industry

Map 2   Britain in 1851

0 40 80 120 160 km

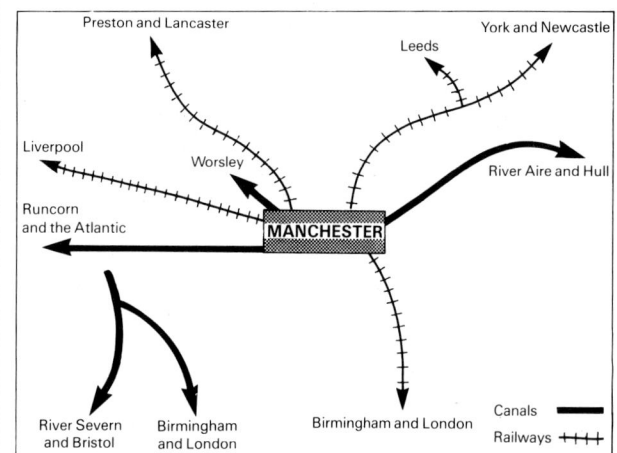

Map 3   Manchester's canals and railway links, 1851

1 Copy the headings below:
   Change and Continuity 1700–1851
   Britain in 1700   *Britain in 1851*
2 List the statements below in the column headed *Britain in 1700*
   a London was by far the largest city in Britain.
   b Manchester was an important industrial centre.
   c Most people lived in the country.
   d Travel was slow and difficult.
   e Britain was becoming richer.
3 Consider each statement that you have listed. If you think that it was still true in 1851, put a tick in the column headed *Britain in 1851*. If you think it was no longer true, put a cross.
4 Ask one person to read his or her answers to the class, giving reasons for each answer. Do the rest of you agree?

2
Population

Part One
Introduction

Population growth 1700–1851

In 1700, according to estimates made by people living at the time, the total population of Britain was probably about 6.5 million.

In 1851, according to an official census, the population had risen to 20 million. So the population in 1851 was more than three times as large as in 1700. This huge increase is one of the most important changes that took place in Britain during this period. Unfortunately there is not enough evidence to show for certain exactly how and why it happened.

Part Two
The Available Evidence

CHURCH REGISTERS

Most of the evidence for population changes before 1801 comes from church registers (see Source 1A). These were meant to contain a record of all the christenings, marriages and burials in parish churches throughout England and Wales.

They do not give a complete picture because some clergymen did not bother to keep their registers up to date, some registers have been lost or destroyed, and some families did not belong to the Church of England and held their own ceremonies which were not recorded in Church registers. By studying registers historians can calculate whether the population was rising or falling, but cannot be certain how big the total population was.

Study

The aim of this study is:

Ev to see how church registers can help a historian studying Britain's population.

Source 1A

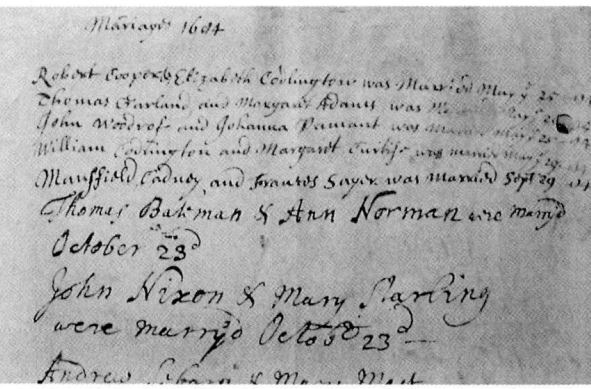

Part of a page from a Cambridgeshire parish register.

1 a Look at the picture of a page from a church register. Why is it difficult to read the information given in the register?
  b What three pieces of information should a clergyman have recorded in his parish registers?
2 Give two or more reasons why we cannot form a complete picture of Britain's population in 1700 by studying the parish registers from that time.
3 Which of these questions can church registers help historians to answer?
  a Was the population of Britain increasing or decreasing between 1700 and 1800?
  b What was the total population of Britain in 1800?
  Give reasons for your answers.

NATIONAL RECORDS

In 1801 the government began to keep reliable national records of the country's population. The two most important were:

The census

Since 1801 a census has been held every ten years (see Source 1B). Before 1841 they only reported the number of people living in a town or village, but since then they have recorded the names, ages and other details of all the inhabitants.

Registers of births, marriages and deaths

Since 1837 all births, marriages and deaths in England and Wales have been recorded in an official register. A certificate is issued to prove that this has been done.

Chronology	
1801	The first census was held.
1837	Births, marriages and deaths in England and Wales had to be registered.
1855	Births, marriages and deaths in Scotland had to be registered.
1874	The cause of death had to be recorded when a death was registered.

Study

The aim of this study is to help you:

Ev to work out what can be learned from census returns and other national records—and what cannot.

Source 1B

A page from an 1851 census form. The black dashes were made by officials in the census office.

1 In what year was the first national census held?
2 Look at Source 1B. What *five* pieces of information does it give about each person in a household?
3 Which *one* of the questions below would it NOT be easy to answer from the information given on census forms?
   a How large was Britain's population in 1801?
   b How many more people lived in Britain in 1821 than in 1801?

   c Did the population increase because the birth rate was rising, or because the death rate was falling?
4 After which year was it possible to give a reliable answer to each of these questions?
   a What is the birth rate in Wales?
   b What is the death rate in Scotland?
   c How many deaths a year in England are caused by consumption?
   Give reasons for your answers.

—————— Part Three ——————
The Growing Population

HOW THE POPULATION GREW

From studying church registers and other evidence, historians have come to these general conclusions:

Table 1   The total population 1700–1851

1700–30	Little change.
1730–80	Slow increase.
1780–1801	Rapid increase.
1801–51	The population doubled.

Table 2   Distribution of population 1801–51

	1801	1851
Where most people lived.	In the countryside.	In towns.
Most densely populated region of Britain.	Southern England.	Northern England, e.g. Lancashire and parts of Yorkshire.

WHY THE POPULATION GREW

Historians have tried to work out why the population grew rapidly between 1750 and 1850.

There is not enough evidence to give a definite answer.

The death rate

Some think that the main cause was a fall in the death rate. This means that the proportion of the population who died each year was falling. They point out that living conditions were improving, so that people were living longer and healthier lives. According to some historians these developments led to a decline in the death rate, and so to an increase in the population. (See Diagram 1.)

The birth rate

Some historians argue that only a few well off people had better food, houses, clothes and medical attention. Most workers were as badly off as ever. Indeed, many of them went to live in crowded, unhealthy towns (see Chapter 10) where diseases such as cholera killed thousands. These historians say that the population grew because more children were born.

According to them, farm labourers and factory workers both had good reasons for wanting large families. (See Diagram 2, page 9.)

Diagram 1

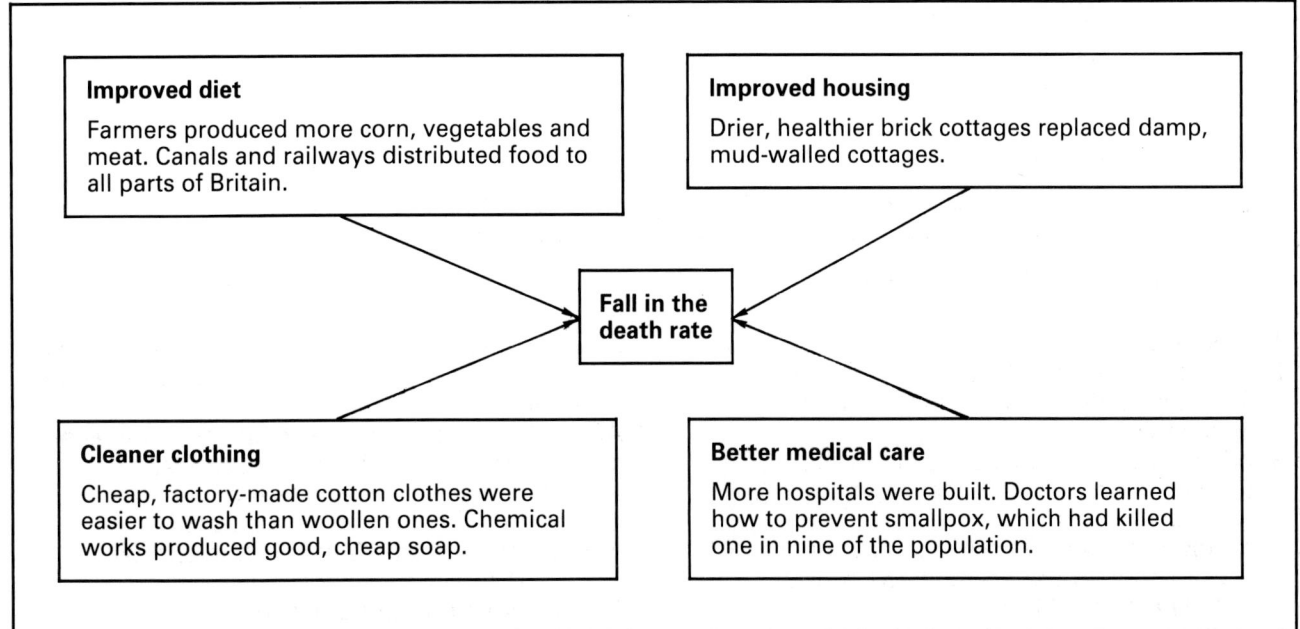

Improved diet
Farmers produced more corn, vegetables and meat. Canals and railways distributed food to all parts of Britain.

Improved housing
Drier, healthier brick cottages replaced damp, mud-walled cottages.

Fall in the death rate

Cleaner clothing
Cheap, factory-made cotton clothes were easier to wash than woollen ones. Chemical works produced good, cheap soap.

Better medical care
More hospitals were built. Doctors learned how to prevent smallpox, which had killed one in nine of the population.

Study

In this study you will be looking at three generations of a family who might have lived between 1752 and 1865. Your aim is:

Ca to see how the conditions in which they lived might have affected their life spans.

You will need the information on pages 7 and 9.

Nathan Thorpe was born in 1752. His father farmed in the open fields surrounding the village. The family lived in a thatched cottage. Its walls were made of wood and clay, and it had an earth floor. Their diet consisted mainly of bread, cheese, some meat and a few vegetables. They wore clothes made of wool from local sheep. They did not wash their clothes very often. Nathan frequently had colds when he was young and died of bronchitis in 1805.

1 a How old was Nathan when he died?
  b Why may the conditions in which he grew up have helped to shorten his life?

■

By the time Nathan was forty five his eldest son, Joseph, born in 1775, was helping him to farm their land. In 1792 they decided to go over to new methods of farming that were being introduced (see Chapter 3). By using the new methods, they were able to produce more food and they sold what they did not eat themselves to a cotton manufacturing town that was growing up ten miles away. Soon they could afford to build

themselves a small brick farmhouse with a wash-house.
Joseph died in 1835.

2 a How old was Joseph when he died?
  b Why may the changes in his way of life have helped him to live longer than Nathan?

■

William Thorpe was born in 1800. He was one of the first children to be vaccinated against smallpox. He went to school until he was ten years old and could read and write. When he left school he helped his father on the land and took over the farm when Joseph died in 1835. In 1840 he sold some of his land to a railway company who were building a line to link two nearby towns. He died in 1865.

3 a How old was William when he died?
  b What reasons might William have given when he was in his fifties to explain why he expected to live longer than either his father or his grandfather?

Diagram 2

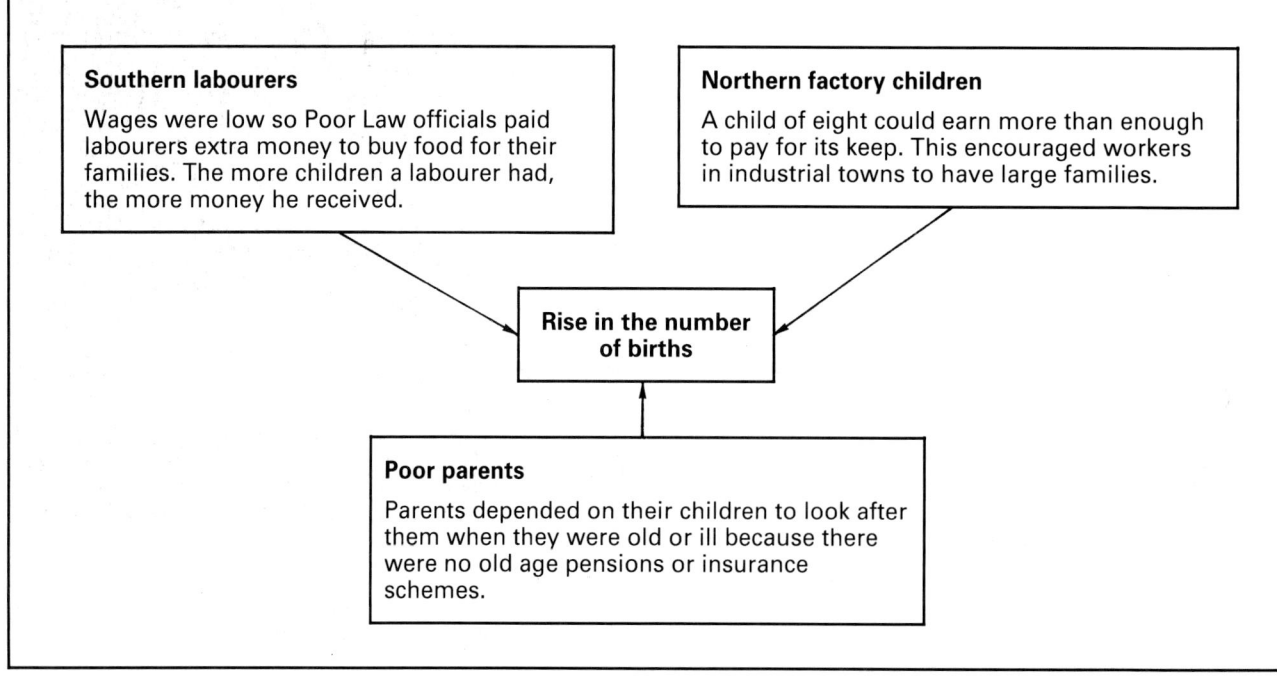

Southern labourers

Wages were low so Poor Law officials paid labourers extra money to buy food for their families. The more children a labourer had, the more money he received.

Northern factory children

A child of eight could earn more than enough to pay for its keep. This encouraged workers in industrial towns to have large families.

Rise in the number of births

Poor parents

Parents depended on their children to look after them when they were old or ill because there were no old age pensions or insurance schemes.

Summing up

It is impossible to decide for certain if the increase in the population between 1780 and 1851 was due to an increase in births, or a decrease in deaths. It may well have been caused by a combination of the two.

RESULTS OF POPULATION INCREASE

The ideas of Malthus

A large increase in population is bound to affect the way people live. Thomas Malthus (see Illustration 2), a clergyman and mathematician, believed that it would bring poverty and misery. In 1798 he published his *Essay on the Principle of Population*. He argued that the number of people was always likely to increase faster than the supply of food and other necessities. So he believed that if the population rose there would always be a larger number of poor people without enough to eat.

Many people at the time agreed with Malthus. Some also thought that as there was bound to be a lot of poor people there was no point in trying to help them.

Why Malthus was wrong

So far as Britain was concerned, Malthus was wrong. It is true that the population eventually increased so much that British farmers could not grow enough to feed everyone, but Britain produced so much wealth that she could afford to buy food from overseas countries which still had a surplus. As a result, the standard of living of the people of Britain towards the end of the twentieth century is much higher than it was at the end of the eighteenth, in spite of the fact that the population is five times as large.

Malthus had not realised all the effects that the increase in population would have. Diagram 3 shows how it encouraged farmers and manufacturers to produce more, which in turn helped the population to increase further.

Diagram 3

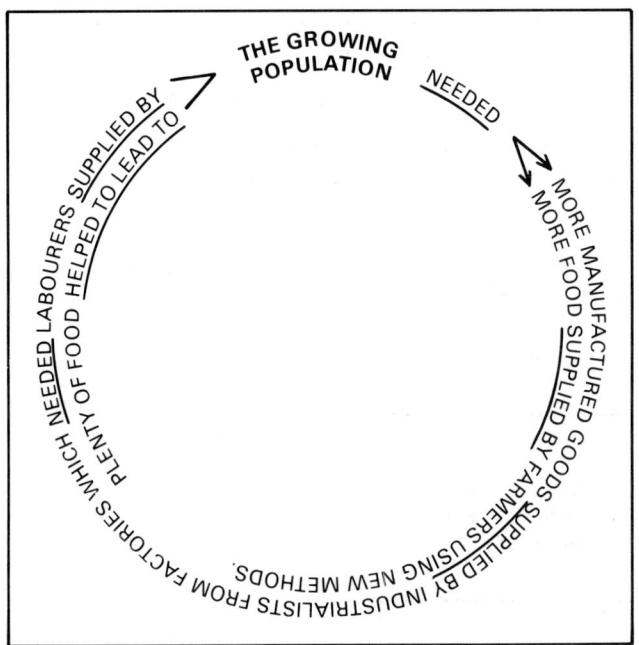

Illustration 1   Thomas Malthus (1766–1834). Some people disagreed with his views on population. One magazine said that the human race would be saved 'not by diminishing their numbers, but by sharpening their intellects'.

Recall

1 a What was the population of Britain in *i* 1700, *ii* 1851?
  b Did the population double between *i* 1700–50, *ii* 1800–50?
2 In what year did the government first order:
  a a national census;
  b the compulsory registration of births, marriages and deaths in England and Wales;
  c the issue of birth certificates in Scotland?
3 Look at Diagram 4. In what ways did Britain's population change between 1700 and 1850? How did the changes in population help Britain to become a great industrial nation?

Diagram 4

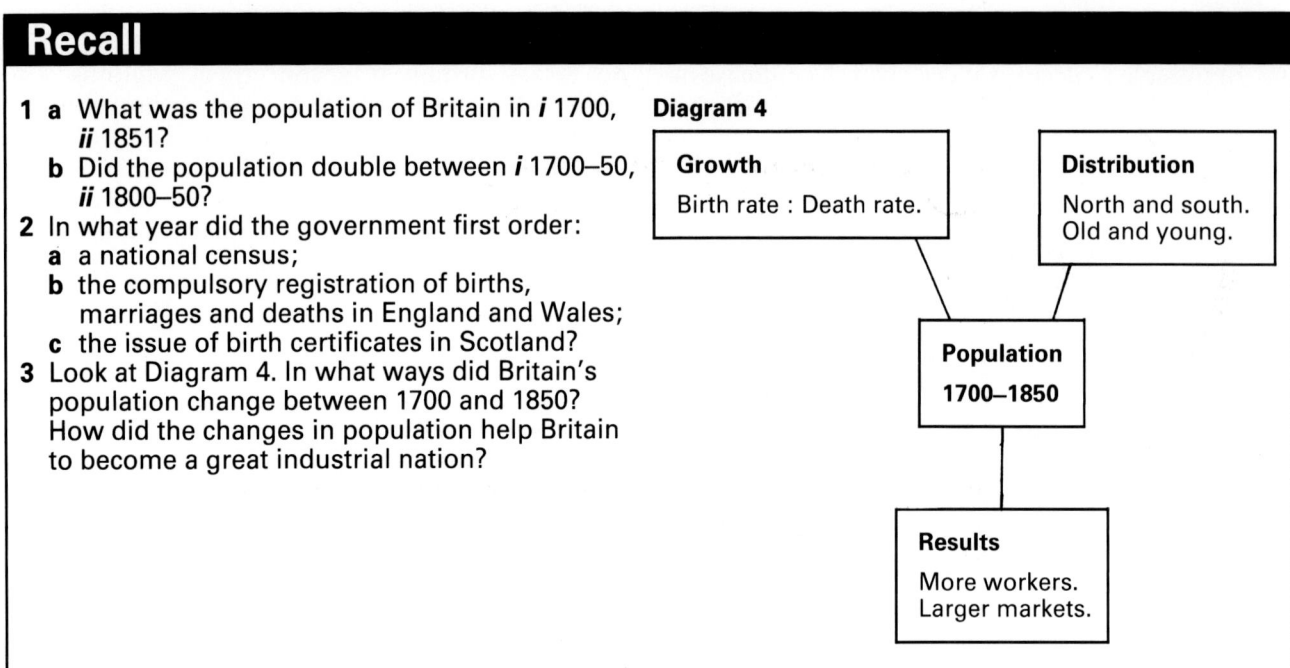

Growth
Birth rate : Death rate.

Distribution
North and south.
Old and young.

Population
1700–1850

Results
More workers.
Larger markets.

3
Farming

The Old System

At the beginning of the eighteenth century, many farmers in England and Wales were using much the same system of farming as in the Middle Ages.

OPEN-FIELD VILLAGES

Layout

Villages on the low, flat lands of the Midlands and East Anglia still had their fields laid out in the old 'open-field system'. (See Diagram 1.)

Working in the open fields

Every day the farmers and their men set out along the village street into the fields, just as their ancestors had done for hundreds of years.

Moving around the fields

Farmers had to spend time tramping from one strip to another. A lot of land was taken up by tracks and paths which wound over the fields to enable the vil-lagers to reach a strip without treading on the grow-ing crops.

Growing crops

In spring the fields were prepared for planting by teams of oxen pulling heavy ploughs through the soil. A sower then walked along the strip, flinging or 'broadcasting' seed to the left and right. A harrow, drawn by horses or oxen followed the sower and covered the seed by dragging soil over them. Seed left uncovered was eaten by birds. Weeds and diseases spread easily from strip to strip.

Harvesting crops

In early summer the grass in the hay meadow was cut and dried to make hay for the cattle to eat in the winter.

In August or September farmers and labourers cut the corn with scythes and sickles, bound it into sheaves and left it to dry. When they were dry the sheaves were loaded onto carts, taken to the farmyard and heaped in ricks (see Illustration 1).

Illustration 1 'Harvest time', a nineteenth-century painting by John Linnell.

Diagram 1 Plan of a typical lowland open-field village

Layout

1 Crops grown on three unhedged 'open' fields, up to 200 ha each.
2 Each field divided into strips about 200 m long and 5 m wide.
3 Poorer land used as meadow to grow hay.
4 Poorest land used as pasture.

Crop rotation

Only grew crops on two of the fields. The other was left fallow to recover fertility. This is the crop rotation they used:

Year	FIELD 1	FIELD 2	FIELD 3
1	Wheat	Fallow	Barley
2	Barley	Wheat	Fallow
3	Fallow	Barley	Wheat

N.B. Some open-field villages had only two fields, which they cultivated alternately. Some had four. They cultivated three each year.

Land ownership and rights

1 All the farmers owned strips scattered over the three fields. In 1763 Richard Derby, a farmer at Hanslope in Buckinghamshire, owned about 10 ha of land. It consisted of twenty four separate strips. (In some places the *demesne* land, which belonged to the lord of the manor, and the *glebe*, which belonged to the rector, was mixed in with the rest. In others, they were in separate, compact fields.)
2 Every farmer had the right to graze cattle and sheep on the pasture. The number depended on how many strips he owned.
3 In most villages some cottagers who owned no land grazed one or two animals on the common.
4 Every farmer had the right to have some hay from the meadow.

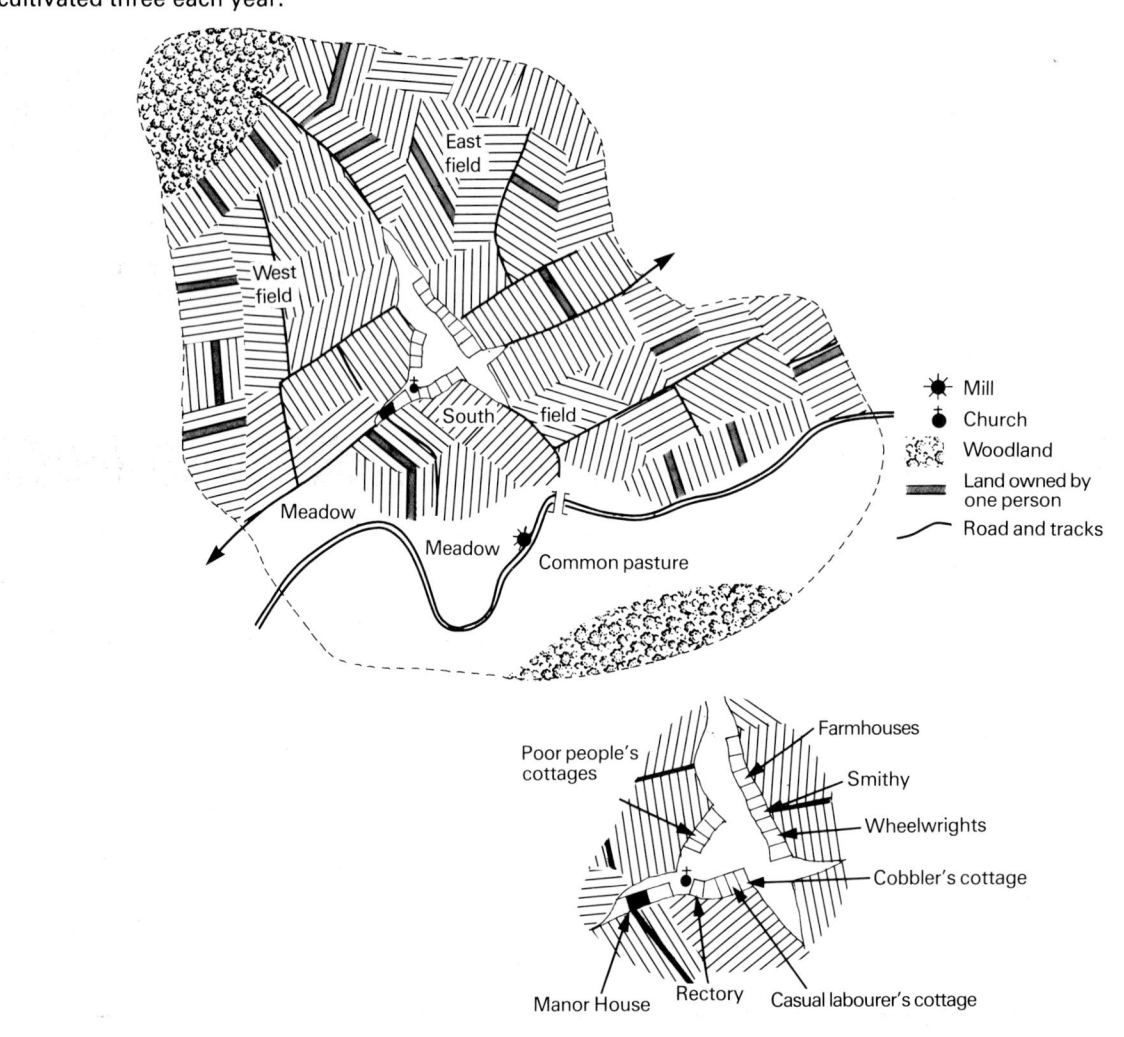

Illustration 2 Labourers threshing corn.

In winter labourers threshed the corn with flails (see Illustration 2) to separate the grain from the chaff. Then the grain was ground into flour for bread-making.

Raising animals

Sheep and cattle grazed on the common pasture. Some were also allowed on the fallow field. Many did not have enough to eat, and disease spread quickly. There was not enough hay for them all, so every autumn some were killed and their carcasses were salted to provide the villagers with meat in the winter. If the owner of a cow wanted to breed from her, he would mate her with one of the village bulls.

How the farmers worked together

The farmers decided among themselves when to start ploughing, sowing and harvesting. They shared ploughs, oxen and labourers at busy times.

Study

Most farmers were content with the old ways. They knew that the open-field system had always provided enough to feed the population.

In this study you will:

K use the information on farming the open fields to work out the advantages and disadvantages of the system.

1 Copy the notes below.
2 Complete your notes by adding more examples to each column.

The open-field system	
Advantages	**Disadvantages**
One field was left fallow every year, so the land was not exhausted.	One third of the land was out of production every year.

A DEVON HILL FARM

In hilly areas, such as Devon or the Lake District, where steep slopes and rocky outcrops made it difficult to plough the land, most country people lived in isolated farms with small fields enclosed by hedges or stone walls.

Diagram 2   A Devon hill farm

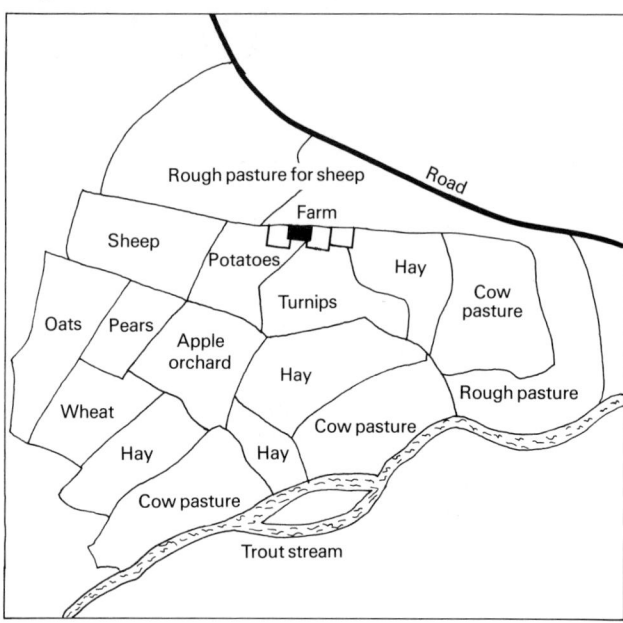

Study

In this study you will be using information from the text and diagrams:

S to work out the similarities and differences in the lives of an open-field farmer and a hill farmer.

1 a Copy and complete the notes below.
  b Complete your notes by adding information on:
    —cattle and sheep;
    —the crops they grew.

| | Types of eighteenth-century farmer | |
	Open-field farmer	Hill farmer
Type of house		Isolated farm house
Type of land	Divided into strips on open fields	

2 Which farmer would have spent more time:
  a walking to and from his crops;
  b opening and shutting gates or climbing stiles?
  Give reasons for your answers.

3 a In what way or ways were the lives of the open-field farmer and the hill farmer similar?
  b What do you think was the greatest difference in their ways of life as farmers?

—————— Part Two ——————
The Need for Change

POPULATION AND PRICES

After 1730 the population of England began to increase steadily.

Table 1   Population of England: 1731–1811 (millions)

1731	5.26
1741	5.58
1751	5.77
1761	6.15
1771	6.45
1781	7.04
1791	7.74
1801	8.66
1811	9.89

As the population increased, farmers found that the demand for their produce grew, and its price went up. (See Table 2.)

Table 2   Prices in Barkham, Berkshire

	1750		1794	
	s	d	s	d
Flour (per bushel)	4	0	8	4
Bacon (per lb)		6		9
Beef (per lb)		3½		5
Mutton (per lb)		3½		5
Cheese (per lb)		3½		6
Butter (per lb)		6	1	0
Wool (per 28 lb)	15	0	30	0

THE IMPROVERS

Encouraged by the higher prices, some farmers began to experiment with 'new' methods of raising animals and growing crops. Most of them were wealthy landowners, who could afford to try out new ideas. Diagram 3 gives details of some of the most famous pioneer farmers.

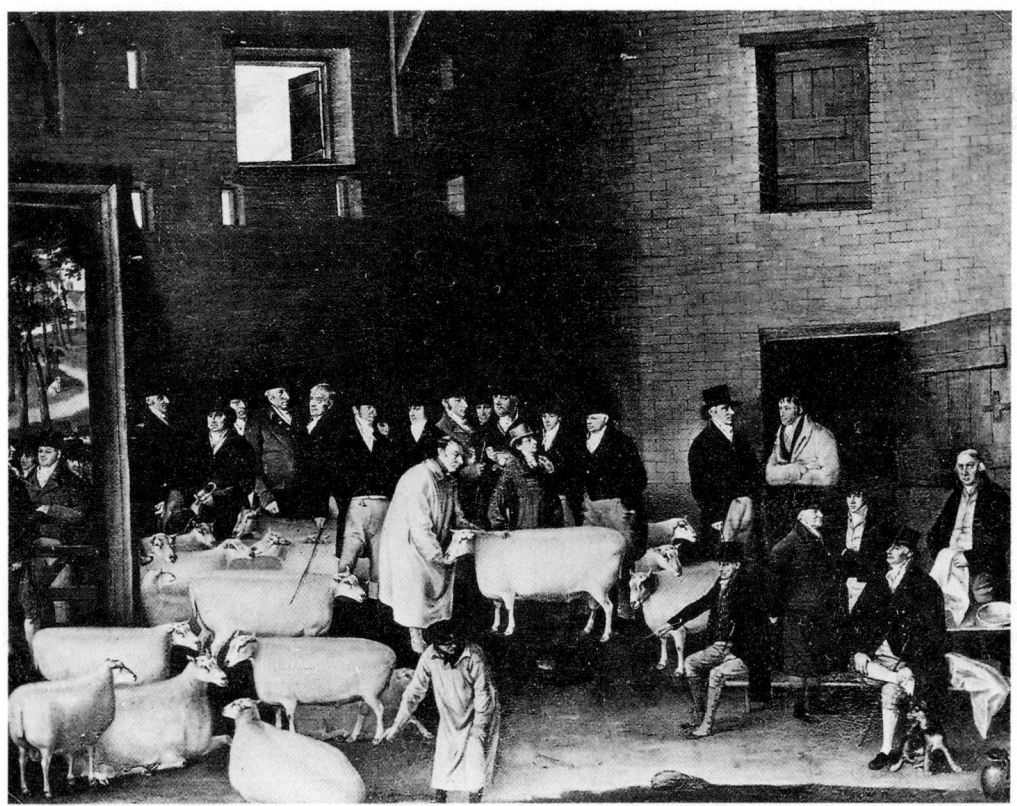

Illustration 3   Rams bred on Bakewell's farm were hired by other farms to mate with their ewes. (See page 16.)

Diagram 3   Improving landlords

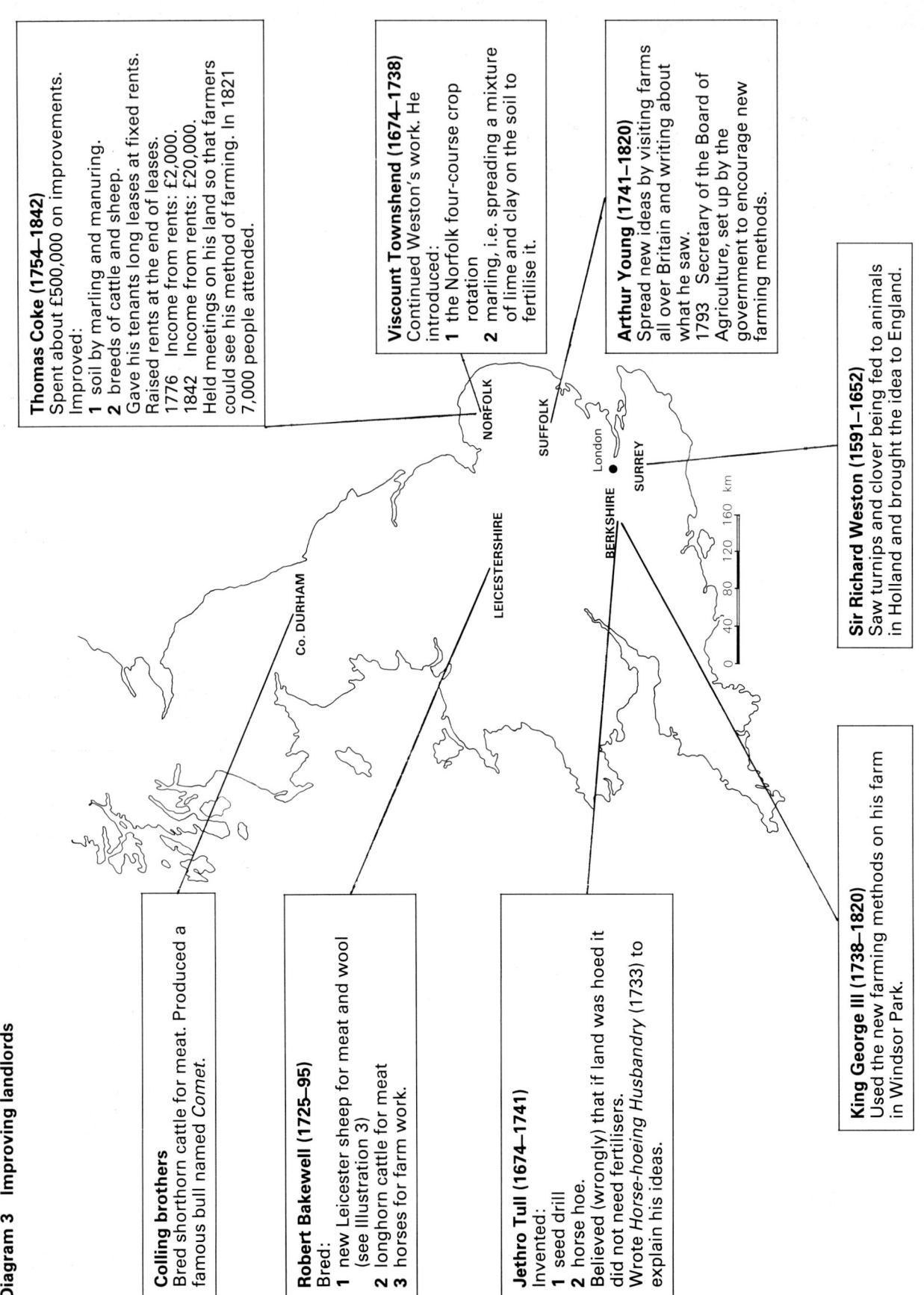

Thomas Coke (1754–1842)
Spent about £500,000 on improvements.
Improved:
1 soil by marling and manuring.
2 breeds of cattle and sheep.
Gave his tenants long leases at fixed rents.
Raised rents at the end of leases.
1776   Income from rents: £2,000.
1842   Income from rents: £20,000.
Held meetings on his land so that farmers could see his method of farming. In 1821 7,000 people attended.

Viscount Townshend (1674–1738)
Continued Weston's work. He introduced:
1 the Norfolk four-course crop rotation
2 marling, i.e. spreading a mixture of lime and clay on the soil to fertilise it.

Arthur Young (1741–1820)
Spread new ideas by visiting farms all over Britain and writing about what he saw.
1793   Secretary of the Board of Agriculture, set up by the government to encourage new farming methods.

Sir Richard Weston (1591–1652)
Saw turnips and clover being fed to animals in Holland and brought the idea to England.

Colling brothers
Bred shorthorn cattle for meat. Produced a famous bull named *Comet*.

Robert Bakewell (1725–95)
Bred:
1 new Leicester sheep for meat and wool (see Illustration 3)
2 longhorn cattle for meat
3 horses for farm work.

Jethro Tull (1674–1741)
Invented:
1 seed drill
2 horse hoe.
Believed (wrongly) that if land was hoed it did not need fertilisers.
Wrote *Horse-hoeing Husbandry* (1733) to explain his ideas.

King George III (1738–1820)
Used the new farming methods on his farm in Windsor Park.

NORFOLK

SUFFOLK

London

SURREY

BERKSHIRE

LEICESTERSHIRE

Co. DURHAM

0   40   80   120   160   km

Study

In this study you will:

K use various books to find out more about the methods used by improving landlords.

The following kinds of books will give you the information you need:
—books about the eighteenth century (look at a book's Contents and Index as well as its title);
—topic books on farming; encyclopedias.

1 Make brief notes on the following:
  a Jethro Tull's methods of planting and hoeing crops;
  b Viscount Townshend's Norfolk four-course rotation;
  c Bakewell and the Colling brothers' reasons for selecting animals for stock breeding;
  d Thomas Coke's farming methods and sheep-shearing festivals.

Study

This study will help you:

K to understand *how* the work of the improvers helped to increase production.

You will need to study the crop rotations below and Diagram 3.

Crop Rotation

The three-course rotation

Wheat → Barley → Fallow → Wheat

The Norfolk four-course rotation

Wheat → Turnips → Barley → Clover → Wheat

1 Improving farmers changed from the three-course to the Norfolk rotation. How did this enable them to:
  a produce more crops from the same amount of land;
  b keep all their cattle through the winter instead of slaughtering some of them?
2 Cattle dung was used to manure the fields. Why would the farmer be able to grow better crops on the same amount of land?

Breeding animals

Improving farmers carefully selected the cattle and sheep they wanted to breed from. Sometimes they used bulls and rams from herds many miles away. They made sure that their animals were properly fed and tried to make sure they were healthy. They kept a careful check on how quickly the animals grew, the amount of meat and, in the case of sheep, the quantity and quality of wool they carried. Every generation they selected the best animals for breeding, until eventually they produced new, heavier, healthier breeds. The following sources show how the weight and appearance of animals increased.

Table 3

	1700	1794
average weight of cattle	370 lb	800 lb
average weight of sheep	28 lb	60 lb

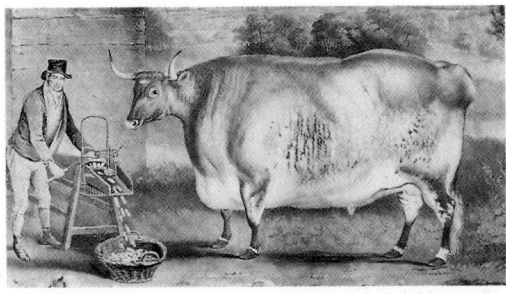

Illustration 4 An engraving of the Newbus Ox.

Illustration 5 A two and a half year old pig, thought to weigh fifty stones (300 kg).

Study

This study will help you:

K to understand why the open-field system hampered the work of improving farmers.

1 Write a brief rough note on why it would have been difficult to use the Norfolk rotation in most open-field villages. (If in doubt, look at the notes under 'Layout' on page 12, and then check on page 17 to find the number of crops grown in the Norfolk rotation.)

2 Read the section on breeding animals on page 17. Note which of the processes used by improving farmers would have been: *i* easy, *ii* difficult, *iii* impossible for farmers in open-field villages to adopt. (Look under the heading *Raising animals* on page 13 if you need a reminder about conditions in open-field villages.)

3 Using the information you have noted in answer to 1 and 2, write a paragraph explaining why farmers in open-field villages who wanted to improve their crops and animals needed to get rid of the open-field system.

—————— Part Three ——————

The Process of Enclosure

Early enclosures

It was much easier for farmers to experiment if all their land was grouped together and enclosed so that they could divide it up as they wished. In some villages, farmers exchanged strips with each other to build up a few solid blocks of land among the strips. This was known as 'piecemeal enclosure'. In other villages all the farmers met and agreed to divide up the three arable fields and the pasture so that each had his share in one solid block. This was known as 'enclosure by agreement'.

Parliamentary enclosure

In most villages there were at least one or two farmers who would not agree to have their land enclosed. To deal with them, it was necessary to pass a special Act of Parliament.

Diagram 4 shows what happened when 'Parliamentary Enclosure' took place.

Diagram 4   The process of enclosure

1   Local landowners
A *meeting* was held at which the owners of at least three-quarters of the land had to agree to enclose the land of the village.   A *petition*, drawn up by the landowners, asked Parliament to pass an Act ordering all the farmers in the village to enclose their land.   A *notice*, displayed on the church door for three weeks in August or September, told the villagers that the petition was being sent to Parliament.

2   Parliament
A *Committee of MPs*, appointed by Parliament, considered the petition.   *Parliament*, following the Committee's recommendations, passed a special Enclosure Act, and appointed three commissioners to supervise the enclosure.

3   The Commissioners
The commissioners arrived in the village and asked each farmer: 'Which strips do you own in each field?'   'How many animals do you keep on the common?'   They instructed *surveyors* to measure and map the strips and common pasture. They then drew up a new map showing how they had re-divided the land to give each farmer a compact holding.

Study

The aim of this study is to:

Ch explore how the layout of the land around a village changed when it was enclosed.

You will need to look carefully at Diagrams 5A and 5B and to remember what you have already learned about open-field farming.

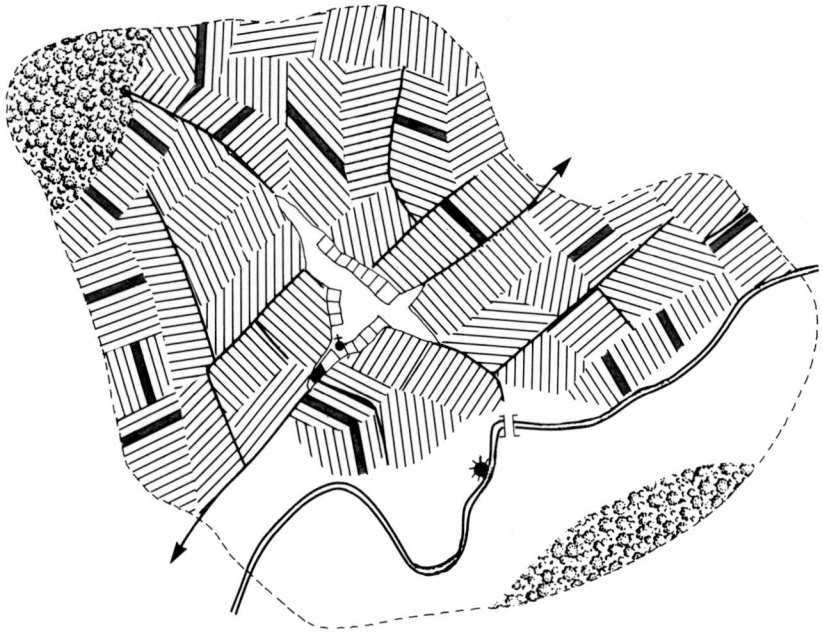

Diagram 5A   Village before enclosure

■ Land owned by one person

▦ A compact enclosed farm

✳ Mill

☗ Church

〰 Road

▣ New Farmhouses

🌳 Woodland

— Hedge

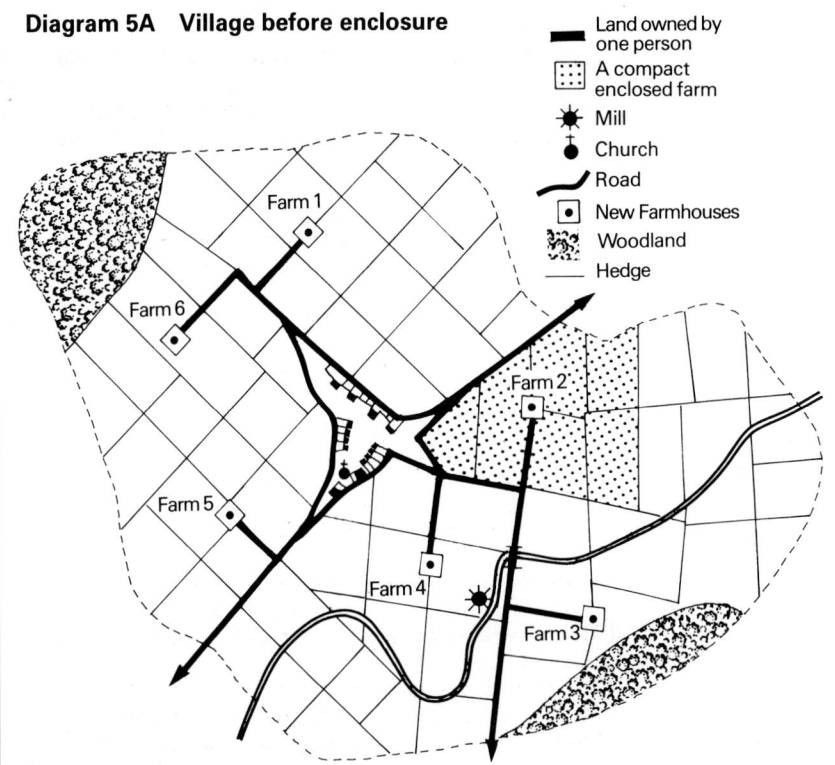

Diagram 5B   The same village after enclosure

1 **a** What changes have been made to the layout of the fields round the village as a result of enclosure?
   b What other changes can you see?
2 What has remained unchanged?
3 What effect did the changes have on:
   a the amount of land cultivated around the village
   b the villagers' ability to move freely round the countryside?

Study

This study will test:

K how well you understand the procedure by which a village was enclosed.

Refer to Diagram 4 if you need to.

1 a How many landowners in a village had to agree to enclose their land before a petition could be sent to Parliament?
  b How did the villagers find out that the landowners wanted to enclose the open fields?
2 a Which people considered the landowners' petition?
  b Whom did Parliament send to see that the Enclosure Act was carried out fairly?

3 a What kind of information did the surveyor need to draw up the new map of the village?
  b What kind of holding did each farmer have after land had been re-divided?

The cost of enclosure

Enclosure Acts ordered farmers to fence their new holdings within a year. Farmers had to pay for this. They also had to pay the lawyers, commissioners, surveyors and Parliamentary officials who had helped to get the Act through. Then, if they wished to improve their farms, they had to buy expensive new animals, good new seed and fertiliser for the land. Often, if their new fields were far from the centre of the village, they had to build themselves a new house as well (see Illustration 6). All this was expensive. The total cost for a farm of forty hectares might well be more than £1,000.

In 1801 Parliament passed a General Enclosure Act. This allowed the fields of any village to be enclosed so long as the owners of at least three-quarters of the land agreed. It was no longer necessary to pass a separate Enclosure Act for each village. This made enclosure cheaper and easier, but it was still very expensive to improve the land and increase output.

Illustration 6   An 'enclosed' farmhouse near Leicester.

Part Four

The Effects of Enclosure

FOOD PRODUCTION

Enclosures helped to make the country more prosperous. Over a million hectares of pasture and waste were enclosed, and with the new crop rotations, none of the arable land was left fallow. So farmers cultivated more land. They also found that if they fed the new breeds of cattle and sheep properly they could produce bigger and heavier animals. Farmers used the dung from these animals to fertilise their arable fields. This helped the yield of wheat to increase fourfold. So the amount produced by Britain's farmers increased, providing enough food for the increasing population.

FARMERS AND EMPLOYMENT

Increased prices meant that farmers who could afford to improve their farms and increase their crops soon got back the money they had spent. But in every village there were poor farmers who only owned a small amount of land and could not easily afford to pay to enclose and improve their holdings. Historians used to think that many sold their farms to richer neighbours, and either became labourers or moved to towns to look for work. But we now know that most 'small' farmers paid their share of the costs and continued to farm. They found it difficult to compete with richer farmers who could afford to buy all the latest machinery and pay to have their land drained and manured. So gradually the number of small farms decreased as their owners sold up and retired.

At the time people thought that enclosures would put labourers out of work because farmers would bring in machinery and increase the efficiency of their farms. The study below helps you see if these fears were justified.

We now know that there were just as many labourers after enclosure as before. Enclosed farms provided extra work hedging and ditching. Also, most farmers grew turnips which labourers had to spend many hours weeding. Finally, the new machines were expensive and unreliable, so very few farmers used them.

The misunderstanding arose because the population in the countryside was rising. This meant that even though the number of jobs remained the same, there were still not enough to go round, and people had to leave their villages and go to new industrial towns to look for work. People at this time took it for granted that labourers were leaving the countryside because there were fewer jobs there.

Study

In the study you will:
Ev test your skill in using a secondary source to help you consider a primary source.

Think about the information in each source, what it tells us about enclosures and employment, and how reliable it is.

Source 2A

A more ruinous effect of this enclosure will be the almost total depopulation of their town [village] now filled with bold and hardy husbandmen . . . driving them from necessity and want of employ . . . into manufacturing towns.

From a petition against enclosure sent in 1797 to the House of Commons by the villagers of Raunds in Northamptonshire.

Source 2B

The census figures . . . confirm that agricultural employment was expanding, not declining. In 1831, for instance, 761,348 families were reported as employed in farming as compared with 697,353 families twenty years earlier.

J. D. Chambers and G. Mingay, *The Agricultural Revolution* (1966). (In the nineteenth century, census officials visited every house and noted down on an official form details of all the people living there, including what they did for a living.)

1 Which source is primary, and which is secondary?
Give reasons for your answer.

2 a What did the villagers of Raunds think would happen to them if their land was enclosed?

   b Does the evidence in Source 2B:
   suggest that the villagers were wrong;
   prove that the villagers were wrong?
   Give reasons for your answer.

3 a What further evidence could historians use if they wanted to find out whether the number of villagers in Raunds who were employed in farming increased or decreased after 1797?

   b Do you agree or disagree with this statement:
   'If the number of families employed in farming in Raunds increased as a result of enclosure, it would show that Source 2A is unreliable, and of no use to historians.'
   Give reasons for your answer.

THE POOR

In many villages, enclosures hit poor people hard. Usually there were a few cottagers who owned no land, but before enclosure they were allowed to graze a cow or a couple of sheep on the common pasture. They had no legal right to do this, and when the commissioners divided up the common pasture they only gave a share to villagers who could prove that they had a legal right to graze animals there. So poor cottagers got nothing, and had nowhere for their animals to graze.

Arthur Young sympathised with them. In 1801 he wrote, 'By nineteen enclosure acts out of twenty the poor are injured'. In 1808 the Board of Agriculture published a general report on enclosures. They agreed with Young. For example, they noticed that at Letcombe in Berkshire the poor could 'no longer keep a cow, which before many of them did'.

Most poor people could not write so we do not have much direct evidence of what they felt when the fields, commons and woodlands were enclosed. But Arthur Young wrote, 'The poor . . . may say with truth, "Parliament may be tender of property. All I know is I had a cow and an Act of Parliament has taken it from me"'.

Study

This study gives you the opportunity to discuss whether or not an open-field village should be enclosed. It will help you:

Em to see the debate from the point of view of four different landowners who might have lived in the eighteenth century.

Remember what you have learned about open-field farming, the methods used by improving farmers, the rules about sending an enclosure petition to Parliament, and the likely effects of enclosures.

The four landowners

In 1795, four landowners in the parish of Littleover meet to decide whether or not to petition Parliament to pass an Act allowing them to enclose the land around the village. They are:

1 **Michael Cavendish**, a wealthy landowner, who lets out some of his land and farms the rest as a compact holding. His income comes from his rents and the profit he makes selling farm produce in the neighbouring market town. He reads articles on the new farming methods, and has attended several sheep-shearing festivals.
2 **Richard Rogers**, who farms on strips of land in the open fields and keeps a small herd of cattle on the common. He produces enough food to feed his family and leave a small surplus to sell at the market. He has no income apart from this, and rarely travels further than the nearest market town.
3 **Henry Standforth**, who farms a small amount of land, but also has an income from some money he inherited from his uncle. He takes an interest in the poor families of the village, and knows that several of them will be worse off if the land is enclosed, because they will no longer be able to keep a cow or a pig on the common. They are too poor to buy milk and meat.
4 **Amos Briggs**, who has already exchanged some of his strips for some that belonged to Henry

Standforth. He now has a compact holding and is pleased with the crops he grows on it. He would like to experiment with selective cattle breeding. He keeps a note of food prices, can show that they have risen over the last ten years, and thinks that they will probably go on doing so.

What to do

1 Divide into groups of four and let each person take one of the characters described above.
2 For about ten minutes make brief notes, listing the reasons why you think the character you have taken would or would not vote for sending a petition to Parliament asking for the land to be enclosed.
3 Hold a meeting with the other people in your group at which each character gives his reasons for supporting or opposing enclosure, and discuss any matters about which you disagree. Then take a vote. (Cavendish and Briggs own enough land between them to carry the vote if they both support enclosure.)
4 Ask one group to summarise its reasons for voting for or against enclosure. What do the rest of you think?

—————— Part Five ——————
Nineteenth-Century Farmers

Rich farmers in the nineteenth century

As farmers grew richer, many either built new houses or added extra rooms to their existing homes. They bought expensive furniture and hired servants. They wore fashionable clothes, gave parties and, like other rich people, sent their sons away to school and had their daughters taught to sing, draw and play the piano. They no longer wanted to share their homes with labourers, so they paid them money wages and sent them to live in their own cottages.

Study

In this study you will be:
Ev examining two primary sources, one by John Gillray, a cartoonist, the other by William Cobbett, a journalist.

You will see how they showed their opinion of the rich farmers and how their opinions may have influenced people who lived at the time.

Source 3A

John Gillray published this cartoon in 1809. He called it: *Farmer Giles and his wife showing off their daughter Betty to their Neighbours on her return from school*. People used the name 'Farmer Giles' when they were talking about farmers in general.

1 Judging from the way in which the parlour is furnished, is Farmer Giles a rich farmer? Give reasons for your answer.

2 Why do you think Farmer Giles and his wife are so proud of their daughter, Betty?

3 Would you expect people living in 1809 to form a high or a low opinion of farmers from looking at Gillray's cartoon? Give reasons for your answer.

Study continued

Source 3B

Everything about this farmhouse was formerly the scene of *plain manners* and *plentiful living* . . . Oak tables to eat on, long, strong, and well supplied with . . . stools . . . [Now] there was a *parlour*. Aye, and a *carpet* and bell-pull too! One end of this once plain . . . house had been moulded into a '*parlour*'; and there was the mahogany table, and the fine chairs, and the fine glass . . . And, there were the decanters, the glasses, the 'dinner set' of crockery-ware, and all just in the true stock-jobber style . . . Why do not farmers now *feed* and *lodge* their work-people as they did formerly? Because they cannot keep them *upon so little* as they give them in wages. That is the real cause of the change.

William Cobbett, writing in 1825 of a farmhouse he had just visited in Reigate in Surrey. 'Stock-jobbers' were men who made money by dealing in stocks and shares. Cobbett despised them because they did not produce anything.

4 What changes did Cobbett say had been made to:
  a the structure of this farmhouse;
  b the way in which it was furnished?
5 How can we tell that Cobbett had a low opinion of the farmer from the way in which he described his furniture, glasses and crockery?
6 a Why may some people living in 1825 have thought that farmers should pay their workers higher wages, after reading what Cobbett wrote?
  b Why may other people have felt that Cobbett was unfair to the farmers?

Part Six

Nineteenth-Century Labourers

SOUTHERN LABOURERS

Living accommodation

Southern labourers' cottages were usually very primitive (see Illustration 7). A Poor Law official from Ampthill in Bedfordshire described them as 'very miserable places, in which it is impossible to keep up the common decencies of life'. He described how a man, wife and nine children lived in a two room cottage. The parents slept in one room in a bed which they shared with four or five of their children. The rest of the children slept in a bed in the other room, where the family cooked, washed and ate its meals.

Work and wages

Many southern labourers were employed from week to week, or even from day to day. When there was no work, the farmers sent them home and paid them nothing. In the past many had spent their spare time making cloth for local merchants. But the new factories made such cheap cloth that country merchants could not compete. So they closed down and labourers lost their part-time work.

In the south, labourers and their families were in a hopeless situation. Farmers paid such low wages that even labourers who were working full time could not afford to feed themselves and their families, and as the population increased there were too few jobs for them all.

Illustration 7 The interior of a labourer's cottage at Blandford in Dorset, drawn by an *Illustrated London News* artist in 1846.

Study

In this study you will be using information from a survey carried out in 1787 by the Rev David Davies, Rector of Barkham in Surrey. Davies asked labourers in his parish how much they earned and how they spent their money.

The aim of the study is:

Em to see what life was like from the point of view of a farm labourer's family living in Barkham at the end of the eighteenth century.

Source 4A Wages

**In southern England wage rates were low.
In Barkham, the average weekly wage for a labourer was eight shillings a week.
Labourer's wives could earn about six pence a week.**

(There were twelve pence in a shilling.)

Source 4B Expenses

Davies found that a labourer, his wife and two children spent the following amounts of money on goods each week.

	s	d
Flour, 5 gallons	4	2
Yeast and salt		3
Bacon, 1.5lb @ 8d	1	0
Tea, 1oz, 2d; sugar, ½lb, 4d; butter, ½lb, 4d		10
Soap, ¼lb, 2d; candles, 3d; worsted, 3d		8
TOTAL	6	11

Davies reckoned that for rent, fuel, clothing, medical and funeral expenses the family needed to set aside about 2s 7d a week.

1 a Use the information that Davies gives us about the family's income and weekly expenses to explain why labourers' children often wore ragged clothes, and looked undernourished.
   b Labourers in the south were often accused of being lazy. Why would a man living on the kind of diet that Davies describes have found it difficult to do a hard day's work?

2 Why might a labourer have felt worse off after the farmers enclosed the land around the village, even though he still had a job?

3 Davies found that labourers' wives did not usually go out to work. If they did, any money they earned belonged, by law, to their husbands.
   Why may a labourer's wife have rarely gone out to work:
   a between the ages of 17 and 40;
   b when she was older?

The Swing riots

In the past, many labourers had worked in the winter, threshing the autumn grain crops. By 1830 most rich farmers had bought threshing machines which did the job much more quickly, and put labourers out of work.

In the summer of 1830 there were riots across the south of England from Norfolk to Dorset and Somerset. Labourers banded together and visited all the farms in turn. They asked farmers to destroy their threshing machines (see Illustration 8), and to promise to pay higher wages. If a farmer refused, they smashed his thresher themselves and set fire to his ricks. Most farmers did as they were asked and for a time, labourers' pay in the south increased.

NORTHERN LABOURERS

Labourers in the north were better paid than in the south. This was because factories had been established in the north. The factories needed labourers, and farmers had to pay higher wages to compete with them. A visitor to the north noticed that ploughmen looked 'vigorous and well-fed'. In addition, threshing machines had less effect in the north, because less grain was grown there.

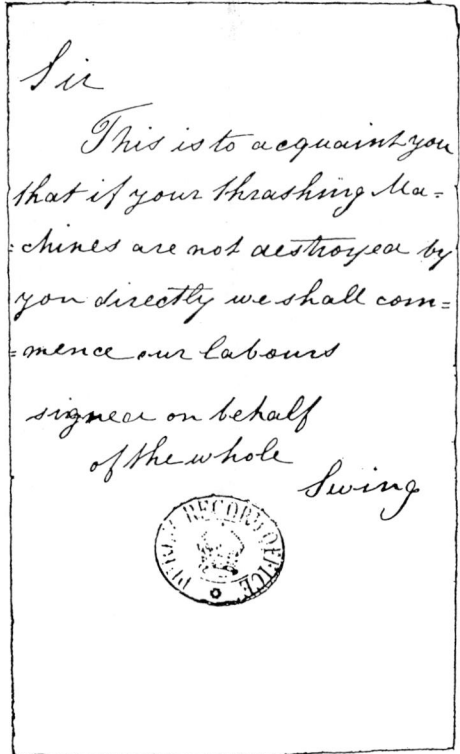

Illustration 8 The farmer who received this 'Swing' letter gave it to a magistrate, who sent it to the Home Secretary. It is now kept in the Public Record Office.

Study

Riots are often sparked off by a particular incident, but the rioters usually have grievances that have been building up for a long time as well. The aim of this study is:

Ca to consider the causes of the Swing riots.

Remember what you have learned about southern labourers' lives after enclosures and what you have just read about the Swing riots.

1 The list below gives you some of the causes of the Swing riots. Re-write the items in the list under the headings. Leave out items you think did *not* help to cause the riots.

a After enclosures, many farmers' standard of living improved, but labourers were worse off.

b There were bad harvests in 1828 and 1829.

c Britain and France were at war from 1793 to 1815.

d The population in industrial towns was increasing.

e By 1830 most rich farmers had bought threshing machines.

Causes of the Swing Riots	
Long term	**Short term**

f After the middle of the eighteenth century it was increasingly difficult for labourers to earn money by spinning or weaving.

g Unemployment was increasing and many parishes were cutting the amount spent on poor relief.

h People wanted change, and in 1830 a revolution in France and a change of government in Britain made them expect rapid reforms.

2 Ask one person to read his or her list to the class. Do the rest of you agree?

Recall

1 Explain the meaning of the following terms in your own words: agriculture; arable; enclosure farming.
2 Re-write the lists opposite, matching each improving landlord with the method of farming.
3 *Discussion:* It was said that the changes in agriculture led to 'fat beasts but thin men'.
  a Do you think this was true? Write down the reasons for your answer.
  b Ask one person to read his or her answers to the class. Do the rest of you agree?

Landlord	Method
Jethro Tull	Marling soil to improve its quality
Viscount Townshend	*Horse Hoeing Husbandry*
Robert Bakewell	Norfolk four-course rotation
Thomas Coke	Breeding New Leicester sheep

4
The Cloth Industry

The Domestic System

ORGANISATION

At the beginning of the eighteenth century, cloth was made by workers and their families in their own homes on hand-powered machines. This system of working is usually known as the domestic system.

During one of his journeys, Daniel Defoe visited West Yorkshire, one of the busiest manufacturing areas in the country. The hillsides were covered with a patchwork of small fields dotted with houses, each supplied with water from a small stream. These houses were the homes of clothmakers, and the cloth was produced in small workshops attached to the houses themselves.

Clothmakers bought wool from nearby sheep farmers. Every week or so they set out on horseback with loads of this raw wool. They took it to small cottages in the neighbourhood. Here women and girls spun it into thread.

When the clothmakers handed over the raw wool, the spinners gave them the thread they had made since the last visit. The clothmakers paid them for their work and took the thread back home where, with the help of their families and one or two hired labourers, they made it into cloth.

The woven cloth was dyed and washed. Then it was stretched and put outside to dry. When the cloth was finished, the clothier took it to market to sell, or in some places, sold it in a shop at the front of the house (Illustration 1).

In the west country the cloth industry was organised differently. The master clothiers lived in towns and had the processing done in nearby villages.

Clothmaking was a family affair. Children grew up with the work going on around them and learned the various processes by watching their parents. They were expected to do a share of the work as soon as they were able. Defoe said that children earned their keep at four or five years of age, and some parents made their children work cruelly long hours.

Illustration 1   A clothmaker's house at Wigston, near Leicester. At the front there was a shop where he sold his cloth. His weaving shed was behind the house.

WHEELS AND LOOMS

Woollen thread was made on small spinning wheels, driven by a foot pedal. The thread was woven into cloth on hand looms. A number of threads, called the *warp*, were stretched out side by side on a loom. Then another, finer, thread (the *woof*) was woven through the warp at right angles. The woof was carried on a shuttle, and at the beginning of the eighteenth century, weavers threaded the shuttle through the warp by hand. On small looms one weaver could do the job, but two weavers had to work on wide looms, passing the shuttle to and fro between them.

Study

This study will help you to:

K understand how the cloth industry was run in Defoe's time.

Use Source 1 and the information on pages 28 and 29.

Source 1

Winding, warping and weaving in the family shop, 1798.

1 How can we tell that the picture shows the domestic system of manufacturing cloth?

2 In which part of England might Defoe have seen a cottage like the one shown in the picture? Give reasons for your answer.

3 What does the picture *i* show us, *ii* not show us, about the role of children in the domestic system?

————— Part Two —————

The New Machines

INCREASED DEMAND FOR CLOTH

As the population grew during the eighteenth century, demand for cloth increased. Lancashire cotton merchants imported more raw cotton. Soon there was too much for the spinners and weavers to process, so inventors tried to improve spinning wheels and hand looms to speed up the work.

Table 1   Inventions in the cloth industry 1733–1787

Date	Inventor	Invention	Power used	Effect on production
1733	John Kay (living in Colchester)	Flying shuttle for hand loom	Hand	Speeded up weaving. Increased demand for thread.
1764	James Hargreaves (Blackburn)	Spinning jenny	Hand	Increased supply of thin, weak thread.
1769	Richard Arkwright (Bolton)	Water frame	Water then steam	Increased supply of strong, thick thread.
1779	Samuel Crompton (Bolton)	Spinning mule	Water then steam	Increased supply of high quality strong fine thread.
1787	Edmund Cartwright (Notts)	Power loom	Water then steam	Speeded up weaving. Weavers able to use all that spinners could produce.

Study

The aim of this study is:
K to help you understand why the various inventions in the cloth industry, 1733–1787, were important.

Find the answers

In pairs, use the table above to find the answers to the following questions. You need not write down your answers.
1 a Who invented the water frame?
  b Name the machine that Edmund Cartwright invented.
2 a Give an example of an invention that speeded up spinning.
  b Give two examples of inventions that were driven by water.
3 a The thread from the spinning jenny was unsuitable for the warp of a loom. Explain why.
  b By the end of the eighteenth century, fine, strong cloth, made out of thread spun in Britain, could be produced rapidly. Name the two inventions that made this possible.

Hold a quiz

With the help of the table above, make up two questions each on the inventions in the cloth industry, 1733–1787. Write each question on a separate sheet of paper.
Give in your questions and hold a class quiz.

Test your memory

Divide a double page in your notebook into the same number of columns as the table of inventions.
Copy the heading to each column.
From memory, fill in as much correct information as you can.
Check the work in your notebook with the table of inventions and give yourself a mark for every space that you have filled in correctly.
Copy any information that you could not remember.

— Part Three —
Cloth Mills

SETTING UP MILLS

The new machines destroyed the domestic system. Only the smallest jennies and mules could be used in people's homes. The rest were too big, too complicated and needed too much power.

To use the new machines, cloth manufacturers set up mills on the banks of streams with a good flow of water and used the water power to turn a wheel to drive the machines. It was difficult to find sites. Arkwright travelled all around Derbyshire, Yorkshire and Lancashire looking for suitable streams. When a manufacturer came across a head of water in a deserted valley he was quite prepared to buy land, build a factory, move machines into it, bring in workers from miles away and put up houses for them to live in. It was the stream that mattered, not the people. It was an expensive business to set up a factory, and to make a profit, the manufacturer had to keep it working for long hours.

WORKING IN THE MILLS

Cloth workers had to leave their homes and go to work in mills. It was very different from working at home. At home, spinners and weavers worked at the speed which suited them best, and took occasional rests when they were tired. In a mill they had to keep up with the machine.

Factories were kept very warm because cold, dry air makes cotton thread brittle. Fine thread was spun at 27°C, and when it was dark the mills were lit by gas lamps, which made them even hotter.

Many women worked in the cloth mills. Skilled, well-paid jobs such as mule-spinning were reserved for men. All the managers and supervisors were men. But there were plenty of jobs for women looking after spinning frames, power looms and carding machines. Some worked in cloth mills for most of their lives.

Study

In this study use Map 1 to work out
K why Jedediah Strutt, who was Arkwright's partner for a while, built a water-powered spinning mill at Belper in Derbyshire.

When Strutt was looking for a suitable site for a factory he had to consider these items:
Water   Did the stream flow with enough force to drive the water frames?
Communications   Could the site be reached easily by road, river or canal?
Workers   Could he recruit workers who were used to working in the cloth industry?

In pairs, find Belper on the map. Consider each of the items listed above. Why may Strutt have decided to build a factory at Belper?
   Choose one person to read his or her answers to the class. Do the rest of you agree?

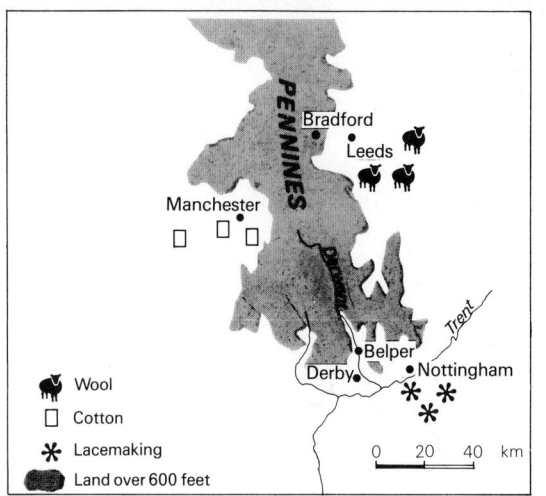

Map 1   Belper and the surrounding region

The piecers

Most work in cloth factories consisted of feeding machines with raw material, taking away finished products, and mending faults such as broken threads. Some jobs could be done by children as well as adults, and almost every spinning mill employed young children as 'piecers'. Their job was mending broken threads. They had to watch the machines and, when a thread broke, they went up to the spindle, stopped it spinning, pulled the end of thread off, and mended it by twisting the two broken ends together. If the machines were running well, piecers had little to do, but if the engine ran roughly or they had a bad batch of cotton, piecers were always on the move, slipping between machines, stopping spindles, bending and stretching to get at the ends of the threads.

Study

In 1816 Parliament became concerned about children in factories and set up a committee to investigate their working conditions. In the sources below two mill owners, Peter Noialle and Robert Owen, give their views on the employment of young children.

Your aims are to:
S compare their ideas;   **Em** consider what other mill owners thought of them.

Source 2A

Peter Noialle, a silk manufacturer from Sevenoaks, Kent.

Q At what age do you take children?
A From six to seven and eight; we never refuse anybody.
Q Why do you take them at so early an age?
A They more easily acquire the facility of handling silk, and it is an advantage to themselves and their parents to take them at those early ages.
Q If you did not take the children at that age, how would they be employed, do you suppose?
A In running about the country, and in all sorts of mischief; at least such is the case with the children I do not employ in the neighbourhood.

Source 2B

Robert Owen, a factory owner from New Lanark, Scotland. (Owen had just suggested that children under 10 should not be employed in factories.)

Q What employment could be found for the children of the poor . . . till ten years of age?
A It does not appear to me that it is necessary for children to be employed, under ten years of age, in any regular employment.
Q If you did not employ them in any regular work, what would you do with them?
A Instruct them, and give them exercise.

Study continued

Q **Would there not be a danger of their acquiring . . . vicious habits, for want of regular occupation?**

A **. . . I have found quite the reverse, that their habits have been good in proportion to the extent of their instruction.**

(Owen set up a school for workers' children at New Lanark where they learned a variety of subjects and were encouraged to enjoy music, art and physical exercise.)

1 How old were the youngest children who were regularly employed at:
Peter Noialle's mill in Sevenoaks;
Robert Owen's mill at New Lanark?

2 What answer might *i* Noialle and *ii* Owen have given to this question:
'How will the way you treat young children help them to become skilled adult workers?'

3 Suggest reasons why most mill owners agreed with Noialle and disagreed with Owen.

ILL-TREATMENT AND INJURY

Study

In this study your aims are to use the primary sources 3A–G:

K to decide why some children in cloth factories were cruelly treated and likely to become crippled or ill;

Em to understand why some people saw nothing wrong with factory conditions.

You will find other information you need on pages 32–3.

Source 3A

Children working in cloth mills suffered in various ways. In 1833 a commissioner sent by Parliament to investigate conditions in factories interviewed Alexander Barr, aged 15, who worked in a flax mill near Edinburgh. Afterwards he wrote:

The long hours tire him, and make him sleepy in the evening, and the dust from the flax plagues his eyes . . . He had his leg hurt by the machinery . . . He has been two or three times strapped on the hand by the overseer for acts of negligence or inattention.

Source 3B

Sometimes there were serious accidents. Leonard Horner, a factory inspector, described how a young girl, working close to a revolving vertical shaft,

. . . was caught by her apron, which lapped round the shaft, and being tight round her body, she was whirled round and repeatedly forced between the shaft and the carding engine.

(Her severed right leg was found some distance away.)

Source 3C

Many children complained of being beaten. A sixteen-year-old girl working in a Manchester mill said that if she arrived late for work or made mistakes she was 'licked',

. . . generally with a strap—either with a strap or a rope—very seldom with the hand . . . The spinners all beat the piecers. You see it throws them behind of their work if they an't there.

Source 3D

Mrs Marsden, who lived in Nottingham and had several children working in cotton mills, said:

For my part I think children won't do without beating. It's better to beat them than fine 'em. The parents only suffer for the fining, the children don't mind it.

Source 3E

Carding machines prepare the raw cotton for spinning.

Study continued

Source 3F

Some children were crippled by the work. Joseph Rayner, aged 16, had worked in a Bradford wool mill for six years for 12 or 13 hours a day. He said:

I never was a very strong boy. I got a very bad set of frames to mind . . . It was too hard work for me. The flies [spindles] were very large ones, my hands got sore, and I was obliged to stop them with my knee. I did it with my left knee and it got bent outwards as you see, and the other got bent inwards.

At the age of sixteen he could hardly walk.

Source 3G

I have worked here half a year . . . I get 3s 6d. I was gathering 'tatoes before I came here. I got 3s at that. When the 'tatoes were in I had nothing to do, and I came here. I have no father. This suits me very well. We have very good masters and very good overlookers here. I have never been strapped here once. It tires me standing a little now and then, but not half as much, no, not a quarter as much, as I used to be in getting in 'tatoes, with my back. I used to get leathered a deal when I was gathering 'tatoes. I like this a good deal best.

In pairs, answer the following questions in brief notes.

1 List the conditions in cloth mills which might have led children to be cruelly treated, fall ill, or be crippled.
2 Who, do you think, could have done most to protect the children:
    millowners
    adult mill-workers
    parents?
Give reasons for your answer.
3 In 1833 William Munton, aged ten, talked to a commissioner visiting cloth mills in Nottingham (Source G). Many people could see nothing wrong with the conditions in which children in cloth mills had to work. How does William Munton's evidence help us to understand their point of view?
4 Ask one person to read his or her answers to the class. Do the rest of you agree?

Part Four

The Lancashire Riots: A Study in Depth

Factory-made cloth was cheaper than that produced at home. So people working in their own homes could no longer make a living. Occasionally, driven by hunger and want, gangs of them marched on cloth mills and tried to destroy the new machines. Usually they first sent letters asking the mill owners to destroy the machines themselves. Some of these letters were signed 'Ned Lud', or 'King Lud'. So the machine breakers were known as 'Luddites'.

At the beginning of the nineteenth century, Haslingden and Chatterton were prosperous Lancashire cotton manufacturing communities. The demand for cotton was increasing. Manufacturers produced more thread by setting up mills equipped with new spinning machines, but they still depended on hand loom weavers to make thread into cloth, so they encouraged weavers to produce more by raising their pay.

Weavers and their families saw the chance to make easy money. They cleared spaces in their cottages and outhouses and set up hand looms. A family of weavers could earn between two and five pounds a week, depending on how many looms they had.

By 1826, all this had changed and in April there was unrest in the two towns. A troop of cavalry stationed in the area to keep order was on the alert, and on 26 April it had to deal with riots in which several people were killed and many wounded.

Study

In this study you are asked to:

Ev see what you think of the Luddites after looking at a nineteenth-century cartoon; reconsider your opinion when you have studied various sources on the Lancashire riots of 1826.

Source 4A

A cartoon of a gang of Luddites on their way to break machines.

1 What did Luddites do?
2 Judging from the cartoon, what kind of people were the Luddites?

Source 4B

At present a boy or girl, 14 or 15 years of age, can manage two steam power looms, and with their help can weave three and a half times as much cloth as the best hand loom weaver . . .
In 1818 there were in Manchester, Stockport, Middleton, Hyde, Staley Bridge and their vicinities 14 factories containing about 2,000 [power] looms.
In 1821 32 factories containing 5,732 looms . . .
Now there are more than 10,000 [power] looms.

Richard Guest, *A compendious History of the Cotton Manufacture* (1823).

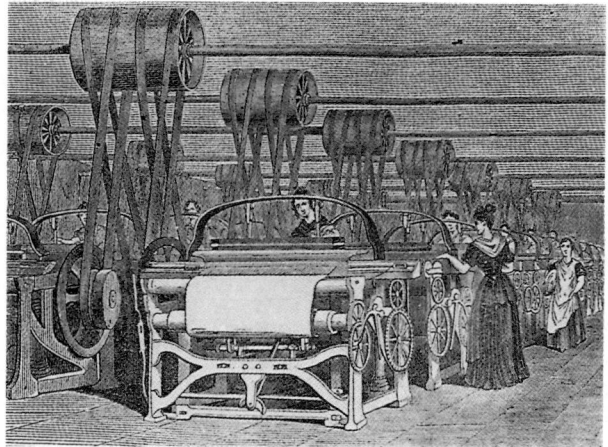

Illustration 2   A power loom shop with unguarded belts driving the machines.

3 **a** How many power looms were there in Manchester and the surrounding area by 1823?
  b How many had there been in the area five years earlier?
4 Give two reasons why you would expect there to be less work for hand loom weavers in 1823 than there was in 1818.

5 Would you expect the information in Source 4A to be reliable?
Give reasons for your answer.

Study continued

Source 4D

A good workman, who formerly earned from six shillings to eight shillings a day, cannot now earn six shillings a week by labouring sixteen hours a day. Many manufacturers have put weavers on half work—say three shillings a week and with that miserable pittance we have to meet the needs of our hungry and naked families . . . a solitary meal each day of oatmeal and water is absolutely more than a man with a family of small children is able to obtain.

Statement issued by the Bolton Weavers, 27 February 1826.

6 What are we told to suggest that, by 1826:
   the rate of pay for hand loom weavers had fallen;
   there was less work for hand loom weavers;
   some hand loom weavers were not earning enough money to support their families?
7 What kind of evidence would you look for if you wanted to find out if the Bolton weavers were giving a biased account of their hardships in 1826?

Source 4E

So come all you cotton weavers, you must rise up very soon,
For you must work in factories from morning until noon:
You mustn't walk in your garden for two or three hours a day,
For you must stand at their command, and keep your shuttle in play.

From a ballad written in about 1820.

8 What changes brought about by the introduction of power looms does the writer of the ballad dislike?
9 Would you expect the hours of work and play given in the ballad to be accurate? Give reasons for your answer.

Source 4F

That morning we [a crowd of hand loom weavers] set off to the loom-breaking. When we had got on the road we saw horse soldiers coming towards us. There was a stop then. The soldiers came forward, their drawn swords glittering in the air. The people opened out to let the soldiers get through. Some threw their pikes over the dyke and some didn't. When the soldiers had come into the midst of the people, the officers called out 'Halt!' All expected that the soldiers were going to charge, but the officers made a speech to the mob and told them what the consequences would be if they persisted in what they were going to do. Some of the old fellows from the mob spoke. They said, 'What are we to do? We're starving. Are we to starve to death?' The soldiers were fully equipped with haversacks, and they emptied their sandwiches among the crowd. Then the soldiers left, and there was another meeting. Were the power-looms to be broken or not? Yes, it was decided, they must be broken at all costs.

From *Reminiscences of Thomas Duckworth*, describing the events of 25 April 1826. Thomas Duckworth was a hand loom weaver in Haslingden. He was sixteen at the time of the riots.

10 What did the hand loom weavers of Haslingden set out to do on the morning of 25 April 1826?
11 What are we told that suggests that the soldiers sympathised with the weavers?
12 Do you believe Thomas Duckworth's account of the events of 25 April 1826? Give reasons for your answer.

Source 4G

At Haslingden yesterday, notwithstanding the . . . troop of cavalry [in the area], a mill was attacked and the machinery destroyed . . . This morning as early as seven o'clock . . . almost 3,000 [people] successfully destroyed the power looms of three mills. Having been applied to most earnestly by the proprietors of two other mills for protection . . . the military were . . . placed in a position to defend a mill at Chatterton . . . where they were immediately assailed with volleys of stones, which placed the colonel in the necessity of ordering them to fire. Several of the mob were killed and it is to be feared from the incessant firing, which was kept up for more than a quarter of an hour, that a considerable number must have been wounded . . . The populace then dispersed gradually, but with the avowed intention of returning with an overbearing force. They were supplied mostly with bludgeons, clubs, etc., but no arms were observed. The obstinacy and determination of the rioters was most extraordinary, and such as I could not have credited had I not witnessed it myself.

Report for the Home Secretary written by an army officer, 26 April 1826.

13 What further information are we given about the events at Haslingden on 25 April 1826?
14 What are we told that supports Thomas Duckworth's statement that the weavers:
    met a troop of cavalry at Haslingden on 25 April;
    aimed to destroy power looms;
    were determined to destroy power looms 'at all costs'?

Study continued

15 What reason or reasons may the army officer have had for stressing the obstinacy and determination of the rioters in his report?

Now that you have studied the Lancashire riots, look again at the cartoon (Source 4A).

16 Do you think the cartoonist's view of the Luddites was biased? Give reasons for your answer.
17 If his view was biased, does this mean it was wrong? Give reasons for your answer.

Part Five

The Factory Acts

THE FIRST FACTORY ACTS

At the beginning of the nineteenth century, many people believed that factory workers' health was gradually undermined by the long hours they worked. They tried to persuade MPs to pass a law limiting the working day.

Most MPs believed they had no right to limit working hours for adults. They thought that workers and employers ought to be free to bargain and agree whatever hours of work they liked. So they refused to interfere.

But MPs were concerned when they heard that children were expected to work more than twelve hours a day. They knew that some factory owners took batches of orphans from workhouses (see Chapter 11) to work in their mills. These children were fed, clothed and housed by the mill owners and were entirely in their power. They had no parents to speak up for them. MPs decided that they needed protection, so in 1802 they passed an Act limiting their hours of work. Later, between 1819 and 1831, other Acts were passed limiting the hours of work for all children in most textile factories to twelve a day.

Study

This study asks you to consider:
Ev the reliability of the evidence in Source 5.

John Freestone was ten years old when he was questioned by the Parliamentary commissioner who was gathering evidence about children working in factories.

Source 5

I come to work at half past five in the morning; stay till eight o'clock. It is twelve and a half hours without meal time . . . I was very tired of standing just at first, for about a week. Yes, and some time after that too; a good deal at the end of the day; felt as if I could drop. It is not quite so bad now. I'm very tired when I go home at night. I'm tired now (five o'clock) . . .

If I went away now I should go in the yard and play. I shall go and do so now when I've done my victuals, and you've done talking to me. I never play after going

away at eight. Go to bed at nine. Fall asleep sometimes before going to bed. Never fall asleep here. Mother calls me in the morning. I never feel tired when I come in the morning. Can always eat my supper when I go home.

John Freestone, a piecer in a Leicester spinning mill, answering questions in 1833.

1 Do you believe John Freestone's evidence on the following:
the number of hours he worked a day;
the way in which he spent his time when he was not working;
whether or not he ever fell asleep at work?
Give reasons for your answers.
How might you check that his statements were reliable?

Illustration 3 An illustration from *The Life and Adventures of Michael Armstrong, the Factory Boy*, a novel by Frances Trollope.

Unfortunately the magistrates whose job it was to enforce the Factory Acts often owned factories themselves, so the laws were not properly enforced. In 1832, therefore, the House of Commons appointed a committee to investigate conditions in cloth mills, and in 1833 a Royal Commission also took evidence. Some of the extracts quoted in this chapter (for example, Source 3A) come from their report.

These enquiries proved that in spite of the laws, many children were working more than twelve hours a day, that some were cruelly treated, and that the health of a large number suffered as a result of their work.

FACTORY ACTS 1833–50

In 1833 Parliament passed a new Factory Act. This applied to all textile mills except lace and silk factories. More Acts were passed between 1836 and 1850 (see Table 2).

Table 2

Date	Terms of Act	Comment
1833	**1** *Hours of work* Children under nine years old not to work in textile mills Children aged nine to thirteen to work no more than nine h.p.d. (hours per day) Young people aged thirteen to eighteen to work no more than twelve h.p.d. No one under eighteen to do night work.	It was difficult to enforce the law because it was difficult to prove how old a child or young person was.
	2 *Government inspectors* Four inspectors were appointed by the government to make sure that factory owners were keeping the law.	Not enough inspectors to check all the mills. One of them, Robert Rickards, died of overwork.
1836	Births, marriages and deaths had to be registered.	Made it easier to check the age of workers.
1844	**1** *Hours of work* Children aged eight to eleven to work no more than six and a half h.p.d. Children aged twelve to sixteen to work no more than nine h.p.d. Young people aged thirteen to eighteen and women to work no more than twelve h.p.d.	Allowed children of eight to work in mills, but cut the h.p.d. for children under thirteen, and for women.
	2 *Safety precautions* Machinery to be fenced in.	Made factories safer.
1847	Young people and women to work no more than ten h.p.d.	Reduced h.p.d. for young people and women. They now worked shifts. Some men worked two shifts p.d.
1850	Prohibited use of 'relays' of women and young people. Increased hours to ten and a half h.p.d.	Men could work no more than ten and a half h.p.d. because it was impossible to run the mills without women and young people.

Study

In this study you are asked to consider three factory inspections that might have taken place between 1836 and 1851, and to discover:

Ch what major charges were brought about by the Acts over that period.

In pairs, use Table 2 on page 38 to answer the questions set on each inspection.
   Ask one person to give his or her answers to the class and see if the rest of you agree.

Inspection of a cotton mill in Manchester, 1836

An inspector arrives to carry out an inspection of the factory under the terms of the 1833 Factory Act.
   In his report the inspector said that he suspected that:
   some children working as piecers were under nine years of age;
   some young women on the night shift were under eighteen years of age.

1 Why could the mill owner have been prosecuted if the inspector's suspicions were correct?
2 The inspector could not prove that his suspicions were correct. Explain why not.

Inspection of a Bradford wool mill, 1846

An inspector has come to Bradford to make sure that the mill owners are carrying out the terms of the 1844 Factory Act. He arrives at 7 a.m., when the workers are starting the day shift.

3 At what time, allowing an hour's break for dinner, and twenty minutes for tea, would the inspector expect the following workers to stop work for the day:
   children aged eight to eleven;
   young people aged thirteen to eighteen;
   women over the age of eighteen?

4 Polly Wilkins, who works a twelve hour day, claims she is thirteen. The inspector is sure she is no more than eleven but cannot prove that she is lying. Why is the inspector unable to prove that Polly is lying?

Inspection of a Nottingham cotton mill, 1851

An inspector comes to see a factory in Nottingham that he remembers inspecting in 1843.
   In his report the inspector comments that, compared with his 1843 visit:
   workers seem more alert;
   the number of accidents has decreased;
   men work a ten hour day, even though no law has been passed limiting their hours of work.

5 What reasons may the inspector give to explain these changes?
6 What, do you think, were the main aims of the Factory Acts passed between 1833 and 1850? Why was it difficult to enforce these Acts?

Recall

1 Re-write this list of inventors and inventions, matching them correctly:

Inventors	Inventions
John Kay	Water frame
James Hargreaves	Power loom
Richard Arkwright	Flying shuttle
Samuel Crompton	Water frame
Edmund Cartwright	Spinning mule

2 In what year did an Act of Parliament:
   a limit the hours of work of orphan children in textile mills;
   b limit the hours of work of women employed in textile mills to twelve hours a day;
   c make it impossible for men employed in textile mills to work more than ten and a half hours a day?
3 A spinner living in 1850 would have been doing similar work to one who lived in 1700. In what ways would their working conditions have been different?

5
Power

—— Part One ——
Power in 1700

In 1700, four kinds of power were in common use. Table 1 gives some details.

Table 1

Source	Uses	Limitations	Cost
Manpower	Most used. Could work small machines, and shift small loads.	Needed breaks for rest. Might fall ill. Did not develop much power.	Expensive. Needed food, clothing and shelter.
Horsepower	Moving heavy loads in carts and wagons. Worked some machines.	Needed breaks for rest Might fall sick or be lamed.	Expensive. Needed food, shelter and care.
Wind	Grinding & pumping.	Unreliable. Would not work on calm days.	Cheap.
Water	Many uses. A water wheel could drive machinery to grind corn (Illustration 1), pump water, work bellows for furnaces, hammer iron, etc.	Reliable. Always worked unless there was a very hard frost or a long drought. Would work by any stream with a strong enough flow to turn a water wheel.	Cheap.

Illustration 1   The most common use for water power was driving corn mills.

40

——— Part Two ———
Steam Power

NEWCOMEN'S STEAM PUMP

Steam engines were first developed to pump water out of Cornish tin mines. By the end of the seventeenth century, most shallow seams of tin had been worked out and miners were having to sink deeper shafts. These shafts quickly filled with water and existing horse or water-powered pumps could not pump them dry.

Thomas Newcomen (1663–1729), an ironmonger from Dartmouth in Devon, improved these early engines and invented the first practical steam pump. It consisted of a huge beam like a see-saw.

One end was connected to a pump: the other to a piston which moved up and down in an open-topped cylinder.

Newcomen invented his pump in 1708. His first working engine was installed at a colliery at Dudley in Worcestershire in 1712. Its cylinder was 48 cm in diameter, and nearly two metres in length. It worked well, and in the next fifty years Newcomen pumps were set up at mines all over the country. They were expensive. In 1733 it cost about £850 to install one at a colliery near Newcastle-on-Tyne. But they were very strong and easy to maintain. Some remained in use for nearly two hundred years.

Study

Your aim in this study is:

K to understand how Newcomen's steam pump worked.

When a steam pump was installed, a skilled worker, called an 'engineer' or 'engine-man', was put in charge. The engineer was responsible for controlling the steam by opening and closing taps.

Instructions

To lower the pump piston:
Open Tap A
1 Steam from the boiler rises to fill the steam cylinder, allowing the piston to rise.
2 The counterweight pulls the other end of the beam down, sending the pump piston down the shaft.
3 Tap 'A' is closed.

To raise the pump piston:
Open Tap B
1 A jet of cold water from the tank is let into the steam cylinder.
2 The steam in the cylinder condenses (turns into water) and creates a vacuum. Air pressure now drives the piston down, pulling the end of the beam down.
3 The pump piston is pulled up, drawing water up the shaft with it.
4 Tap 'B' is closed.

In pairs

1 **a** Study the diagram of Newcomen's engine and the instructions on how it works for five minutes.
  b Cover the instructions and, with the help of the diagram, take it in turns to explain to each other how the engine works.

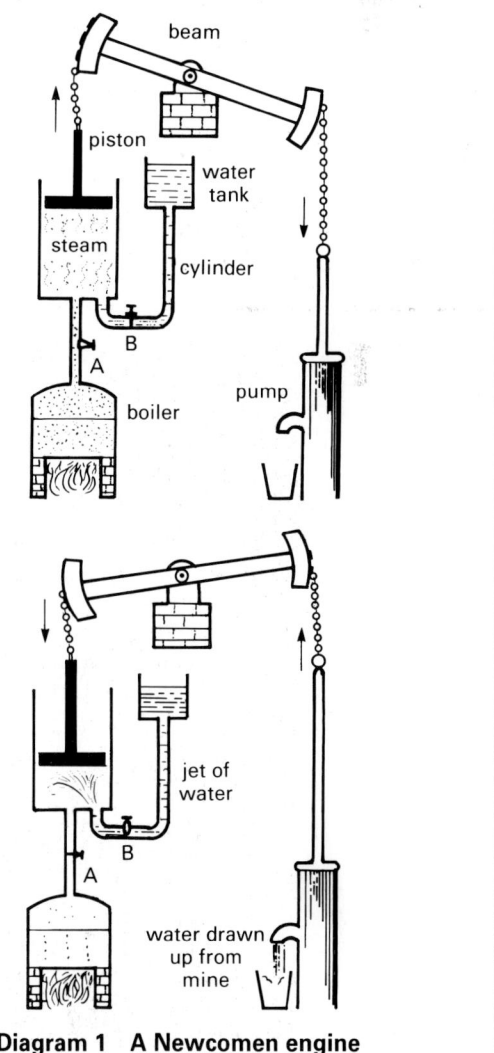

Diagram 1   A Newcomen engine

BOULTON AND WATT

James Watt and the separate condenser

James Watt (1736–1819) improved Newcomen's engine and eventually made it suitable for driving machinery. Watt was born at Greenock in Scotland. In 1763 he was working at Glasgow University making scientific instruments. One day he had to repair a model of Newcomen's engine, and noticed that the cylinder heated up every time steam entered it and then cooled down again when the water spray condensed the steam. He reckoned that alternately heating and cooling the cylinder wasted fuel. So he designed a separate chamber to draw the steam into when it was time for it to condense. He surrounded this 'condenser' with a water jacket to keep it cool and kept the cylinder hot by putting a steam jacket round it. Watt also decided to close in the top of the cylinder and used steam instead of air pressure to drive the piston down the cylinder.

Watt's improved engine

Watt made various improvements to his steam engine.

Chronology	
1769	Watt patented the separate condenser, but could not find skilled workmen to build his engine.
1773	Watt moved to Birmingham and went into partnership with Matthew Boulton (1728–1809). Boulton introduced him to John Wilkinson. He helped Watt to build two full-sized engines, which worked well, and consumed less than a third of the coal used by Newcomen's engines (see Illustration 2).
1782	Watt designed and patented the 'sun and planet wheel' which enabled his engines to drive machinery. Watt developed a 'double-acting' engine, in which the steam pushed the piston both up and down the cylinder.
1788	Watt adapted the 'centrifugal governor' used on windmills to control the speed of his engines automatically.

Study

Watt's engine was more efficient than Newcomen's. Your aim in this study is:

K to use the information in Source 1 below to work out why.

Source 1

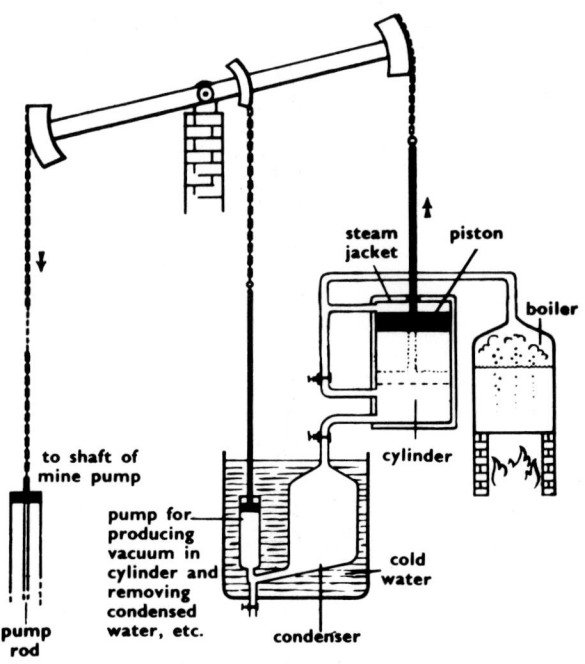

James Watt's improvements to Newcomen's steam engine.

In pairs, study Source 1, then jot down your answers to the questions below, and compare them with your partner's.

1 a In Watt's engine, did the steam condense in:
      the steam cylinder;
      a separate condenser?
   b By this stage of their development, steam engines had valve gear which opened and closed the taps automatically. Which tap would have opened to:
      let steam from the boiler into the steam cylinder;
      allow steam from the cylinder to pass into the condenser;
      draw off condensed water from the condenser?
2 Why was the steam cylinder still hot when Tap 'A' was turned off?
3 Write a paragraph of four or five sentences explaining why Watt's engine could be run on less coal than Newcomen's.

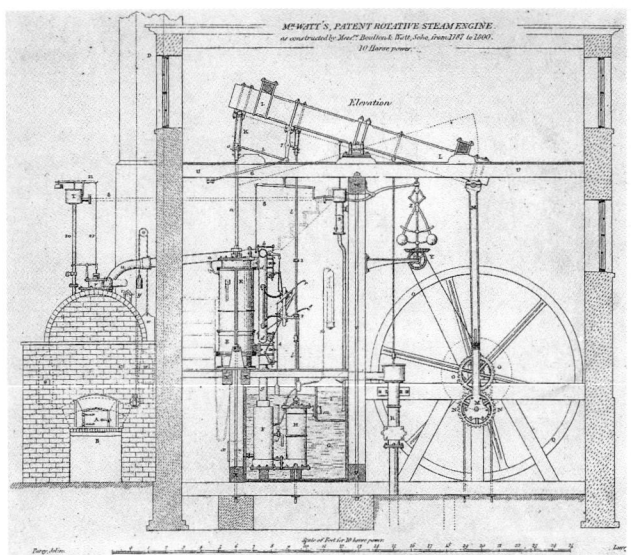

Illustration 2 An improved Boulton and Watt engine.

Study

By the end of the eighteenth century, steam was beginning to replace other forms of power. This was partly due to the partnership between James Watt and Matthew Boulton. In this study you will:

Ca use the information on pages 42–3 to work out why this partnership was so successful.

1 Rewrite the list below in the order of their importance to Boulton and Watt's success:
   a Boulton was a good businessman
   b Watt was a skilled inventor
   c Britain had plentiful supplies of coal
   d Wilkinson could make the cylinders that Watt needed
   e Britain's industries were expanding.
2 Ask one person to read his or her list to the class. Do the rest of you agree?

Boulton's deal

When Boulton realised that Watt's engines used so little fuel, he offered to adapt existing Newcomen engines in return for a yearly fee equal to a third of the savings made in the owner's fuel bill. This was a good deal for both sides. Within a few years all the engines in Cornwall, where coal was expensive, had been converted.

THE RESULTS OF STEAM POWER

The steam engine was one of the most important inventions of modern times. By 1850 it was used in a variety of ways. Diagram 2 shows you some of the results.

Diagram 2

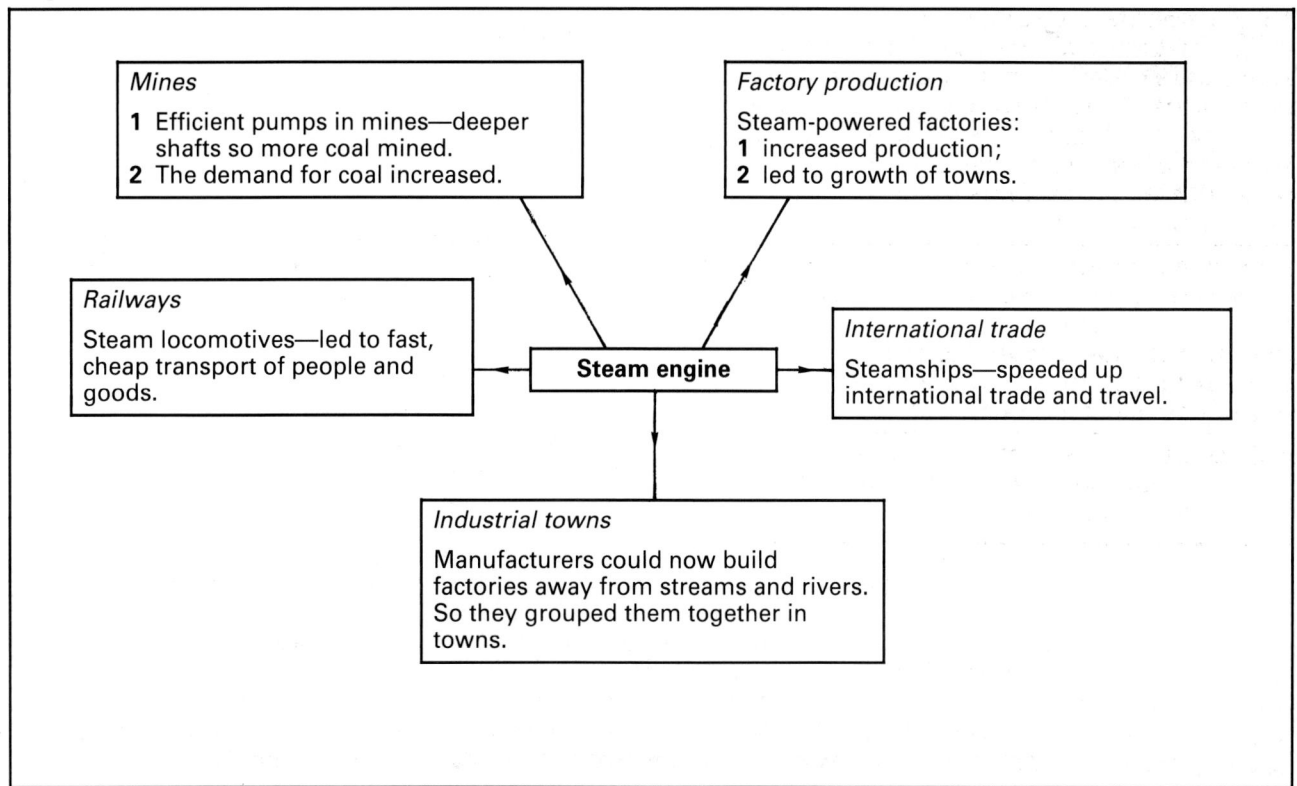

Mines
1 Efficient pumps in mines—deeper shafts so more coal mined.
2 The demand for coal increased.

Factory production
Steam-powered factories:
1 increased production;
2 led to growth of towns.

Railways
Steam locomotives—led to fast, cheap transport of people and goods.

Steam engine

International trade
Steamships—speeded up international trade and travel.

Industrial towns
Manufacturers could now build factories away from streams and rivers. So they grouped them together in towns.

Study

In this study you will be considering:

Em how various people who lived between 1750 and 1850 might have felt when they saw steam power taking over.

You will have to:
remember what you have learned about steam power;
use the information in Diagram 2.

Would you expect each of the following people to have welcomed or disliked the change to steam power?

1 A barge owner who used horse-drawn barges to transport goods to and from industrial towns.
2 A young man who wanted to be an engineer.
3 A manufacturer who wanted to set up a factory in an area where there were no fast-flowing streams.
4 A sail-cloth maker.
5 A poor but contented middle-aged farmer whose fields lay over a rich seam of coal.
Give reasons for each of your answers.

Recall

1 Which kind of power was considered the cheapest and most reliable in 1700?
2 Why are these years important in the history of the steam engine: 1712; 1773; 1788?
3 What could steam engines be used for after Watt invented the 'sun and planet wheel'?
4 What forms of power were used in 1700? Show how steam had become the most widely used source of power by 1850.
Include:
    examples of how each type of power was used;
    the advantages and disadvantages of each type of power;
    examples to show how steam power was used by 1850.

5 Write an account of the work of James Watt.
Include:
    his improvements to Newcomen's engine;
    his partnership with Matthew Boulton;
    two or more improvements he made to the steam engine.
6 'Steam is an Englishman' (an anonymous Frenchman).
'I sell . . . what all the world desires—*power*' (Matthew Boulton).
What reasons might each speaker have had for saying what he did about steam power?

6
Iron and Steel

Part One
Charcoal Iron

INTRODUCTION

To understand the development of the iron industry you need to know how an early eighteenth century blast furnace worked, and the difference between the various grades of iron.

At the beginning of the eighteenth century, iron was made in charcoal blast furnaces (see Diagram 1). When it was first lit, a charcoal furnace took about three days to heat up before the blast was put on. The blast made the interior of the furnace white-hot, turning the ore into iron. Furnaces were often kept in blast for months at a time.

Diagram 1   A charcoal blast furnace

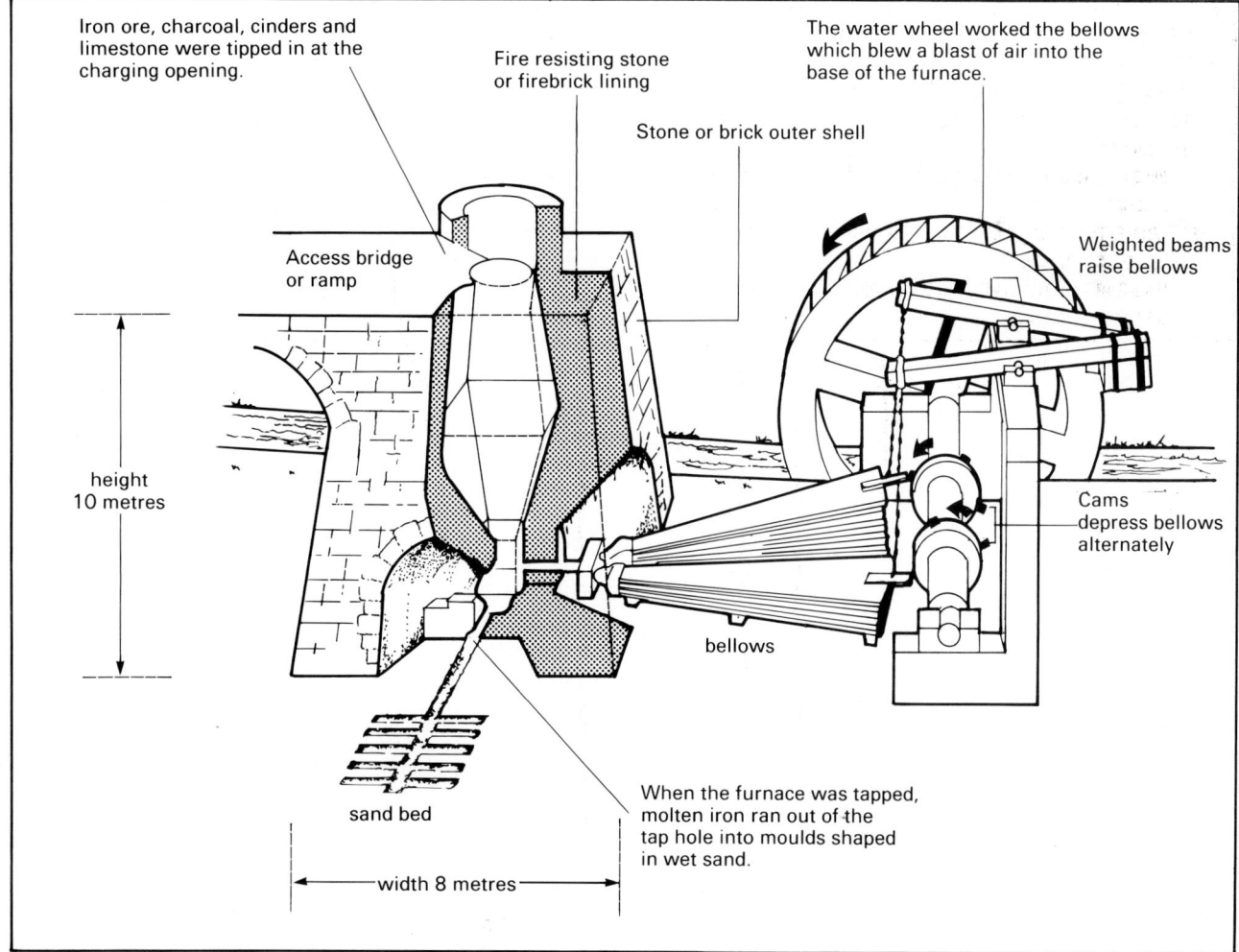

Iron ore, charcoal, cinders and limestone were tipped in at the charging opening.

Fire resisting stone or firebrick lining

Stone or brick outer shell

The water wheel worked the bellows which blew a blast of air into the base of the furnace.

Weighted beams raise bellows

Access bridge or ramp

height 10 metres

Cams depress bellows alternately

bellows

sand bed

When the furnace was tapped, molten iron ran out of the tap hole into moulds shaped in wet sand.

width 8 metres

Table 1   Grades of iron

Type	Description	Use
Pig or cast iron	Iron that has been smelted (extracted from the iron ore by melting) but not processed further.	Pots, kettles, pans.
Wrought iron	Iron that has been heated and hammered to get rid of impurities. This makes it tougher and more flexible.	Ploughshares, tools, cannons.
Steel	Iron with a high carbon content which has been heated and hammered until it is highly malleable.	Swords, springs, razors.

Study

This study will help you:

K to understand and use the information given in Diagram 1 and Table 1.

1 What kind of:
fuel was mixed with iron ore and tipped into the charging opening

power was used to work the bellows that blew the fuel in the furnace to a high temperature

iron would have been produced when the molten iron had run into the moulds and set?

2 All the substances fed into the charging opening contained impurities.
  a Why did these impurities have to be removed before the iron could be used to make wrought iron or steel?
  b How were the impurities removed?
3 Why would you expect a ton of steel to cost more than a ton of cast iron?

THE DEVELOPMENT OF THE IRON INDUSTRY

Centres of production in 1700

At the beginning of the eighteenth century there were fewer than 100 furnaces in England and Wales. Nearly half were in Sussex, Kent and Hampshire. The industry had grown up there because there was iron ore, lime and timber to feed the furnaces, and it was easy to transport the finished goods to sell in London or to one of the south coast ports.

Uses of iron

Most of the iron was used to make cooking pots, nails and tools. Some was also used to make weapons such as cannons. Britain was involved in the following wars during the eighteenth century:

1739–48	War of the Austrian Succession.
1756–63	Seven Years War.
1776–83	War of American Independence.
1793–1815	Revolutionary and Napoleonic Wars.

Population and production

As the population grew and prospered, the demand for iron products increased. In addition, iron was being used in buildings and to make machines. Sussex, Kent and Hampshire ironmasters could not easily increase production because they were short of timber to make into charcoal. They had to put their furnaces out for several months every year because they did not have enough wood to fuel them.

Production costs increase

Ironmasters in other areas also found it difficult to get enough timber. So they set up new furnaces in areas where timber was plentiful. Some shipped iron ore all the way to furnaces in the Highlands of Scotland because there was plenty of wood there. The cost of transporting ore to Scotland and bringing iron back to England made it very expensive, but it seemed the only way to increase production.

—— Part Two ——
Coke Iron

THE DARBYS OF COALBROOKDALE

The Darbys were a Quaker family who owned an ironworks at Coalbrookdale in the Severn Valley in Shropshire. They made several important discoveries and inventions.

Abraham Darby I, 1678–1717	
1708	Moved to Coalbrookdale to make cooking pots.
1709	Converted some local coal into coke and used it instead of charcoal in his furnace. It made hard, brittle iron.

Abraham Darby II, 1711–63	
1750	Produced a batch of tough, malleable iron smelted with coke. Installed wooden wagonways on which one wagon pulled by three horses could move as much as twenty packhorses on the old paths. Gradually replaced wooden ways with metal rails.

Abraham Darby III, 1750–89	
1779	Erected an iron bridge over the Severn (Illustration 1). It was the first iron bridge in the western world.

Illustration 1　An engraving of the Iron Bridge near Coalbrookdale.

Study

In this study you will:

Ev consider the reliability of pictures as evidence.

Remember what you have learned about Coalbrookdale.

Source 1A

Coalbrookdale is itself a very romantic spot. It is a winding glen between two immense hills . . . all thickly covered with wood, forming the most beautiful sheets of hanging wood. Indeed too beautiful to be much in unison with [the] . . . horrors . . . at the bottom; the noise of forges, mills etc., with all their vast machinery, the flames bursting from the furnaces with the burning of the coal and the smoke of the lime kilns.

Arthur Young, *A Tour of Shropshire* (1776)

Source 1B

Abraham Darby's ironworks at Coalbrookdale.

1   What are we shown in Source 1B that suggests this picture of Coalbrookdale was painted: after 1709; before 1750?
2   Some artists who painted industrial scenes made them look more romantic and attractive than they really were. Do you think that Source 1B shows us what Coalbrookdale was really like when the artist painted this picture? Give reasons for your answer.
3   Would the picture be of any use to historians if it exaggerated the beauties of Coalbrookdale? Give reasons for your answer.

THE DEVELOPMENT OF COKE IRON

It was many years before the majority of ironmakers used coke in their furnaces, partly because news of the discovery spread slowly, and partly because most coal was unsuitable for making iron. But as the demand for iron increased, more and more ironmasters had to use coal, because there was no longer enough wood to go round. So they worked hard to improve the quality of the iron they produced. Table 2 gives details of what three of the most important ironmasters achieved.

Huntsman lived in Sheffield, which was famous for producing edged tools such as knives, shears and scissors. Only steel was hard enough to keep an edge, and flexible enough not to snap when in use. So Sheffield craftsmen needed large quantities of steel, all of which had to be made in very small furnaces, like that used by Huntsman. It took a long time to produce the amount of steel they needed. This made it very expensive. It was not until 1856 that it became possible to produce steel cheaply and quickly (see page 172).

Table 2

Name	Discovery	Results
Benjamin Huntsman (1704–1776). Quaker clockmaker. Lived in Yorkshire	Made 'crucible steel'.	Produced small amounts of steel for making razors, springs, etc.
John Wilkinson (1728–1808). 'Iron-Mad' Wilkinson. Staffordshire ironmaster.	Used steam engines to blow bellows of furnaces. In 1774 he invented a machine for boring gun barrels, cylinders, etc. Specialised in munitions.	Furnaces heated more efficiently. Boulton and Watt used only Wilkinson's cylinders because they were so accurate. Wilkinson became very rich.
Henry Cort (1740–1800). Businessman and ironfounder from the south of England.	In 1784 he produced wrought iron by heating it in a special coke furnace—a puddling furnace—and rolling it out into rods.	Speeded up production of wrought iron fifteen fold. Made production of large amounts of good quality cheap wrought iron possible.

Study: Library work

In this study you will be finding out:

K how the work of the three ironmasters mentioned in Table 2 helped the development of the iron and steel industries.

1 List the sections in your school or local library where you might find the answers to these questions:
   a How did the methods introduced by *i* Huntsman and *ii* Cort help to reduce the impurities in iron and steel?
   b Why did these methods help to increase the number of goods that were made of iron?
   c Give three or more examples to show how 'Iron-Mad' Wilkinson earned his nickname.

2 Find the information you need and answer the questions in brief notes.
3 With the help of your notes and the information in Table 2, write an essay on: 'Huntsman, Wilkinson and Cort—three great ironmasters'.

Study

In this study you will see:

Em why puddlers—the workers who ran 'puddling furnaces'—were respected in iron-manufacturing towns.

Source 2A

A puddling furnace.

Source 2B

The puddler dare not relax his efforts for a single minute. Though the perspiration trickles from his face and arms, and oozes through his scanty clothing, he must toil on. His eye is never removed from watching the contents of the furnace . . . [Puddling] is the severest kind of labour voluntarily undertaken by men.

David Bremner, *The Industries of Scotland* (1869).

Source 2C

The puddler was looked up to as one standing somewhat higher in the social scale than most in his own department of the works. Many young puddlers refused promotion to managerial positions. They made more money and were more independent than the 'gaffers'.

Anonymous contribution to *Recollections of Merthyr's past.*

Source 2D

[He] filled the whole chapel with his presence . . . and he made a greater flutter as he swaggered down the aisle than did the minister and his family.

(Of a puddler going to Chapel in Merthyr). Reminiscences by 'Merlin' in *Red Dragon*, a magazine (1883).

1 Why would a foreman who was hiring puddlers have looked for strong, fit, alert men?
2 Why might a puddler who refused promotion when he was young have accepted it when he reached middle age?
3 Why, do you think, did people living in iron-manufacturing towns have so much respect for puddlers?

RICHARD CRAWSHAY (1739–1810): AN EIGHTEENTH-CENTURY IRONMASTER

Crawshay was one of the first ironmasters to take advantage of Cort's discovery. He was born near Leeds in Yorkshire. At the age of fifteen he went to London to make his fortune. He married the daughter of an ironmonger and eventually inherited his shop. The business prospered and Crawshay decided to invest his money in an ironworks. He realised that there would be a large demand for cheap wrought iron, which was tougher and more flexible than cast iron. So in 1786 he took over a small works at Cyfartha, near Merthyr in South Wales, where there was plenty of iron ore, coal and limestone. He built new furnaces, forges and rolling mills, and in 1803 the Cyfartha works were said to be the biggest in Britain. Crawshay employed almost 2,000 men and his works produced about 10,000 tonnes of iron a year, most of which he made into shells and cannons, Cyfartha was such a success that Crawshay set up several other iron-works in neighbouring valleys, and when he died he left a fortune of £1.5 million.

Study

In this study you will:

Ch see what effect the iron industry had on Merthyr Tydfil and the people who lived there.

Source 3A

Rolling mills at Merthyr by night, painted by Thomas Hornor in 1817.

Source 3B

Speculators of various kinds seem to have built courts, alleys and rows of houses wherever opportunities presented themselves, in order to meet the demand for the rapid increase of the town . . . without any control as to lines, the form of streets, or to arrangements for drainage . . .

The rarity of privies is one of the marked characteristics of the town . . . In some localities, a privy was found common to 40 or 50 persons and more . . . The cinder heaps, as the lines of refuse slags from the iron works are termed, and the river sides are frequented by persons of all ages and sexes, who manage the best way they can.

Report on Merthyr Tydfil by Sir H. T. De La Beche (1845).

Source 3C

During the time I was in Merthyr, I saw nothing in the shape of public brawling or disturbance, either by night or day. The streets are full and the public houses also, through the greater part of Saturday and Monday. On other days the town appeared to be as quiet as any place of equal size. On Sundays, public Worship was the most frequented in the evening from six to eight o'clock. From eight to ten o'clock the streets are as full as Saturday, there being a public promenade by the working classes. At this time their houses are for the most part deserted. On the Sunday I was in Merthyr, they walked about in a manner both sufficiently quiet and decorous.

Report of the Council of Education (1847).

Source 3D

In 1801 there were   7,704 people in Merthyr
    1849   45,016
    1853   50,579

In 1854, 527 out of every 1,000 children born in Merthyr died before they reached the age of five. Only Liverpool was worse, with 528.

Public Health reports by Merthyr Officer of Health, 1855.

Source 3E

Women and girls had been employed at the Dowlais Works since its earliest days, as limestone girls, tippers, cokers and pilers. Exposed to extremes of hot and cold and all sorts of weather, they broke up limestone, also coke, with heavy hammers. Pilers stacked piles of bars in the Puddling Mills.

F. Vaughan, *The Women of Merthyr in the Nineteenth Century* in *Recollections of Merthyr's Past* (1979) (secondary source).

1 In 1760 Merthyr Tydfil was 'a tiny village inhabited by shepherds and farmers'. How had the appearance of the village changed by 1845?
2 a Why may so many children in Merthyr have died before they were five years old?
   b How might you check to see if your suggestion is correct?
3 Why may women have been willing to live in Merthyr in spite of the poor housing and high rate of infant mortality?

Part Three
The Growth of the Iron Industry

COKE-FIRED FURNACES

The wars in the second half of the eighteenth century encouraged industrialists to set up new ironworks. In addition, extra furnaces were added to existing works. By 1800 there were nearly four times as many furnaces as in 1700.

Almost all new furnaces were coke-fired. This was partly because most ironmasters installed steam engines to blow their furnaces. Steam engines produced a strong, constant blast. This made furnaces hotter than before, and burned away more impurities. So the quality of coke-smelted iron improved rapidly. Gradually charcoal furnaces closed down. By the end of the eighteenth century there were very few left and most ironworks were near coal mines.

In the early nineteenth century only good quality coal was coked for use in blast furnaces. Poor coal produced less coke, which made the iron more expensive. Most Scottish coal coked badly, so Scottish iron was much dearer than Welsh or English.

Illustration 2   This photograph, taken in 1851, shows James Nasmyth and the steam-powered hammer he invented. His hammer made it easier, quicker and cheaper to shape large pieces of iron, and so helped to increase the production of iron goods.

THE HOT BLAST

In 1828 James Neilson, a Scottish engineer, discovered that furnaces worked much more efficiently if the air blasted into them was heated. He was able to halve the amount of coke he used. He also found that, using a hot blast, he could load furnaces with a mixture of coal and iron ore and produce good cast iron. It was the first time uncoked coal was used to fuel furnaces.

Neilson's discovery was vitally important for the Scottish iron industry, because the Scots were now able to use blackband ironstone, a mixture of iron ore and coal, in their furnaces. There were huge quantities of this ironstone in Lanarkshire, and new ironworks were built to take advantage of it. Between 1830 and 1860 the amount of iron produced in Scotland increased from 37,000 tonnes to more than a million tonnes a year.

SUMMING UP

By 1851 the British iron industry was the most advanced in the world. Indeed, Britain was producing more than half the world's iron. It was turned into a huge variety of products, ranging from pins and inkstands to ships and railways.

Study

In this study you will consider:

Ca why the iron industry expanded between 1750 and 1850.

The list below gives a number of reasons why the iron industry in Britain was able to expand between 1750 and 1850. Rewrite them in what you think is the correct order of importance.

1 Britain was at war for long periods between 1750 and 1850.
2 The use of the steam engine to blow furnaces meant that impurities in iron were burned away more efficiently.
3 Cort's puddling furnaces were coke-fired.
4 Neilson found that if hot air was blasted into furnaces, coal could be used as a fuel without converting it to coke.
5 Britain had large deposits of coal.

Ask one person to read his or her list to the class. Do the rest of you agree?

Recall

Test your memory

1 Name the first man to:
use coke to smelt iron successfully;
make crucible steel;
use the 'puddling' process.
2 Give two examples to show how steam power
was used in the iron industry.

Table 3
Iron production 1720–1850
(tonnes per annum)

1720–40	c25,000
1788	c68,000
1796	125,000
1806	244,000
1823	455,000
1830	677,000
1840	1,400,000
1850	2,200,000

3 a Copy the headings below.

The Iron Industry	
1720	*1850*

b Copy the list below under the heading *1720*:
The industry produced c25,000 tonnes of
iron a year.
Production was concentrated in areas with
supplies of iron ore and timber, e.g. Kent,
Sussex and Hampshire.
Wrought iron and steel took a long time to
make and were expensive.
Iron was used to make household utensils
and munitions, but was not used for large
structures, e.g. bridges.

c Complete your notes by showing how each
item listed in the *1720* column had changed
by 1850.

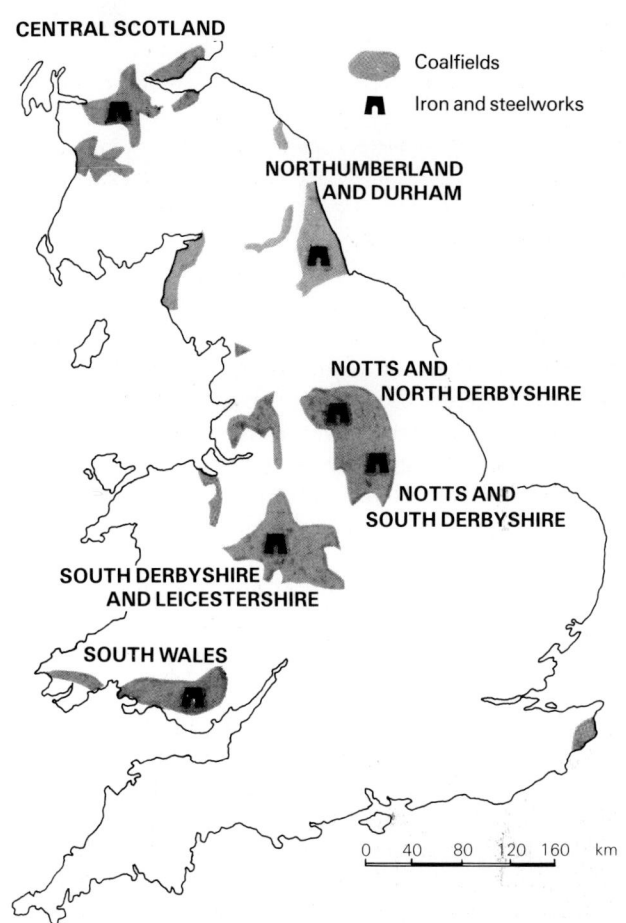

Map 1   Iron-producing areas, 1850

7
Coal

Part One
Mining in 1700

GETTING THE COAL

Pits

At the beginning of the eighteenth century Britain probably produced about 2.5 million tonnes of coal a year. Some came from drift mines (mines driven into hillsides). The rest came from pit shafts.

By modern standards, mines were small and simple. Pit shafts were lined with wooden planks. At some mines, horses harnessed to an 'engine' hauled the coal to the surface in 'corves', which were baskets made of hazel twigs woven onto a wooden framework. At others the 'winding' was done by men and women (see Diagrams 1A and 1B).

Mine workers

Hewers worked underground. They hacked out coal with pickaxes, levered it out with wedges or blasted it out with gunpowder. Hewers were paid piece work—about one old penny for each corf that they filled.

Barrow men or bearers loaded coal into the corves and pulled them to the bottom of the pit shaft on rough wooden sledges. In some parts of the country this work was done by women. Barrow men were paid about 1s 8d a day.

Difficulties

The work of the barrow men was slow and hard. If the hewers were working more than about 200 metres from the pit shaft, the barrow men took so long to haul the coal that they could not clear all that was cut. So when the hewers had cut all the coal within about 200 metres of the shaft, the mine owner sank another about 400 metres away from the old one and worked from that. In shallow pits the bearers or barrow men had to carry the coal up ladders to the surface.

About half the coal in a seam had to be left in the mine. This was because the hewers did not bother to put in props. Instead they left columns of coal standing to support the roof.

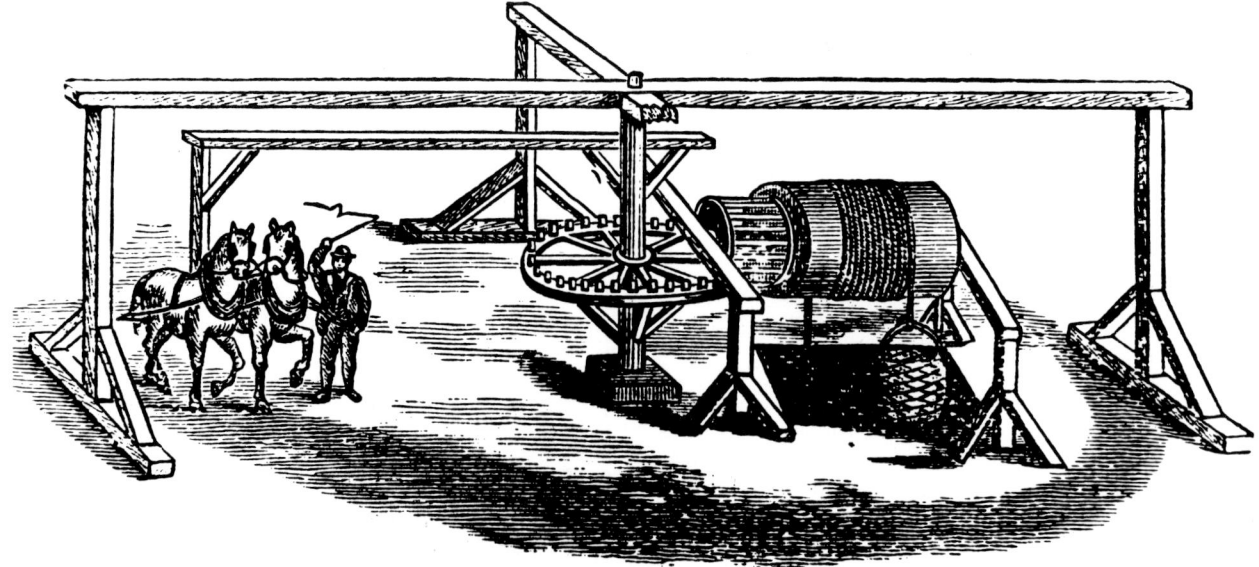

Illustration 1   A horse-gin for hauling coal to the surface.

Dangers

Gas was one danger. It was difficult to keep the air fresh. If there was choke-damp (carbon monoxide) in the pit, the miners might suffocate. If there was fire-damp (methane), the whole mine might be destroyed by underground explosions set off by the candles the miners used to light the pit.

Flooding: very few pits were completely dry, and many had two or three underground springs or 'feeders' leaking into them. Before the invention of the steam pump (see Chapter 5), horse gins (Illustration 1) or water-powered pumps were used to remove the water. They were not very effective, and many mines had to be abandoned when a sudden rush of water 'drowned' them.

TRANSPORTING COAL

Coal is heavy and bulky. At the beginning of the eighteenth century, the only ways to move it by road were on packhorses or in small carts. Both were very expensive. The only cheap way to carry coal was by boat, so most mines were either very near to the place where the coal was burned, or close to a sea port or navigable river.

Sea coal

The most prosperous mines in Britain were in Northumberland and Durham. Most of the coal they produced was taken by sea to London where it was known as 'sea coal'—the most popular fuel for heating homes and other buildings.

Study

The aim of this study is to help you to understand:

K how coal was mined in about 1700

Em why a miner's work was difficult and dangerous.

Diagram 1A   A drift mine

Diagram 1B   A pit

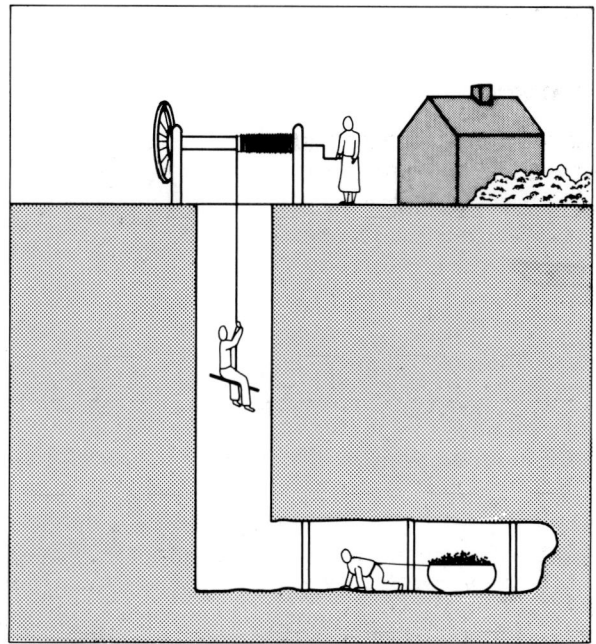

1 a Draw Diagram 1A and Diagram 1B.
   b Compare the diagrams with the information on page 54 and label them correctly.
2 Give three or more reasons why working down a pit was more dangerous than working in a drift mine.

3 a Why would bearers in Diagram 1B have found it difficult to do their work when the hewer at the coal face had cut another few metres of coal?
   b Why, do you think, would work in both a drift mine and a pit have been dirty and difficult?

Part Two

Output Increases

THE NEED FOR COAL

In 1700 coal was used as a fuel in houses and by salt makers, soap boilers, sugar refiners, brick makers and brewers. Between 1750 and 1850 the output of coal increased. Diagram 2 gives the figures, and shows how most of the extra coal was used.

Diagram 2

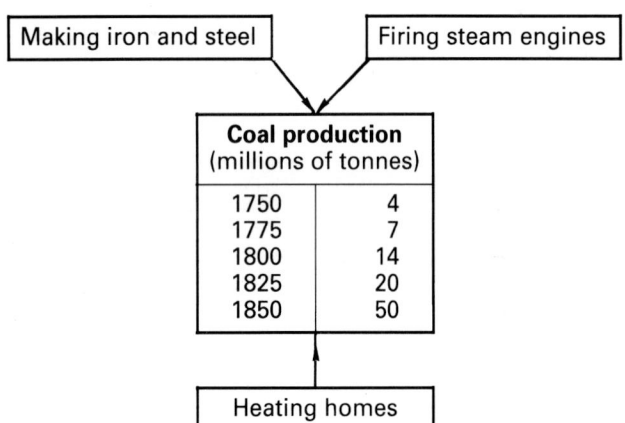

Coal production (millions of tonnes)	
1750	4
1775	7
1800	14
1825	20
1850	50

THE EFFECT ON MINES

To get the extra coal, mine owners sank deeper pit shafts and drove longer passageways underground.

Dealing with dangers

Methane: many mines still had pockets of methane gas. To deal with this a man dressed in wet clothes crawled along the passages, holding a long pole with a lighted candle on the end. When the candle flame hit a pocket of methane there was an explosion which cleared the methane. Usually the long pole and the wet clothes kept the man safe.

Carbon monoxide: the miners took canaries down the mine. A very small amount of gas would kill a canary, so when the miners saw the bird die they got out.

Flooding: mine owners installed steam pumping engines to clear the water.

Part Three

Miners at Home

WAGES

Miners could earn high wages. In 1840 their pay was about 3s 6d a day. Mine owners expected them to work six days a week, but many worked only five. Even so their pay was nearly double that of many farm workers, and as most miners' wives worked down the pits with their husbands, miners and their families had plenty of money to spend.

LIVING CONDITIONS

Villages

Most miners lived in squalor. A visitor to the 'Black Country' in the West Midlands described pit villages as 'very unsightly and unsavoury', and wrote of the 'disgusting' smell rising from rubbish heaped outside the doors of cottages.

Houses

Most houses consisted of two rooms—a living room and a bedroom. The women were expected to look after the home, but miners' wives also worked down the pit all day, and had no time or energy to do housework. 'I was so tired', said a Scottish miner's wife, 'that I had no heart for it.' So there was no one to clean the house. A Lancashire doctor said that the cottages were 'wretched in the extreme', with the children covered in lice. One doctor in Scotland noticed 'a fearful amount of filth, dust etc. accumulated on the walls, floors and furniture' of miners' cottages, and a commissioner visited a miner's house in Scotland where the total furniture for a family of nine consisted of two bedsteads, two chairs, three stools and a table.

Study

In this study you will be:

Ch considering changes that took place in the coal industry as a result of the increased demand for coal.

Use the sources below and remember what you have learned about the increase in coal output.

Source 1A

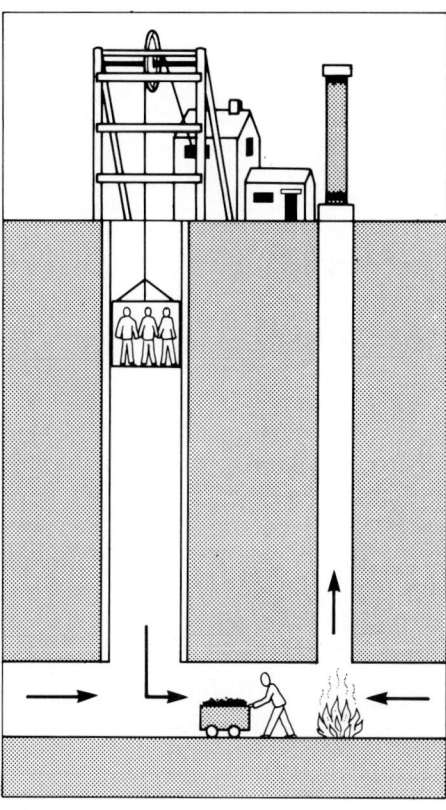

A ventilated pit shaft.

Source 1C   Coal production

Date	Millions of tonnes
1750	4
1775	7
1800	14
1825	20
1850	50

Source 1D

Covered in filth . . . ragged and beastly . . . half-naked, blackened all over with dirt . . . they looked like a race fallen from the common rank of man, and doomed . . . to wear away their lives in these dismal shades.

Richard Ayton describing workers he saw down a pit in Cumberland in 1813.

Source 1B

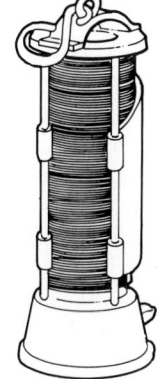

A Davy lamp, invented by Sir Humphrey Davy in 1815. Its flame turned blue when gas was present.

1 Compare Source 1A with Diagram 1B. List at least two changes that had taken place in pits by 1850 as a result of increased demand for coal.

2 a Why was mining a safer job after 1850?
  b In what ways was the work still hard, unpleasant and dangerous?

3 a What evidence is there to suggest that between 1750 and 1850 there was a great increase in the number of people employed in the coal industry?
  b Consider the ways in which coal was used by 1850. Why might it have been said that coal mining had become the most important industry in Britain?

Food

Miners ate well. They bought expensive cuts of meat and enjoyed roast duck or goose with vegetables such as asparagus and green peas.

Leisure

Miners lived a rough life. Some never washed their bodies. They believed that too much washing would make them weak. They were paid once a fortnight, and many at once spent most of their money on drink. When they were bored they organised prize fights, cock fights, or went bear baiting. Most did not care what their houses were like. Only a few stayed at home in their free time, cultivating their gardens and, perhaps, breeding pigeons. It was said that they were very generous, glad to share their food and their money with a passing tramp.

Part Four

The Mines and the Government

THE 1840 ENQUIRY

In 1840 the government decided to investigate working conditions in mines, and appointed commissioners to interview mineworkers all over the country. They were shocked by what they discovered.

Underground workers

Trappers

They found that some children as young as five or six worked underground as 'trappers', opening doors in passageways to allow coal trucks to pass through to and from the shaft.

Thrusters

As they grew older the children had harder work to do. Thomas Moorhouse described how when he was nine years old he began 'thrusting' in a mine, that is, pushing loaded trucks along the passages. When they were fully grown most of the boys became hewers.

Bearers

Girls were employed as bearers or 'drawers' who crawled along on all fours pulling loaded coal trucks behind them. Even pits which had horses needed a few bearers because some of the passages were too low for pit ponies to enter.

Bearers went on working after they were married, and even while they were pregnant. This sometimes caused miscarriages, but if they were fit some women worked almost until their baby was due. One woman told a commissioner that she once gave birth down the pit, and carried her baby up to the surface wrapped in her skirt.

The commissioners were horrified when they discovered that most women and girls working underground only wore a ragged pair of trousers, while many of the hewers with whom they worked were completely naked. The commissioners concluded that women ought not to be allowed to work underground.

Pit-bank girls

At many mines, young women worked at the pit head. They loaded the coal which came up the shaft into wagons and drove them away. The commissioners found that these girls were well grown, healthy and strong. One wrote: 'They drive coal carts, ride astride upon horses ... drink, swear, fight, smoke, whistle and sing, and care for nobody'. Another noticed that the girls 'often enter the beer shops, call for their pints and smoke their pipes like men'.

One commissioner did not know what to think of pit-bank girls. He wrote: 'Being very happy they are certainly no objects for pity, but surely their circumstances are of a kind in which girls should never be placed'. He thought they ought to be working as domestic servants.

Study

In this study you will be considering some of the evidence collected during the 1840 enquiry. Your aim is to decide:

Ev how reliable the evidence was;
why the commissioners might have included that evidence in their report to Parliament.

Source 2A

A young woman bearer at work in a mine.

Source 2B

The work is far too hard for me; the sweat runs off me all over sometimes. I am very tired at night. Sometimes when we get home at night we have not power to wash us, and then we go to bed. Sometimes we fall asleep in the chair . . . there is naught else for us to do . . . I don't know my letters. I never learnt nought.

Ann Eggley, aged eighteen. She worked as a bearer from four in the morning till four in the afternoon at a Yorkshire pit.

Source 2C

They are allowed no light, but sometimes a good-natured collier will bestow a little bit of candle on them, as a treat. On one occasion as I was passing a little trapper, he begged me for a little grease from my candle. I found that the poor child had scooped out a hole in a great stone, and having obtained a wick, had manufactured a rude sort of lamp; and that he kept going as well as he could by begging contributions of melted tallow from the candles of any Samaritan passers-by.

J. C. Symons, a commissioner appointed by Parliament.

Source 2D

I'm a trapper in the Gawber pit. It does not tire me, but I have to trap without a light, and I'm scared. Sometimes I sing when I have a light, but not in the dark; I dare not sing then. I don't like being in a pit . . . I would like to to be at school far better than in the pit.

Sarah Gooder, aged eight.

1 a Would you expect the evidence of the following people to be reliable:
   Ann Eggley (Source 2B);
   J. C. Symons (Source 2C);
   Sarah Gooder (Source 2D)?
   Give reasons for your answers.
  b What are we told about Sarah Gooder's working conditions (Source 2D) that appears to be confirmed by Source 2C?
  c Why is it difficult to know whether Source 2B is reliable or not?
2 The commissioners included a number of drawings in their report. Suggest a reason or reasons why they included the drawing shown in Source 2A.
3 Suggest a reason or reasons why J. C. Symons included the account of his meeting with the trapper (Source 2C) in his report to Parliament.

Study

In this study you will be:

Em looking at the work of a pit-bank girl from the point of view of three people who might have lived in 1840.

Consider the information on page 58 and in Table 1. Also remember what you have learned about a bearer's work.

Source 2E

A 'pit bank girl', photographed in 1864.

Table 1

	Pit-bank girl	Maid of all work
Work	Loading coal from shafts into wagons and driving it away. Worked with a group of girls. Went home after work.	Cleaning, mending, cooking and other housework. Worked alone. Lived in.
Days off	Sunday and part of Saturday.	Half a day or a day a week.
Pay per week	Twelve years old—four shillings. Eighteen years old—eight shillings.	About five shillings plus board and lodging.

1 Why might a commissioner have thought that being a maid of all work was more suitable for a girl than working at the pit-bank?
2 Why might a pit-bank girl have preferred working at the pit-bank to being a maid of all work?
3 Why might a bearer have thought she would rather be a pit-bank girl?

THE MINES ACT 1842

Terms

In 1842 the commissioners reported to Parliament. MPs were shocked to learn that conditions were so bad. As a result they passed the Acts shown opposite.

Table 2 Mines Acts

Date	Terms of Act
1842	No women, or children under ten were to work underground.
1843	No one under the age of fifteen was to be put in charge of pit winding gear.
1850	Inspectors were appointed to see that the law was obeyed.

Illustration 2   A row of miners' cottages in Lanarkshire, photographed in about 1900.

Study

In this study you can show your skill in using primary sources to work out:

Ev why the 1842 Act may not have been obeyed in some areas;
how you might follow up the effects of the Act on the employment of women in a particular area.

Use the information you have been given about the Mines Acts as well as the sources below.

Source 3A

In all parts of the coal districts where women had been employed, complaints were numerous of the hardships that the Act had occasioned to elder females, widows, orphan daughters of mature age, families where there were no sons to aid a father who was old and ailing; and other similar cases.

Mining commissioners' report, 1844.

Source 3B

We had about 100 females in our pits when the Act came into operation. Many of these have got work in brick fields and out-door labour from the farmers; some have gone into service; one or two are married. Some are maintained by their relations; others earn a little by sewing . . .

The women earned in the pit from 10d to 1s 1d a day. Now the men draw the coal for themselves. We give them the same as before for hewing, and pay them over and above for the putting. Being no longer dependent on the women . . . and [with] our horses, which we have since introduced assisting them, the men can now earn as much as before.

F. Grier, manager of a colliery in Fife, 1844.

Source 3C

In April 1849 Robert Smith, mineral agent of Blaenavon Colliery, went down the pit. He turned out 70 women and girls, as many as 20 . . . being not more than eleven or twelve years of age. He has no doubt that since then many have gone back from time to time. He gave notice that he would fine any man whom he found employing them again, and he has fined seven or eight from 5s to 10s each.

Report of a Parliamentary commissioner on the South Wales mining districts, 1850.

1   What evidence is there to suggest that between 1842 and 1850 the 1842 Mines Act was not obeyed in some areas?
2   What reasons can you suggest to explain *why* the Act may have been obeyed in some areas, but not in others?
3   How might the following help you to find out how women in mining areas earned a living between 1842 and 1850:
    photographs and drawings of people at work;
    the mining commissioners' reports;
    the census returns for 1841 and 1851?

Changes in mining areas, 1842–50

At the mines

Pit winding gear was improved. Steel wires were used instead of iron chains and hemp ropes, and wooden corves were replaced by iron cages which ran up and down the shafts on metal rails and carried whole wagons loaded with coal.

Before 1843, anyone was allowed to control pit winding gear, and it was quite common for young boys to be given the job because it did not need much strength. But sometimes the boys forgot what they were doing, and caused serious accidents. After the 1843 Act the accident rate fell.

In the villages

In 1850 a traveller noticed that pit villages looked 'far better' than they used to. The houses were cleaner and better furnished. Many had mahogany bedsteads and chests of drawers, eight-day clocks, good chairs, china, and polished brass candlesticks.

A government inspector who visited mining villages in 1850 noticed that many miners owned books. He thought that miners had 'greatly improved'.

Recall

1 What was: a drift mine; a corf; a horse gin; sea coal?
2 What work did women do in the coal industry before 1842? How and why did the situation change in that year?
3 In pairs, answer the following questions in brief notes.
   a Between 1842 and 1850, which of the following *i* changed, *ii* did not change?
   The size of houses in mining villages.
   The standard of comfort and cleanliness in the villages.
   The amount of time miners spent at home as a result of accidents caused by the winding gear.
   The way miners used their leisure time and money.
   b What reasons can you suggest to explain *why* these changes took place?
   c In 1842 many people believed it was wrong for the government to interfere in running industries. Do *you* think the results of the Acts passed between 1842 and 1850 justified the government's interference in the mining industry? Give reasons for your answer.
   Ask one person to read his or her answers to the class. Do the rest of you agree?

8
Communications

— Part One —
Roads

THE ROADS DEFOE TRAVELLED

Soil and roads

In 1725 Defoe wrote a report on England's roads. In some areas, where the soil was light and drained easily or there was plenty of stone and gravel to repair the roads, he found them 'hard and pleasant'. But wherever there was clay soil, roads were quickly churned into mud and became almost impassable.

Transport problems

Defoe described a stretch of road near Baldock in Hertfordshire which was so bad that travellers used to pay farmers to let them ride through their fields alongside the road rather than 'plunge into sloughs and holes which no horse could wade through'.

Defoe noticed that it was very difficult to move heavy goods. He saw tree fellers in Kent moving a tree trunk down to the shipbuilders at Chatham. They used a huge cart called a 'tug', pulled by twenty-two oxen. He wrote: 'sometimes 'tis two or three years before it gets to Chatham; for if once the rains come in it stirs no more that year, and sometimes a whole summer is not dry enough to make the roads passable'.

Travelling to market

Fortunately most people did not have to travel further than the nearest market. Poor people walked. Prosperous people rode on horseback. Animals were driven 'on the hoof', and goods were carried on packhorses.

TURNPIKES

The need for better roads

The increase in population, improvements in farming and the growth of industry all added to road traffic. Improving farmers produced more corn and cattle to send to market, and industrialists had to bring in raw materials and take their products to market. They needed good roads, and were prepared to pay for them.

Turnpike trusts

Parliament devised a new system for financing roads. They appointed groups of people known as 'trustees'. Each group was responsible for maintaining a short stretch of road. The trustees set up gates on their road and made all those who passed through pay a small amount of money to help maintain the roads (a toll). The toll gates were known as 'turnpikes', and the roads were called 'turnpike roads'.

The roads

The first turnpikes

The first turnpike was set up in 1663. By 1750, 400 Turnpike Acts had been passed, and by 1830 there were 1,116 trusts controlling 35,000 km of roads. Some trustees improved their roads dramatically. Defoe noticed that the roads from London to Harwich which were 'formerly deep, in time of floods dangerous, and at other times in winter scarce passable', were, after they had been taken over by turnpike trustees, 'so firm, so safe, so easy to travellers and carriages as well as cattle, that no road in England can yet be said to equal them'.

Bad turnpike roads

Sometimes, however, turnpikes were still in a bad state. Travellers usually blamed the trustees for not doing their jobs properly, and resented having to pay. Occasionally furious mobs attacked the gates, and at Bristol in 1749 anti-turnpike riots lasted for a fortnight. It is true that some trustees let their roads go to rack and ruin. Others tried their best, but their roads were so badly made that it was impossible to repair them. The only answer was to make a new road. To do this properly the trustees needed the help of a road engineer.

Study

Your aim in this study is to use the map, table and sources below:

Ca to work out why goods were often sent by water instead of road in the early eighteenth century.

Source 1

Six or eight men, by the help of water carriage, can carry and bring back in the same time the same quantity of goods between London and Edinburgh, as fifty broad-wheeled wagons, attended by 100 men and drawn by 400 horses.

Adam Smith, *The Wealth of Nations* (1776).

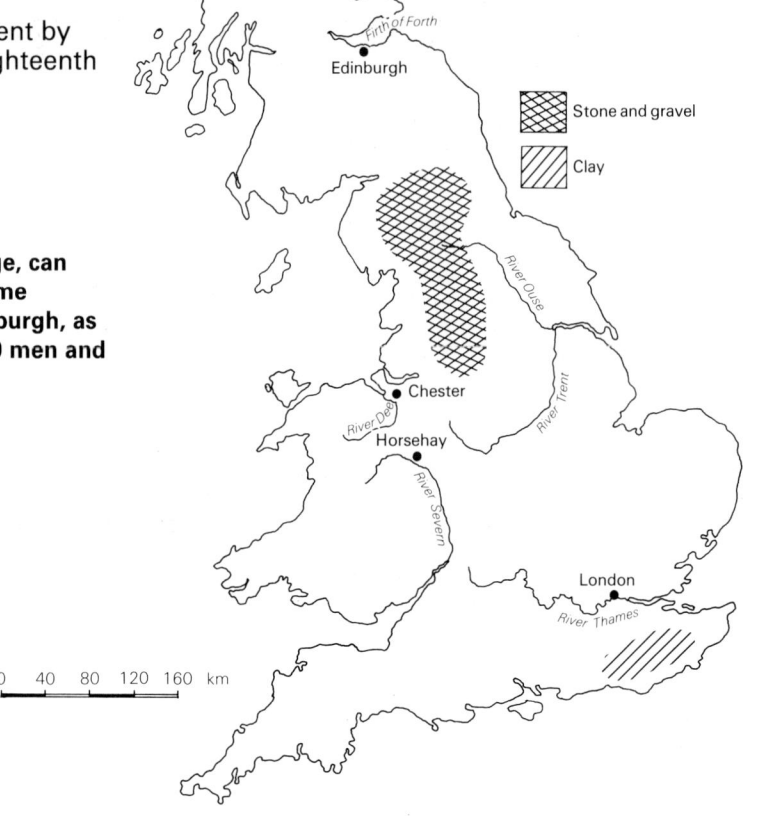

Stone and gravel

Clay

0   40   80   120   160   km

Map 1   British rivers

Road maintenance	
Authority	*Duties*
Parish magistrates	Responsible for maintaining all roads running through it. Appointed a surveyor. Levied rates to pay for road maintenance.
Surveyor	Supervised work on roads.
Parishioners	Worked on roads six days a year, or sent a labourer instead.

N.B. It was easier to maintain roads in parishes where there was plenty of stone and gravel than in parishes where there was 'deep clay'.

1 a Copy Map 1.

  b Why might the roads in the stone and gravel region have been better than those in the clay region?

2 The Horsehay Iron Company in Shropshire regularly sent pig iron to Chester by way of the River Severn, round the coast of Wales, and up the River Dee.

  a Draw a dotted line on your map to show the route taken by the iron.

  b By water, the route is about 700 km. By road the distance was less than 100 km. Suggest reasons why the company chose the longer route.

3 a On your map, mark the route that you think a London merchant would have used to send goods to Edinburgh.
Why do you think he would have chosen this route?

  b What kind of evidence would you look for if you wanted to prove that the route you have marked *was* used by merchants at the beginning of the eighteenth century?

ROADBUILDERS

Table 1   The road engineers

Road builder	Method	Area	Comment
John Metcalf of Knaresborough (Blind Jack) (1717–1810)	Laid good foundations, e.g. on boggy ground he put down: **1** a layer of heather, **2** a layer of large, jagged stones **3** a thick layer of gravel. His roads were drained by gullies or ditches.	Yorkshire	His roads were expensive, but lasted well.
Thomas Telford of Dumfriesshire (1759–1834)	Laid good foundations: **1** a layer of large stones, **2** a layer of smaller stones, **3** a layer of gravel.	*Shropshire* Made County Surveyor in 1776. *Scotland* Engineered 1,400 km of roads in the Highlands.	Also designed: London–Holyhead Rd; Menai suspension bridge to carry it over the Menai Straits; docks and bridges. Engineers copied his ideas and turnpike trusts consulted him.
John McAdam of Ayrshire (1756–1836)	Did not bother about foundations: **1** covered subsoil with 30 cm layer of either sandstone or limestone; **2** traffic using the road ground stones together. This bedded them down and filled crevices with fine powder.	*Bristol* Surveyor of the Bristol Turnpike Trust, 1816–18. *London* Surveyor of the General Metropolis Turnpike Trust.	McAdam's roads were good and cheap. His system was copied all over Britain.

Diagram 1   Metcalf's, Telford's and McAdam's systems of roadmaking

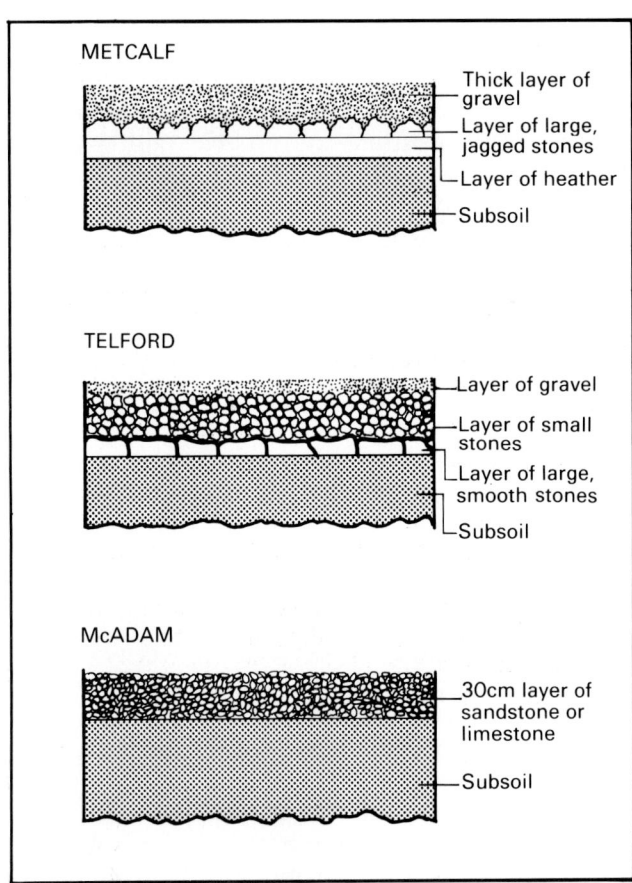

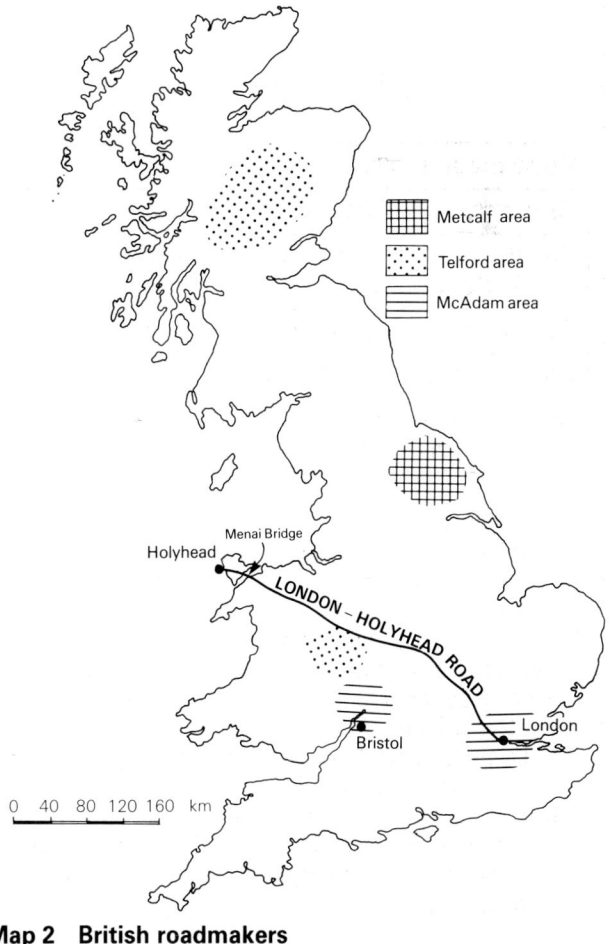

Map 2   British roadmakers

THE GOLDEN AGE OF ROAD TRANSPORT

By using Metcalf's, Telford's and McAdam's techniques, turnpike trusts steadily improved Britain's roads, and by 1830 travel by coach was much easier and quicker than before.

Post coaches

The best coaches were run by the Post Office. In 1784 John Palmer (1742–1818), a businessman from Bath, was given a contract to carry mails in fast coaches. Palmer's coaches carried the mail, a guard with a gun and posthorn and six passengers.

Advantages

They were fast and reliable because turnpike gates had to be opened in good time to let them through, fresh horses were waiting at every stage and other traffic had to give way to let them through.

Disadvantages

They were expensive and they only carried a few passengers.

Study

Your aim in this study is:

K to understand some of the items that turnpike trustees had to consider if they wanted their trust to be a success.

Remember what you have learned about turnpike trusts and roadbuilders.

In pairs

1 From the following items, select and list the five which you think were most necessary if a turnpike trust was to be successful:
   a list of tolls displayed where travellers could see them;
   honest tollgate keepers;
   wealthy trustees who could pay for the road to be built;
   a competent road engineer;
   ready supplies of stone and gravel;
   a growing industrial town on or near the line of the road.
2 List the items you have chosen in order of their importance. Let one person read their list to the rest of the class. Do the rest of you agree?

In 1798 Matthew Boulton travelled in a mail coach from London to Exeter. The swaying of the vehicle made him feel sick, and he had to stop at Axminster and go to bed 'very ill'. Boulton was rich. Next day, when he felt better, he hired a small private carriage, called a post chaise, and a driver to take him on to Exeter. This cost about eleven old pence a kilometre. Most rich people either travelled in their own private carriages or hired a chaise.

THE COACHING INDUSTRY

Employment

By 1830 coaching was an important industry.

Coaching statistics

In 1830 there were:
   3,000 coaches
   150,000 horses
   50,000 coachmen, guards, ostlers, stableboys.
(Parliamentary Committee Report)

Many inns depended on coach passengers.

'A Hell for horses'

A French traveller described England as 'a Hell for horses'. G. Gray, a travel writer at the beginning of the nineteenth century, agreed. He said that the weight of a coach, its passengers and their luggage was 'far too much for four horses at the rate they are forced to go'. Three or four years coaching wore horses out. Gray thought that chaise horses were even worse off, because they had no settled rest periods, and often set out on a new job before they had recovered from their previous journeys. He described their lives as 'most pitiable'.

The effects of railways

Within a few years, the 'iron horses' of the railways had taken over and put many coach firms out of business. In 1839 Edward Sherman, a coach proprietor, told a House of Commons committee that he used to work nine coaches a day between London and Birmingham. But now that the railway had opened, there were only two, carrying 'that part of the public who are timid, and not disposed to go by the rail road'.

He thought that only lower turnpike tolls could save him. There was no hope of this, because turnpike trustees also lost money when a railway

Study

Your aim in this study is:

Ev to use various sources to explore what road travel was like between 1760 and 1830.

Source 2A

A stage wagon.

Source 2B

A post coach.

Table 2   Passenger transport

Date	Vehicle	Speed (kph)	Cost (d per k)	Other comments
Up to 1760	Stage wagon	2	depended on driver	Mainly for goods. Very uncomfortable.
	Stage coach	8	1.5	Carried up to sixteen passengers.
1784–1800	Stage coach	9	1.5	Improved roads led to increased speeds.
	Mail coach	10	2	Fewer passengers than stage coach, so lighter and faster.
1800–1830	Mail coach	up to 15	2	Increasing in number. By 1817, 684 regular mail coach services started from London. Most daily.
	Post chaise	up to 15	15–18	Available for private hire.

Source 2C

A cartoon by Thomas Rowlandson.

1 Which of the vehicles listed in Table 2 is shown in Sources 2A and 2B?
2 **a** Between which dates was the type of vehicle, shown in Source 2B, built?
   b What are we shown in the picture that might help you to date the period that it shows more accurately?
3 What can we tell from Rowlandson's painting (Source 2C) about the dangers of travelling by mail coach?

Study

In the first half of the eighteenth century only one coach a month ran between London and Edinburgh. The journey took twelve to sixteen days. Many travellers made the journey on horseback.

Your aim is to use the sources below:

Ch to see how travelling conditions changed between 1739 and 1836.

Source 3

UNEQUALLED TRAVELLING TO

EDINBURGH

AND ALL PARTS OF SCOTLAND,

BY THE

PEVERIL of the PEAK,

New & Superior Patent Safety Coach.

The Public are respectfully informed that this new superior Patent Safety Coach, called the PEVERIL OF THE PEAK, has commenced running from the BLOSSOMS INN, Lawrence Lane, Cheapside, every *Evening at Eight o'Clock*; through BEDFORD, DERBY, LEICESTER, MATLOCK, BUXTON, MANCHESTER, BOLTON, CHORLEY, PRESTON, LANCASTER, MILNTHORPE, KENDAL, PENRITH, CARLISLE, HAWICK, and SELKIRK, to the Star and Crown Hotels, EDINBURGH, where it arrives at Seven o'Clock the second Evening, performing the journey in FORTY-FOUR HOURS! It returns from EDINBURGH every Morning at Seven.

It having been a subject of general regret that there never has been a Light Post Coach properly established throughout from LONDON to EDINBURGH, Passengers having to stop all night at Carlisle, and put up with the greatest inconvenience and expense through the many changes of Coachmen, Guards, &c. the Proprietors are determined to remove the whole of these obstacles by sending this Coach direct through to EDINBURGH changing Coaches only once, whilst only SIX COACHMEN and ONE GUARD will be employed on the journey, which must give it a most decided advantage over every Coach that has ever travelled on the North Road, not even excepting the Mail, and after a minute calculation it is determined the fares shall be full *one third less*.

The same punctuality and speed will be attended to as is observed by the Mail. The Proprietors place their confidence upon the Nobility and Gentlemen along the line of road, and Travellers and Merchants in general, for their support and patronage, which alone can ensure its permanency.

WILLIAM GILBERT, Blossoms Inn, London.

JOHN KNOWLES, Peacock, Market Street, Manchester.

JOHN CROALL, General Coach Office, 2, Princes Street, Edinburgh.

London, August 1st, 1831.

Alexander Mackie is a businessman who travels regularly between Edinburgh and London. In August 1831 he is handed this leaflet (Source 3).

1 List the reasons why Mackie might have decided to try the new service instead of the mail coach he usually used.

■

Alexander Mackie finds that 'Peveril of the Peak' usually lives up to the claims made for it in the advertisement, so he continues to use it. In October 1836 he sees the following article in *The Essex Standard*, a newspaper he has taken to read on his journey:

'In 1739 . . . two gentlemen going from Edinburgh to London state that they rode the journey on horseback; that there was no turnpike road till they came to Grantham within 110 miles of London; that up to that point they travelled upon a narrow causeway with an unmade soft road on each side of it; that they met from time to time strings of packhorses, from thirty to forty in a gang . . . The leading horse of the gang carried a bell, to give warning to travellers coming in the opposite direction; and they said that when they met these trains of horses with their packs across their backs, the causeway not affording them room to pass, they were obliged to make way for them, and plunge into the side road, out of which they sometimes found it difficult to get back again upon the causeway.'

2 Why may Mackie have thought he was lucky compared with the two travellers in 1739?

opened. Goods and passengers both moved from the road to the railway.

Value of tolls at gate on Liverpool–Manchester road	
1829	£1,700
1830	Railway opened
1831	£800

Some turnpike trusts went bankrupt, and were taken over by other trustees who increased the tolls. This upset local people who used the roads for short journeys.

By 1850 many trusts had gone out of business, and their roads were once again under the care of the parish authorities.

Study

Your aim in this study is to consider the information on the coaching industry on pages 67–9 to work out:

S the effects the changes had on different people.

1 In what way or ways did the methods used to speed up travel by land in the eighteenth and early nineteenth centuries make life:
    better for most travellers;
    difficult for some people in the short term;
    'a Hell' for some animals?

Study

In this study you will be:

Ev using the information in Source 4 to work out what you think happened during the Rebecca Riots; check to see if your ideas were correct.

Source 4

A contemporary picture of the 'Rebecca Riots'.

1 Consider the people in the picture.
  a Do most of the rioters seem to be men or women?
  b What do they seem to be attacking?
2 Consider the clothes the people are wearing. Do you think the riots took place in the years:
    1700–50
    1750–1800
    1800–50?

3 **a** Write an account of the Rebecca Riots, saying when you think they took place and what happened during them.
  b List the sections in your library where you might find out more about the Rebecca Riots, and see what information you can find about them. How correct were the impressions you formed from looking at the picture?

— Part Two —

Canals

WATER TRANSPORT

Canals for coal

Road transport was not suitable for heavy, bulky goods such as coal. A horse and cart could only move about a tonne along most eighteenth-century roads. But a horse could pull forty tonnes on a barge. So by 1750, mine owners with coal pits a long way from navigable water were considering the possibility of making canals to carry their coal.

Engineering a canal

It is difficult to engineer a canal. The bed has to be dead level and lined with kneaded clay to make it waterproof. To cross a hill, a canal has to go round it; through it in a tunnel or cutting; or over it in a series of locks. These have to be well built or they leak badly. Canals need a plentiful supply of water at their highest point to maintain their level, because a certain amount is always lost by evaporation and leakages. What is more, every time a boat passes through the locks a whole lockful of water—about 250,000 litres—flows out of the top level and has to be replaced. So canals need their own reservoirs.

The first canal

The first canal, the Sankey Navigation, opened in 1757 and was 16 km long. It ran from St Helens to the River Mersey, and carried cheap coal to Liverpool. It was paid for by Liverpool Corporation.

THE BRIDGEWATER CANAL

The second canal to be made was paid for by one man, the Duke of Bridgewater. He owned mines at Worsley and sold most of the coal in Manchester, 11 km away. The Duke's coal cost seven old pence for fifty kilos in Manchester. This was expensive, and transport costs made up more than half the price. The Duke decided he could cut the cost of transport by making a canal from Worsley to Manchester, and in 1759 he persuaded Parliament to pass an Act giving him the power to buy the necessary land and make the canal.

The Duke put James Brindley (1716–72), a local millwright, in charge of making the canal. Brindley was rough and uneducated, but he understood machines and was famous locally for solving practical mechnical problems. In 1758 he had surveyed a route for a canal from the Trent to the Mersey for Lord Gower, a local landowner, but he had never actually built a canal before.

Brindley started work on the canal and by 1761 it was finished. It was an outstanding success. One end of the canal was driven into the coal workings so that miners could load coal straight onto the barges, which were then pulled at a steady 3 kph into the middle of Manchester. At Barton the canal had to cross the Irwell valley. Brindley took the canal over on an aqueduct. Visitors found the idea of building a canal 'in the air . . . truly astonishing' and looked at the aqueduct 'with a mixture of wonder and delight'.

The Duke was also delighted with his canal. He had to borrow huge sums of money to pay for it, but it was worth while. Using the canal he could sell coal in Manchester at three and a half old pence for fifty kilos and still make a profit. His coal sales increased enormously, and so did his income.

Study

In this study you are asked:

Em to put yourself in the place of the Duke of Bridgewater as he explains his reasons for building the Bridgewater Canal.

You will need to refer to the information on water transport and the Bridgewater Canal.

1 In pairs, make brief notes under the headings below for a talk which the Duke of Bridgewater might have given to a group of businessmen, explaining his scheme to build a canal.

   The Bridgewater Canal
   route of the proposed canal;
   reasons for building the canal;
   reasons for employing James Brindley;
   why the canal will be costly;
   why the costs should soon be recovered.

   As an example, your first note might be:
   Route of the proposed canal:
   Worsley–Manchester, c 11 km.

2 Let one person give his or her talk to the class. After the talk the speaker may be asked to answer up to three questions.

Study

EXTENDING THE SYSTEM

The Bridgewater Canal was so successful that it encouraged businessmen to build more.
In this study you will discover:
Ca how the canal system that developed during the eighteenth and early nineteenth centuries made it easier to move goods around Britain.

1 Which canal would an industrialist have used to transport goods from:
the North Sea, across England to the Irish Sea;
the North Sea, across Scotland to the Atlantic;
the Midlands to London?
2 Industrialists who used the canal network could cut transport costs. What effect would you expect this to have on:
the price of their goods if other costs did not rise;
the number of goods they sold?
3 What reasons can you suggest to explain why Birmingham became the centre of a canal network by 1800?
4 *Library work*
Look up *Josiah Wedgwood* in an encyclopedia or in the index of a history book on the eighteenth century.
a Which canal did Wedgwood partly own?
b Why was the canal useful to him?

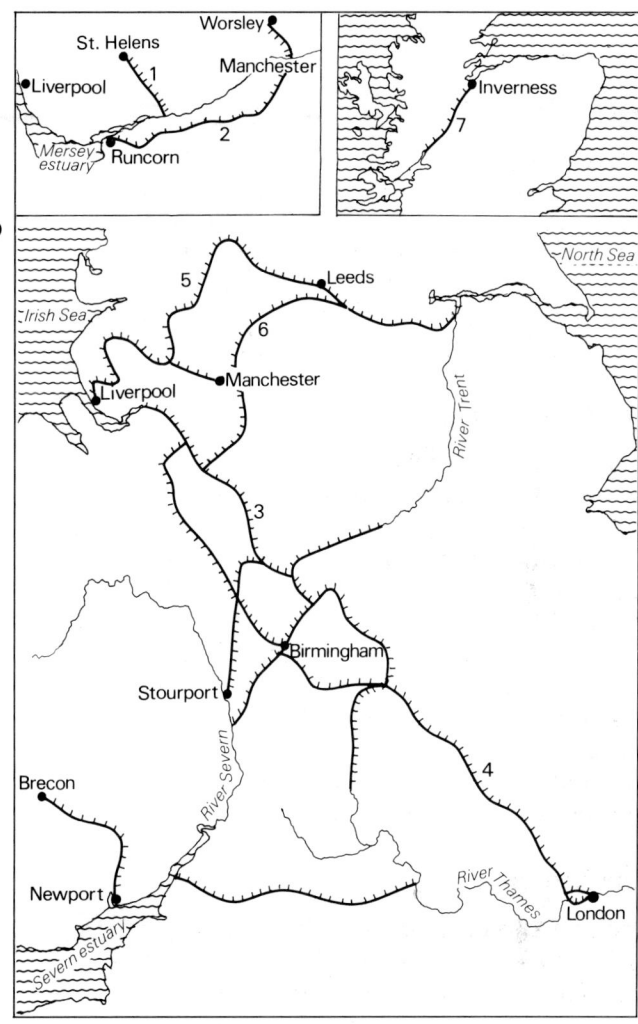

1. Sankey Canal
2. Runcorn Canal
3. Grand Trunk Canal
4. Grand Junction Canal
5. Leeds-Liverpool Canal
6. Huddersfield Canal
7. Caledonian Canal

Map 3   Principal canals in Britain

Table 3   Later canals

Date	Name	Importance
1772	Manchester–Runcorn Manchester–Stourport	Linked Worsley Canal to sea at Runcorn and, via Severn, with Bristol.
1777	Grand Trunk	Linked Severn, Trent and Mersey. So joined the North Sea, Irish Sea and the Bristol Channel.
By 1800	Network of canals round Birmingham, London and main coalfields (see Map 3).	
1805	Grand Junction	Linked the Midlands with London.
1816	Leeds–Liverpool	Linked the Yorkshire and Lancashire industrial areas. 200 km long and took 46 years to complete.
1822	Caledonian Canal	Linked Moray Firth with the Atlantic.
By 1830	More than 6,500 km of navigable rivers and canals.	

Illustration 1 The Trent and Mersey canal, with Wedgwood's pottery works in the background.

THE IMPACT OF CANALS

Advantages of canals

Canals made it cheaper and easier to transport heavy, bulky goods. Some also carried passengers. Canal barges were slow, but were smooth and comfortable and many people preferred this to being bumped and jolted in a coach. Some towns benefited greatly from canals. Many Midlands manufacturers moved to Birmingham because it was the centre of a good canal network, and the town of Stourport grew up round the junction of Brindley's canal with the river Severn.

Disadvantages

Canals had disadvantages. They were slow, particularly if they had a lot of locks, and in freezing winter weather they sometimes had to close altogether.

They were also badly organised. Each canal had been designed by a separate company, with its own ideas. So they differed in width, depth, and the size of their locks. This made it very difficult for barges to move from one canal to another. When there was through traffic, the various companies quarrelled over sharing out the tolls. They very rarely combined to act together.

Closures

A few canals closed down as a result of the development of railways, but most managed to compete, at any rate for a time. Canals cut their prices, and charged less for bulk cargoes than railways did. But canal profits fell, and the companies could not afford to maintain and modernise the system. Many canals were bought up by railway companies, which then neglected them. In time, railways took over most of the canals' traffic.

— Part Three —
Railways

EARLY LOCOMOTIVES

Railways had been developed during the eighteenth century to carry coal wagons from mines. Early railways consisted of lines of wooden planks, and horses pulled the wagons along. But by 1800 most had iron rails, and inventors were beginning to design steam engines, or locomotives, to pull the wagons (see Table 4 below).

LINKING TOWNS

The success of steam locomotives encouraged engineers to build new railways. Here are details of the most important.

Illustration 2 Mount Olive cutting on the Liverpool–Manchester railway.

The Stockton and Darlington Railway

Joined Stockton to Darlington—length 17 km.
Opened 1825.
Engineer George Stephenson.
Financed by Edward Pease, a Darlington wool merchant, and other local businessmen.
Traffic Mostly coal, but also some passengers.
Special features Used Stephenson's steam locomotives to haul some of the trains.
Importance
1 Proved that steam locomotives were reliable enough and fast enough for freight and passenger trains.
2 Made a profit.

The Liverpool and Manchester Railway

Joined Manchester to Liverpool—Length 48 km.
Opened 1830.
Engineers George and Robert Stephenson.
Financed by Liverpool businessmen. Cost £800,000.
Traffic Passengers and general freight.
Special features A cutting 3 km long and 25 m deep through Mount Olive (see Illustration 2), and a 6 km mat of heather and brushwood laid on Chat Moss, a peat bog, to carry the line.
Importance
1 Used only steam locomotives. Trials at Rainhill in 1829 won by Stephenson's *Rocket*, which pulled a load of thirteen tonnes at 23 kph, and reached a top speed of 47 kph.
2 Made good profits, especially on passenger traffic.

Table 4 The first locomotives

Inventor	Place and date	Description of engine
Richard Trevithick (Cornwall), (1771–1831)	Coalbrookdale, 1802	Used on railways at Coalbrookdale works. No details survive.
	Merthyr Tydfil, 1804	Used to pull trucks at Penydarren ironworks. Broke the track. Too heavy.
	London, 1808	*Catch-me-who-can* Travelled at 20 kph round a circular track. Gave rides to public at a shilling a time.
William Hedley (Northumberland), (1770–1843)	Wylam 1813	*Puffing Billy* Worked at Wylam colliery, pulling coal wagons.
	Wylam 1814	*Wylam Dilly* Worked at Wylam colliery, pulling coal wagons.
George Stephenson (Northumberland), (1781–1848)	Killingworth, 1814	A rough and clumsy engine. Pulled 30 tonnes at walking pace at Killingworth colliery.
	Killingworth, 1815	A smoother, faster engine.
	Killingworth, 1820	An engine which could pull a train of loaded wagons at 15 kph.

Illustration 3 Robert Stephenson (1803–59), son of George Stephenson, became famous as a railway engineer and bridge designer. In 1847 he became an MP. He was buried in Westminster Abbey.

Following the success of the Liverpool and Manchester railway, a number of short lines were opened, mostly linking towns to nearby collieries. Two much longer lines were also built.

The London and Birmingham Railway

Joined London to Birmingham—length 180 km.
Opened 1838.
Engineer Robert Stephenson (see Illustration 3).
Financed by London and Birmingham businessmen. Estimated cost £2.5 million. Final cost £4.5 million.
Traffic Passenger and general freight.
Special features Numerous embankments, cuttings and eight tunnels, including *Kilsby Tunnel* (Northamptonshire) 2,300 metres long. (Expected cost £99,000. Actual cost £300,000. Extra cost due to quicksands and underground streams. Needed steam pumps to keep the workings dry.)
Importance The biggest and most expensive piece of engineering ever undertaken in Britain. The first long-distance railway line in the world.

Study

Men who financed railways between towns risked losing a lot of money. In this study you will:

Em try to see why they thought it was worth taking the risk.

1 a In pairs, list the points below in the order of their importance to the backers of the Stockton to Darlington railway.
  i The rail distance between Stockton and Darlington is 17 km.
  ii Local businessmen were willing to put up the capital to build the line.
  iii George Stephenson would design the railway.
  iv There was a growing demand for coal to power Darlington's woollen mills.
  v The railways would carry passengers as well as goods.
  vi Stephenson's *Locomotion* could travel faster than a stage coach.
b Ask one person to read his or her list to the class. Do the rest of you agree?

2 a In pairs. A number of points about the Liverpool and Manchester Railway are listed below. Rewrite the list in the order of their importance to a group of businessmen thinking of building a similar railway, linking two industrial towns 80 km apart by road, separated by a range of hills and a marshy valley.
  i It is 48 km from Liverpool to Manchester by rail.
  ii Several engineers entered locomotives at the Rainhill trials.
  iii *The Rocket* could pull heavy loads at a speed of 47 kph.
  iv The Liverpool and Manchester railway crossed Mount Olive and Chat Moss.
  v The Liverpool and Manchester line was making a profit, especially on carrying passengers.
  vi The line cost £800,000 to build.
b Ask one person to read his or her list to the class. Do the rest of you agree?

The Great Western Railway

Joined London to Bristol—Length 192 km.
Opened 1841.
Engineer Isambard Kingdom Brunel (see Illustration 4).
Financed by Bristol and London businessmen.
Traffic Passenger and general freight.
Special features
1 Designed for high speed operation. So used a broad gauge (2.1 m (7ft)) to reduce swaying instead of Stephenson's 1.41 m (4ft 8.5in) gauge. Also had long, level stretches with gentle curves.
2 *Box Tunnel* (Wiltshire) 3 km long, made on a 1 in 100 slope. Took two years to make.
Importance First railway designed for comfort and high speed.

RAILWAY NAVVIES

It was hard work to make a railway. Most of it was done by navvies, who dug out cuttings, heaped up embankments and burrowed in tunnels using pick-axes, shovels and wheelbarrows as their main tools. They usually worked in gangs, contracting to cut and shift so much earth for a given price. They worked hard and fast. A fit navvy reckoned he could shovel away twenty tonnes of 'dirt' in a day. They took great risks to get their jobs finished quickly, and were often involved in accidents. They lived in rough huts near the line where they worked. When the line was finished, they tramped to another and started again.

If they worked hard they could earn good money —up to £1 a week. They spent most of it on food and drink, and on pay days they often went on a 'rampage' in a nearby town, drinking, singing and fighting until most of their money had gone. When work ran short in Britain they went abroad, and Joseph Locke, an engineer working with British navvies on the Paris to Rouen railway, remarked that French peasants used to come and watch them, muttering: 'My God, how these English work!'

THE RAILWAY MANIA

For a few years after 1840 there was a 'railway mania' in Britain. People believed that if they invested in railways they were bound to make a fortune, so whenever a company asked for money to build a new line, the public willingly handed over their money. Many investors lost money because:

1 Some companies were over-optimistic. They built lines which never carried enough traffic to make a profit.
2 A few companies were dishonest. They took the money, but never built the railway.
But many companies succeeded and by the time the mania died down in 1848 most of the British railway system had been made or was being built.

Illustration 4 Isambard Kingdom Brunel (1806–59), son of Sir Marc Isambard Brunel, a famous civil engineer, was educated in France. He designed railways, ships, bridges and docks.

Study

Robert Stephenson and Brunel both designed railways, but there were several differences between them. This study asks you:

S to spot the similarities and differences in their work.

The information on pages 73–5 will help you. Write a report that might have appeared in a newspaper in 1841 comparing the work of Stephenson and Brunel.

Include:
1 the name of the railway that each of them has recently completed
2 the total cost of each line, and the reasons why railways are expensive to build
3 the reasons why it is more comfortable to travel in Brunel's trains than in Stephenson's
4 the difficulties that may arise in the future if a company wishes to link a line designed by Stephenson with one designed by Brunel.

Study

In this study you will:

Ev consider various types of evidence about navvies' work and living conditions.

Source 5A

Navvies making a cutting.

Source 5B

We are pained to state that a labourer who was working in the excavation of the rail-road . . . was killed on Monday last. The poor fellow was . . . undermining a heavy load of clay, fourteen or fifteen feet high, when the mass fell on him.

Liverpool Mercury, 10 August 1827.

Source 5C

Suppose a place . . . about twenty-eight feet by twelve feet wide, and along one side of it, facing the door, a range of beds in two tiers, but no curtains, no separation between the beds; in short, a child wishing to walk into one bed from another might scamper over the whole tier. In one bed you may find a man and his wife and one or two children; in the next one adjoining, probably a couple of young men; again on top of them, another man and his wife and family; that is the sort of arrangement.

Single men paid 1s 6d per week for this accommodation, and married men with families 2s. The hut-keeper's wife prepared any food the navvies gave her to cook.
Evidence given by Alexander Anderson, manager of Edinburgh Waterworks, to a House of Commons Select Committee on Railway Workers, in 1846. He had visited huts built by the North British Railway for their navvies.

Source 5D

I stood and looked down, and there were the chaps, ever so far below, and the cuttings so narrow. And a lot of stone fell, it was always falling, they were bound to be hurt. There was no room to get away, nor mostly no warning. One chap I saw killed while I was there.

Elizabeth Garnett, *Our Navvies* (1885), quoting a navvy.

1 a Re-write the list below, matching the source with the type of evidence correctly.
   Source 5A   A book by an author who was not a navvy.
   Source 5B   Evidence given to a government committee.
   Source 5C   A book illustration.
   Source 5D   A newspaper report.
 b Most navvies spent most of their money on food and drink. Does the evidence in the sources above help us to understand *why* they did this? Give reasons for your answer.
2 a Is the evidence given in Source 5D primary or secondary?
 b Do you think the evidence in Source 5D reliable? Give reasons for your answer.
3 Why do historians need to know if a source is primary or secondary?

GOVERNMENT CONTROL

At first the government did little to control railway companies, but in 1844 and 1846 they passed two important Acts.

The 1844 Railway Act

This Act ordered companies to run at least one train a day which
  i carried third class passengers for a penny a mile (0.62p a kilometre) in covered coaches with seats
  ii stopped at every station
  iii averaged at least 20 kph.
These *Parliamentary Trains* were cheaper and quicker than coaches.

The 1846 Gauge Act

The government realised that in the long run, the railway system would work better if all lines were the same gauge. Most companies had adopted Stephenson's 1.41 metre gauge, and the 1846 Act declared that all future lines had to be built to this gauge. Eventually the Great Western decided to convert their 2.1 metre track to 1.41 metres, but the work was not finished until 1892 (see Illustration 5).

GEORGE HUDSON, THE 'RAILWAY KING'

The railway system in Britain developed piecemeal. Every line was sanctioned by a separate Act of Parliament, and was developed by a separate company. As time passed, richer and larger companies began to take over smaller ones. The process began in the 1840s when George Hudson (1800–71), one of the founders of the North Eastern railway, bought up so many companies that by 1848 he

Illustration 5 Through passengers from other parts of the country had to change trains when they travelled on the Great Western Railway, because the gauges of the lines were different.

controlled about a third of the entire network and was known as 'the Railway King'. But some of his deals were illegal. In 1849 he was forced to resign, and his empire collapsed, but the separate companies still co-operated to run long distance trains.

THE IMPACT OF RAILWAYS

Benefits of railways

Cheap mass transport

At first, trains were slow and uncomfortable. Only first-class passengers (Illustration 6) had closed coaches. Second-class passengers (Illustration 7) sat on wooden benches in open-sided trucks, while third-class passengers had to stand without any protection from the weather and the fumes of the engine. But these conditions improved after the 1844 Railway Act. For the first time, people could travel cheaply and quickly.

Illustration 6 First class on the Liverpool–Manchester railway.

Illustration 7 Second and third class on the Liverpool–Manchester railway.

Study

In this study you will:

Ch consider how far the railway system improved between 1841 and 1851.

Use the information on pages 75–7 and Map 4.

1 a Copy the list below.
   Railways in 1841
   i   Most companies owned short stretches of line, many of which were unprofitable.
   ii An efficient national system could not be developed because each company could decide what gauge to use.
   iii Trains built for a narrow gauge could not run on a wide gauge.
   iv Most parts of Britain did not have a rail service.
   v   Passengers could travel more cheaply by stage coach than by rail.
   b Put a tick against the items on the list that had changed by 1851 and a cross against those that had not.

2 Write two paragraphs on: *The railways of Britain, 1851*. Include:
   a description of the railway system in 1851, showing why it provided the public with a better service than it had in 1841,
   the reasons why some parts of Britain still could not claim to have an efficient railway service.

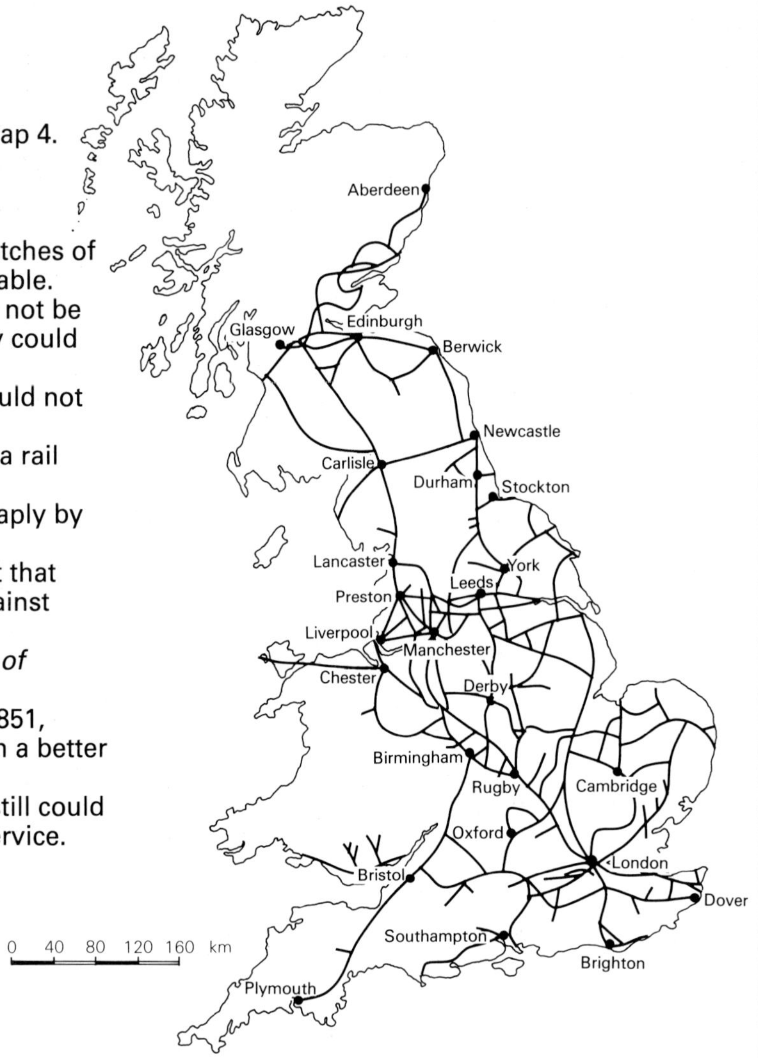

Map 4   The railway system, 1851

Suburbs and resorts

Railways enabled people to live further away from their work than ever before. This encouraged new suburbs to develop along railway lines on the outskirts of industrial towns. Railways also made it possible for people to go on trips during their holidays. This led to the growth of seaside resorts such as Bournemouth and Blackpool.

Railway towns

Some towns, like Crewe and Swindon, grew up round railway workshops. Crewe was designed by the Grand Junction Railway's architect, and controlled by a committee of the company.

Trade and industry

Railways provided hundreds of jobs and consumed huge quantities of iron and coal. The railway network helped factory owners by carrying raw materials and finished goods quickly and safely.

Farming

Farmers also benefited. They could send perishable items such as milk, eggs and vegetables long distances and be certain that they would still be fresh at the end of the journey. They also used railways to transport animals to market instead of herding them along the road.

Study

Your aim in this study is:

Em to consider plans for a new railway from the points of view of the people most affected by it.

In 1844 a group of businessmen are thinking of forming a company to build a railway from Smoketown, a large industrial town, to Broadfields, a small market town thirty kilometres away. Just outside Broadfields there is a lake, some woods and a small inn.

A public meeting is called to discuss the matter. It is attended by the following people:

Sir Humphrey Marchmont, through whose estate the proposed line would run. Sir Humphrey likes privacy, and is angry to learn that the line would cross his estate and be visible from the windows in the south wing of his mansion. It costs Sir Humphrey a great deal to maintain his standard of living, and the company would pay him for a right of way across his land, and build a halt where trains would pick up produce from his estate.

Frederick Jessop, a farmer who rents his land from Sir Humphrey. He is afraid that his herd of cattle will be frightened by passing trains and that sparks from engines will set fire to his crops.

Robert Fulton, who owns a prosperous coaching inn on the road between Smoketown and Broadfields. He has saved £500 and is thinking of investing it in a business project. Fulton employs ten people and cares about their welfare.

Dr Luxford, who works in Smoketown, but will soon retire to Broadfields because it is quieter than Smoketown. He believes that many of his patients would benefit from fresh air and exercise. He also thinks that the human body cannot stand the strain of travelling at 40 kph in a train.

Peter Harris, a lawyer who lives in Broadfields. He has been asked to chair the meeting and to make sure that points for and against the proposed line are discussed. He has a casting vote.

In groups of five

1 Choose a character each and decide what you think his views might have been when the meeting began. The chairman can be listing the points that he thinks should be considered, e.g. will people in the area benefit from the railway?

2 Hold the meeting, making sure that everyone has a chance to give his views on the points raised by the chairman. At the end of your discussion, take a vote on whether or not you think the railway should be built.

— Part Four —

Shipping

SAILING SHIPS

The Channel crossing

Source 6

In the eighteenth century, the only way to travel overseas was in a sailing ship. In 1791 Joseph Haydn, the composer, crossed from Calais to Dover. He wrote afterwards in a letter:

I boarded the ship at Calais at 7.30 am, and at 5 pm I arrived, thank God! safe and sound in Dover. At the beginning for the first four whole hours, we had almost no wind, and the ship went so slowly that in these four hours we didn't go further than one single English mile and there are twenty-four between Calais and Dover. Our ship's captain, in an evil temper, said that if the wind did not change, we should have to spend the whole night at sea. Fortunately, however, toward eleven o'clock a wind arose and blew so favourably that by four o'clock we covered twenty-two miles.

Sailing to India

Many ships traded between Britain and India. To try to ensure a favourable wind they crossed the Atlantic to the coast of Brazil before turning east to round the Cape of Good Hope. This was much further than the direct route, but it was quicker than sailing down the coast of Africa into the teeth of the prevailing southerly wind. It usually took about six months to sail to India, sometimes much longer. In 1743 the ship in which Robert Clive was travelling was driven aground on the Brazilian coast, and the voyage took fourteen months.

Study

In this study you will:

S compare two voyages made along sea lanes that were frequently used by British ships in the eighteenth century.

You will find the information you need in Source 6.

1 Make brief notes on Joseph Haydn's voyage under these headings:
   a Date of voyage
   b Type of ship
   c Starting and finishing points
   d The wind's influence on the voyage.
2 Using the same headings, make notes on Robert Clive's·voyage.

3 Write a paragraph saying in what ways the voyages were:
   similar
   different.
4 Consider what you have learned about sea travel by comparing the two voyages. What do you think was the greatest difficulty that designers had to overcome before a ship's captain could say with any certainty when his ship would reach its destination?

STEAMSHIPS

Early steamships

At the beginning of the nineteenth century, inventors began to build steam-powered ships. Table 5 gives details of some of the most important. Before 1830, steam engines consumed so much fuel that on long voyages, steamships would need all their cargo and passenger space to carry coal. So all steamships had sails, and only used their engines when the wind dropped. The *Savannah* is famous because in 1819 it became the first steamship to cross the Atlantic. But it only steamed for eighty five hours during the four week voyage.

Illustration 8   A contemporary picture of the *Comet*.

Table 5

Designer	Name of ship	Comment
William Symington	*Charlotte Dundas* (1802)	A canal boat. Trials were successful, but canal directors feared wash from paddles would damage canal banks, so refused to buy it.
Robert Fulton	*Clermont* (1807)	Built in America, using a Boulton & Watt steam engine. Carried passengers along the Hudson River. First commercial steamer in the world.
Henry Bell	*Comet* (1812)	Carried passengers on River Clyde for eight years. First steam passenger boat in Britain (see Illustration 8).
David Napier	*Rob Roy* (1818)	Eight times as powerful as *Comet*. Carried passengers between Scotland and Ireland. Similar boats used between England and France.

Illustration 9 The *Great Eastern* on her maiden voyage.

Brunel's ships

By 1830, steam engines were more efficient and it was possible to build ocean-going steamships. I. K. Brunel (1806–59), the engineer of the Great Western Railway, designed three of the most famous.

The *Great Western*	
Launched	1837
Hull	Wood
Weight	1,340 tonnes
Length	72 m
Power	Sail and 750 hp steam engines
Driven by	Paddles
Use	Transatlantic passenger ship

When it was launched the *Great Western* was the biggest and most powerful steamship afloat.

The *Great Britain*	
Launched	1843
Hull	Iron
Weight	3,720 tonnes
Length	98 m
Power	Sail and 1,500 hp steam engines
Driven by	Screw propeller
Use	Transatlantic passenger and cargo boat

The *Great Britain* was the first large iron ship to be built, and the first ocean-going ship to be driven by a screw propeller.

The *Great Eastern* (Illustration 9)	
Launched	1858
Hull	Iron
Weight	19,000 tonnes
Length	213 m
Power	Sail and 83,000 hp steam engines
Driven by	Paddles and propeller
Use	Passenger traffic to Australia.

The *Great Eastern* was by far the biggest ship in the world. By the time it was launched, the number of people wanting to go to Australia had fallen. As a result, the ship was never used on the Australia run. Instead it was used to lay cables.

Clydeside

Brunel's ships were built in the south, but many shipowners preferred to buy Clyde-built ships. Samuel Cunard, who set up a transatlantic steamship service in 1839, had his first four ships built on Clydeside. By 1860, it was the most important shipbuilding centre in Britain.

Clydeside had several advantages as a shipbuilding centre. There was plenty of coal and iron in the area to provide the raw materials for building steamships. There were skilled engineers who knew how to build the high pressure, fast-running steam engines needed to drive ship's propellers, and the river Clyde had recently been deepened so that it was safe to launch boats of all sizes.

Map 5   Clydeside

Part Five
The Post and Telegraph

THE POST

The old postal system

Before 1840 the cost of sending a letter depended on how far it had to travel and how many sheets of paper it contained. For example, up to 24 km the charge was four old pence a sheet. For 80 km it was eight pence. (The fee had to be paid on delivery.)

The system was cumbersome and wasteful because every letter had to be checked to see how many sheets it contained, and when it was delivered the postman had to wait until he had been paid before he could hand it over.

The Penny Post

In 1839 Rowland Hill (1795–1879) devised a new system, which came into effect in 1840. Any letter weighing less than half an ounce (about 14 g) could be sent to any part of the UK for a penny. The fee was paid by the sender, who bought a stamp from a post office and stuck it on the letter to show that the fee had been paid.

The new Penny Post led to an enormous increase in the number of letters posted. The old mail coaches would not have been able to carry them all, but trains coped easily, and Britain soon had a cheap and efficient postal service, which was copied by other countries.

THE ELECTRIC TELEGRAPH

In 1837 Professor C. Wheatstone and W. F. Cooke patented a device which used electrical impulses to send messages along wires (see Illustration 10). Brunel installed the system on the Great Western Railway. Station masters and signalmen used it to tell one another where the trains were, but it was

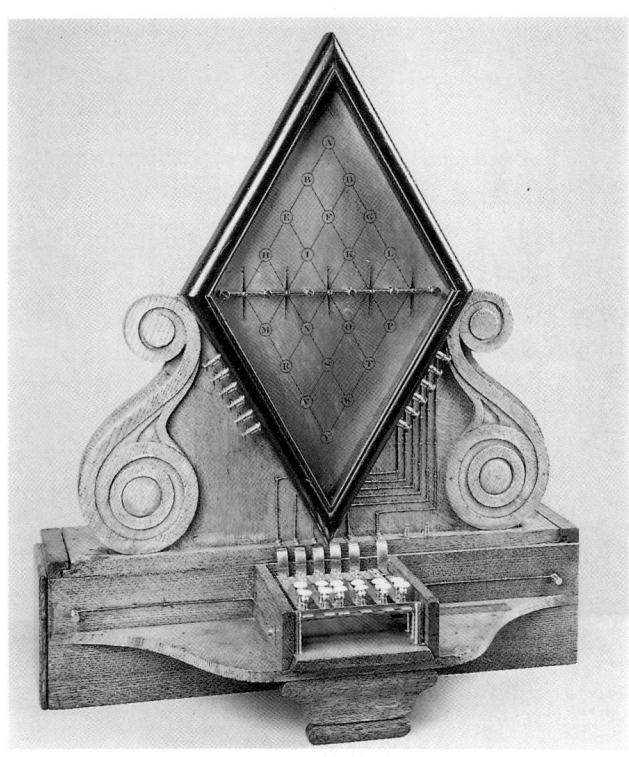

Illustration 10 An early telegraph receiver.

also used to send other messages. In 1844 news of the birth of one of Queen Victoria's sons was telegraphed to London, and in 1845 a murderer seen boarding a train at Slough was captured at Paddington after his description had been telegraphed along the line.

In 1846 the Electric Telegraph Company was set up with the idea of establishing a system to carry messages sent by the public. The system spread slowly throughout Britain, and in 1851 a telegraph cable was laid across the Channel to France. This was the first of many submarine cables.

Recall

1 What was: a turnpike trust; a navvy; a narrow boat; the *Savannah*?

2 Why was the work of these men important in the history of communications?
John McAdam, David Napier; Robert Stephenson; Wheatstone and Cooke.

3 In 1700 heavy goods often had to be transported by water. How had this situation changed by 1850? Give examples to illustrate your answer.

Diagram 1

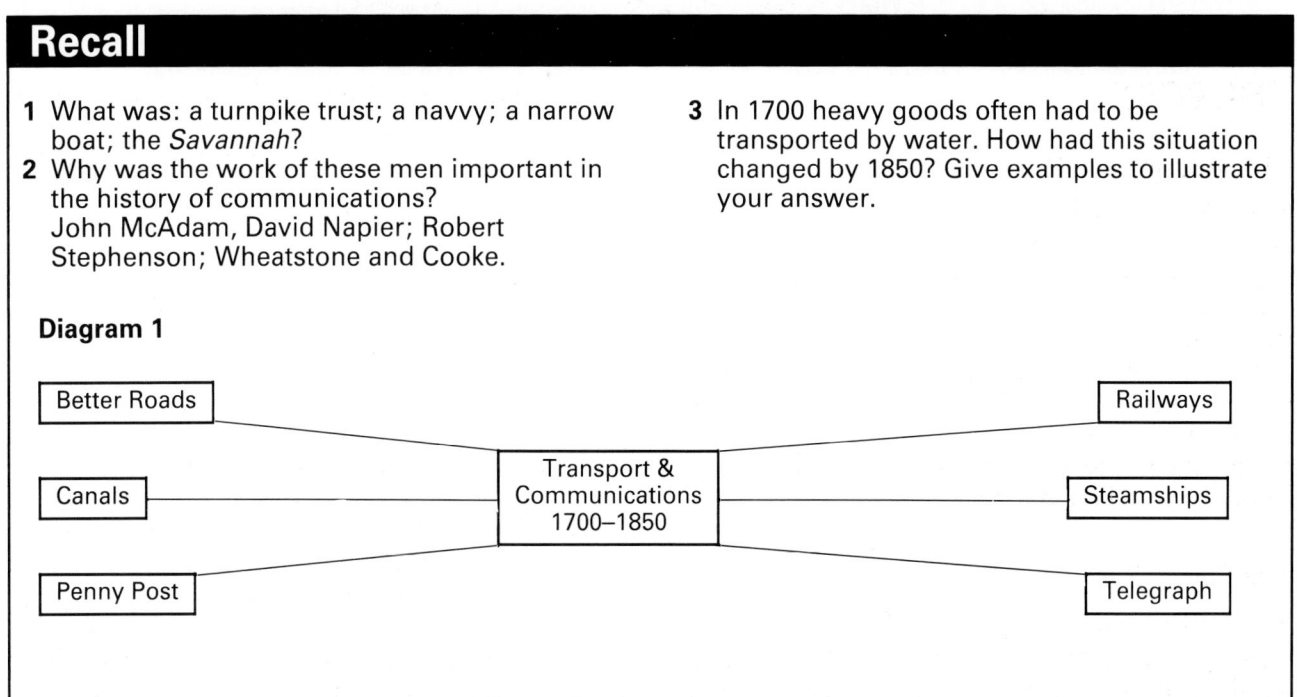

9

Overseas Trade

Trade in 1700

COUNTRIES AND COMMODITIES

In 1700 Britain traded with countries all over the world. The following tables describe Britain's trade in 1700. Hemp, timber, iron and tar were all needed to build the ships which carried Britain's trade. Some salt was exported to Newfoundland for salting cod. Then the salt cod was shipped to the West Indies.

MERCANTILISM

The mercantile system, or mercantilism, was a system used by governments in the eighteenth century to control overseas trade.

Why the government controlled trade

1 Much of the money the government used to run

Table 1   Goods imported by Britain

From Europe	Goods
The Baltic France, Spain, Portugal	Hemp, timber, iron, tar Wine
From colonies and trading posts	**Goods**
West Indies America The East India Company (EIC) (India, China, East Indies)	Sugar Cotton, tobacco, pig iron Cotton cloth, spices, tea

Table 2   Principal goods exported by Britain

White and coarse salt Refined sugar Leather goods Coal Earthenware Wool, cotton and linen cloth Metal products, e.g. iron nails Glass Hops

Table 3   Quantity of imports and exports

Imports	
£1.4 million	Imports from the colonies (including EIC)
£2.8 million	Imports from other overseas countries
Exports	
£4 million	Exports produced in Britain
£2 million	Re-exports (goods imported from the colonies and re-exported to Europe)

Table 4   Destination of exports

	(Figures in £million)
North Europe	3.42
Spain and Portugal	0.41
Mediterranean countries	0.6
Africa	0.1
East Indies	0.11
West Indies	0.31
North America	0.27

Illustration 1 Broad Quay at Bristol in the eighteenth century. Many of the ships calling at Bristol were West Indiamen, trading with the West Indies.

the country came from taxes or *duties* on imports, and it needed to control this source of income.

2 Governments thought of international trade as a competition in which each country tried to get more of the available wealth than the others. The government thought that Britain was more likely to do well in this competition if it 'protected' British traders and manufacturers from foreign rivals.

How the system worked

1 *The government* passed laws to help British manufacturers. For example, it helped cloth manufacturers by refusing to allow foreign cloth to be imported and British-made textile machinery to be exported.

Study

In this study you will:

K use the information in Tables 1, 2, 3 and 4 to make brief notes for an essay on *one* of the following:

1 Goods imported by Britain in 1700
2 British trade in 1700
3 The importance of Britain's trade with the colonies in 1700.

Begin your essay, 'By 1700 the British were trading with Europe and other countries as far apart as . . .'
Include two or more paragraphs, using information in your notes.
End your essay with one or two sentences saying why Britain's trade with the Baltic became increasingly important as trade with other regions increased.

2 *The government* paid 'bounties' or subsidies on British exports, e.g. corn and beer.

3 *The government* aimed to import cheap raw materials such as pig iron and raw cotton, and to export finished goods such as cooking pots and cloth, which could be sold at a higher price than the raw materials. For example, they refused to allow American colonists to manufacture any goods made of iron. The colonists were only allowed to smelt iron ore into pig iron. They then had to ship this to Britain, where British manufacturers made it into pots, pans and stoves which the Americans needed. These finished goods were then shipped back to America.

4 *The Navigation Acts* laid down:
   a only British ships could trade with the colonies
   b all imports to Britain had to be carried either in British ships, or in ships of the producing country.

The government believed that this would help to increase the number of British ships and seamen. This had two advantages:

   a it made it easier to defend the country, because in wartime the Admiralty conscripted thousands of sailors from British merchant ships to serve in the navy
   b owners of British ships carrying goods from the colonies usually insured cargoes in Britain, used British bankers and stored goods in British warehouses. This benefited British businessmen and brought more wealth to Britain.

Smuggling

High import duties encouraged smuggling. Smugglers brought in:

a French brandy   In France, a five gallon tub of brandy cost about seven shillings. It cost the smugglers about eight shillings to ship it across to England, and about six shillings to run it inland—a total cost of just over £1. But brandy on which import duty had been paid cost well over £2 a tub. So the smugglers could make a profit of about £1 a tub on their brandy, and still sell it cheaper than brandy which had been imported legally.

b Tea   In the middle of the eighteenth century the Board of Customs reckoned that more than 10,000 kg of tea was smuggled in every year.

c Gin, tobacco and snuff   The Board of Customs reported that the Dutch had set up a special distillery to supply smugglers with gin.

Study

In this study you will use the information on pages 84–5:

Em to understand why many people in eighteenth-century Britain supported mercantilism and some believed that it led to wars.

1 Mercantilism is sometimes described as 'a system of protection'. Why is this a good description of the system?

2 Would you have expected the following people who might have lived in the eighteenth century to have supported or opposed mercantilism:
   a member of the British government,
   a Birmingham manufacturer of iron goods,
   a Bradford cloth manufacturer,
   a London banker,
   the captain of a Liverpool merchant ship?
   Give reasons for your answers.

3 During the eighteenth century the British:
   won the Seven Years' War against the French and took over their colonies in India and America,
   lost a war against their American colonists who then formed the United States of America.
   a Some people believed that mercantilism helped to cause these wars. Suggest a reason or reasons why they believed this.
   b Why may some people have supported mercantilism, even though they believed it led to wars?

Illustration 2   Smugglers unloading goods on the south coast.

Study

In this study you will be looking at a traditional story, said to date from the eighteenth century. Your aim is:

Ev to decide if an unreliable source can still be of use to historians.

Source 1

In the first half of the eighteenth century, many villages along the Sussex coast were too small and poor to support a full-time clergyman, so they shared one with a neighbouring parish. This meant that the vicar was away every other Sunday, and on that day no one in the village went to church.

One Sunday the vicar of a poor fishing village arrived at his church, which was close to the sea, and was stopped by the verger.

'Why, sir,' said the verger, 'What are you doing here? You've come on the wrong day!'

The vicar insisted it was the right day, and they had a long argument. Finally, the verger said,

'Anyway, you can't hold any services today, because the pulpit's full of tea and the choir stalls are stacked with brandy.'

1 Why may the villagers who attended the church have become smugglers?
2 Does the story suggest that people along the Sussex coast thought smuggling was a serious crime? Give reasons for your answer.
3 a What questions would you ask to try to test the truth of the story?
  b Is the story of any use to historians if it is *not* true? Give reasons for your answer.

Customs patrols

The government tried to prevent smuggling by appointing customs officers to patrol the coast, and sometimes bands of customs men and smugglers met and fought pitched battles. But the officers could not check every inlet where a smuggler's ship might land, and smugglers had lookouts on shore who signalled to them to keep away when customs men were on the prowl. In any case, many customs men turned a blind eye to the smugglers. This was partly because smugglers were supported by the local population, who enjoyed the cheap goods they brought. So smuggling continued, and the government lost many thousands of pounds in unpaid duty.

———— Part Two ————

Trade 1750–1815

CHANGES AFTER 1750

Growth of trade

The pattern of Britain's trade altered between 1750 and 1815. In the first place the quantity of goods traded increased (see Source 2). As Britain's population grew, more consumer goods such as sugar and tea had to be imported, and as industries developed they had to import more raw materials such as cotton. At the same time Britain's empire, particularly in India, was growing. So it exported more to Britain, and took more goods in return.

Source 2   Overseas trade 1700–1850

Year	Exports	Imports
1700	6.5	6.0
1720	6.9	6.1
1740	8.2	6.7
1760	14.7	9.8
1780	12.6	10.8
1800	40.8	28.4
1820	40	17
1850	150	70

The figures refer to the quantity of goods traded, not to their value.

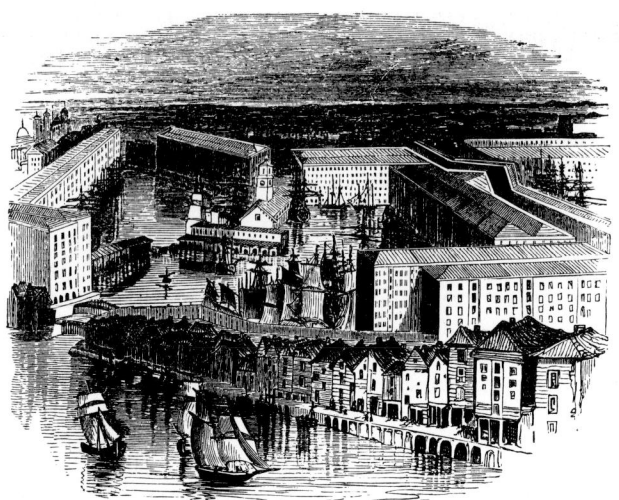

Illustration 3   St Katherine's dock in London. New docks were built to cope with increasing trade.

The effects of war

Sometimes wars disrupted trade, but as a rule their effects did not last long.

The War of American Independence (1776–83)

It stopped Britain's trade with her American colonies, but as soon as they had won their independence, America began to trade with Britain again.

The French Wars (1793–1815)

French troops invaded most of Europe during the French Wars, and the French government ordered the occupied countries not to trade with Britain. But British ships, protected by the navy, managed to smuggle goods into Europe. In fact, in some ways, the war in Europe helped British trade because the fighting on the continent prevented industrialists setting up new factories there, while factory owners in Britain were left in peace to manufacture goods to sell overseas, for example, to North America.

THE SLAVE TRADE

Slaves were one of the most important cargoes carried on British ships. The slave trade was centred on Bristol and Liverpool. Ships sailed from Britain loaded with cloth and ironware to the west coast of Africa. Here the traders met slave merchants, who exchanged the cloth and iron for black slaves, most of whom had been captured in inter-tribal wars, or had been sold into slavery as a punishment. The traders shipped the slaves across to the West Indies or America, to work on cotton, sugar and tobacco plantations. When the traders had sold the slaves, some picked up cargoes of sugar, rum or timber to take back to Britain, but most sailed back empty.

The slave trade was profitable. Most merchants reckoned to make about ten pounds a year for every hundred that they invested. This was a good return. But the trade was cruel and inhuman. It took it for granted that some human beings were commodities to be bought and sold.

On the voyage across the Atlantic, slaves were packed into dark and stinking holds. The only air and light came through gratings in the ships' decks, and even these were covered up in wet and stormy weather. One ship took on 562 slaves in Africa. In seventeen days at sea, fifty-five of them died, and their bodies were thrown overboard. On some voyages a quarter of the slaves died before the ship reached the West Indies.

Slave traders were always afraid that the slaves might break out and take over the ship. To prevent this they chained them together in pairs, and watched them carefully. If the traders discovered that any of the slaves were plotting to escape, they punished them severely. But traders rarely killed any slaves. They wanted as many as possible left alive to sell at the end of the voyage.

Respectable merchants in Bristol and Liverpool made a good living out of the slave trade. They took it for granted, and so did most people in Britain.

Study

This study tests:

K your understanding of the information on pages 87–8 on the growth of Britain's trade and the effects of war.

1 For what reason or reasons did Britain's trade with these regions increase between 1750 and 1815?
   a India and America
   b Europe
   c other regions overseas?

Study

In this study you will be considering:

Ev what the sources below tell us about the slave trade, and whether or not they are reliable.

Source 3A

Loading slaves onto a ship.

Source 3B

Question after question was put . . . to these witnesses; and from their own mouths they dragged out . . . the following melancholy account:

Every slave, whatever his size might be, was found to have only five feet and six inches in length, and sixteen inches in breadth to lie in. The floor was covered with bodies stowed or packed according to this allowance. But between the floor and the deck or ceiling were often platforms or broad shelves in the mid way, which were covered with bodies also . . . The men were chained two and two together by their hands and feet. Their allowance consisted of one pint of water a day to each person, and they were fed twice a day with yams and horse beans.

Thomas Clarkson, *History of the Abolition of the African Slave Trade* (1808) (reporting what witnesses told MPs about conditions on slave ships).

Source 3C

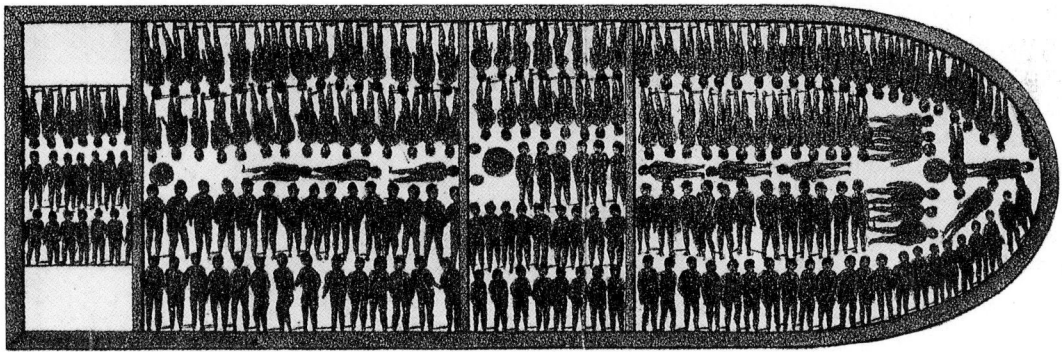

A plan of an eighteenth-century slave ship showing how slaves were packed in.

1 Do Sources 3A, 3B and 3C support the statement on page 88 that the slave trade 'took it for granted that some human beings were commodities to be bought and sold'? Give reasons for your answer.
2 a Look at Source 3A. Why may the artist have painted this?
  b What further information would you need before you could decide whether Source 3A is primary or secondary evidence of how slaves were loaded onto ships?
3 Thomas Clarkson is considered to be biased in his reporting of the slave trade. Do you think that the information in Source 3B is reliable? Give reasons for your answer.

—————————————— **Part Three** ——————————————

The Growth of Free Trade

THE WEALTH OF NATIONS, 1776

In 1776 Adam Smith (1723–90), a professor at Glasgow University, published a book called *The Wealth of Nations*. He said that governments ought not to control trade. He thought most customs duties ought to be abolished. He said that if trade was free, every country would grow crops which suited its climate best and manufacture goods for which it had the raw materials. It would sell some of its produce abroad, and buy anything it needed from other countries.

Smith believed that 'free trade' would bring down prices. This would encourage people to buy more goods, so manufacturers would build more factories and employ more workers. Then everybody would be better off. Many people agreed with Smith. Factory owners in particular were in favour of free trade, because they believed that British factories were more efficient than those abroad, and would undercut their prices. But farmers and landowners were not so sure that they would be able to compete against imports of foreign corn if the duty was removed.

THE DEVELOPMENT OF FREE TRADE

Between 1786 and 1860 Britain gradually became a free-trade country.

Study

This study will test:

K how well you understand the arguments for and against free trade.

This list jumbles together points that might have been made by a supporter of Adam Smith and by supporters of the mercantilist policy of protection.

A If Britain relied on cheap imported food, an enemy could cut off supplies in wartime.

B Duties lead to smuggling and a loss of revenue for the government.

C Each country should grow crops that suit its climate, and manufacture goods for which it has the raw materials.

D The government's income will fall if it abolishes import duties so it will have to raise other taxes.

1 Rewrite the list, putting each point under the appropriate heading: *Free Trade* v. *Protection*.

2 Add two or more points to each list.

3 Ask one person to read his or her list to the class. Do the rest of you agree?

Humane Man Traps

Illustration 4 Many labourers hunted for hares, rabbits and other game on local farmers' land. This was illegal, and some farmers set mantraps to catch them.

Table 5 Britain becomes a free trade nation

Date	Minister	Free trade measures	Comment
1786	William Pitt (Prime Minister)	*Trade Treaty with France* **Britain** cut duties on French wines and spirits **France** cut duties on British cloth and iron	Pitt hoped to reduce many more duties but in 1793 war broke out with France. Pitt had to increase duties to pay for the war.
1815	The war with France ended, but the government still needed revenue from customs duties to repay money borrowed during the war.		
1823–28	William Huskisson (President of the Board of Trade)	1 System of Reciprocity. Duties were cut on goods from countries which cut duties on British goods. 2 Duty on most manufactured goods cut from 50% to 25%. 3 Duty on colonial goods cut. 4 Navigation Acts reformed. Foreign ships could carry goods to British ports.	Huskisson was MP for Liverpool. By 1828 he had reduced the duty on many everyday items. This helped to cut the cost of living and encouraged trade.
1841–46	Robert Peel (Prime Minister)	1 Cut import duties on manufactured goods by 10%. 2 Abolished the duty on corn (see page 91). 3 Abolished duties on 520 everyday items.	The government's income from customs duties was reduced. To make up for this, Peel introduced Income Tax for three years. It has never been removed.
1853 and 1860	William Gladstone (Chancellor of the Exchequer)	His two budgets abolished all remaining duties except those on tea, sugar, beer, wines, spirits and tobacco.	Gladstone kept some customs duties in order to bring in some revenue for the government.

THE DUTIES ON CORN— A SPECIAL CASE

The Corn Law of 1815

In 1815, to prevent imports of cheap foreign corn, British farmers persuaded Parliament to pass a law forbidding imports of foreign wheat until the price of British wheat reached eighty shillings a quarter— a price which farmers thought would give them a fair profit.

This 'Corn Law' was unpopular because when wheat was dear, bread was expensive, and working men hated having to pay a high price for bread just to benefit farmers.

In fact the 1815 Corn Law did not have much effect on the price of wheat. In most years harvests were good and the price remained below seventy shillings. But most farmers still managed to make a living.

The sliding scale, 1828

The government realised that the fixed price of eighty shillings was too high, and in 1828 they persuaded Parliament to impose a sliding scale of duties to replace the 1815 law. As the price of British wheat rose, the duty fell, until at eighty shillings foreign wheat was allowed in duty free.

The sliding scale made little or no difference to the price of wheat. It continued to vary between forty and seventy shillings a quarter, depending on the size of the crop.

The end of the Corn Laws

The Corn Laws were still very unpopular. Many people believed that it was wrong to tax food. Manufacturers who wanted to sell goods abroad argued that foreigners would not buy goods from Britain so long as we refused to buy their wheat.

When Peel reduced or abolished duties on many raw materials and manufactured goods he left the duties on wheat. This annoyed factory owners. They thought it was unfair to protect farmers from imports of foreign wheat while manufacturers had to compete with imported foreign goods.

The Anti-Corn Law League

In 1839 a number of Lancashire merchants had set up the Anti-Corn Law League to campaign against the Corn Laws. Its leaders were Richard Cobden and John Bright, who both owned cloth mills.

At first the league relied on public meetings and pamphlets to get its message across, but in 1841

Study

In this study you will:
K see how well you understand the reasons for and the results of the Corn Laws.

In each pair of the following sentences, one sentence contains accurate information and one does not. Choose the accurate sentence from each pair. You may need to refer to the information on page 90–1.

1 **a** In 1815 British farmers persuaded Parliament to pass a Corn Law which said that no foreign corn could be imported until British corn reached eighty shillings a quarter.
  b In 1815 British farmers persuaded Parliament to pass a Corn Law which said that no foreign corn could be imported until its price reached eighty shillings a quarter.

2 **a** Working men thought the Corn Law made bread expensive, but in fact bread was dear because farmers had to charge high prices to cover their costs.
  b Working men thought the Corn Law made bread expensive, but in fact the size of each year's harvest had the greatest influence on the price.

3 **a** In 1828 a sliding scale replaced the fixed price of eighty shillings, so that a low tax was charged on imported wheat when British wheat was cheap, and a high one when British wheat was dear.
  b By 1828 a sliding scale replaced the fixed price of eighty shillings so that a high tax was charged on imported wheat when British wheat was cheap, and a low one when British wheat was dear.

4 **a** The price of wheat on sale in Britain continued to vary between forty shillings and seventy shillings a quarter, so the sliding scale made little or no difference to the price of wheat and bread.
  b The price of wheat on sale in Britain continued to vary between forty shillings and seventy shillings a quarter because the sliding scale made the price move up and down.

Cobden was elected to Parliament, and in 1843 so was Bright. They spent many hours in the House of Commons arguing against the Corn Laws, and they succeeded in convincing Peel himself that the Corn Laws would eventually have to go.

The repeal of the Corn Laws

In 1845 and 1846 the potato crop in Ireland failed. The population of Ireland was over eight million, and most relied on potatoes for their food. When the crop failed they faced starvation. Peel therefore decided to repeal the Corn Laws at once to allow foreign corn to be imported duty-free to feed the Irish. So in 1846 Parliament abolished all duties on imported corn.

Results of repeal

The repeal of the Corn Laws upset farmers and landowners. They thought it showed that the government no longer cared about their welfare. They believed that Peel had betrayed them in favour of factory owners, and shortly after the repeal his government was defeated in a vote in the House of Commons. He had to resign, and never took office again.

Study

In this study your aim is to:
Ca consider why the events between 1839 and 1846 led to the repeal of the Corn Laws.

1 The list below gives some possible factors that led to the repeal of the Corn Laws:
  a Poor people disliked the Corn Laws because they thought they made bread expensive.
  b The Anti-Corn Law League was well organised and had good leaders.
  c The supporters of the Anti-Corn Law League had the vote and elected MPs who put their case in Parliament.
  d By 1841 Peel had decided to repeal the Corn Laws at some time in the future.
  e In 1846 Peel thought the best way to help the starving Irish was to repeal the Corn Laws.
  In pairs, list the events in order of their importance as causes of the repeal of the Corn Laws, adding any other items you think were important.
2 Ask one person to say which items he or she thinks were the least and most important and explain why. Do the rest of you agree?

Study

Your aim in this study is to decide:
- **Ev** how people might have reacted to the cartoon (Source 4) when it was first published; whether or not the view it gives is a fair impression of farmers at that time.

Remember what you have learned about the Corn Laws when you are doing this work.

Source 4

A cartoon published in 1849 showing gloomy farmers after the repeal of the Corn Laws.

1 What impression does the cartoon give of:
   the farmers' standard of living;
   the farmers?
   Give reasons for your answers.
2 Why might the following people have been angry if they had seen the cartoon:
   a factory worker;
   a factory owner;
   a farmer?
3 Do you think each of them would have had a right to be angry? Give reasons for your answers.

Part Four

Changes in Trade by 1850

PROFITS AND PAYMENTS

Exports: by 1830 manufactured cotton goods made up nearly 50% of Britain's exports.

The value of cotton goods exported was not all profit because cloth manufacturers had to import huge quantities of raw cotton from America and India.

Imports: after 1830 the total value of goods imported into Britain was always greater than that of goods exported.

To pay for imports: Britain had to rely partly on money earned abroad by British service industries, for example, banks, insurance companies and British ships carrying foreign goods.

Table 6   Changes in items traded by 1850

Goods	Imports	Exports	Comment
Slaves	None	None	**1787** Committee for the Abolition of the Slave Trade set up. William Wilberforce and Thomas Clarkson collected evidence against the slave trade. **1807** Parliament abolished the slave trade.
Corn	Greatly increased	None	**1750–1850** Britain's population rose from five and a half million to twenty million. More food was needed.
Iron	No pig iron after 1800	Manufactures greatly increased	Developments in the iron industry and engineering meant that Britain could produce more pig iron, iron goods and machinery.
Coal	None	Increased	Britain produced more than enough coal to supply its industries.
Wool	Little change	Little change	Supplies of raw wool just kept up with increased demand in Britain.
Cotton	Raw cotton— greatly increased	Cotton goods greatly increased	Improved machinery driven by water and steam power speeded up the manufacture of cotton cloth.

Study

Your aim in this study is:

Ch to use the information on pages 87–94 to work out how Britain's trade had changed between 1750 and 1850.

1 By 1830:
   what type of manufactured goods made up nearly half of Britain's exports;
   which service industries helped to pay for Britain's imports?
2 By 1850, which commodity that had been an important item in Britain's trade in 1750 was:
   no longer traded at all;
   imported in greatly increased quantities but not exported;
   imported and exported in greatly increased quantities?
3 How did each of the following developments help to change the pattern of Britain's trade between 1750 and 1850:
   setting up the Committee for the Abolition of the Slave Trade
   the increase in Britain's population
   the growth of the iron and engineering industries?

Recall

1 What was: a duty; a bounty; the sliding scale; protection?
2 Rewrite the lists below, matching the dates and events correctly:
   1776   The Corn Laws are passed.
   1786   The Corn Laws are repealed.
   1815   Pitt signs a Free Trade Treaty with France.
   1828   *The Wealth of Nations* is published.
   1846   The sliding scale is introduced.
3 In 1700 Britain was a mercantilist nation. How did *i* the ideas of Adam Smith and *ii* the Irish Potato Famine 1845–6 help to change Britain into a free trade country?

10
Towns and Public Health

Part One

The Growing Towns

NEW TOWNS

As industry grew, so did the size and number of towns. Some were new settlements which developed round coal mines and ironworks.

Administrative problems

The sudden growth of new towns led to many problems. In the countryside, parish councils were responsible for dealing with matters such as roads, policing and caring for the poor. They could cope with problems which arose in a small village with a few scattered farms, but had no idea what to do when a factory or mine was established in their parish, and hundreds of workers suddenly moved in.

EXISTING TOWNS

Existing towns also grew. The development of steam engines (see Chapter 5) enabled manufacturers to site their factories where they liked. Most chose towns, because there were plenty of people to man their machines, and roads, canals or railways to bring in fuel and other raw material and take away the finished products. When factories were established in a town, anyone in the area who was out of work went there, because they knew there might be jobs available. So the towns grew.

OVERCROWDING

The growth of towns caused problems. Coventry and Nottingham were both surrounded by fields belonging to the town corporations. They would not allow anyone to build on this land. Newcomers had to find a place to live within the old town. So owners of orchards and gardens divided them up and sold them for building (see Diagram 1). Soon every open space had gone. Instead there were rows of three-storey, back-to-back houses. In some parts of Nottingham 2,000 people lived on one hectare of ground. A government commissioner who visited the town in 1845 wrote: 'I believe that nowhere else shall we find so large a mass of inhabitants crowded into courts, alleys and lanes as in Nottingham'.

Nottingham and Coventry were more overcrowded than most industrial towns. But in all of them houses were packed closely together, partly because the more houses there were on a piece of land, the more rent the landowner would get. It was also convenient for workpeople to live as close as possible to the factories where they worked. They had to walk to work, and did not want to waste time and energy getting there.

Diagram 1

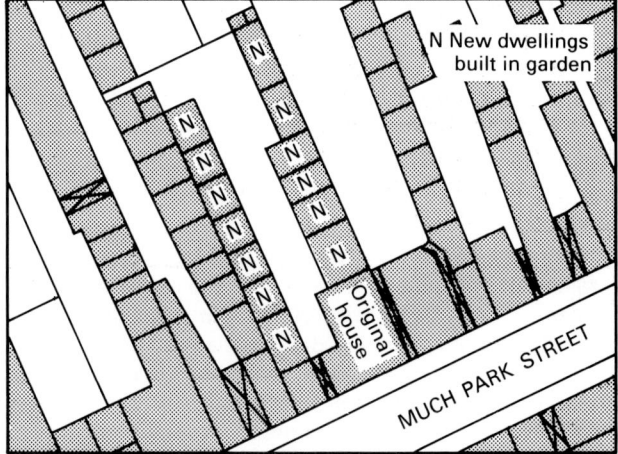

The plan shows new dwellings built in the gardens of houses in Much Park Street, Coventry.

Study

In this study you will:

Ca consider the reasons why workers in Coventry and Nottingham in the nineteenth century had to live in overcrowded conditions.

The information you need is on page 95.

1 In pairs, rewrite the list of points below in the order of their importance as causes of overcrowding in Coventry and Nottingham.
   a Britain's population increased rapidly between 1700 and 1850.
   b The population of Coventry and Nottingham increased rapidly.
   c Workers wanted to live within walking distance of their workplace.
   d Manufacturers built factories in Coventry and Nottingham.
   e The town councils would not let the towns expand in area.
   f Some landowners were greedy and crammed as many houses as possible onto the land available.

   Ask one person to read his or her list to the class. Do the rest of you agree?
2 From memory, write a paragraph on 'Overcrowding in Coventry and Nottingham in the nineteenth century'.

—————— Part Two ——————
Homes for the Workers

Study

In this study you will:

Em consider what people who lived, or could have lived, at the time thought about working-class living conditions in the first part of the nineteenth century.

The evidence quoted all comes from government commissioners' reports published in 1843 and 1845.

LODGING HOUSES

Source 1A

When workers first moved into a town, they often stayed in a lodging house. This source describes a house at Ashton-under-Lyme, in Cheshire in 1843:

each house consists of four rooms, of the average size about 15 feet [4.5 m] square by 7.5 feet [2.25 m] high, two of these rooms being on the ground floor and two on the upper floor . . . Generally the front lower room is reserved as a kind of kitchen, and the remaining three filled . . . completely with beds . . . In some instances the floors are covered with filth of a wet, pitchy consistency, the walls with vermin of the most noxious kind, and the bedclothes and furniture with filth and nastiness . . . Ventilation is never attended to, and . . . the atmosphere is absolutely suffocating.

WORKERS' HOUSES

Structure

Source 1B

Most houses built for workers were small, dark, damp and flimsy. In 1845 workers' houses in Derby were described as:

badly built, with the usual 4.5 inch [115 mm] party walls . . . The interior is generally dark and filthy, the light and sun being excluded by the neighbouring walls and buildings. There is usually one room on the ground floor, in which the family cook, eat, and pass the day, with one or two sleeping rooms over it. The dimensions of the apartments vary from about 12 feet by 10 (3.6 by 3 m) to about 14 feet by 12 (4.2 by 3.6 m), and the height ranges from 7 to 10 feet (2.1 to 3 m). The ground floor is usually of brick or stone, and the upper floors of plaster.

▶

Source 1C

An 1868 photograph of slum houses in Glasgow.

The rent for such houses in Derby was about two shillings a week. The average number of people living in them was five, though some families took in lodgers, and occasionally there were as many as ten people living in a two-roomed house.

Some families lived in cellars, described in 1796 as 'holes where the light of the sun never reaches, and where pure and wholesome air is not admitted'. A Manchester doctor visiting the sick found some had no beds, but were lying on damp earth floors, dressed only in 'rags'. The cellars where they lived were so dark that, even during the day, he had to examine patients by candlelight.

1 Thomas Crocker is an unemployed farm labourer with a wife and two children. He comes to Derby and boards at a lodging house for two months while he looks for work and a house to rent. He is given a job in a stocking mill, finds a house within walking distance of his work, and moves his family to Derby. Why might he and his family think he was fortunate to have found the house?
2 Why might a landlord have been willing to buy up property in Glasgow slums like those pictured in Source 1C?

Furnishings

Source 1D

Most working class families had very little furniture. In 1833 a factory commissioner interviewed a Manchester housewife. Her husband was a skilled spinner and they had five children, one of whom worked as his piecer. The commissioner wrote:

The house consists of four rooms, two on each floor; the furniture consists of two beds in the same room, one for themselves and the other for the children; [they] have four chairs, one table in the house, boxes to put clothes in, no chest of drawers, two pans and a tea-kettle for boiling, a gridiron and frying-pan, half a dozen large and small plates, four pairs of knives and forks, several pewter spoons.

3 What may the commissioner have found surprising about the information that the spinner's wife gave him?
4 Why may the spinner's wife have felt that her family's house and furniture were adequate for their needs?

The smells

Source 1E

Many middle class people had no idea of the conditions in which workers lived. A Manchester doctor tried to explain how bad their houses were. He wrote:

Let anyone accustomed to better conditions of life put his head into one of them, and he will be met with a mephitic [foul-smelling] atmosphere, the like of which is not to be found in the domicile of any other animal. Stables and shippons [cow sheds] and even pig sties have their peculiar smells, but they are not as poisonous, or repulsive, or offensive as these. No animal could live in them and flourish.

5 a Why may the doctor have known a good deal about working class housing in Manchester?
  b Why may the doctor have compared the smell in working class houses with the smell of cowsheds and pigsties?

——— Part Three ———
Water and Air

WATER AND DRAINS

The countryside

Very few communities in the eighteenth century had piped water or main drainage. Most people in the countryside got water from a nearby spring or pump. Their lavatories, which they called 'privies', or 'necessaries', were usually outside the house. Some emptied into a 'cess pit', but most were earth closets, which had to be cleaned out regularly.

Towns

Water and washing

Householders in towns had to buy drinking water from water-carriers at three gallons a penny. For washing they carried water from the nearest river or canal, and a doctor in Whitechapel in London said, 'they merely pass dirty linen through very dirty water. The smell of the linen itself when so washed is very offensive'.

Waste disposal

Householders tended to throw most of their slops and rubbish, including the contents of the earth closets, into the street, and town councils arranged for street cleaners to gather up the rubbish and sell it to local farmers to use as fertiliser.

Most councils only had the main streets cleaned. They did not bother with areas where factory workers lived. A doctor in Leeds reported:

'The ashes, garbage and filth of all kinds are thrown from the doors and windows of the houses upon the surface of the streets and courts, and in some cases where a gallery . . . has been erected for the inhabitants of the second floor, the whole of the slops and filth are thrown over the gallery in front of the houses beneath, and as the ground is often sloping towards the doors of the lower dwellings, they are inundated with water and filth . . . The privies . . . are few in proportion to the number of inhabitants. They are open to view both in front and rear, are invariably in a filthy condition, and often remain without the removal of any portion of the filth for six months.'

Study

This study helps you:

S to compare living conditions today with those of working class people in the nineteenth century.

1 a Give three ways in which your family uses water in the house during a normal week.
b Give two or more examples to show why you might find life difficult if:
   your water supply was cut off for a week,
   your dustbin was not emptied for a month.
2 Look at Source 1F.
a If five people, on average, lived in each house (marked 'h'), how many people:
   lived in the court,
   had to share a lavatory?
b Refuse was not collected regularly and the court did not have piped water. What problems may this have caused the people who lived in the court?

Source 1F

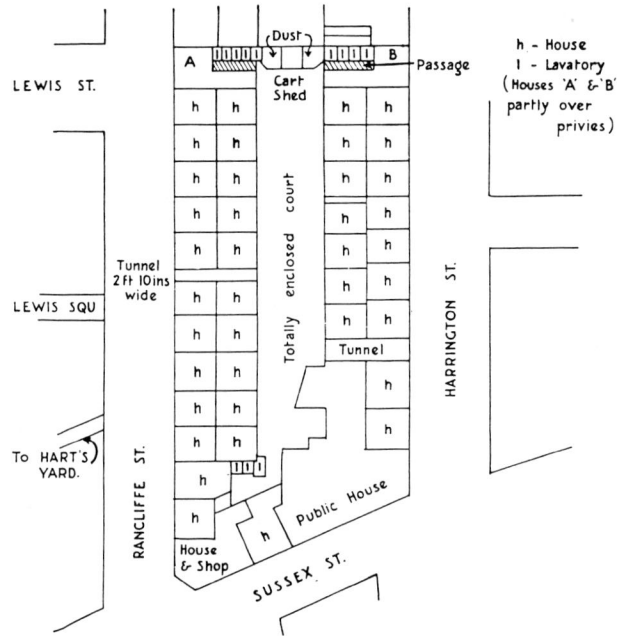

This plan of a Nottingham court comes from a government report published in 1845.

SMOKE AND SMELLS

The air in most industrial towns was polluted. Hippolyte Taine, a visitor from France, noticed that in Manchester it was 'impregnated with fog and soot'. Many towns were built in narrow valleys which filled with smoke from domestic fires and factory chimneys. But even in Newcastle-on-Tyne, which is on an open, sloping site, the inhabitants complained of the 'smoke from manufactories, gas from alkali works, slaughter houses, burning of bones and animal matter, manure in cow-keepers' premises, pig-sties, tanneries etc.'

—————— Part Four ——————

Urban People

Study

In the first half of the nineteenth century, London was the largest city in the world, and there were more industrial towns in Britain than in any other country. In this study you will be looking at London and Manchester through the eyes of two French visitors, Gustave Doré and Hippolyte Taine, and considering:

Ev how useful and reliable their evidence is.

THE POOR

Source 2A

An engraving of a London street by the French artist Gustave Doré.

Source 2B

Hippolyte Taine went into some of the poorest parts of London and Manchester. In Shadwell, in London, he reported:

the whole place is alive with street boys, bare-footed, filthy, turning cartwheels for a penny. They swarm on the stairs down to the Thames, more stunted, paler, more deformed, more repulsive than the street urchins of Paris . . . Among them, leaning against the festering walls, or crouched inert on the steps, are men in the most astonishing rags. Nobody who has not seen them can imagine what layers of filth a frock-coat or a pair of trousers can carry. They doze and day-dream . . . It was in this district that families were discovered whose only bed was a heap of soot; they had been sleeping on it for some months.

1 Is the impression given by Taine's description of London similar to or different from that given by Doré's picture? Give reasons for your answer.
2 Does Taine give the impression that the poor of Paris were better or worse off than the poor of London? Give reasons for your answer.

Source 2C

In Manchester Taine saw:

women and children swarming in the filthy air. Their clothes are dirty: many of the children are bare-footed; the faces are drawn and dismal . . . We follow them: what dreary streets! Through half-open windows we could see wretched rooms at ground level, or often below the damp earth's surface. Masses of pale children, dirty and swollen, crowd every doorway and breathe the foul air of the street, less foul than that inside.

3 What can you see in the picture of London that is similar to Taine's description of Manchester?

▶

Study continued

THE PROSPEROUS

Source 2D

While he was in Manchester, Taine walked into the suburbs. After leaving the poorest areas he came to:

a more open space where rows of small cheap houses have been built by speculators. The black streets were paved with ironstone slag . . . But at least each family has its own home, and the fog they breathe is not so contaminated.

These were the homes of skilled workers and craftsmen. Further out still, he came to:

wide streets, quiet and devoid of shops, in which each house, surrounded by its plot of green, is isolated and contains only a single family.

These were the houses of the managers and factory owners, and most of them were built to the west of the town, so that the prevailing westerly winds blew the smuts and smells away from their homes.

4 a Why might French people who only knew about Britain from Doré's picture and Taine's descriptions of London and Manchester have thought that:
most British people had not benefited from the wealth produced by Britain's industries,
Britain was an unattractive country?
b Give an example of something that: *i* Doré might have drawn, *ii* Taine might have described, that would have given a better impression of British life in the middle of the nineteenth century.

———————— Part Five ————————

Cholera and Public Health

THE URBAN DEATH RATE

The death rate in industrial towns was very high. Children were particularly at risk. In 1841 the death rate among babies under the age of three in Manchester was four times what it was in Dorset. Working class children did worst of all.

Table 1   Percentage of children under five dying in Preston, 1843

	Percentage
Upper class families	18
Tradesmen's families	38
Workers' families	55

THE COMING OF CHOLERA

In 1832 a terrifying new disease called cholera appeared in Britain. It struck without warning, and killed up to half the people who caught it. Its main symptoms were continual diarrhoea and vomiting, with convulsive cramp-like pains in the stomach. Sufferers excreted so much fluid that their bodies seemed to shrink, their blood thickened and their skin turned blue. Cholera spread steadily through England, Wales, Scotland and Ireland. By the time the epidemic died down in 1834, it had killed 56,852 people.

REACTIONS TO CHOLERA

Cleaning up the towns

The authorities could not prevent cholera because they did not know what caused it. Most doctors believed it was caused by impure air. They pointed out that most cases occurred in poor, overcrowded districts which stank because there were no drains or sewers, and all the rubbish lay rotting in courts and alleyways. They decided that to prevent further outbreaks of cholera, these areas had to be cleaned up.

The Municipal Corporations Act 1835

In a few towns, such as Liverpool and Manchester, Improvement Commissioners had been set up by Parliament. Some had the power to have the streets cleaned and to install a system of drains and sewers. But in most towns nobody had this power. Then in 1835 Parliament passed the Municipal Corporations Act. This abolished all the old corporations. Instead towns could apply for a charter, which would give them permission to set up a council elected by the ratepayers. These new councils had the power to organise street-cleaning and sewer-laying. But as the memory of the cholera epidemic faded, many were unwilling to spend the necessary money.

The Chadwick Commissions

Some members of Parliament were still concerned about the state of Britain's towns.

In 1839 the House of Lords ordered the Poor Law Commissioners to investigate the 'Sanitary condition of the Labouring Population'. Most of the work was done by the commissioners' secretary, Edwin Chadwick.

In 1842 Chadwick published his report. This gave the first detailed account of the filthy conditions in which many working people had to live. It sold more than 10,000 copies, and persuaded many politicians and town councillors that conditions had to be improved.

In 1843 the government decided to set up a Royal Commission on the Health of Towns. This published two reports, parts of which were quoted earlier in the chapter.

The Health of Towns Association 1844

In 1844, after the publication of the Commission's first report, an organisation called *The Health of Towns Association* was set up.

Study

In this study you will:

K investigate attitudes to Public Health following the cholera outbreak of 1832.

1 a What did the majority of doctors think caused cholera?
  b Why did they think that the best way to prevent cholera was to clean up overcrowded streets and to install sewers and drains?
2 a In which year did the government: encourage councils to improve sanitary conditions in towns, make it compulsory for councils to improve sanitary conditions in towns?
  b Why were: some councils unwilling to spend money on improvements in the early 1840s, most MPs prepared to make councils spend money on improvements by 1848?
3 a How did the work of Edwin Chadwick help to convince some politicians and town councillors that sanitary conditions in towns had to be improved?
  b How did the work of the Health of Towns Association put pressure on Parliament to pass laws forcing local authorities to improve sanitary conditions in towns?

The association:
  published fact-sheets,
  sent letters to MPs and councillors,
  set up local branches,
  organised a petition to Parliament demanding a new law to force local authorities to pave and cleanse towns.

At first Parliament refused to act because many MPs did not think the government ought to be given so much power over local authorities. But in 1848 cholera once again spread across Europe. This frightened Parliament, and in August they passed the Public Health Act.

The Public Health Act 1848

The 1848 Act made town councils responsible for cleansing streets, laying sewers and providing a supply of drinking water. (Towns which had no councils could be made to set up local Boards of Health, elected by the ratepayers, to do the job.) It also set up a National Board of Health for England and Wales for five years to control the system.

THE 1848 CHOLERA EPIDEMIC

Chadwick's work

In October 1848 cholera broke out in Britain for the second time. Edwin Chadwick was on the Board of Health. He was very energetic and sure of himself. He believed that 'all smell was disease', and was certain that cholera was caused by impurities in the air. As the disease spread he sent out hundreds of letters telling local boards to clean streets and lay drains. Some doctors doubted if he was right. They thought cholera was infectious, and believed that sufferers ought to be isolated. But Chadwick thought that isolation was a waste of time and money.

Results

1 In spite of all the money spent on drains and sewers, the 1848–9 cholera epidemic killed well over 100,000 people—about double the number who died in 1831–4.
2 In 1853 the town of Croydon, which had just installed an up-to-date sewerage system, was struck by the worst epidemic of typhoid fever it had ever known.
3 So people lost confidence in Chadwick and the Board of Health. In 1854, when the board's five year term came to an end, Parliament refused to extend it. As a result the Board of Health was abolished.

Study

In this study you can:

Ev show your skill in combining what you have learned about Edwin Chadwick with the information in Source 3.

Source 3

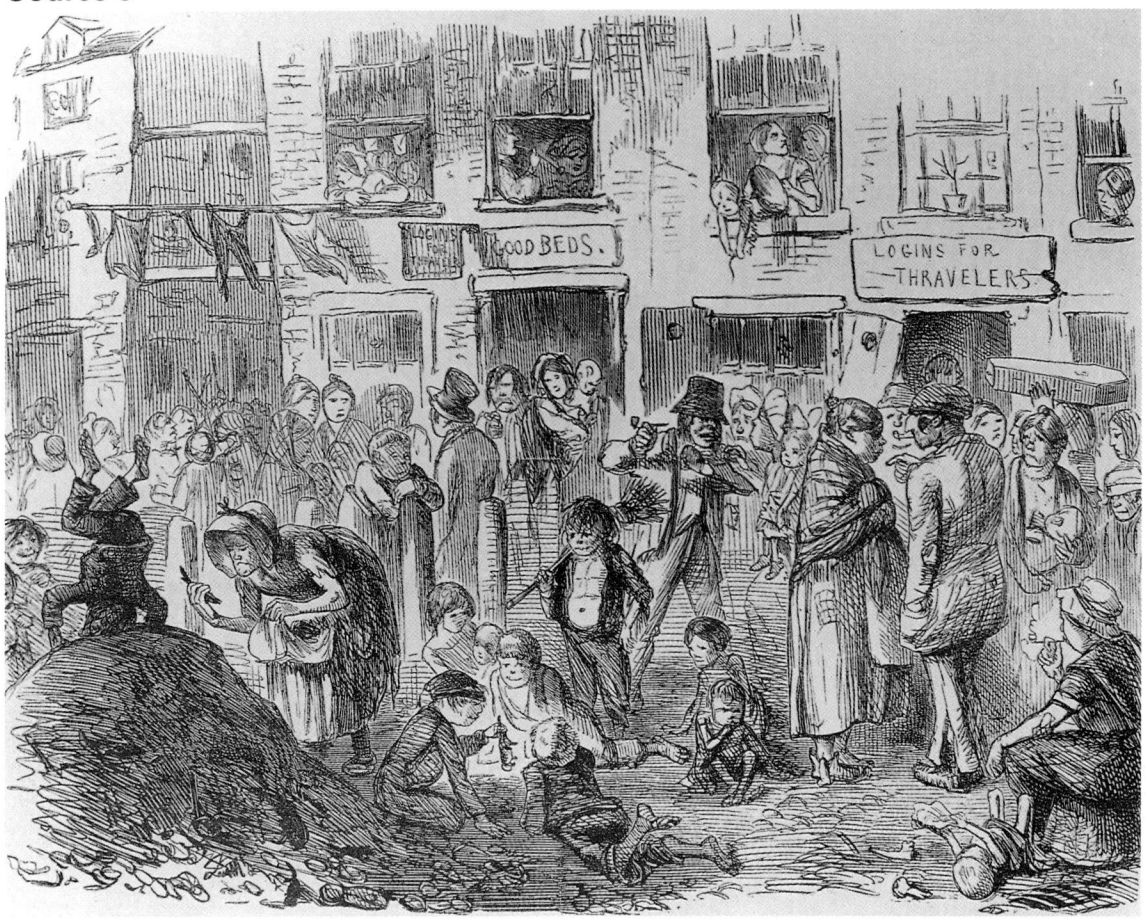

A cartoon, published in 1852, called 'A Court for King Cholera'.

1 a What did Edwin Chadwick believe caused cholera?

b What can you see in the cartoon which suggests that the artist supported Chadwick?

2 a How many years had the National Board of Health left to carry on its work when the cartoon was published?

b What reason or reasons may the artist have had for publishing his cartoon when he did?

3 If the artist's ideas on the causes of cholera proved to be wrong, would his cartoon:
   have shown anything of importance about living conditions in the 1850s,
   be of any use to modern historians?
Given reasons for your answers.

SEWAGE AND CHOLERA

The new drains

By 1854 many towns had been provided with sewers to carry the waste away. In most cases the sewage was simply piped into the nearest river (see Illustration 1). In 1859 an article in *The Times* described how London was drained:

> All the sewers in London on both sides of the river run due north and south, all discharging themselves into the Thames, all within a length of five or six miles [8 or 10 km] . . . This was the arrangement 10 years ago, and is so still . . . From that time to the present 700 or 800 miles [1100 or 1300 km] of sewers and drains have been constructed . . . providing . . . the means for all cesspools to flow into [the Thames] regularly day by day. By this 'improved' drainage upwards of 200,000 gallons [900,000 litres] of sewage has been daily added to the Thames at low water . . . But . . . the Thames has not been the only sufferer. Wherever a stream could be found, no matter how pure its waters . . . drains have been made into it.

John Snow's theories

Many towns and villages drew their drinking water from streams into which sewage had been piped. So long as the water appeared clean and sweet, nobody cared. But in 1855 John Snow, a London doctor, published a book containing good evidence that cholera was spread by infected sewage getting into drinking water 'either by permeating the ground and getting into wells, or by running along channels and sewers into the rivers from which entire towns are sometimes supplied with water.'

The 1866 cholera outbreak

At first few people believed Snow, but in 1866 cholera broke out in east London. An investigation showed that just before the outbreak a workman had opened the wrong valve at the East London Water Company's works and had let unfiltered water from the River Lea into the mains. And the River Lea carried sewage from a house in Bromley where a man had recently died of cholera.

After 1866 local authorities began to treat sewage before they piped it into rivers, and were careful to provide a reliable supply of pure water. As a result cholera died out in Britain.

Illustration 1 Southwark Water Works drew drinking water from the Thames, just where the city's main sewers emptied into the river. This shows what the cartoonist, George Cruikshank, thought about it.

Study

This study:

Ca tests your understanding of the connection between cholera and the water supply.

1 Copy the table below and fill in the spaces correctly:

Table 2   The pollution of rivers 1832–66

Date	Event
1832	Cruikshank's cartoon drew attention to the pollution of the .... Thames.
1833 1848	Acts of Parliament to improve drainage and sewage disposal in towns.
1855	John .... published evidence that cholera was spread by infected .... getting into .... water.
1866	An investigation of the .... outbreak showed a connection between cholera and .... water let into the mains.

2 Look at the article published in *The Times* in 1859.
  a When the author of the article wrote about 'improved' drainage, did he mean that:
    no real improvements had been made to the drainage of London,
    London had a better drainage system, but some of the results were disastrous?
  b Were the views put forward by John Snow in 1855:
    completely supported by *The Times* article,
    partly supported by *The Times* article,
    unsupported by *The Times* article?
    Give reasons for your answer.

3 a Was the 1866 cholera epidemic caused by:
    infected sewage entering the River Lea;
    the East London Water Company's failure to provide a filter for water entering the mains;
    human error?
    Give reasons for your answer.
  b Did any good come from the 1866 cholera epidemic?
    Give reasons for your answer.

Illustration 2   An engraving, published in *The Builder* in 1862, showing people queueing to collect water from a tap in a London alley.

Recall

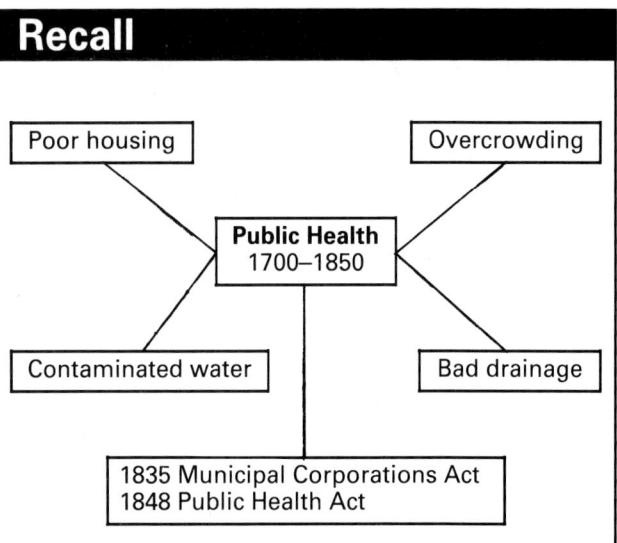

1 Why was there so much disease in eighteenth and nineteenth century industrial towns? How did the government try to make towns healthier places to live?

11
Social Welfare

Part One
The Poor Law

THE POOR LAW IN THE EIGHTEENTH CENTURY

The parish overseer

In the eighteenth century every parish in England and Wales had an overseer of the poor. Overseers were appointed by local magistrates, and they had to look after people who were too poor to fend for themselves. Such people were known as 'paupers'. Overseers' money came mostly from a 'poor rate' which every householder had to pay. Sometimes, in addition, there was money left by rich men and women in their wills.

Indoor and outdoor relief

Able-bodied paupers lived in their own homes and were given money to keep them going. This was known as 'outdoor relief'.

Old, sick, or disabled paupers were put into hospitals or workhouses, where they were fed and clothed. This was known as 'indoor relief'.

Gilbert's Act 1782

Workhouses were expensive to build, and sometimes two or more parishes clubbed together to build one for them to share. Before 1782, parishes wishing to do this had to pay for a special Act of Parliament. Then Parliament passed 'Gilbert's Act', which allowed parishes to group together into 'Unions' to build workhouses. But less than 1,000 of the 15,000 parishes in England and Wales had formed Unions before 1834. (See Illustration 1.)

The law of settlement

To be entitled to receive help, a pauper had to be 'settled' in a parish. The law of settlement was very

Study

Your aim in this study is to:

K see how well you can use the information about the system of poor relief before 1782.

1 In 1709 Widow Bleat lived in the Bedfordshire village of Eaton Socon. Her house was falling down, and she could not afford to have it repaired. Which parish official would Widow Bleat have gone to for help?

2 The parish official paid workmen to patch up her house, and afterwards recorded in his accounts the amount he had spent.

For wood	5s	6d
For nails		8d
For straw and spits	4s	0d
For thatch ropes and reed		10d
For carpenter's work	2s	3d
For thatcher and server	2s	6d
Total	15s	9d

a Did Widow Bleat receive outdoor or indoor relief?
b How was the money raised to pay for the repairs?

3 At the same time Widow Bleat's son needed a new coat and waistcoat. So the official bought cloth for 10s 2d, paid a local woman a shilling for making the two garments and added these expenses to his accounts.

a The parish official had to show his accounts to the local magistrate if he asked to see them. Explain why.
b What name was given to people like Widow Bleat and her son whose expenses were entered in the official's accounts?

Illustration 1   In some towns workhouses were old, decaying buildings. This drawing, made in 1820, shows King's Lynn workhouse.

complicated, but poor people who wandered from place to place and never lived anywhere for long were, according to the law, 'settled' in the parish where they were born.

Paupers' work

Overseers tried to give able-bodied paupers useful work to do. They made unemployed labourers repair roads (see Illustration 2), or offered them to local farmers to work for reduced wages.

Pregnant women

Unmarried pregnant women who wandered into a village were particularly unwelcome, because an illegitimate baby was automatically 'settled' in the parish where it was born, and the local ratepayers might have to pay to maintain it for several years. Sometimes women were bribed or bullied to marry a man from a neighbouring parish, because then the child would be 'settled' in the husband's parish. Sometimes they were moved on. In 1722 an Essex overseer paid 17s 7d to have a pregnant woman nursed for several days and, when she was strong enough, to have her moved into the next parish 'to prevent her lying in [having her baby] here'.

Pauper children

Most pauper infants were farmed out to local families, who were paid a small sum for looking after them, or were apprenticed to local businessmen and factory owners. Some parishes clubbed together and set up special workhouses for them. If the children died, the overseers did not care, because it meant they would no longer have to pay for their keep. On average infants under three years old only survived for a month in London workhouses in the middle of the eighteenth century.

THE SPEENHAMLAND SYSTEM

Pauperised labourers

Until the end of the eighteenth century it was taken for granted that only people who were unemployed could apply to the parish for help. But in the 1790s there were several bad harvests, the price of bread rose, and farm labourers could not earn enough money to feed themselves and their families. So they applied for relief. In many parishes the magistrates decided that, as it was an emergency, they would help, and in 1795 those at Speenhamland in Berkshire worked out a system of supplementing wages which was copied over much of southern England (see Source 1A).

Illustration 2   A road gang at work.

Effects of Speenhamland

The system encouraged farmers to underpay their labourers. If they paid low wages they made more profit. They knew that their labourers would not suffer, because they got enough money out of the rates to keep them and their families alive. So wage rates remained low and labourers had to rely on regular hand-outs from the rates. This annoyed other ratepayers. They thought it unfair to have to pay high rates because farmers would not give labourers a living wage.

The system was also bad for labourers. They had to depend on the poor rates so they lost their self-respect. There was no reason why they should work hard, because the amount they were paid depended entirely on the size of their families. A single man got very little. A man with a large family got much more, however little he did. Indeed, Thomas Malthus (see Chapter 2) said that the Speenhamland system encouraged labourers to marry at an early age and have large families.

Even in areas where the Speenhamland system was not in use, people complained about the cost of the Poor Law. In particular they complained about outdoor relief. Ratepayers were dissatisfied, and in 1832 the government appointed a commission to investigate the Poor Law and suggest how to improve it.

Study

Your aim in this study is:

K to understand how the Speenhamland system worked and some of the criticisms made of it.

Consider the sources below and the information on farmers and pauperised labourers on page 106.

Source 1A   The Speenhamland system

	Entitlement	
Price of loaf	**Labourer**	**Each dependent**
1s	3s	1s 6d
1s 1d	3s 3d	1s 7d
1s 2d	3s 6d	1s 8d
1s 3d	3s 9d	1s 9d and so on

If a man's pay was less than his family's entitlement, the magistrates made it up to the required amount out of the rates. The loaf was a 'gallon loaf' weighing about 4 kg.

Source 1B   Cost of the Poor Law

1784   £2 million
1803   £4 million
1818   £8 million

Source 1C

One hundred and sixty-seven families and single persons at present receive an . . . allowance of sixpence per head to the smaller, ninepence to the larger families, and this added to their wages, about eighteen pence a day . . . is barely sufficient to furnish them with bread only. Nor does any other mode of relief seem likely to prove effectual . . . except a rise of the labourer's wages proportioned to the price of corn.

A gentleman living in Stoke-by-Nayland in Suffolk in about 1800.

Source 1D

The magistrates do a great deal of harm by their scales of allowance. For instance, a man by the name of Robert Smith is now on the road, only works half what he ought to do, has 11s by order of the magistrates and has five children living in the house with him some of whom work, and he gets their wages. He . . . says he will not try to get work anywhere else, as he cannot have such good masters anywhere as the magistrates.

A Derbyshire overseer in 1831.

1 a When the Speenhamland magistrates were deciding how much poor relief to pay a labourer, what information did they need about *i* bread, *ii* the labourer's family?
  b Did the gentleman from Stoke-by-Nayland (Source 1C) think that the best way of helping labourers was to:
    find a better system of poor relief,
    pay the labourers enough wages to buy bread?
2 What evidence is there to suggest that:
    the number of labourers applying for relief increased after the Speenhamland system was introduced,
    for many years no-one could think of an alternative system of poor relief?
3 Do you think that the example of Robert Smith (Source 1D) proves the overseer's statement that 'The magistrates do a great deal of harm by their scales of allowance'? Give reasons for your answer.

Illustration 3 Wisbech Union workhouse in Cambridgeshire.

THE POOR LAW AMENDMENT ACT 1834

In 1834 the Poor Law commissioners reported, and Parliament passed an Act based on their report.

Terms of the 1834 Poor Law Amendment Act

Workhouses and paupers

1 Old or sick people receiving help from the rates could live in their own homes.
2 Able-bodied paupers had to enter a workhouse if they wanted help from the rates.
3 Conditions of inmates in workhouses had to be worse than those of the lowest paid workers in their own homes.

Organisation of system

1 Parishes were grouped into Unions.
2 Each Union was administered by a Board of Guardians elected by the ratepayers.
3 Boards of Guardians had to see that a workhouse was built in each Union and supervise the way it was run.

Supervision of Unions

1 Three commissioners in London supervised Unions throughout England and Wales.
2 Regional inspectors appointed by the commissioners inspected workhouses in their regions.

The new workhouses

The first workhouses

The first workhouses were built in the south of England. It was not until 1837 that they were put up in the north. Every town had its own workhouse, usually on the edge of town where land was cheap (Illustration 3). As a rule there were several villages in a Union, so rural workhouses were sometimes situated in the open country within easy reach of all of them.

Diet

In some workhouses paupers did not get enough to eat. In 1846 there was a scandal at Andover in Hampshire when starving paupers fought over scraps of gristle sticking to bones they had been given to crush as part of their work. But in most Unions paupers had regular, plain meals (see page 110) which had to be eaten in silence.

Work

Men and women were expected to work for ten hours a day. They pumped water, ground corn in hand mills, and divided old tarred rope into separate fibres to use for caulking boats. Men dug the workhouse garden and broke stones. Women worked in the laundry and kitchen. If a workhouse was full, there was often not enough work to go round, and the paupers had nothing to do.

Study

In this study you will:

Ca consider the effects that the three Poor Law Commissioners thought the Poor Law Amendment Act would have on rates and on agricultural wages.

Remember what you have read about poor relief and the Poor Law Amendment Act.

The story of Elijah Wheeler

Some Berkshire parishes had already abolished outdoor relief when the Poor Law Amendment Act was passed in 1834. Edwin Chadwick, one of the commissioners, gave examples of the good it had done. He mentioned 'Elijah Wheeler, a man with a large family, who prior to the present system of management of the poor laws received constant and very considerable relief, but he has now provided himself with a horse and cart and has taken up the business of common carrier . . . and lives in credit without any parochial relief.'

1 a Elijah Wheeler and his family would have been sent to the workhouse if he had not found a way to earn his living. What point do you think Edwin Chadwick was making when he told this story?

b Does the story *i* prove or *ii* illustrate Chadwick's point? Give reasons for your answer.

2 The Poor Law Commissioners believed that once the new workhouses were built:

a ratepayers would spend less on running them than they had on the Speenhamland system

b farmers would be able to pay their labourers higher wages.

Suggest reasons why they believed this.

Workhouse children

Most children born in workhouses were illegitimate. Many 'respectable' people disapproved of unmarried mothers, and were unwilling to pay for them to be cared for. Often the mothers were undernourished and ill, so the death rate among both mothers and babies was very high.

A third of the inmates of workhouses were under sixteen. Three quarters of the children were either illegitimate, orphaned, had been deserted by their parents or had a father in prison. Most of the rest were the children of other inmates. Boys and girls had to work. At Preston, able-bodied boys broke stones for three and a half hours a day, and the girls helped in the kitchen. For the rest of the day they went to the workhouse school where they were taught reading, writing and arithmetic.

Their health

Workhouse children were very unhealthy. The diet was unsuitable for growing children, and at night they were crammed together in overcrowded dormitories, sometimes as many as five to a bed. In one workhouse in 1840, 100 children slept in a room 39 by 21 feet (11.9 m by 6.4 m). Diseases spread quickly, and the children infected one another with lice, ringworm and especially 'sore eyes', a highly infectious condition in which their eyelids were covered with itching scabs and scales.

Effects of the new Poor Law

Continuation of outdoor relief

In some ways, the new Poor Law had less effect than expected. In many areas guardians still provided

Illustration 4 A casual ward in a London workhouse in 1860. This was provided for men who needed somewhere to sleep for a night or two.

Study

According to one official, the aim of the new law was to make workhouses 'a terror to the poor, and prevent them entering'. Your aim in this study is to:

Ev use the sources below to see how the authorities made life in workhouses unpleasant.

Source 2A

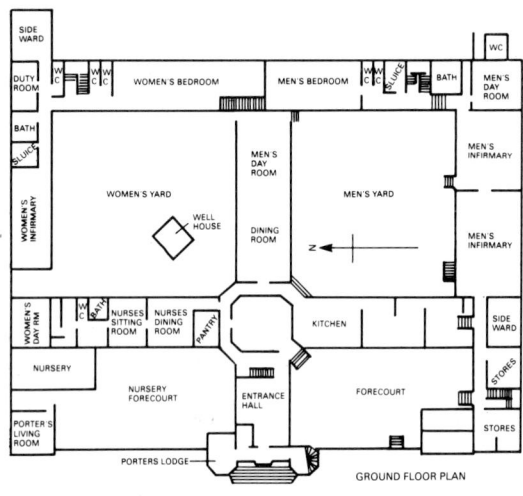
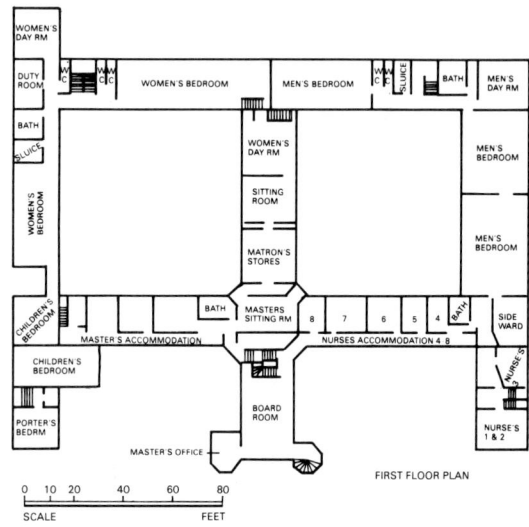

Plan of Downham Market workhouse.

Source 2B

STOCKTON UNION.

Dietary for able-bodied Men and Women.

		BREAKFAST		DINNER				SUPPER	
		Bread.	Boiled Milk with Oatmeal.	Cooked Meat.	Potatoes.	Suet Pudding.	Soup or Rice Milk.	Bread.	Boiled Milk with Oatmeal or Broth.
		Ozs.	Pints.	Ozs.	lbs.	Ozs.	Pints.	Ozs.	Pints.
Sunday	Men	6	1½	....	....	14	....	6	1½
	Women	6	1½	....	....	14	....	6	1½
Monday	Men	6	1½	5	½	....	....	6	1½
	Women	6	1½	5	½	....	....	6	1½
Tuesday	Men	6	1½	....	....	....	1½	6	1½
	Women	6	1½	....	....	....	1½	6	1½
Wednesday	Men	6	1½	....	...	14	....	6	1½
	Women	6	1½	....	....	14	....	6	1½
Thursday	Men	6	1½	....	....	....	1½	6	1½
	Women	6	1½	....	....	....	1½	6	1½
Friday	Men	6	1½	5	½	....	....	6	1½
	Women	6	1½	5	½	....	....	6	1½
Saturday	Men	6	1½	....	....	....	1½	6	1½
	Women	6	1½	....	....	....	1½	6	1½

Old People above 60 years of age, may be allowed Tea, Coffee, Butter, and Sugar, (not exceeding 1 oz. of Tea, 2 oz. of Coffee, 3½ oz. of Butter, and 4 oz. of Sugar, per week each) in lieu of Gruel to Breakfast. Greens, occasionally, in lieu of Potatoes.

4 oz. of Bread to Soup and Rice Milk Dinners, to each Person.

Children under 9 years of age dieted at discretion. Sick dieted as ordered by the Medical Officer.

A mid-nineteenth century workhouse diet sheet.

Source 2C

A workhouse yard in the 1840s.

1 a How many meals a day were able-bodied paupers given?

b Which groups of workhouse inmates did not count as able-bodied?

c Were paupers given what we would think of as a balanced diet?

d What evidence is there to suggest that families were split up when they entered a workhouse, and rarely met while they were there?

2 a What do you notice about the clothes the women are wearing in Source 2C?

b What reasons may the workhouse authorities have had for making the women dress in this way?

3 a What do the sources tell us about the life of workhouse children?

b Do you think that the artist of Source 2C was biased? Give reasons for your answer.

4 *Library work.* Find a copy of *Oliver Twist* by Charles Dickens, and read from the section in Chapter 2 which begins: 'The room in which the boys were fed . . .', to the end of the chapter. Do you think the events Dickens describes:
really happened in a workhouse,
could have happened in a workhouse,
could not have happened in a workhouse?
Give reasons for your answer.

outdoor relief. This was partly because there was often no room in the workhouse for all the paupers. Many inmates had to stay in workhouses permanently because they were too frail to live on their own. This did not leave enough accommodation for able-bodied paupers, especially if there was a slump in trade, and large numbers were put out of work. In any case, many guardians thought it was more sensible to pay labourers cash in their own homes for a few weeks, than to bring them and their families into the workhouse.

Money saved

The new law seemed to save money. In 1831 poor rates amounted to £7 million. By 1851 they had fallen to less than £5 million, in spite of the fact that the population had risen by twenty nine per cent. The number of paupers also fell. This was partly because there was plenty of work available: for instance, navvies were needed to build railways. In addition, the 1834 Act had altered the settlement law to make it easier for men to leave their own parishes to look for work.

Support for Chartism

Working people hated the new system. In some ways paupers were better off in workhouses than many labourers at home (see Chapter 10). In the workhouse they had a sound roof over their heads, dry clothes and regular meals. But they resented having their families split up, being made to wear a uniform, being forced to work like convicts, and having to eat meals in silence. They often called workhouses 'Bastilles' after the French prison that was destroyed by the Paris mob at the beginning of the revolution in 1789. The new Poor Law persuaded many workers to support the Chartists (see later in this chapter).

Later reforms

Gradually the system was reformed. In 1842, paupers were allowed to speak at mealtimes and husbands and wives were permitted to live together in workhouses. Then in 1847 the three commissioners were replaced by a Poor Law Board who continued to improve conditions.

Study

In this study you will:

Ch consider the changes brought about by the 1834 Poor Law Amendment Act.

You will need the information on pages 105–11.

1 a Copy the headings below.

Poor Relief	
Before 1834	**After 1834**

b Copy this list under the heading *Before 1834*
i Most paupers received outdoor relief
ii The poor rate was rising
iii The number of paupers was increasing
c Under the heading *After 1834*, show how the situation changed after the Poor Law Amendment Act was passed.

2 For what reasons, apart from the passing of the Poor Law Amendment Act, did changes **ii** and **iii** on your list take place?

3 What evidence is there to suggest that:
conditions in the workhouse made many workers dissatisfied with the way in which laws were made;
the authorities were prepared to be kinder to inmates once the number of paupers claiming poor relief dropped?

Part Two

Legal Reforms

LAW AND ORDER IN THE EIGHTEENTH CENTURY

The death penalty

In 1689, fifty crimes were punishable by death in England and Wales. During the eighteenth century, as the population and the number of large towns increased, the number of crimes committed multiplied. So Parliament increased the number of offences punishable by death. By 1800 there were more than 200. They included:

pick-pocketing goods worth more than a shilling,
stealing goods worth more than five shillings from a shop,
going out at night with faces blackened,
sending threatening letters,

and scores of more serious offences. Women could be sentenced to be burned at the stake for murdering their husbands, and a girl of seven was hanged at Norwich for stealing a handkerchief.

The police

Parish constables

The police system was out of date and inefficient. Every parish had an unpaid constable to keep the peace. He was elected to serve for a year. If a rich man was elected he paid a deputy. Deputies were usually craftsmen or labourers, who, for a few shillings a month, would give up their ordinary jobs for a few hours to chase thieves or help at the local magistrate's court.

Keepers and watchmen

In London there was a different system. During the day every parish was patrolled by a 'keeper of the streets' to stop people obstructing roadways and footpaths. At night, watchmen patrolled the streets. They wore long, heavy overcoats and carried lanterns, rattles, and wooden sticks. Most were old men. They trudged round the parish, following the same route every night, stopping every twenty minutes to call out the time and say what the weather was like. If a watchmen saw a thief or a housebreaker at work, he would use his rattle to summon help, and if the criminal ran off, he would chase him as far as the parish boundary.

Informers

Watchmen did not catch many criminals. The authorities relied on informers to tell them who had committed a crime. To encourage people to inform, they offered a reward for every criminal convicted and allowed anyone who gave information leading to the return of stolen goods to claim a proportion of their value. Some people, known as 'thief-takers', made a living out of rewards. The most famous was Jonathan Wild (1682–1725), who organised a large gang of highwaymen, pickpockets and housebreakers. If any were arrested, he paid witnesses to give them alibis, but he betrayed any thief who was not a member of his gang. Wild became very rich, but in 1725 he was arrested for receiving stolen goods and hanged.

Study: Library work

In this study you will:
K find out about a new police force established in London in the eighteenth century.

Henry Fielding's police force

Henry Fielding was a London magistrate. He trained as a lawyer, and also worked as a writer. One of his novels was based on the life of Jonathan Wild. He believed that London needed a full-time police force, and in 1749 he recruited seven men to work as detectives.

1 List the sections in your school or local library where you might find the answers to these questions:
  a What name was given to the police force set up by Fielding in 1749?
  b Why was it given this name?
  c How were the men in Fielding's police force paid?
  d Did other London magistrates copy Fielding's idea?
  e What was the name of Fielding's novel based on Jonathan Wild's life?
2 **a** Find the information you need and answer the questions in brief notes.
  b Write two or three paragraphs on *Henry Fielding's Police Force*.

Study

In this study you will:

Em explore what various people in the eighteenth century thought about public hangings.

Remember the list of crimes that were punishable by death.

Source 3A

The English artist William Hogarth drew this picture of an execution at Tyburn in London.

KEY: **1** The condemned man   **2** The gallows   **3** The stands for spectators   **4** A pickpocket

Source 3B

One often sees criminals going to their death perfectly unconcerned . . . When all the prisoners arrive at their destination they are made to mount on a very wide cart made expressly for the purpose, a cord is passed round their necks and the end fastened to the gibbet, which is not very high. The chaplain . . . makes them pray and sing a few verses of the Psalms. The relatives are permitted to mount the cart and take fare well. When the time is up . . . the chaplain and the relations get off the cart, which slips from under the condemned men's feet, and in this way they all remain hanging together.

de Saussure, *A Foreign View of England in the Reigns of George I and George II* (c. 1720).

Source 3C

They object that the old method draws together a number of spectators. If they did not draw the spectators they would not answer the purpose. The old method is most satisfactory to all parties; the public is gratified with a procession; the criminal is supported by it. Why should all this be swept away?

Dr Samuel Johnson, an eighteenth century writer, commenting on reasons why some people objected to 'the old method' of executing criminals in public.

1 In spite of the law, few people were executed. Juries sometimes found thieves not guilty, even when there was clear evidence against them, and many condemned criminals were reprieved. By the end of the eighteenth century, only a third of those sentenced to death were actually hanged. Suggest reasons to explain this.

2 Some people wanted to abolish public executions. They said it was almost as if the government had turned hangings into a free entertainment for the mob. Is there any evidence to support this view? Give reasons for your answer.

3 Do you think that:
a Dr Johnson (Source 3C),
b Hogarth (Source 3A),
believed that public executions succeeded in making people too frightened to commit crimes? Give reasons for your answers.

Prisons

Eighteenth-century prisoners

In the eighteenth century very few criminals were sent to prison as a punishment. At the Old Bailey in 1770, fewer than three per cent of those convicted were imprisoned. The rest were hanged, transported, whipped, fined, or bound over. Most people in prison were either waiting to be tried, or were there because they could not pay their debts.

Fees

Prisons were expected to make a profit. The money came from the prisoners. When they were imprisoned they were asked to pay various fees to the jailers.

Fees payable at Newgate		
Transfer out of Stone Hold	2s	6d
Transfer to Master's side	14s	10d
For coals	1s	6d
For other prisoners	1s	0d
For a visit	1s	6d
For a bed, per week	3s	6d

In 1708 it was said that the governor of Newgate prison in London had paid £8,000 for the post.

Comforts for cash

Prisoners who paid all the fees and provided plenty of wine and brandy for the jailers could often have rooms of their own, as much to eat and drink as they liked, and as many visitors as they wanted. Most of the time they could wander freely round the prison, and there was always plenty of drink available.

According to one prisoner, 'the Press Yard of Newgate at night-time was like the taproom of a common inn'.

'Free' accommodation

Prisoners who could not or would not pay were put in irons, and thrown into a dark, damp, filthy, overcrowded dungeon, where they were fed on rotting bread and stinking water. One example in Newgate was 'The Stone Hold', described by an ex-prisoner as, 'a terrible, stinking, dark and dismal place, situate underground, into which no daylight can come. It was paved with stone; the prisoners had no beds, and lay on the pavement.' Illustration 5 shows another example of how poorer prisoners were treated.

Illustration 5   Sometimes prisoners were chained together to prevent them escaping.

Study

This study asks you:
S to compare the prison system in Britain today with that of the eighteenth century.

Refer to the information on this page and remember what you know about the legal system in the eighteenth century.

1 Today, a large percentage of convicted criminals are sent to prison. What percentage of prisoners convicted at the Old Bailey in 1770 were sent to prison?

2 Today, taxpayers provide the money to pay prison staff. Why, in the eighteenth century did: men pay to be made prison governors, jailers treat poor prisoners worse than those with money?

3 Copy the statements below and say why you agree or disagree with each of them.
Compared with prisons today, prisons in the eighteenth century:
contained a smaller number of inmates serving sentences for crimes of violence;
allowed prisoners more freedom to do as they liked inside the prison walls.

THE FIRST REFORMERS

John Howard (1726–90)

His travels

Between 1773 and 1776 John Howard, a prosperous English gentleman, toured Great Britain visiting prisons. He was shocked by what he found.

The debtors' prison at Knaresborough in Yorkshire was typical. It consisted of 'one room, about twelve feet (3.5 m) square: window seventeen inches by six (430 by 150 mm). Earth floor: no fireplace . . . a common sewer from the town running through it uncovered'. He found that most prisons stank so badly that the smell lingered in his clothes long after he had left them.

In most prisons young people awaiting trial mingled with debtors, hardened criminals and prostitutes. In some towns, however, debtors were housed in separate prisons (see Illustration 6).

The State of English Prisons, 1777

In 1777 Howard published his findings in a book called *The State of English Prisons*. Howard's book shocked MPs, and Parliament made new laws ordering different classes of prisoners to be kept apart, and telling magistrates to inspect prisons regularly. Unfortunately many magistrates ignored these laws, so conditions did not improve.

Elizabeth Fry (1788–1845)

The Newgate women

Accommodation. Men and women shared the same prisons. In 1813 there were nearly 300 women in Newgate. They were crammed into two stinking 'wards'. They had no beds, but there was a low platform round the walls on which they could lie at night, wrapped in blankets.

Behaviour. According to a male prisoner, women in Newgate behaved much worse than men. He was particularly shocked by a group of women waiting to be transported. They knew they would not be spending long in their ward, so they did not bother to clean it. He said they lived 'rather worse than swine, for they are poisoned by their own filth, and their conversation is nothing but . . . swearing, cursing and debauchery'.

In 1813 Stephen Grellet, an American Quaker, asked to visit the women. The jailer warned him that they were 'unruly and desperate', and would probably attack him. Grellet insisted and went in. Many women were drinking and cursing. Some

Illustration 6 The Fleet prison in London was the biggest debtors' prison in England.

were fighting. Some were ill, and were lying on heaps of old straw. Some had babies, most of whom were cold and crying. Some had been sentenced to death, others had not yet been tried.

Mrs Fry's first visit

Grellet wanted to help the Newgate women, so he told an English Quaker, Elizabeth Fry (see Source 4A), what he had seen. Elizabeth went back to Newgate with him, carrying as much warm flannel cloth as she could find. Over the next few days she visited the prison regularly. She helped the women to make clothes for their children, and chatted and prayed with them.

The Newgate committee

A few days later Elizabeth left London but she did not forget Newgate. In 1816 when she came back she set up a committee of twelve to work with the prisoners. They set up a school for prisoners' children, and taught the women to sew and make their own clothes. The women worked well. They trusted Elizabeth, because she always consulted them and never did anything without their permission. She helped them to draw up a set of rules, which banned 'begging, swearing, gaming, card-playing, quarrelling and immoral conversation'. Every morning at nine they gathered to hear a reading from the Bible. Then they worked at needlework, knitting, 'or any other suitable employment'. At six in the evening there was another reading from the Bible, and the day's work was collected. Most of it was sold, so the women earned some money.

Study

In this study your aim is:

K to see how much you can deduce about Elizabeth Fry's character by considering her work at Newgate.

Remember what you have already learned about Elizabeth Fry from reading pages 115–17.

In pairs

1 The following list gives four pieces of information about Elizabeth Fry's work at Newgate. Write brief notes saying what each item tells us about her character. For example, you might think that the first shows that she was not too proud to work among ragged, dirty and drunken women.

a In 1813 she went to Newgate with Stephen Grellet after he told her about the conditions there.

b She left London in 1813 but set up a committee to help her at Newgate when she returned in 1816.

c She encouraged prisoners to make clothes for themselves and their children.

d When she wanted to make changes she discussed them with the prisoners and asked for their opinions.

Source 4A

Elizabeth Fry reading to prisoners in Newgate.

Source 4B

The looks of tender reverence the women cast on her, as she moved among them, and the way in which some whispered a blessing after her, testified to the influence she had obtained over them.

A clergyman who saw Elizabeth Fry at work in Newgate.

Source 4C

It was more terrible to be brought up before Mrs Fry than before the judge.

A Newgate prisoner who broke one of the rules made by Mrs Fry and the other prisoners.

2 a What impression do you think the artist in Source 4A wanted to give of Mrs Fry's character? Gives reasons for your answer.

b Do *i* Source 4B and *ii* Source 4C support the artist's view of Mrs Fry's character? Give reasons for your answer.

3 Ask one person to read his or her answers to the class. What do the rest of you think? Jot down any ideas you had not thought of.

4 *With the help of your notes only* write a character sketch of Elizabeth Fry.

Results of her work

A visitor to the prison was taken to the women's ward:

'At the head of a long table sat a lady belonging to the Society of Friends [Quakers]. She was reading aloud to about sixteen women prisoners who were engaged in needlework ... Each wore a clean-looking blue apron and bib ... They all rose on my entrance, curtsied respectfully, and then, at a signal, resumed their seats and their employment.'

Elizabeth Fry wrote in her own diary 'from being like wild beasts, the prisoners appear harmless and kind'.

Elizabeth's work at Newgate became famous. It seemed to show that if prisoners were correctly treated, they behaved well and might lead better lives after they were released.

SIR ROBERT PEEL'S REFORMS, 1822–30

Criminal law reform

In 1808 Sir Samuel Romilly (1757–1818) persuaded Parliament to abolish the death penalty for picking pockets. His work was carried on by Sir Robert Peel who became Home Secretary in 1822. He believed that the law would be easier to enforce if the penalties were not so harsh, and between March 1822 and the end of 1823 he persuaded MPs to abolish the death penalty on more than 100 offences. They also decided that in most cases where the death penalty was still in force, judges could pass a less severe sentence if they thought fit. Previously if someone had been found guilty of a capital offence, the law had forced judges to sentence him to death. So after 1823 fewer people were sentenced to death.

Peel resigned in 1830, but Parliament continued to reduce the number of offences punishable by death. After 1838, criminals were only hanged for treason, murder and attempted murder.

The Metropolitan Police, 1829

At first, Peel's reforms did not seem to work. The number of crimes increased. Peel was not surprised.

He knew that punishments only deter criminals if they think they are likely to be caught. This means there has to be an efficient police force. But in 1822 MPs refused to approve 'an effective system of police' because they believed that the government would use the police to harass their political opponents.

In 1828 the House of Commons appointed a committee to enquire into crime in London, and into the state of the police. The committee decided that Peel was right, and told MPs that a new police force was urgently needed. Peel immediately drew up plans to reorganise the London police. Parliament approved and in June 1829 a new Metropolitan Police Force came into existence.

Peel's new police force consisted of just over 1,000 officers and men. Peel, as Home Secretary, was in overall charge. The constables were young and fit. They wore blue uniforms, and were armed with truncheons. They were paid twenty one shillings a week, and a special police rate was levied to provide the money. They were nicknamed 'Peelers', or 'raw lobsters', and at first they were very unpopular. Their officers tried hard to win over the public. They told policemen to be 'civil and attentive to all persons, of every rank and class', and to do their duty 'in a quiet and determined manner'.

In 1839 an Act of Parliament allowed similar police forces to be set up in every county in England and Wales.

Prison reform

The fact that fewer people were hanged after 1823 meant that more were sent to prison as a punishment, so Peel decided that prisons would have to be reformed (see Table 1).

Table 1   Prisons: government action 1823–78

1823	Robert Peel's reforms: 1 Local magistrates were made responsible for inspecting prisons and reporting regularly to the Home Secretary. 2 First offenders were separated from hardened criminals. 3 Jailers were paid regular salaries.
1835	The Home Office appointed inspectors of prisons controlled by the government.
1878	All prisons were put under direct government control.

Study

In this study you will show your skill in using the sources below and the information on pages 112–17:

Ca to work out why the 'Peelers' gradually replaced the 'Charlies'.

Source 5A

A 'Charlie', or London watchman.

Source 5B

An early photograph of a 'Peeler', taken in about 1850.

Source 5C

In 1817 an MP asked a gentleman living in Soho if London watchmen would go to help those in the next parish. He answered:

'No . . . it is a difficulty that frequently occurs.'

'So that if any disturbance occurs in the same street, if out of his parish, the watchman would not think it his duty to interfere?'

'No he would not; perhaps he would stand and look on.'

Source 5D

Money stolen in London:
1829   £900,000
1834   £20,000

1 Do you think that Londoners respected the Charlies? Give reasons for your answer.
2 Why, do you think, did Londoners dislike the Peelers when they were introduced in 1829, but respect them by 1839?
3 Why, do you think, did local authorities throughout England and Wales begin to set up Peelite police forces after 1839?

NINETEENTH-CENTURY PRISON LIFE

Partly as a result of Elizabeth Fry's work, the treatment of prisoners changed. Attempts were made to reform convicts, as well as punish them. Some experts believed that convicts corrupted each other, so they set up a 'separate' system. Each convict had a separate cell, in which he slept, ate, and worked (see Source 6). When convicts met at exercise they wore masks, and were forbidden to speak. Other prisons organised a 'silent' system, where the prisoners were allowed to mix, but were forbidden to speak.

Prisoners were properly clothed and fed, but they had to work during their sentence. They unpicked old rope, made mats and wove cloth. Convicts sentenced to hard labour worked on treadmills, or did shot drill, which involved doing exercises with heavy iron cannon balls.

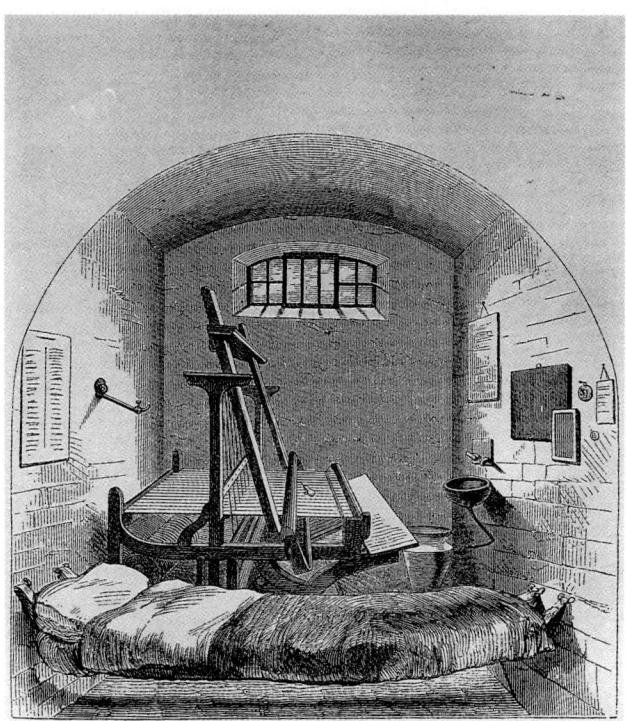

Illustration 7 A 'separate' cell in Pentonville. During the day the bed was folded away and the prisoner worked at the loom.

Convicts who made trouble were punished. For minor offences they lost some of their meals for a few days. For more serious offences they were locked up in total darkness for several days. If they still offended they might be flogged. Most convicts soon learned to behave well while they were in pri-son. But as soon as they were released, most went back to a life of crime.

Between 1830 and 1850 many prisons were built to accommodate the increased number of convicts. Most are still in use.

TRANSPORTATION

In the eighteenth and early nineteenth centuries, many criminals were transported to the colonies. At first most were sent to America and the West Indies, but in 1786 the government decided to ship convicts to special settlements in Australia. Between 1788 and 1867 162,000 prisoners were transported to New South Wales and Tasmania.

Prisoners were transported for seven years, fourteen years, or for life. In Australia some worked in government 'gangs' on jobs such as building or roadmaking. The rest were 'assigned' to farmers to work as labourers.

Government labour gangs were very strictly controlled, but some farmers treated convict labourers very well, and they were better off than they had been at home. When their sentences were over, convicts were allowed to return to Britain, but most stayed in Australia, and some became very rich.

Peel wanted all convicts sentenced to transportation to be treated alike. He increased the number working in government gangs, and tried to lay down detailed rules for those working on private farms. This upset the farmers, who wanted to use convict labour as they thought best. The colonists and the government also argued about who should pay the costs of convict settlements. They could not agree, and as a result the system of transportation was brought to an end in 1867.

Study

The changes made in prisons after 1823 were described as *reforms*. In this study your aim is:

Em to see these reforms through the eyes of a prisoner, a jailer and a reformer. Would they think these reforms improved conditions in prisons?

You will need to refer to the information on prison life on pages 114–19.

In pairs, make brief notes in answer to the following questions.
1 In what way or ways might a prisoner have considered that his life in prison was:
  better after 1823,
  worse after 1823?
2 For what reason or reasons might a jailer have preferred his job:
  before 1823,
  after 1823?

3 Elizabeth Fry believed that prisoners' behaviour would improve if they were made to feel they mattered as people and were given worthwhile work to do. Choose three ways of reforming or punishing prisoners under the 'separate' and 'silent' systems. Do you think Elizabeth Fry would have agreed or disagreed with each of them? Give reasons for your answers.
  Ask one person to read his or her answers to the class. What do the rest of you think?

Study

In this study you will be looking at extracts from Dickens's novel, *Great Expectations*:

Ev to see whether or not historians can learn anything from it about crime and punishment in the nineteenth century.

Background information

Charles Dickens, the novelist, lived from 1812 to 1870. His novel, *Great Expectations*, was published in 1861, six years before transportation was abolished. In it he tells how a boy named Pip helped an escaped convict named Magwitch. The convict was recaptured, taken back to the hulks, which were old ships used to house convicts waiting to be transported. Magwitch was transported to Australia, but later played an important part in Pip's life.

Source 6A

A hulk, the *Defence*, at anchor off Woolwich.

Source 6B   Pip's first impression of the convict

A fearful man, all in coarse grey, with a great iron on his leg. A man with no hat, and with broken shoes, and an old rag tied round his head.

(Chapter 1.)

Source 6C   Pip asks his sister about the hulks

'And please what's Hulks?' said I.
'There's the way with this boy!' exclaimed my sister . . . 'Answer him one question, and he'll ask you a dozen directly. Hulks are prison-ships . . .'
'I wonder who's put into prison-ships, and why they're put there?' said I . . .
'I tell you what, young fellow,' said she '. . . People are put in the Hulks because they murder, and because they rob, and forge, and do all sorts of bad; and they always begin by asking questions. Now, you get along to bed!'

(Chapter 2.)

Source 6D   Pip sees a hulk

By the light of the torches, we saw the black Hulk lying out a little way from the mud of the shore, like a wicked Noah's ark. Cribbed and barred and moored by massive rusty chains, the prison-ship seemed in my young eyes to be ironed like the prisoners.

(Chapter 5.)

1 What information does Charles Dickens give us about the hulks and the prisoners in them?
2 Do you think that the information is reliable? Give reasons for your answer.
3 a How would you try to check whether or not the information is reliable?
  b Would the novel tell us anything useful about crime and punishment in the nineteenth century, if the information was shown to be unreliable?

---- Part Three ----
Workers and the Vote

THE REFORM ACT OF 1832

The unreformed Parliament

In the eighteenth century:
1 only property owners could become MPs;
2 in most constituencies (districts returning an MP to Parliament) only property owners could vote;
3 most large manufacturing towns were not represented in Parliament;
4 very few people had the right to vote;
5 voting was public, which made bribery and intimidation easy.

Parliamentary reform 1832

In 1830 a new government in favour of reforming Parliament was elected. In 1832 they passed the Great Reform Act. After 1832:
1 only property owners could become MPs;
2 prosperous tenants and householders were given the vote;
3 large manufacturing towns were represented in Parliament;
4 the number of people with the right to vote increased by about fifty per cent;
5 voting was still open, so bribery and intimidation were still easy;
6 property owners and prosperous tenants controlled Parliament.

THE CHARTISTS

Beginnings

Many workers were disappointed by the Reform Act. Then the new Parliament reformed the Poor Law. Most workers feared and hated the new system. So workers' leaders demanded further reforms to give workers control over the House of Commons.

Their chance came in 1836. There was a poor harvest, and food prices rose. There was widespread discontent, and William Lovett (1800–77), a London cabinet-maker, and a few friends set up the London Working Men's Association to demand further reform. Its members got in touch with the Birmingham Political Union, which had been fighting for reform of Parliament since 1830. Together they drew up a document which they called the People's Charter. It was published in 1837.

Study

In this study you will:
Em look at Parliament before and after the Reform Act of 1832 from the point of view of three men who might have lived at the time.

You will need the information on this page.

Miles Campion, a wealthy landowner, owns a large estate in the south of England. For the last 200 years a member of his family has been the MP for the constituency in which his mansion and estate are situated. The MP who represents the nearby market town is usually nominated by the Campions, who pay his election expenses. In Parliament Campion puts forward the views of the other landowners in his constituency and does what he thinks is best for the people in the area.

Henry Apthorpe owns an engineering works in a Midlands town. The town has doubled in size during the last fifty years, and the goods it exports contribute to Britain's wealth, but it has no MP to represent it in Parliament. Apthorpe is able to vote because he has bought a house and land near the town.

Walter Atkins works for a London printer and rents a small house near the works. He went to school until he was eight so he can read and write. As a young man he became interested in the ideas of Tom Paine, a writer who supported the French and American revolutions and declared that everyone should have the same rights. Atkins decided he agreed with Tom Paine and joined the London Radical Reform Association—a club for workers interested in politics.

1 Which of the men described above do you think would:
   have been satisfied with the Parliamentary system before 1832,
   have wanted Parliament to be reformed?
Give reasons for your answers.
2 Which of the men do you think would have been:
   satisfied with the reforms made to Parliament in 1832,
   dissatisfied with the reforms?
Give reasons for your answers.

Study

In this study you will use Source 9A:

K to understand what the Chartists hoped to achieve through their Charter.

Source 7A

The Six Points
OF THE
PEOPLE'S
CHARTER.

1. A VOTE for every man twenty-one years of age, of sound mind, and not undergoing punishment for crime.

2. THE BALLOT.—To protect the elector in the exercise of his vote.

3. No PROPERTY QUALIFICATION for Members of Parliament —thus enabling the constituencies to return the man of their choice, be he rich or poor.

4. PAYMENT OF MEMBERS, thus enabling an honest trades-man, working man, or other person, to serve a constituency, when taken from his business to attend to the interests of the country.

5. EQUAL CONSTITUENCIES, securing the same amount of representation for the same number of electors, instead of allowing small constituencies to swamp the votes of large ones.

6. ANNUAL PARLIAMENTS, thus presenting the most effectual check to bribery and intimidation, since though a constituency might be bought once in seven years (even with the ballot), no purse could buy a constituency (under a system of universal suffrage) in each ensuing twelvemonth; and since members, when elected for a year only, would not be able to defy and betray their constituents as now.

Subjoined are the names of the gentlemen who embodied these principles into the document called the "People's Charter," at an influential meeting held at the British Coffee House, London, on the 7th of June, 1837:—

Daniel O'Connell, Esq., M.P.,	Mr. Henry Hetherington.
John Arthur Roebuck, Esq., M.P.	Mr. John Cleave.
John Temple Leader, Esq., M.P.	Mr. James Watson.
Charles Hindley, Esq., M.P.	Mr. Richard Moore.
Thomas Perronet Thompson, Esq., M.P.	Mr. William Lovett.
William Sharman Crawford, Esq., M.P.	Mr. Henry Vincent.

W. COLLINS, PRINTER, "WEEKLY TIMES" OFFICE, DUDLEY

A Chartist leaflet printed in 1837. The names of those who drew it up are printed at the bottom left.

1 a Would the Chartists have given the vote to:
   all adults;
   all adult men?

   b Which points in the Charter aimed at preventing voters from being bribed or intimidated? Give reasons for your answer.

   c Explain in your own words why points **3** and **4** were included in the Charter.

2 Did all the leaders of the Chartist movement belong to the working class? Give reasons for your answer.
3 The Chartists believed that if the six points of the People's Charter were granted, Parliament would never again be able to pass laws such as the Poor Law Amendment Act. Why, do you think, did they believe this?

The Birmingham meeting 1838

In August 1838 a meeting was held in Birmingham to launch the Charter. Lovett and his friends wanted to win over the 'most intelligent and influential portion' of the working class by reasoned argument. But a number of delegates from north-east England opposed this view. Many belonged to trades such as hand loom weaving which had been hit hard by the growth of factories. They had no time for reasoned argument. They wanted the government to put the Charter into effect at once, and threatened to organise strikes and rebellions if it was not done. These men were known as 'physical force' Chartists.

Their leader was an Irishman named Feargus O'Connor, a big man with a powerful voice. He said he spoke for those with 'blistered hands and unshorn chins'. He was a popular speaker at Chartist meetings and ran a weekly newspaper called *The Northern Star*. This became the official Chartist paper. By the end of 1838 it had a circulation of 50,000 copies.

Most of the people at the 1838 meeting supported O'Connor. They decided to call meetings all over the country to elect members of a National Convention. This would meet in London and draw up a petition to Parliament in favour of the Charter.

The Chartist Convention 1839

The Convention met in February 1839. The members had to decide what to do if Parliament rejected their petition. Some called for a general strike. A few wanted an armed rebellion. Others were so frightened by such talk that they went home. So nothing was decided.

The first petition 1839

The Chartists presented their petition to Parliament, but the House of Commons rejected it by 235 votes to 46. To prevent a Chartist rebellion, the government arrested some of the southern leaders, including Lovett, while in the north General Napier invited Chartists to a demonstration of artillery fire. He told them that if they did rebel they would easily be defeated. 'We have the physical force, not they', he wrote afterwards. In September the Convention was dissolved. There were no strikes and no major rebellion.

The Newport rising

The only disturbance was in South Wales, where John Frost, a one-time Mayor of Newport, led a band of miners in an attack on the town. He had been at the Convention, and thought that O'Connor would support his rebellion by leading a revolt in northern England. But O'Connor was visiting Ireland when Frost marched on Newport. Frost's attack failed. Twenty four of his followers were killed, and three, including Frost, were captured and put on trial. At first they were condemned to death, but later the sentences were changed to transportation for life.

The National Charter Association

In 1840 trade improved, the country was more prosperous and there was less discontent. To keep support for the Charter alive, the National Charter Association was set up. This founded local branches, and helped them to organise meetings. Chartists held lectures and discussions. In addition, on public holidays, they organised open-air rallies, with brass bands and market stalls. In winter they had torchlight processions through the streets.

These provided good publicity and attracted people who might not have bothered to go to lectures and discussions.

The second petition 1842

In 1842 trade slumped again, and support for Chartism increased. O'Connor decided to draw up another petition to Parliament. He told his supporters that the petition was bound to succeed, and by May he claimed to have collected three million signatures (see Illustration 7). Once again the House of Commons refused to consider it, this time by 287 votes to 49.

Many disappointed Chartists went on strike, and in Lancashire gangs of workers stopped factories working by knocking drain plugs out of boilers. Troops had to be sent to restore order. O'Connor disapproved of these strikes and riots, but he could not suggest any other way for workers to make their feelings known.

The Chartist land scheme

After 1842 trade improved and support for the Charter fell. In 1845 O'Connor tried another scheme to benefit working men. This was the Chartist Co-operative Land Society. Members subscribed money to buy land which was then let to some of the members. The scheme made O'Connor very popular, and in 1847 he was elected MP for Nottingham. But the land scheme was badly administered, and in 1848 it was found to be bankrupt.

The third petition 1848

The 1848 Convention

In February 1848 there was a successful revolution in France. This encouraged Chartist leaders, and they called a convention to meet in April to present another petition to Parliament. The members of the convention organised a mass meeting on Kennington Common in south London on 10 April (Illustration 8). After speeches those present were to march in procession to Parliament and present the petition.

The revolution in France frightened the government. They banned the procession, and asked the Duke of Wellington to defend London against the Chartists. He decided to rely on special constables armed with staves, and on the day of the demonstration he stationed them on the bridges over the Thames which the procession would have to cross to reach Parliament.

Illustration 8 Thomas Duncombe trying to persuade MPs to consider the Chartist petition in May 1842. The petition is heaped up in front of the table.

Study

In this study you will be looking at two speeches made in the House of Commons during the debate on the second Chartist Petition in 1842. Your aim is to consider:

S why each MP supported or opposed the Chartists;
why each MP cared what happened to Parliament

You may wish to refer back to the points of the People's Charter (p. 122).

Background information

In the nineteenth century many people believed that it was the duty of men who owned property, for example landowners and manufacturers, to give up some of their time to help to govern the country. They thought that property owners were responsible, educated men who were used to making decisions and who would pass laws that would benefit the country as a whole. MPs were not paid and many of them considered it was an honour to sit in Parliament, one of Britain's most important institutions.

Source 7B

It is my opinion that property, intelligence, and knowledge should form the qualification of a constituency . . . I . . . think that in the present state of popular education . . . there might . . . be . . . Members returned to this House whose votes would be favourable to the destruction of our institutions and would shake the security of property.

Lord John Russell, speaking in the same debate in the House of Commons in 1842.

Source 7C

. . . What can you expect but that they should make their way to this House, and, as you will do nothing for them, endeavour to do something for themselves.

T Duncombe, MP for Finsbury, presenting the 1842 petition to the House of Commons.

1 a Why did Mr Duncombe (Source 7C) think that the Members of Parliament were not doing their job properly?
  b What reasons may he have had for thinking that Parliament would improve if it accepted the points of the People's Charter?
2 a Why may Lord John Russell (Source 7B) have thought that property owners were the people best qualified to become MPs?
  b What reasons might he have given for thinking that British institutions such as Parliament would be destroyed if the People's Charter was accepted by the government?
3 Which man do you think cared most deeply about Parliament and the way in which MPs carried out their duties? Give reasons for your answer.

Illustration 9   An engraving of the Kennington meeting in 1848.

The Kennington meeting

On 10 April about 23,000 Chartists gathered on Kennington Common. They had expected 100,000. O'Connor told them that they had no chance of getting through to Parliament, and advised them to go home. The petition, said to contain six million signatures, was taken to Parliament in a cab, escorted by a few delegates who travelled in a van drawn by six farm horses.

The petition fails

When the House of Commons received the petition, they appointed a committee to examine it. There were only two million signatures, pages of them in the same handwriting. Queen Victoria, Mr Punch and the Duke of Wellington had all signed, and so had people with names like 'Pug-nose', or 'No-cheese'. It was now difficult to take Chartism seriously. The demonstration had failed, the petition was a fraud, and the land scheme was bankrupt. O'Connor never recovered from the humiliation. In 1852 he had a mental breakdown, and he died in 1855. Ernest Jones replaced him as leader, but in 1860 the National Charter Association closed down.

Importance of Chartists

The Chartists were important. In the long run five of their six points were granted. In addition, working class leaders learned from the mistakes the Chartists made. Afterwards they always understood the importance of unity and good organisation.

Study

This study aims:
K to give you an overall view of the Chartist movement.

Revise the information on the Chartists and remember what you have learned about the Great Reform Act and the Poor Law Amendment Act.

The Chartist Movement 1837–1860	
Date	**Event**
1837	The People's .... is drawn up.
. . . .	First petition to .... is rejected. John .... rebellion at .... fails.
1842	Second .... to Parliament is rejected. Chartists protested by removing .... from boilers in ....
1845	Chartist .... Land .... is set up to buy .... which can be .... to workers.
1848	.... petition to Parliament is ....
1860	The .... Charter .... closes down.

1 Copy and complete the time chart above.
2 a Why, in 1837, were working class people disappointed in:
the Reform Act of 1832;
the reforms carried out by the new Parliament?
 b What reasons might a worker have given for:
joining the Chartists in 1842;
leaving the Chartists in 1848?

3 Name the Chartist leader who favoured:
winning the support of influential people by using reasoned arguments;
using force to make Parliament grant the Chartist's demands but failed to support John Frost's rebellion.

Recall

1 What was: a Peeler; a pauper; a Chartist; the Speenhamland system?
2 Why are these people famous?
Henry Fielding; Elizabeth Fry; William Lovett; Feargus O'Connor.
3 **a** In pairs consider this list of reasons for the Chartists' failure:
  i Many workers would only attend meetings and organise petitions when they were badly off. After 1845 there was plenty of work available and food was cheap.
  ii The government took prompt action to prevent violence; for example, in 1848 Wellington recruited special constables.
  iii The leaders could not agree on detailed, long-term plans to gain their demands— some wanted to use violence, others would only use peaceful persuasion.
  iv Lovett wanted to use industry for the benefit of the workers when the Chartists came to power, but O'Connor wanted to destroy the industrial system.
  v After 1850 many workers turned to the co-operative and trade union movements.
  vi Only a few MPs supported the Chartists.
b Write down the item on the list that you think was the most important reason for the Chartists' failure.
c Ask one person to read his or her answer to the class. What do the rest of you think?

12
Britain from 1851 to the Present Day: Introduction

Part One

The Great Exhibition

THE IDEA OF PROGRESS

In 1851 an exhibition was held in Hyde Park. Its aim was to celebrate the progress that had been made in arts and science in the recent past and to encourage artists and engineers to continue working for the good of mankind.

THE CRYSTAL PALACE

The exhibition took place in a building specially designed by Joseph Paxton, the Duke of Devonshire's head gardener. The building was like a huge greenhouse, covering more than seven hectares. It was 578 metres long, and 34 metres high at its highest point. The Crystal Palace, as it was called, was so large that several huge elm trees growing in the park were enclosed in it like greenhouse plants. The building was enormously strong, but it looked light and delicate, and had been designed so that it could be dismantled and rebuilt elsewhere when the exhibition was over (Illustration 1).

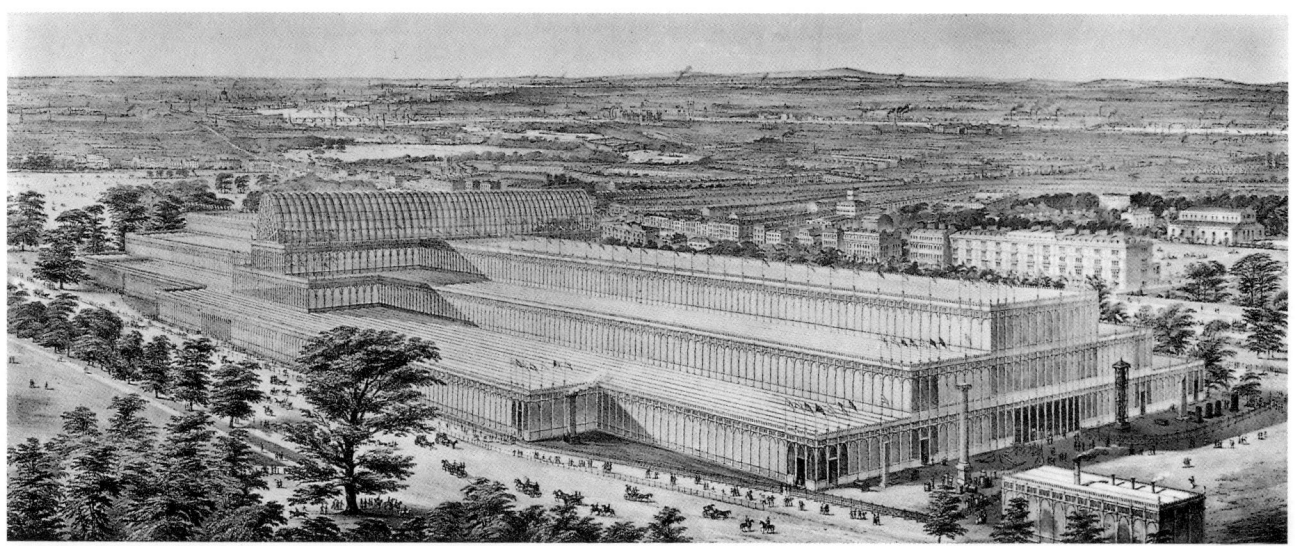

Illustration 1   A so-called 'aeronautic' view of the Crystal Palace.

THE EXHIBITS

Exhibits from abroad

Inside the Palace there were exhibits from all over the world.

Table 1

Country	Main items sent
France	silk, porcelain, tapestries, carpets
Belgium	cutlery
Austria	carved furniture
Switzerland	watches
Russia	silver plate
India	jewels and precious stones
USA	gold ornaments, photographs, Colt revolvers, a new reaping machine, articles made of vulcanised rubber

British engineering exhibits

These included:
the latest cotton spinning machinery;
Daniel Gooch's broad gauge express locomotive, 'Lord of the Isles', built for the Great Western Railway;
James Nasmyth's steam hammer;
Applegarth's vertical printing press, turning out 10,000 sheets of newsprint an hour (Illustration 2);
examples of the latest electric telegraphs.

Illustration 2   Applegarth's printing press produced pages of *The Illustrated London News* while visitors watched.

Household goods

There were also displays of furniture and household goods such as baths, cooking stoves and fireplaces. There was even an 'alarm bed' which dumped the sleeper into a bath of cold water in the morning.

Decorative work

Most items on display were covered in elaborate carving and decoration. In the eighteenth century a craftsman had to work for many hours to carve decoration on furniture. By 1851 a machine did it in a few minutes. Most people enjoyed elaborate machine-carved or cast decorations (see Illustration 3), but a few did not. An article in a London magazine complained about 'the indiscriminate addition of ornament everywhere'.

Illustration 3   A cast-iron fireplace exhibited at the Crystal Palace in 1851.

Fine arts

In the fine arts section of the exhibition there were several huge statues, including a zinc figure of Queen Victoria nearly seven metres high. The most popular statue was a Greek girl slave 'exposed for sale to some wealthy Eastern barbarian'. Many statues were imitations of the kind of work done by ancient Greek and Roman sculptors. Some were very sentimental, like that of a small boy crying because he had broken his toy drum. This appealed to many visitors.

RESULTS OF THE EXHIBITION

The exhibition was a great success. By the time it closed in October 1851, more than six million people had been round, paying total fees of £356,000. The exhibition made a profit of £86,000. This was used to buy land in South Kensington and establish several museums there, including the Science Museum and the Natural History Museum.

Study

The pictures below show the Great Exhibition of 1851 as it was portrayed by two artists living at the time. Your aim is to:

S identify the similarities and differences between the two pictures and their artists' view of the Great Exhibition.

Source 1A

Cotton machinery at the Great Exhibition.

Source 1B

Farm labourers visiting the exhibition.

1 a What can we learn about the Great Exhibition from looking at Source 1A that we cannot learn from Source 1B?

b What can we learn about the Great Exhibition from looking at Source 1B that we cannot learn from Source 1A?

2 How does each artist show us that the Great Exhibition was impressive?

3 The Great Exhibition was held to celebrate the progress that had been made since the beginning of the nineteenth century and to show visitors what a wonderful future was in store for them. Which picture do you think best illustrates this idea? Give reasons for your answer.

——— Part Two ———

Life in 1851

1801 AND 1851: A COMPARISON

The standard of living

Most people living in Britain in 1851 felt that they had plenty to celebrate. The editor of *The Economist* magazine published a series of articles comparing life in 1851 with life in 1801. He said that people were more prosperous in 1851.

Table 2

		1801	1851
Population of UK		15 million	30 million
Total taxation paid		£63 million	£50 million
Prices:	Meat per stone (6.4 kg)	5s 8d	3s 4d
	Bread per loaf	1s 10d	6d
	Tea per pound	5s	3s 4d
	Coffee per pound	2s	1s
	Sugar per pound	8d	4d
	Cotton cloth per yard	1s	3d

Living and working conditions had improved. The average number of people living in each house had fallen from 5.6 to 5.4, and there were many new houses, which were bigger than old ones. Hours of work in factories had fallen from seventy four to sixty a week. The population was healthier. The expectation of life had increased by five years.

Brutality and good manners

The Economist said that a journey back from 1851 to 1801 was 'a descent into barbarism':

'Executions taking place by the dozen; the stealing of five shillings . . . punished as severely as rape or murder; slavery and the slave trade flourishing . . . freedom of discussion and writing . . . frequently in jeopardy, religious rights trampled under foot . . . Parliament was unreformed'.

Since 1801 drunkenness had decreased. In 1851 'a drunken gentleman is one of the rarest sights in society', while in 1801 'many got drunk every day'. All ranks of society now had 'a higher sense both of duty and of decency'.

Education

Education had improved. Since 1801 huge numbers of schools had been founded, a Committee of the Privy Council had been set up to supervise them, and in 1850 the government had granted £150,000 a year to schools.

Communications

The editor of *The Economist* reckoned that the greatest improvements had taken place in communications:

Table 3

	1801	1851
Voyage to America	eight weeks	ten days
Fastest journeys on land	16 kph	100 kph
Letter, London–Edinburgh	seven days cost 13.5d	one day cost 1d
Urgent message	man on horseback	telegraph

He believed that railways had given the poor new freedom. 'How few among the last generation ever stirred beyond their own village? How few among the present will die without visiting London?'

Hopes for the future

The editor concluded, 'when we refer to a few only of the extraordinary improvements of the half-century just elapsed . . . we become convinced that it is more full of wonders than any other on record'. What was more, he was sure that things would continue to improve. Endless progress was 'the destined lot of the human race'.

Study ▫

In this study you will be:

Ch looking at three generations of a family that might have lived between 1766 and 1876 and seeing how life changed during that time.

You will need the information about Britain in 1851 on page 130.

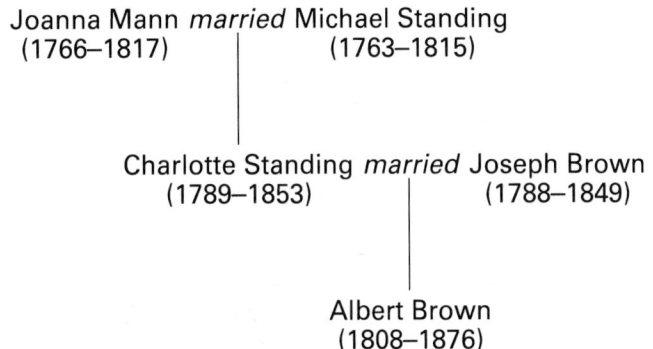

Joanna Mann *married* Michael Standing
(1766–1817)   (1763–1815)

Charlotte Standing *married* Joseph Brown
(1789–1853)   (1788–1849)

Albert Brown
(1808–1876)

1 Charlotte Standing lived longer than either of her parents. Give three changes that took place between 1801 and 1851 that may have helped to prolong her life.

2 Charlotte could not read or write, and never travelled more than twenty five miles from her birthplace. What changes took place between 1801 and 1851 that made it possible for her children to know more about the world than she ever could?

3 When Charlotte married Joseph Brown in 1807 she moved to a village ten miles from her parents' home. When her son Albert grew up, he went to work in a town fifty miles from the village where he grew up. Why was it easier for Albert to keep in touch with his parents than it had been for Charlotte to keep in touch with her parents?

4 Albert's first grandchild, William, was born in 1852. Albert believed that life could only get better during William's lifetime. Do you think that most people in Britain would have agreed with Albert? Give reasons for your answer.

13
Population 1851–1981

Births and Deaths

Study

In this study you will use the information below and what you learned about population records (on page 6) to consider:

Ch changes in population, 1851–1981; **Ca** some results of these changes.

HOW BIRTH AND DEATH RATES HAVE CHANGED

In 1851 the population of Britain was about twenty million. In 1981 it was about fifty five million. In 1851 both the birth rate and the death rate were very high—about double what they are today. We know by studying the registers that the birth rate rose slowly between 1850 and 1870. The death rate at the time was much lower, so the population was increasing very rapidly and a large proportion were young people.

1 How many more people lived in Britain in 1981 than in 1851?
2 a What documents would a historian use to work out the following information for England, Wales and Scotland:
the population in 1851 and 1981;
the birth rate and death rate in 1981?
  b Why is it difficult to work out the birth rate and the death rate for the whole of Britain in 1851?
(Look on page 6 if you cannot remember the answers to these questions.)

3 Look at Table 1.
  a In 1872, what was:
the birth rate per thousand of the population;
the death rate per thousand of the population?
  b Why would very young people have formed a large proportion of the population in 1872?
  c Give one reason why Britain's population has continued to increase since 1872, even though the birth rate has fallen.

Discussion

Between 1850 and 1930 Britain's population doubled.
In pairs, make brief notes on the answers to these questions.
1 What changes may people have seen in the areas where they lived as a result of this increase?
2 What problems may the rapid increase in population have caused?
3 Ask one person to read his or her answers to the class. What do the rest of you think?

Table 1   Birth rate and death rate, 1872

Birth Rate	🐤🐤🐤🐤🐤🐤🐤🐤🐤🐤🐤🐤🐤🐤🐤🐤🐤🐤 🐤🐤🐤🐤🐤🐤🐤🐤🐤🐤🐤🐤🐤🐤🐤🐤
	per thousand people (🐤 = 1 birth)
Death Rate	☠☠☠☠☠☠☠☠☠☠ ☠☠☠☠☠☠☠☠☠☠
	per thousand people (☠ = 1 death)

Since 1872 the birth rate and the death rate have both fallen.

Why the birth rate has fallen: 1870–1981

Economic reasons

Until about 1870 Britain was the most up-to-date manufacturing country in the world and British factory owners could sell all they produced. It was easy to find a job, and this encouraged parents to have large families. But gradually foreign manufacturers caught up and began to produce goods to compete with the British. This meant that British producers could no longer sell everything they made. Some dismissed workers, or even closed factories.

At the same time, foreign farmers were exporting cheap food to Britain. In order to compete, British farmers changed their farming methods and dismissed some of their workers (see Chapter 14). People who are likely to be out of work think twice before they have children, because they might not be able to feed and clothe them properly. So, as Britain's farms and factories slowed down, the birth rate began to fall (see Diagram 1).

New laws

Changes in the law also discouraged workers from having large families. Children were forbidden to work in factories, so parents could no longer send their children out to earn their keep in a mill. Then after 1870 schooling was made compulsory. In many places children had to stay at school until they were thirteen, fed and clothed at their parents'

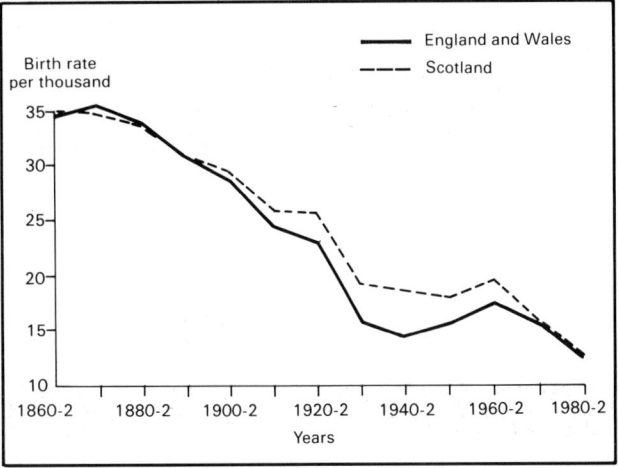

Diagram 1 Birth rates, 1860–1980

expense instead of earning a regular wage. It cost so much to maintain children until they could go out to work that many parents decided to have only two or three.

Birth control

Annie Besant and Charles Bradlaugh

Since 1870 it had been easier to limit the size of families because more people understood birth control. This was partly due to Annie Besant and Charles Bradlaugh. In 1877 they published a new sixpenny edition of a pamphlet entitled *The Fruits of Philosophy* which gave clear advice on birth control. The pamphlet had been written in 1833, but

Study

The diagrams below show two families who might have lived in 1875. Your aim in this study is:

Em to write a paragraph explaining why the parents of each family might have decided that they could not afford to have any more children.

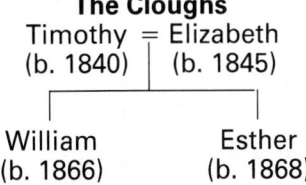

The Cloughs
Timothy = Elizabeth
(b. 1840) | (b. 1845)

William (b. 1866)   Esther (b. 1868)

Timothy is an unemployed weaver. Elizabeth works in a spinning mill. In the town where they live, three mills have closed during the last five years and two more mill owners are on the verge of bankruptcy.

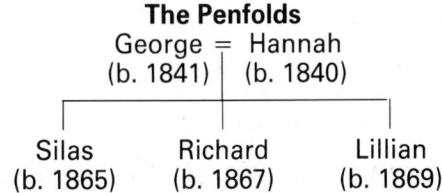

The Penfolds
George = Hannah
(b. 1841) | (b. 1840)

Silas (b. 1865)   Richard (b. 1867)   Lillian (b. 1869)

George is a farm labourer. His wife does the washing for the farmer's family. Their cottage goes with George's job. The farmer who employs him is considering using more machinery on his land in order to cut down on the number of labourers he employs.

this was the first cheap edition. Some people thought it was obscene, so Besant and Bradlaugh were prosecuted. Their case lasted three months, and in the end they were acquitted because the accusation against them had not been properly worded.

Newspapers printed long reports of the case, and while it was going on, 125,000 copies of the pamphlet were sold. Previously it had sold about 700 copies a year.

Marie Stopes

Gradually, easier and safer contraceptives were devised and in 1918 Marie Stopes, a doctor, wrote a book called *Married Love* to publicise them. She also set up birth control clinics where people could go for advice. The number of people using contraceptives rose steadily, even though the use of contraception was opposed by Roman Catholic clergy and some other churchmen. There is no doubt that cheap and easy contraception has kept the birth rate down.

Why the death rate has fallen

Diagram 2   Death rates, 1860–1970

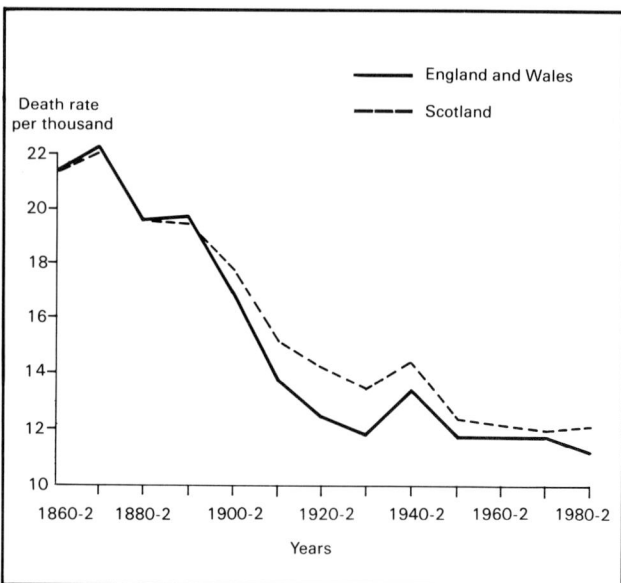

Study

The aim of this study is:
K to understand more about attitudes to birth control;
Ev to use a contemporary photograph as historical evidence.

You will need to refer to the section headed 'Birth control' on page 133 and look at Source 1.

Source 1

Marie Stopes' mobile birth control clinic.

1 Give two or more reasons why Source 1 might have encouraged women who wanted advice on birth control to attend a mobile clinic.
2 Do you think Source 1 was taken:
   at the beginning of the nineteenth century;
   in the middle of the nineteenth century;
   at the beginning of the twentieth century?
   Give reasons for your answer.
3 What evidence is there to suggest that at the time:
   some people would have disapproved of a mobile clinic visiting their area;
   other people would have welcomed the visit?

Table 2   Infectious diseases common in industrial towns before 1870

Diphtheria Scarlet fever } Smallpox	Spread rapidly when people live closely together.
Typhus } Cholera	Caused by impure water supplies.
Since 1930 new drugs have been discovered to prevent or cure most infectious diseases.	

Table 3   Laws passed by Parliament

1853	All children to be vaccinated against smallpox (deaths from this disease then fell rapidly).
1872	No dangerous chemicals to be added to food or drink.

Infant mortality

These changes saved the lives of people of all ages, but babies have benefited most. In 1870 fifteen per cent of all babies died before their first birthday. In 1970 the number was less than two per cent.

In the nineteenth century many babies died because their mothers were too weak to feed them properly. Others were killed by stomach diseases due to dirty, unhealthy houses. So as diet and living conditions improved, the number of babies dying fell steadily (see Table 4). This altered the balance between the number of men and women in the population.

THE BALANCE OF THE POPULATION

Male babies are more delicate and difficult to rear than females, so more boys than girls died during the first few months of life. In the nineteenth century, women always made up over half the population. As the death rate among babies has fallen, the proportion of men has risen, until the numbers of the two sexes below the age of seventy are now about equal. World War I (1914–18) slowed the process. It killed about seven per cent of all men aged between 19 and 53 when the war broke out. World War II (1939–45) had much less effect, because fewer men died and more women were killed than in the 1914 war.

The fall in the death rate reflects the fact that people are living longer. There are more old people than there used to be. At the same time the birth rate has fallen and there are fewer young people. So today old people make up a much greater proportion of the population than ever before.

Table 4   Infant death rates

(deaths under one year per 1,000 births)					
	England & Wales	Scotland		England & Wales	Scotland
1860	148	118	1920	80	94
1870	156	127	1930	64	84
1880	141	118	1940	55	77
1890	149	125	1950	29	37
1900	146	124	1960	22	26
1910	110	109	1970	18	19

Study

In this study you will use the information in Diagram 2 and Tables 2 and 3 to work out:

Ca why deaths from disease decreased between 1850 and 1930.

1 Look at Diagram 2.
  a Did the death rate rise or fall between 1860 and 1970?
  b Why did the population continue to rise after 1870, even though the *birth rate* fell?
2 A person who lived in an industrial town between 1850 and 1930 might have seen the following changes in his or her lifetime:
  overcrowded, badly drained courts replaced by streets with main drainage,
  impure drinking water replaced by water piped from a reservoir;
  patients with infectious diseases treated in an isolation hospital built away from the town.
  a Why would you expect the diseases listed in Table 2 to have become less common by 1930?
  b What effect would you expect these changes in industrial towns to have on the death rate?
3 Look at Table 3.
  a Before 1853 parents were not forced to have their children vaccinated against smallpox. Some refused because vaccination damaged the health of a few children. Was the government justified in making it compulsory? Give reasons for your answer.
  b What are we told in Table 2 that suggests that before 1872 many people were unable to resist disease because their health was undermined by the food they ate?

Study

Use the information on pages 133–5 to work out:
Ca why the balance of Britain's population changed between 1870 and 1970.

1 Copy and complete the following sentences:
In the nineteenth century, fifteen per cent of children died before their first birthday because . . .
By 1970 the number of children who died before their first birthday had fallen to two per cent because . . .
Until recently there were more women than men in the population because . . .

2 Copy the statements below.
Between the second half of the nineteenth century and the second half of the twentieth century:
the number of men and women in the population became about equal;
the proportion of old people in the population increased.

a Did the numbers of men and women equalise because:
the birth rate for boy babies increased;
the death rate for boy babies decreased?

b Did the proportion of old people increase because:
the birth rate decreased;
the death rate among older people decreased;
the birth rate decreased and so did the death rate among old people?

3 Copy this statement.
The two World Wars delayed but did not reverse the process by which the number of men and women in the population became more equal.
Do you agree or disagree with the statement? Give reasons for your answer.

Part Two

Emigration and Immigration

The number of people living in a country is increased by foreigners coming to settle there (immigration) and decreased when people go to live abroad (emigration). In some cases people emigrate because life is bad. Famine, ill-treatment and unemployment all drive people to leave their countries. On the other hand a country such as the USA attracts immigrants because it is very rich, and even people with secure jobs elsewhere believe that they will be better off if they go to live in the USA.

EMIGRATION

Since 1700 more people have left Britain than have come to live here. Most emigrants from Britain have gone to settle in former British Colonies, and there are very large numbers of people of British descent in countries such as the USA, Canada, Australia, New Zealand and southern Africa. In all these countries the climate suits the British. Others went to tropical countries such as India or West Africa to work as government officials, traders or missionaries. But most of them did not settle for life. They returned to Britain when they retired.

IMMIGRATION

Table 5 shows the three short periods when the number of immigrants has been greater than the number of emigrants. Immigration can bring problems, especially when the newcomers belong to a different race and are used to a different way of life from that lived by the majority. The immigrants may feel insecure and isolated, while some of the inhabitants of the host country may fear that the newcomers will take all the available jobs and alter the areas where they live to suit their customs. The fears and suspicions of both sides can lead to bad feeling and sometimes even to violence. In Britain we are still trying to solve these problems.

Table 5

Dates	Countries of origin	Reasons for coming to Britain
1846–50	Ireland	To escape starvation when the potato crop in Ireland failed.
1930–40	Europe	To escape persecution by Hitler and other fascists.
1950–65	Commonwealth countries, e.g. Pakistan, West Indies	To look for work, which was difficult to find in their own countries.

In 1965 and 1968 Parliament passed laws to limit the number of immigrants to Britain, and since then the number of emigrants has always been higher than the number of immigrants.

Study

In this study you will be considering:

Ca what the sources tell us about reasons for emigration from the Scottish Highlands between 1763 and 1854;

Ev whether or not the sources are reliable.

Source 2A

According to John Knox, the London bookseller who toured the Highlands in the seventeen-eighties, twenty thousand people left for the Colonies between 1763 and 1775. In one year alone fifty-four emigrant ships sailed from the western sea-lochs . . . Most [of the emigrants] were led . . . by small tacksmen who wished to escape the rack-renting of their chiefs . . . A growing population, a decaying economy, recurrent famines and bitter poverty made exile inevitable for increasing numbers.

John Prebble, *The Highland Clearances* (1963).
(In the eighteenth century Highland chiefs rented out land to tenants called *tacksmen* who then sub-let it to the clansmen. If a chief charged a very high rent he was said to be rack-renting.)

Source 2B

Emigrants on board ship. Their sleeping quarters are on the right.

Source 2C

We have no country to fight for, as our glens . . . are laid desolate, and we have no wives nor children to defend as we are forbidden to have them . . . Our lands have been taken from us and given to sheep farmers, and . . . we are told we should leave the country.

From a statement made by the young men of Sutherland in 1854. (During the nineteenth century, many Highland chiefs found it more profitable to turn their tenants off the land and use it to raise sheep. Chiefs had great power over their clansmen.)

1 a Consider Sources 2A, 2B and 2C. Which of these types of people do you think would have been passengers on an emigrant ship: poor Highlanders and their families; Highland chiefs and their families; young unmarried men? Give reasons for your answers.

  b Do you think the highlanders would have been glad to leave Scotland? Give reasons for your answer.

2 a What evidence can you see in Source 2B to suggest that passengers on emigrant ships: were not very comfortable; did not have much privacy?

  b What kind of information might you look for if you wanted to know if the conditions shown in Source 2B were typical of emigrant ships?

3 Source 2A is a secondary source and Source 2C a primary source. Does this mean that 2A is less reliable than 2C? Give reasons for your answer.

Discussion

Often the young, the adventurous and the go-ahead emigrate first. Make rough notes to answer the following questions.

1 What problems may emigrants cause for the country they leave?

2 In what ways may they be an asset to the country where they settle?

Ask one person to read his or her answers to the class. What do the rest of you think?

Study

Countries which have large numbers of immigrants have to help their new citizens to become part of the community. At the same time they have to respect the way of life that the immigrants bring with them. This study asks you:

Em to think about some of the factors that have to be considered.

Source 3   Ethnic rights

'Irish parents in . . . Leeds are demanding that their children be recognised as ethnic minority pupils with special cultural needs.
They want Gaelic taught in schools and say that children have a right to study its literature and music as well as the opportunity to play . . . Irish sports like hurling and Gaelic football . . .'
(Mr Bernard McGrath, the Irish community's representative on Leeds City Council, says that there are 110,159 children with Irish parents attending schools in the city.)

The Times Educational Supplement, 6 June 1986.
(An *ethnic minority* is a group of people who belong to a different race or culture from the majority of the population.)

Discussion

In pairs, read Source 3 and then make brief notes on the answers that you would give to these questions.

1 In what ways might it help children from ethnic minorities if they learned the language and customs of their parents' countries in British schools?
2 In what ways might it help all the children in the school if they learned about the language and customs of the ethnic minority?
3 What problems might arise if children from several ethnic minorities attended the same school?
4 Ask one person to read his or her answers to the class. Do the rest of you agree?

Recall

1 Explain these terms in your own words: mortality rate; immigrant; emigrant.
2 True or false?
   a When Britain began to lose its industrial supremacy, the birth rate fell.
   b Britain's population increased after 1870 because the birth rate increased.
   c Fifty five million more people lived in Britain in 1981 than in 1851.
3 Why did the population of Britain increase between 1870 and 1981 even though more people left the country than came to live here?

Diagram 3

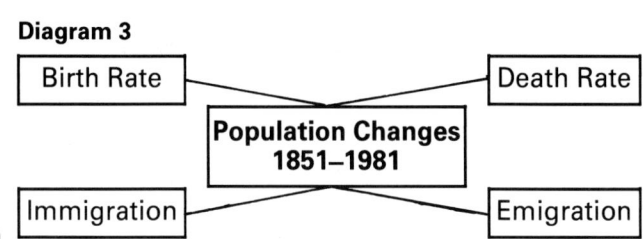

14
Farming 1851–1985

—— Part One ——
The Golden Age

Between 1846 and 1875 farmers prospered. The repeal of the Corn Laws, which many farmers feared would lead to lower wheat prices, seemed to make no difference. The population was still increasing, and trade was booming. So people were prosperous, and had plenty of money to spend on food. British farmers were able to supply most of the extra food that was needed. Several inventions and developments made this possible.

REASONS FOR PROSPERITY

The railway system

By sending produce by train, farmers could deliver fresh meat, milk and vegetables to industrial towns many miles away within a few hours. Foreign farmers could not compete with this.

Field drainage

By 1850 farmers and engineers had discovered effective ways of draining water-logged soil to make it more productive. At a cost of about £12 a hectare, farmers could drain and plough heavy, wet soil which they had never been able to cultivate before.

Drainage money

The government, from 1846 onwards, encouraged farmers to drain land by lending them money. Farmers had only to pay 3.5 per cent interest, and had twenty two years to pay the money back.

Private companies also lent 'drainage money'. By 1878 it was reckoned that, in all, farmers had borrowed about £12 million to pay for drains.

Research and development

In 1838 the Royal Agricultural Society was founded. It organised shows in various parts of the country where farmers could see demonstrations of new methods and all the latest machines. In 1842, John Benet Lawes set up an agricultural research station at Rothamsted in southern England. He and his staff tested new crops and compared methods of cultivation. They also produced artificial fertilisers. The first, superphosphate, went on sale in 1843.

Fertilisers

Farmers used more fertilisers. Animal bones were imported to make into bone meal. In 1823 their value was about £15,000 a year and by 1840 their value was about £250,000. In 1841 2,000 tonnes of guano, a rich manure made from the droppings of sea birds, were imported from Peru. By 1847 the amount had increased to 300,000 tonnes. After 1843 farmers also began to use artificial fertilisers.

Table 1

Date	Name	Invention
c1830	James Smith of Deanston (Perth)	Deep plough which broke up layers of clay under top soil. Water then drained away.
c1830	John Reade (Kent)	Cheap cylindrical tile drain pipe.
1850	John Fowler (Wiltshire)	'Mole' plough—bored a tunnel through earth, and laid string of pipes along it.

Study

MODEL FARMS

In this study your aim is to use the primary sources below to see:

Ev what information they can give us about the 'model' farms built by prosperous farmers after 1845;

S what we can infer from this information about standards of farming in Britain and France.

Source 1A

A farmstead planned in 1850. It contained a large farmhouse, an engine-house, boiler-house, saw mill, dairy unit, cow sheds and pig sties.

Source 1B

. . . a collection of fifteen or twenty low buildings in brick, economically designed and built. [There were] bullocks, pigs, sheep, each in a well-ventilated, well-cleaned stall. [There were] steam engines for all the work of the arable land. A narrow-gauge railway to carry their food to the animals . . . Farming like this is a complicated industry.

Hippolyte Taine, a Frenchman, describing a visit to a model farm in Britain in 1862.

Source 1C

. . . a cool and lofty drawing room. Long curtains held back by gilt loops; two elegantly framed looking glasses; chairs in good taste. In the middle a table with a number of handsomely bound books . . . The farmer's wife came in . . . wearing a dress of narrowly striped grey silk, one or two rings on her fingers, her hands perfectly white, the nails pink and cared for . . . Apart from a few slight faults in manners and speech, she is a lady.

Hippolyte Taine, describing a visit to a farmer's house on a model farm in 1862.

1 What did Taine see that:
shows British farmers were using some of the methods that industrialists had used to increase production;
suggests that these methods were profitable?

2 Do you think the farms he describes in Sources 1B and 1C were typical British farms? Give reasons for your answer.

3 Do you think that farming in Britain was more or less industrialised than farming in France? Give reasons for your answer.

Machinery

New machines speeded up farm work.

John Fowler invented ploughs which were attached to a cable and pulled through the soil by a stationary steam engine.

Patrick Bell, a Scottish divinity student, invented a successful reaping machine in 1828 but did not bother to patent it.

Cyrus McCormick, an American farmer, invented the most successful reaping machine. His horse-drawn mechanical reaper gradually replaced the labourers with their scythes at harvest time.

When the corn had been cut and gathered it was threshed by steam-powered threshing machines which travelled from farm to farm (Illustration 1).

FARM LABOURERS

Food and housing

In the south some rich farmers built new cottages for their labourers, but most southern workers still lived in old, damp cottages. A Dorset doctor reported that labourers in such cottages were 'very dirty, and usually in rags, living almost wholly on bread and potatoes'. In 1863 a survey showed that on average, farm labourers ate 6 kg of bread a week each. Usually the bread was made of a mixture of wheat and barley flour.

The farm labourers' union

Farm labourers in the Midlands and south thought they deserved higher pay and better conditions and in 1872 Joseph Arch, a Warwickshire labourer, set up a farm labourers' union. Afterwards he wrote a description of the first meeting, held at Wellesbourne in Warwickshire in February 1872.

'I mounted an old pig stool, and in the flickering light of the lanterns I saw the earnest upturned faces of these poor brothers of mine—faces gaunt with hunger and pinched with want—all looking towards me and ready to listen to the words that would fall from my lips.'

In 1872 the Warwickshire labourers decided to strike, but the farmers easily broke the new union.

Study: Library work

1. List the kind of library books you might use to find out more about Joseph Arch and the Agricultural Labourers' Union that he founded.
2. With the help of the books in your school or local library, make notes on the reasons why: Joseph Arch formed the Union in 1872; most labourers had left the Union by 1879.

Illustration 1   Hornsby's portable steam threshing machine.

Study

In this study you will:

Ev examine the primary sources below to discover 'bias'.

Source 2A

THE PIG AND THE PEASANT.

Peasant. "AH! I'D LIKE TO BE CARED VOR HALF AS WELL AS THEE BE!"

A cartoon published in *Punch* in 1863.

Source 2B

In 1852 James Caird, who investigated English agriculture for *The Times*, published this weekly budget of a Suffolk farm worker and his wife:

Expenditure			Income		
1 stone (6.4 kg) flour	1s	10d	Weekly wage	8s	0d
8 oz (226 g) butter		6	Less	5s	6d
1 lb (453 g) cheese		7.5	For sundries	2s	6d
1.5 oz (45 g) tea		4.5			
8 oz (226 g) sugar		2			
Total for food	3	6			
Rent of cottage	2	0			
Total	5s	6d			

'Sundries' included clothes, shoes, candles, fuel, soap, yeast, salt, household replacements, medicines and additional food.

Source 2C

. . . dwellings . . . look so pretty in summer, with roses and ivy creeping about their rotten thatch, but . . . often enough are scarcely fit to be inhabited by human beings.

H. Rider Haggard, *Rural England* (1902).

Source 2D

[The bed] stood on the ground floor, which was damp three parts of the year; scarcely one [cottage] had a fireplace in the bedroom, and one had a single small pane of glass stuck in the mud wall as its only window, with a large heap of wet and dirty potatoes in one corner.

A Dorset doctor describing a labourer's cottage in the 1840s.

1 What point do you think the artist was making about *farmers* in the south and Midlands when he drew Source 2A?
2 Does the information in Sources 2B, 2C and 2D suggest that the artist's opinion of farmers was biased? Give reasons for your answer.

3 What further evidence might you look for if you wanted to prove whether or not the artist was biased?

Agricultural gangs

In eastern England, travelling gangs of labourers did much of the farm work. In early spring the gangmasters visited local villages and collected a number of women and children who wanted work. Then they hired their gangs out to farmers for weeding, collecting stones, harvesting hay and picking potatoes. The women and children had to work very hard, and sometimes gangmasters ill-treated them.

Members of Parliament complained about the gangs, and in 1867 they passed the Gangs Act. This said that no children under the age of eight could work in gangs, and set up a system under which all gangmasters had to be licensed. Slowly the number of gangs fell. They finally disappeared when, beginning in 1870, schooling was made compulsory.

Study

In this study you will:

Ca use the information in the photographs below to consider the effect that compulsory education had on the employment of women and children in country districts.

You will need to remember what you have learned about workers in farming areas.

Source 3A

A Norfolk potato-picking gang photographed in about 1910.

Source 3B

Pupils at Waltham-on-the-Wolds Council school in 1909.

1 Consider Source 3A. School registers show that there were many absentees at busy times in the farming year. For what reasons may children have gone to the fields instead of going to school?

2 Consider Source 3B. *Why*, do you think, was this photograph taken?

3 Consider both Sources. What effect do you think compulsory education had on job opportunities for women in country districts? Explain your answer.

Part Two

The Great Depression

CAUSES

Weather

In the late 1870s summers were cold and wet, and grain harvests were very poor. In the past, farmers had still made a profit from a poor harvest because when corn was in short supply, its price rose and they got just as much money from selling a small quantity of expensive grain as they did from selling a large amount of cheap corn when the harvest was good.

Competition

After 1875 it was different. Though the British crop was poor, the price of wheat remained low because huge quantities of cheap wheat were imported from North America. Farmers on the American prairies had better conditions than British farmers for growing good, hard wheat (see Table 2). American wheat was sold in Britain for less than thirty shillings a quarter. Most British farmers could not make a profit selling wheat at this price (see Illustration 2).

EFFECTS OF DEPRESSION

Effects of low wheat prices

Many tenant farmers left their farms, and landowners could not easily find replacements. So a large number of farms were left empty and landowners had to reduce rents in order to let them. Many farmers gave up growing wheat. Between 1874 and 1900 the amount of land used for growing wheat halved. Farmers near large towns made a living by growing fruit and vegetables to feed the townsfolk. There was also a steady demand for meat, eggs and dairy products such as milk and cheese. So farmers grew grass instead of wheat, and kept more cattle, buying cheap grain to feed them when the grass ran short.

A CRUMB OF COMFORT.

JONATHAN. "THEY *DU* SAY WE SENT YOU THIS DARN'D WEATHER! DON'T KNOW 'BOUT THAT! ANYHOW, I GUESS WE'LL SEND YOU THE CORN!!!"
FARMER BULL. "THANK'EE KINDLY, JONATHAN, BUT I'D RATHER HA' DONE WITHOUT BOTH!!!!"

Illustration 2 A *Punch* cartoon published in 1879 showing typical American and English farmers discussing the situation.

Table 2

American farms	British farms
Huge, mostly level fields, ideal for new machines.	Small, mostly undulating fields, awkward for machines.
Used new, cheap barbed wire to fence fields. Needed little maintenance.	Used hedges to fence fields. Needed regular maintenance.
Deep, rich soil.	Variable soil.
Hot, dry summers, ideal for hard wheat.	Variable climate, usually too wet for hard wheat.
Good railroads and shipping links with Europe.	Easy communications with consumers.
Very cheap land.	Comparatively expensive land.

Problems for livestock farmers

Death and disease

Eventually livestock farmers suffered too. The wet weather caused foot rot and liver fluke among sheep. Cattle were attacked by epidemics of pneumonia and foot and mouth disease, and many animals died in the long, cold, snowy winters.

Imports

In 1880 an experimental refrigerated ship, *The Dunedin*, brought a cargo of frozen lamb to London from New Zealand. By 1900, large quantities of cheap New Zealand lamb were coming to Britain and frozen beef was being shipped from Argentina. At the same time the Dutch began to ship cheap cheese to England.

Farmers' economies

Farmers had to economise. They did this in various ways.
1 They dismissed their workers. The number of labourers fell by 300,000 between 1870 and 1900.
2 They did not bother to repair fences, gates and barns.
3 They allowed hedges to grow, and did not clean out ditches.
4 They used less fertiliser than the soil needed, the quality of the land slowly deteriorated, and the yield of crops declined.

Government policy

British farmers complained. They asked the government to put duties on imported foreign food. This would raise its price, and allow them to compete. The government refused because:
1 Farmers and landowners were now less important than manufacturers. In 1867 workers in towns had been given the vote, and they wanted cheap food.
2 Britain was a free trade country, and the government believed it was sensible for Britain to make and export cheap manufactured goods and import cheap food in return.

So the government did nothing to help farmers. By 1914 the country was only growing one third of its own food.

Some official policies made the situation more difficult. For example, the government made schooling compulsory. This hit farmers in two ways. Previously they had used children as cheap labour. Now they had to employ adults, which was much more expensive. In addition, they had to pay increased rates to build the schools and pay the teachers.

Study

This study will help you:

Ca to understand why British agriculture was depressed between 1875 and 1914.

Use the information on pages 144–5.

1 Rewrite the items in the list below in the order of their importance as causes of the depression in British agriculture between 1875 and 1914.
a Town workers were given the vote in 1867.
b Farmers' expenses increased after the 1870 Education Act.
c A succession of cold, wet summers in the late 1870s led to poor harvests.
d After 1875 it was cheaper to import American wheat than to buy British.
e Refrigerated ships came into use after 1880.
f British farmers had less money to spend on making their farms more efficient.
2 Ask one person to read his or her answer to the class. Do the rest of you agree?

Part Three

Twentieth-Century Farming

WORLD WAR I

British farmers and the war effort 1914–18

Chronology	
1914	War began. German submarines sank British merchant ships bringing food to Britain.
1915	Agricultural committees set up in every county by the government. *Aim* to encourage farmers to grow more food.
1917	Corn Production Act—guaranteed farmers sixty shillings a quarter for wheat for five years. Farmers ordered to plough up pasture to produce more grain. Minimum wages laid down for farm labourers.
1918	War ends. About 1.5 million more hectares of land used for growing grain than in 1914.

Study

In this study your aim is:

Ca to understand why the government acted to increase food production in Britain and what happened as a result.

Use the information in the Chronology table above.

1 a Why could the government not rely on imported food to feed the British people after 1914?
b Why were agricultural committees set up in 1915?

2 *The government* wanted farmers to change from producing meat to growing wheat and potatoes, because land produces more food per hectare from growing crops than from grazing animals.
Farmers feared that if they grew more grain, they would lose money after the war when cheap grain was imported again.
What did the government do in 1917:
a to encourage farmers to grow more corn;
b to force farmers to grow more corn?

3 How did the following people benefit from government actions to increase food production during the war:
a agricultural labourers;
b the British people as a whole?

4 Write three or more points that you would include in a paragraph on each of the following.
a Ways in which the government increased food production during the war.
b The need to ensure food supplies in Britain during the war.
c The importance of the work of agricultural committees.

FARMING 1918–1945

British governments and British farmers 1918–39

Chronology	
1920	Agriculture Act confirmed the guaranteed prices begun by the 1917 Corn Production Act.
1921	World food prices fell so the British government: **a** repealed the 1920 Agriculture Act; **b** abolished the minimum wage for farm labourers.
1924	*The Labour government* set up Agricultural Wages Boards in each county to fix labourers' pay.
1925	*A Conservative government* was elected which wanted to reduce food imports and encourage British farmers to produce more. *To do this they:*
1925	paid a subsidy to farmers to grow sugar beet;
1929	abolished rates on farm buildings and land;
1932	put a duty on imported wheat;
1933	set up Milk Marketing Boards to organise the collection and sale of milk, make sure that farmers got a fair price and pay them regularly.

Illustration 3 A reaping and binding machine at work at St Columb Minor, Cornwall, in 1932.

Study

In this study you will consider:

K how the Labour and Conservative parties tried to help agricultural communities between 1918 and 1939;

Em which of the parties two people living at the time might have voted for.

Use the information in the Chronology table on this page.

Source 4A

A labourer talking about his pay in 1921 said:

Farmworkers' wages were about fifty shillings a week. In two cuts they were down to twenty-five shillings. And that's when things started going wrong. That's when times really began to get hard.

1 Why may the labourer have blamed the government of 1921 for the drop in his wages?

Source 4B

A Devon school inspector's report in 1923 said:

Many of the children in country schools are pale-faced, anaemic-looking, with eyes lacking lustre, undersized, under-fed and sad-faced.

2 Why may the labourer have supported the Labour government of 1924 if he had children?

Source 4C

A Devon farmer described his family's situation before Milk Marketing Boards were set up. He said:

My father kept bullocks, milked a few cows, and mother took butter to Exeter and sold it for 1/10d a pound. We probably took £5 a week. It was not a very good way of making a living.

He said that after the boards were set up:

Everybody was paid the same price for milk throughout the country. We were getting the equivalent of double the price for liquid milk . . . We could keep cows and it could be profitable.

3 Which political party do you think *i* the labourer and *ii* the farmer would have supported in the period 1925–33? Give reasons for your answer.

Illustration 4 'Land-girls' at work during World War II.

World War II

In 1939 World War II began. Local committees were set up to make farmers plough up pasture to grow grain and potatoes. 'Land girls' were recruited to take the place of farm labourers who went to the war (Illustration 4). Between 1939 and 1945 the area of cultivated land increased from five million to more than seven million hectares, and the amount of food produced rose by thirty five per cent. The number of sheep, pigs and beef cattle fell.

POST-WAR FARMING

Subsidies

After the war Britain could not afford to import as much as before. So the government encouraged farmers to grow as much food as possible. In the 1947 Agriculture Act they promised to pay farmers subsidies on all the food they produced. So farmers could afford to invest in new buildings and machinery. New, more productive strains of plants

Study

In this study you will be using primary sources:

Ch to consider some changes brought about by the government's decision in 1947 to subsidise agriculture.

Source 5A

They gave farmers subsidies on practically every commodity they had, on all the corn, on the milk, on the cattle, on the fertilisers, the drainage, the ditching, practically everything. . . . Well, they called them feather-bedded farmers and of course they were in those days. They had it jolly good.

A farm labourer talking about the 1950s.

Source 5B

Where I come from there are 72,000 hard working Black Country folk . . . No guaranteed prices for them . . .
There is no ill will for the farmers. We wish them well. We are anxious to have a square deal for the farmers, but we think a square deal for the housewife is getting overdue

S. N. Evans, MP for Wednesbury, 1953.

Source 5C

Total [food] production is now well over 50 per cent above pre-war, and . . . farmers are looking forward with confidence to maintaining and increasing the volume of production.

Sir Thomas Dugdale, Minister of Agriculture, 1953.

Table 3 Subsidies and profits

1947–51	Farmers received £1,200 million in subsidies.
1952	Farmers made a total profit of £883 million.

1 a Copy these headings

British Farming	
The 1930s	**The 1950s**

  b Copy this list of points under *The 1930s* heading:
  i Farming was not subsidised.
  ii Farmers found it difficult to maintain their farms and invest in new production methods.
  iii Food production was falling.
  c Under *The 1950s* heading, show how the situation had changed.

2 MPs who voted for the 1947 Agriculture Act believed it would help the whole country if farming was subsidised.
  a Why could farmers in the 1950s claim that they had used the subsidies to help the country as a whole?
  b Why did some people feel that farmers were the people who had benefited most from the subsidies?
3 After World War II, Britain's industries needed to be modernised to compete for overseas markets. Why may some people have thought that it would have been better to subsidise British manufacturing industries instead of farming?

and animals, new fertilisers, more effective pesticides and better machines were all developed. But farm labourers were still poorly paid.

Farmers and the EEC

In 1973 Britain joined the European Economic Community (EEC). Farmers' lives were now controlled by the Common Agricultural Policy (CAP), agreed by all the member states. The aim of the policy was to encourage farmers to grow enough food to feed the whole Community. So the Community fixed a price for each crop, and guaranteed to buy all that the farmers produced. This encour-

aged farmers to produce more of the most profitable crops. Many grew the same crop year after year. They kept the land fertile by using artificial fertilisers, and sprayed crops regularly to kill pests and diseases. Their machines worked best in large fields, so they created new open fields by grubbing up hedges planted by improvers 200 years ago.

It seemed that many farm animals grew quickest in confined spaces inside a building. So many pigs, hens and calves spent their lives penned up indoors.

These new methods increased crop yields. Between 1939 and 1981, yields of milk, potatoes and sugar beet per hectare doubled and yields of wheat nearly trebled.

Study

In this study your aim is to see how:
Ch farming in Britain changed between 1949 and 1986; these changes may affect Britain in the future.

You will need the information on pages 148–9.

Source 6A

Fields in Leicestershire.

Study continued

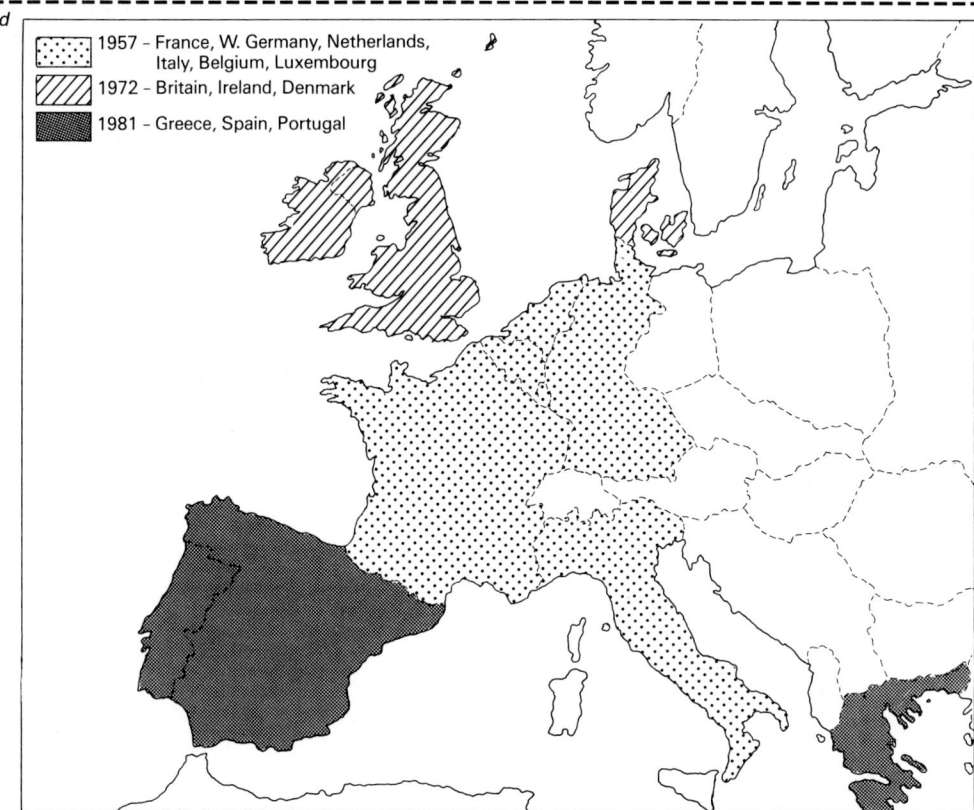

1957 – France, W. Germany, Netherlands, Italy, Belgium, Luxembourg
1972 – Britain, Ireland, Denmark
1981 – Greece, Spain, Portugal

Map 1   The EEC

Source 6B

EEC surpluses by 1986:	
butter	1.5 million tonnes
cereals	18 million tonnes
beef	600,000 tonnes
The Times, December 1986	

Source 6C
FARM MINISTERS AGREE ON SWEEPING CAP REFORMS

The Common Market's agriculture ministers finally submitted last night in Brussels to a sweeping set of reforms to two key parts of the Common Agricultural Policy – reforms which many believed they would never accept.

Following a marathon 90-hour negotiating session, Britain's Mr Michael Jopling finally steered ministers from the 12 EEC member states into accepting substantial cuts in milk production in the next two years, and radical changes to the beef sector which should make surpluses there a thing of the past.

Extract from *The Guardian*, January 1987.

1 Between 1950 and 1986 Leicestershire farmers in the area shown in Source 6A changed from mixed farming to growing cereals subsidised by the EEC. What changes did they have to make to:
the landscape shown in Source 6A;
methods used to keep the land healthy and productive?

2 a Why, after 1973, did British farmers have to obey decisions made in Brussels?
  b What evidence is there that the CAP guarantee to buy all that EEC farmers could produce led to overproduction?
  c What did the EEC ministers agree to do in December 1986 to check overproduction?

3 By 1986 many people feared that the countryside was being destroyed by farming methods that the British government and the EEC had encouraged. They wanted farmers to use less artificial fertilisers, weed killers and pesticides. This would reduce output and make crops more expensive, but they believed that chemicals harmed the soil and killed wild plants and animals.
  a What changes may you see in the British countryside if farmers continue to farm intensively?
  b What changes must you expect in the price of food if farmers stop using intensive methods of production?

Recall

1 Rewrite the list below, matching dates and events correctly.

   1838   The first frozen New Zealand lamb arrived in Britain.

   1872   The Royal Agricultural College was founded.

   1880   Britain joined the EEC.

   1973   Joseph Arch founded the Agricultural Labourers' Union.

2 Was British agriculture prosperous or depressed during these years: 1846–75; 1875–1914; 1914–39; 1939–73?

Discussion

In 1900 George Barlow farmed fifty hectares of land and employed six labourers. In 1986 his grandson, Joe, produced more food on the same amount of land and employed two labourers.

1 *In pairs* discuss:

   a Did Joe Barlow farm his land more efficiently than George?

   b Was he a better farmer than George?

   Give reasons for your answers.

2 Ask one person to give his or her answers to the class. Do the rest of you agree?

Diagram 1

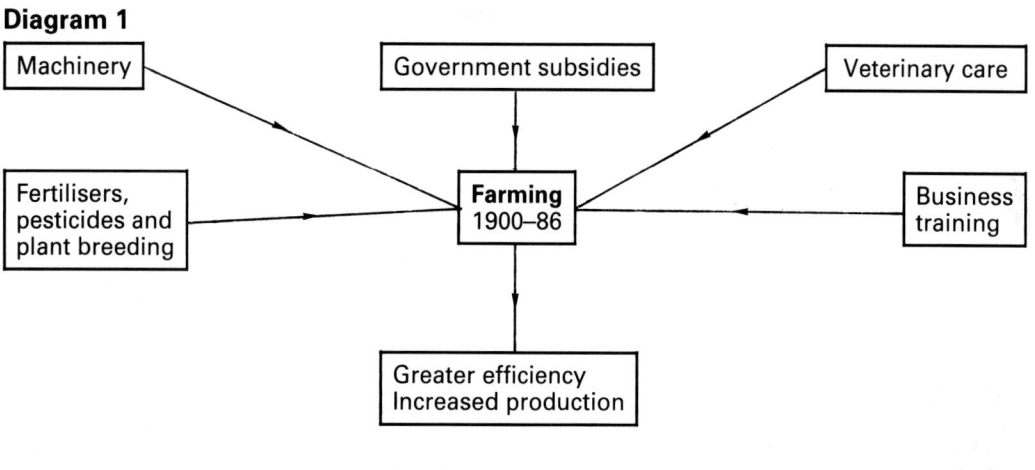

15
Developments in Industry and Trade 1851–1986

— Part One —
Power

INTRODUCTION

Since 1851, the demand for power has increased enormously. This has led to great changes in the ways power is produced and supplied.

GAS

Chronology	
1792–1802	Production of gas from coal developed by William Murdock while working for Boulton and Watt.
1805	Pall Mall in London lit by gas.
1806	First factory lit by gas.
1812	Gas Light & Coke Co. set up in London.
1834	600 miles of gas mains in London. Thereafter gas lighting quickly spread to other towns and cities.
1876	N. A. Otto, a German engineer, invented an efficient gas engine to drive machines—cheaper, cleaner and easier to use than steam engines.
1960	Natural gas discovered under the North Sea. Soon natural gas replaced coal gas in England, Wales and Scotland.

Study

Your aim in this study is:

Ch to understand how sources of Britain's gas supply have changed since the beginning of the nineteenth century.

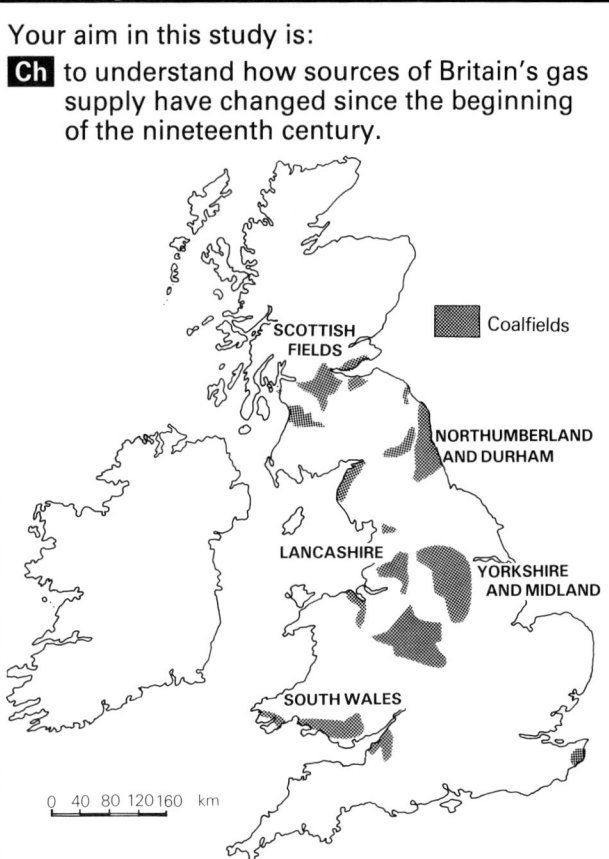

Coalfields

SCOTTISH FIELDS

NORTHUMBERLAND AND DURHAM

LANCASHIRE

YORKSHIRE AND MIDLAND

SOUTH WALES

0 40 80 120 160   km

Map 1   Main British coalfields, 1830

In the nineteenth century, Britain's gas was extracted from coal.

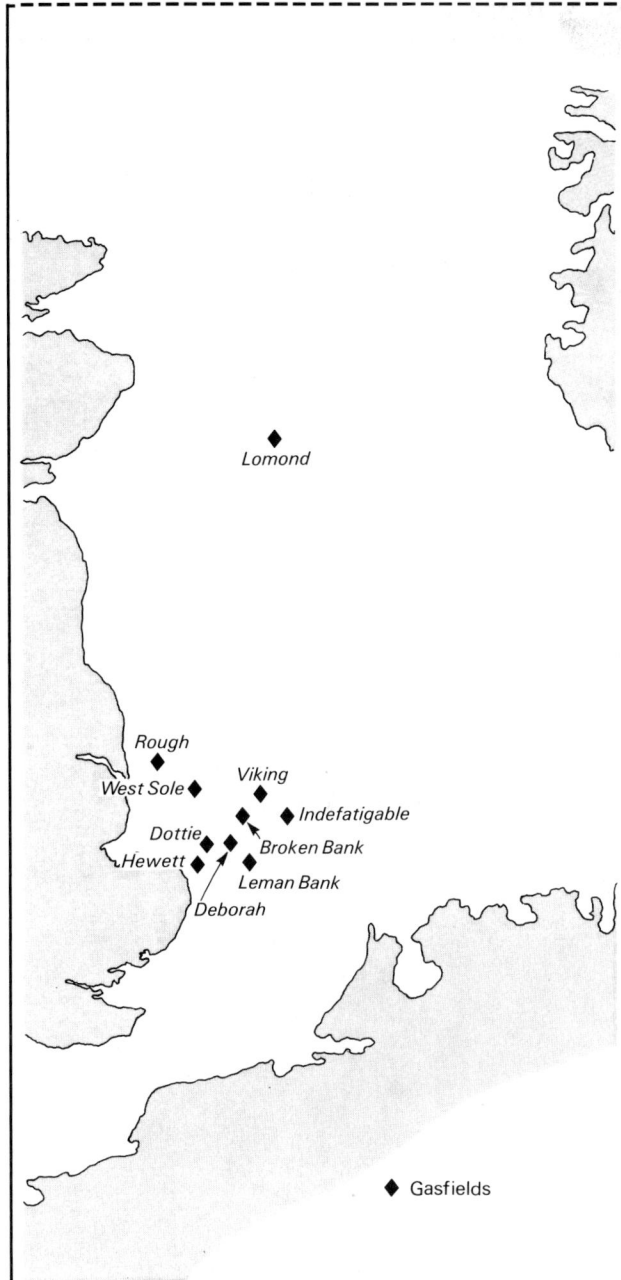

Map 2   North Sea gas fields, 1980

Since the 1960s Britain's gas has come from natural gas beds under the North Sea.

1 Why was Britain able to develop supplies of cheap gas during the nineteenth century?
2 How did the source of Britain's gas change in the second half of the twentieth century?
3 Coal and natural gas are 'fossil fuels' which took millions of years to form. How may this fact influence the amount of gas used in Britain in the second half of the twenty-first century?

ELECTRICITY

Chronology	
By 1831	Michael Faraday had succeeded in making simple model electric motors and dynamos.
1834	First small electric generators produced.
1870	Theophile Gramme invented an improved dynamo in Paris.
1879	R. E. Crompton designed a commercial dynamo, based on the Gramme design. Began to provide sets to light stations, factories and large houses.
1886	The Kensington & Knightsbridge Electric Supply Company set up to provide electricity for a whole housing estate.
1887	Sebastian de Ferranti designed a power station to produce enough electricity to light the whole of London.
1920	730,000 electricity consumers in Britain.
1923	2,000,000 electricity consumers in Britain.
1926	Electricity 'grid' planned to cover the whole country.
1938	9,000,000 electricity consumers.
1947	Electricity industry nationalised.

Driving the generators

All electric generators were driven by conventional steam engines up to 1892. In 1892 the first generator driven by a steam turbine, invented by Charles Parsons, went into service.

Now almost all the electricity produced in Britain is made by steam turbines. But three different fuels are used to produce the steam (see Diagram 1).

Diagram 1   Sources of Britain's electricity, 1985

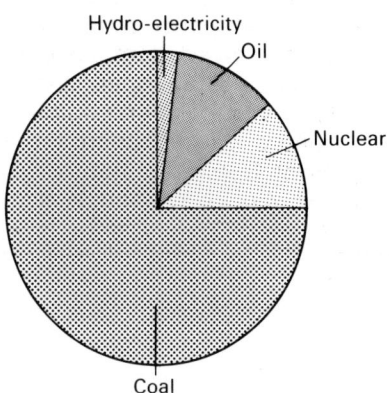

Study

In this study you will use the sources below to explore:

Ca how electrical appliances in the home changed women's lives in the twentieth century.

IMPACT OF ELECTRICITY

Electricity provides a clean, flexible, reliable source of power and light for industry. It has made industry more mobile. It has also provided power for numerous household appliances, making housework and maintenance quicker and easier.

In the home, coal, gas and wood were used for lighting and heating. Lighting was provided by gas or oil lamps which needed frequent cleaning. Cooking was done on kitcheners which constantly had to be stoked with coal or wood. Washing was done with water heated in large coppers or boilers. A well-off household might have employed a cook, scullery maid and housemaid to do the housework.

Source 1A

Washing day, 1910.

Source 1B

A 1930 Servis washing machine with power wringer.

Source 1C

I used to get to work at six in the morning and go home at half past twelve or one. I had all the cleaning to do. I had a hoover but it was hard work. I had to turn out a room every day. Washing machines weren't thought of then. The lady I worked for did all the washing by hand, and she did the cooking. They had electric light.

Ellen Mitchell, talking in 1986 of her work as a daily help in the 1930s and '40s.

Source 1D

Electric cookers made their appearance before 1914, but, like vacuum cleaners and washing machines, did not come into widespread use until about the 1950s.

R. J. Unstead, *Incredible Century* (1974).

1   Why did domestic work in 1900 involve a great deal of *i* cleaning, *ii* carrying?

2   **a** In what ways was Ellen Mitchell's job in the 1930s and '40s easier than a similar job would have been in 1900?

   b In what ways was it just as difficult?

3   **a** What evidence is there to suggest that Ellen Mitchell was wrong when she says that washing machines were not thought of in the 1930s and 40s?

   b Why, do you think, did she say there were no washing machines at that time?

4   In the 1930s most married women did not go out to work. By the 1970s many women continued going out to work after they married. How did the use of electrical appliances in the home help to bring about this change?

Study

Most forms of power damage the environment. In this study you will consider:

Ca three types of environmental damage done in the twentieth century;
ways in which further damage may be prevented.

Source 3A

Smoke from the cottage chimneys in the foreground escaped into the atmosphere. Slag from the mines was dumped on the hills in the background.

Source 3B

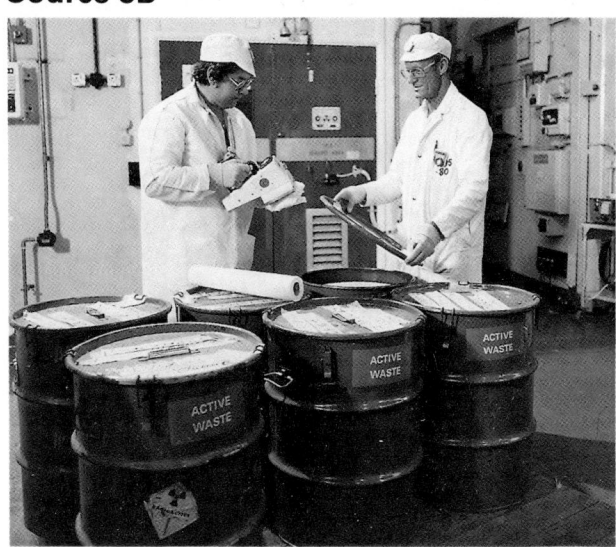

Nuclear waste stays radioactive for hundreds of years and must be sealed carefully before it is buried. This photograph shows scientists checking drums of radioactive waste at Harwell.

Source 3C

Acid rain is caused by sulphur dioxide fumes from power stations and factories. In the 1980s Britain was western Europe's biggest producer of sulphur dioxide.

In pairs

1 How are the problems shown in Sources 3A, 3B and 3C similar?
2 Which of the problems shown in the sources do you think damages the environment most:
   in the short term;
   in the long term?
   Give reasons for your answer.
3 North Sea oil will run out in the twenty-first century and Britain will have to replace it with other energy sources.
   a How might Britain provide this energy while limiting the damage to the environment?
   b What difficulties can you see in carrying out your suggestions?
4 Ask one person to give his or her answers to the class. Do the rest of you agree?

Study

In this study your aim is to see:

Ca why Britain stopped importing foreign oil in the 1970s, and why it may have to find new sources of power after AD 2000.

OIL

Chronology	
1880 onwards	Oil used as a fuel for industrial engines and to power cars and lorries.
1945–73	Plentiful supplies of cheap oil from the USA, Venezuela, and the Middle East led to more oil fuel for heating, more oil fired power stations and diesel railway engines instead of steam or electric. During this period, the world's reserves of oil, a fossil fuel, were being used up very fast.
1970	Oil discovered in North Sea.
1973–4	Oil producers quadrupled the price of oil.
1975	First North Sea oil landed in Britain.
1976–9	Oil producers doubled the price of oil.
1981	Britain self-sufficient in oil.
1986	Oil price halved. Oil provided thirty four per cent of Britain's energy needs.

Source 2

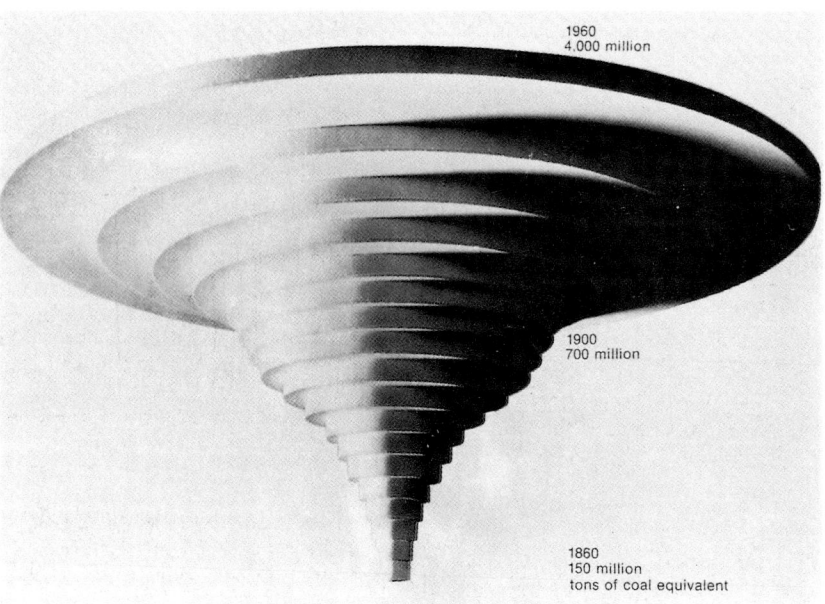

1960
4,000 million

1900
700 million

1860
150 million
tons of coal equivalent

The increasing demand for energy in Britain.

1 a Which areas supplied oil to Britain before 1975?
  b How was this oil used?
2 Why had Britain stopped importing oil from abroad by 1981?

3 Why, by the end of the twentieth century, may Britain have to:
  a import oil from abroad again;
  b find sources of power to replace oil?

Recall

1 Explain these terms in your own words: fossil fuels; natural gas; domestic appliances.
2 Why are these men famous: Sebastian de Ferranti; Theophile Gramme; N. A. Otto; Charles Parsons?
3 Why were Britain's coalfields less important as a source of power in 1980 than in 1900? Why may they be a more important source of power by the beginning of the twenty-first century?

Diagram 1

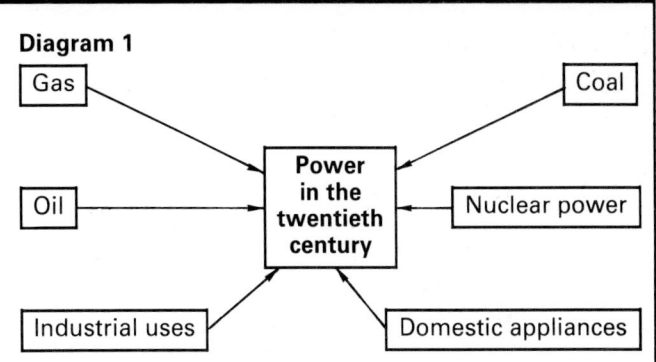

——————— Part Two ———————

Trade and Industry

1851–1914

Industry

In 1851 Britain's industries were the most up to date in the world, and were still growing. But businessmen in other countries were establishing factories. Many had toured British mills and planned their factories to take advantage of good ideas they had seen and avoid the mistakes. By 1870 foreign products were as good and as cheap as British.

By 1900, British manufacturers began to find it difficult to export their products, and increasing quantities of foreign goods were coming into Britain. In 1900 both Germany and the USA produced more steel, machinery, chemicals and electrical goods than Britain. People wondered why foreign manufacturers were doing so well. They found it was partly because many British factories were out of date and inefficient, but they also discovered other reasons (see Diagram 2).

Diagram 2   British and foreign firms: a comparison

Small British family firms had too little cash behind them.

Large foreign firms had plenty of cash.

British firms concentrated on one process: e.g. spinning or weaving or dyeing—slow and expensive. Many foreign firms carried out all the processes in one factory—quick and cheap.

Successful foreign competition.

British firms did not like change—rejected new ideas.
Foreign firms welcomed new ideas.

Illustration 1   The Krupp steel works at Essen in Germany in 1880. Krupp had his own coal mine and owned iron ore deposits.

Study

In this study you will use primary sources to:

S compare British and foreign industrialists at the beginning of the twentieth century;
consider how the attitudes of British industrialists may have helped foreign rivals to overtake them.

Source 4A

In America the manufacturer works *with* his men . . . There the man is colleague of his master, and they run the machine together.

British research report on American industry, c1900.

Source 4B

. . . the German's love of work, love of business . . . plus his thoroughness and scientific training [make him] a menace to easier-going rivals.

The *Daily Mail*, 1902. The reporter had been sent to Germany to find out why German industry was doing so well.

1 Why may the British researcher in America have been so surprised to see American manufacturers working alongside their men?
2 What impression does the *Daily Mail* reporter give of British manufacturers? Give reasons for your answer.
3 How may the way in which British manufacturers treated their work and workers have helped their foreign rivals to overtake them?

Study

In this study you will use the information in the tables to:

Ch work out changes in the pattern of British trade between 1850 and 1914.

Table 1 Principal exports

Goods	1850 Value £m	%	1911 Value £m	%
Textiles	60	60	126	38
Iron and steel	18	18	46	14
Machinery	2	2	24	7
Coal	2	2	33	10

Table 2 Principal imports

Goods	1850 Value £m	%	1911 Value £m	%
Food	49	30	179	32
Raw textiles	50	30	107	19
Other raw materials	26	16	77	14
Manufactured goods	3	2	32	6

Table 3 Overall trade (£ millions)

	Imports	Exports	Invisible exports
1851	116	89	35
1871	201	144	130
1891	227	182	182
1911	489	394	394

Invisible exports consisted mostly of:
a money earned abroad by British ships, insurance companies and banks;
b the interest paid to Britons on money invested abroad.
(British shipping contributed most. In 1913 British ships earned £200 million.)

1 In 1911, which goods formed:
a higher percentage of Britain's exports;
a lower percentage of Britain's exports
than they had in 1850?
2 What reasons can you suggest to explain why, by 1911:
raw textiles and other raw materials formed a lower percentage of Britain's imports than in 1850;
food formed a higher percentage than in 1850?
3 Between 1851 and 1911, Britain's trade with the outside world continued to grow.
a During that period, which increased more:
exports;
invisible exports?
b Throughout the period 1851–1911, Britain's imports cost more than its exports earned. How was Britain able to pay for the imports it needed?

1914–1939

World War I (1914–18)

During World War I the country needed more war supplies such as uniforms, guns, ammunition, chemicals, lorries, tanks, ships and aircraft (Illustration 2). Factories in Britain had to work flat out to produce what was needed, and some industrialists made fortunes. Towards the end of the war, government ministers tried to persuade them to prepare for peace by:

1 combining small firms into larger groups;
2 training managers;
3 learning how to sell goods effectively;
4 re-equipping out-of-date factories with new machinery.

Most manufacturers took no notice. When trade was brisk they said they did not need new machines. When trade was slack they said they could not afford them.

The war disrupted Britain's trade. Exports fell sharply. In 1919 they were only sixty five per cent of what they had been in 1913. This was very serious, because invisible exports had also fallen. During the war fourteen per cent of Britain's merchant fleet was sunk, and the government had to sell some of the country's overseas investments to pay for imports needed for the war effort.

The effects of the slump

In 1920 there was a sudden slump in trade. British firms were hit hard because they were less efficient than overseas rivals. Between 1922 and 1929 trade improved, but in 1929 there was another world-wide slump which lasted for almost ten years. During the slump Britain's exports fell.

Table 4   Exports as percentage of 1913 figure

1920–4	75
1925–9	84
1930–4	60
1935–8	66

At the same time, imports rose. This was partly because Britain was a free trade country. Other countries took advantage of this. They paid bounties (subsidies) to their manufacturers to export goods to Britain. So their exports were very cheap and sold well in Britain. Often they under-cut the price of British goods.

The result of this process, known as 'dumping', was that foreign factories were busy making goods for the British market, while British factories closed down because they could not compete with 'dumped' imports.

Britain's old-established industries such as iron and steel, shipbuilding, coal and cotton all suffered, and more than three million workers lost their jobs, many of them in the areas such as South Wales, north-east England and central Scotland where the coal, steel and shipbuilding industries had grown up. Some parts of Britain remained quite prosperous because 'new' industries such as manufacturing cars, chemicals, aircraft and electrical goods developed. But Britain's major industries did not recover until the country began to re-arm in preparation for World War II.

Illustration 2   Many women went to work in munitions factories in World War I.

Study

The 1930s were a time of mass unemployment. Your aim in this study is to use the information in the maps below and on page 159 to help you to consider:

Ca why so many people were out of work

S why there were more people out of work in some regions than in others.

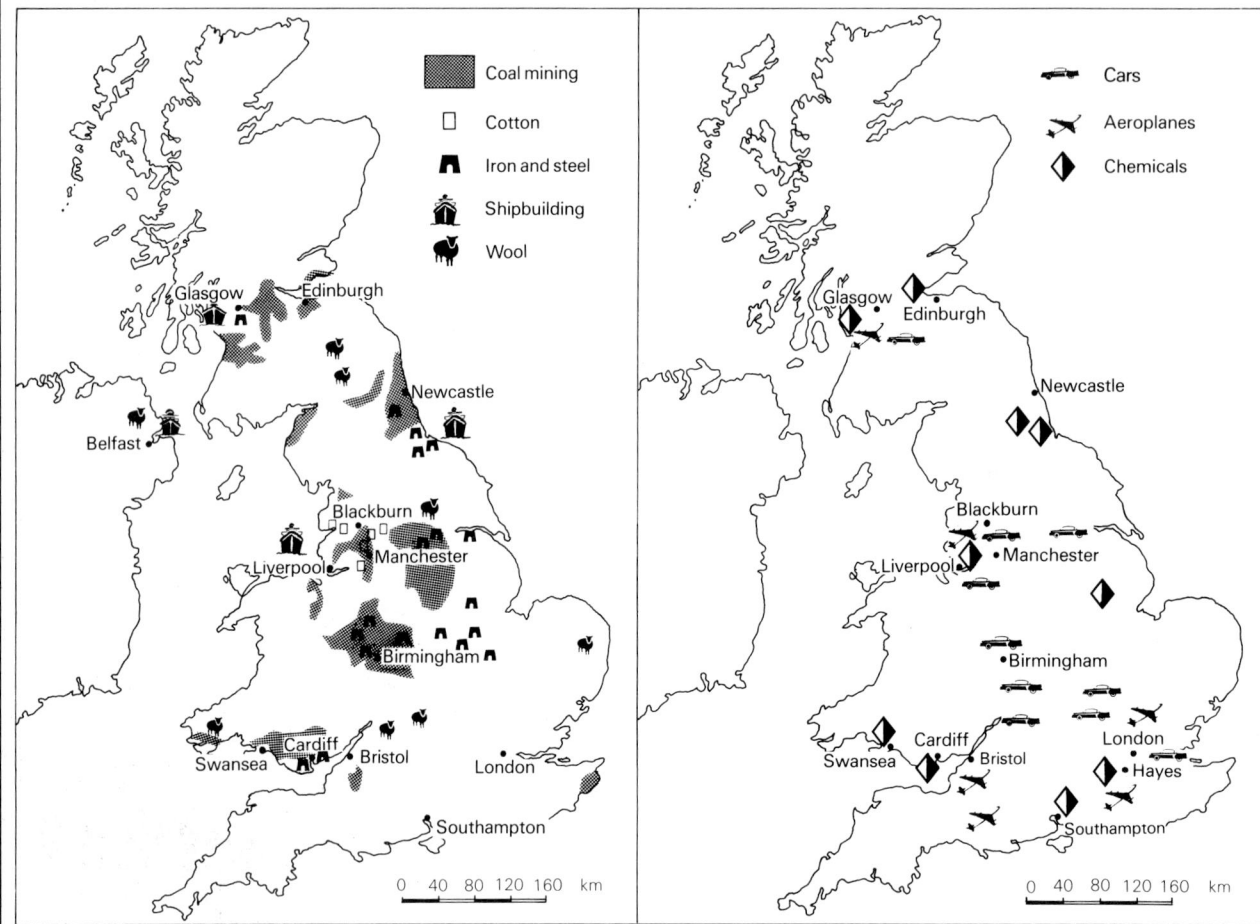

Map 3   Britain's old industries

Map 4   Britain's new industries

1 Name three regions of Britain where, in the 1930s, you would expect:
   a high level of unemployment;
   a low level of unemployment.
   Give reasons for your answer.
2 A number of reasons for the high level of unemployment are listed below.
   a British factories were not modernised after World War I ended and were inefficient compared with foreign factories.
   b Investments overseas were sold during World War I, so the value of Britain's invisible exports dropped.
   c There was a slump from 1920 to 1922 and another from 1929 to 1936.
   d Trade improved during the period 1922–29.
   e Britain had been a free trade country since 1860 so British manufacturers had no protection from foreign competitors who

   'dumped' subsidised goods in Britain in the 1930s.
   f After World War I the British government encouraged manufacturers to modernise but would not give them subsidies to do so.

   Rewrite the list under these headings:

Causes of unemployment in the 1930s	
Long term	Short term

   Leave out any items on the list that you think did NOT cause unemployment.
3 During the 1930s many people believed that there would be less unemployment if the coal, steel and shipbuilding industries were nationalised. Explain why they believed this.

Study

The end of free trade

In this study you will:

Em consider the overseas trade policy of British governments in the 1930s through the eyes of businessmen in Britain and abroad.

Remember what you have learned about British trade 1850–1930.

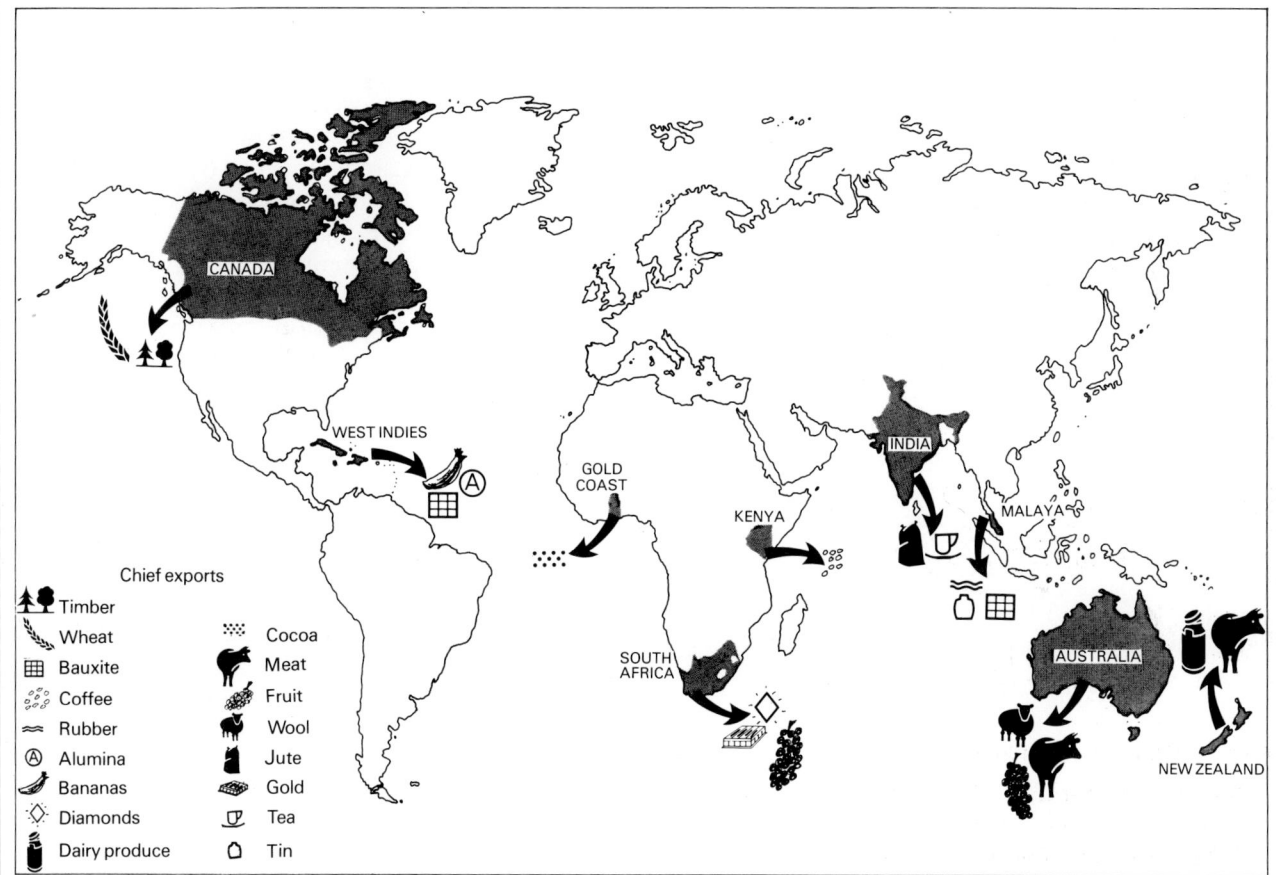

Map 5   The British Empire in the 1930s

Table 5   Government policy 1931–39

1931	The government made imports dearer and exports cheaper by reducing the value of the pound.
1932	A tariff (customs duty) of twenty per cent was put on most imported goods.
1937	At the Ottawa conference, Britain agreed to *imperial preference*, that is to charge lower tariffs on goods imported from the Empire.

1 Would you expect each of the following to have welcomed or disliked the trading policy of British governments in the 1930s? Give reasons for your answers.
   a A British manufacturer of electrical goods.
   b An American car manufacturer.
   c A Polish coal exporter.
   d A Hong Kong cotton manufacturer.
   e A New Zealand butter exporter.

1939–1985

Industry

During World War II (1939–45) the government controlled all aspects of industry, including wages and prices. The shipbuilding, heavy engineering, steel and coal industries all recovered and unemployment disappeared. After the war unemployment remained low and wages increased. This meant that people could afford to buy all that factories could produce.

The export boom

During the war Britain sold most of her remaining overseas investments, and got into debt to countries which supplied the arms, oil and foodstuffs needed during the war. After the war, to pay off this debt, Britain had to try to export more goods than she imported, so factories were busy producing goods for export.

At first the only serious competition came from the USA. Most of Europe's industries had been destroyed in the war, and Far Eastern countries, such as Japan and Korea, had no exporting industries. So British factories were able to export goods to Europe. In 1950, twenty five per cent of the world's manufactured goods came from Britain.

The growth of competition

Between 1950 and 1960 the situation changed. Industrialists in Europe and the Far East began to produce goods cheaper than they could be made in Britain. At the same time British colonies, which had always bought most of their goods from Britain, became independent and began to buy from other countries. In 1961 the proportion of the world's manufacturing goods coming from Britain fell to sixteen per cent. By 1970 it had reached nine per cent. In order to survive, Britain's industries had to compete with overseas manufacturers.

The effects of competition

Many British firms found it very difficult to compete. They were too small to afford up-to-date machinery, which was very expensive. Some firms combined with their rivals to form new, much larger companies. They closed down small, inefficient factories and put money into new buildings, equipped with the latest machinery. To cut costs, many workers had to be dismissed and others had to change their working methods to suit new machines. Unemployment began to increase. Some old industries, such as shipbuilding, could not cope with cut-price competition from the Far East. Almost all the British shipyards closed down. The steel and motor industries had to cut down in size. Some new industries, based on computers, began to develop, but they could not make up for the decline of the rest.

Study

In this study you will consider:

Ca the connection between the level of demand for British manufactured goods and the level of employment in Britain 1939–1980.

You will need the information on pages 160–2.

1 Why was there very little unemployment in Britain between 1939 and 1950?
2 Why would you expect the level of unemployment to have:
   risen slowly between 1950 and 1970;
   risen rapidly between 1970 and 1980?

3 Why would you expect fewer people to be employed in manufacturing industries in the year 2000 than there were in 1950, even if the demand for British manufactured goods increases by the end of the century?

Study

Trading links with Europe

One of the most important decisions that Britain had to make in the second half of the twentieth century was whether or not to join the European Economic Community (EEC).

Your aim in this study is:

K to understand why this decision was so important.

Background information

1939–45   *World War II.* Many homes and factories throughout Europe were destroyed, and millions of people were killed.

1951   *Treaty of Paris.* Six countries set up the European Coal and Steel Community (ECSC). Tariffs were removed from all coal, iron and steel traded between member states. This free trade experiment was a success.

1957   *Treaty of Rome.* The countries of the ECSC set up the European Economic Community (EEC).

The aims of the EEC were:
   to set up a 'Common Market' within which all goods would be traded duty-free;
   to set targets for agricultural production;
   to set up a customs union to protect the EEC from foreign competition;
   to share the cost of developing atomic energy.

The rules governing the EEC were made by representatives of the member states meeting in Brussels, not in the national parliaments.

Many people thought that eventually the EEC would develop into a United States of Europe.

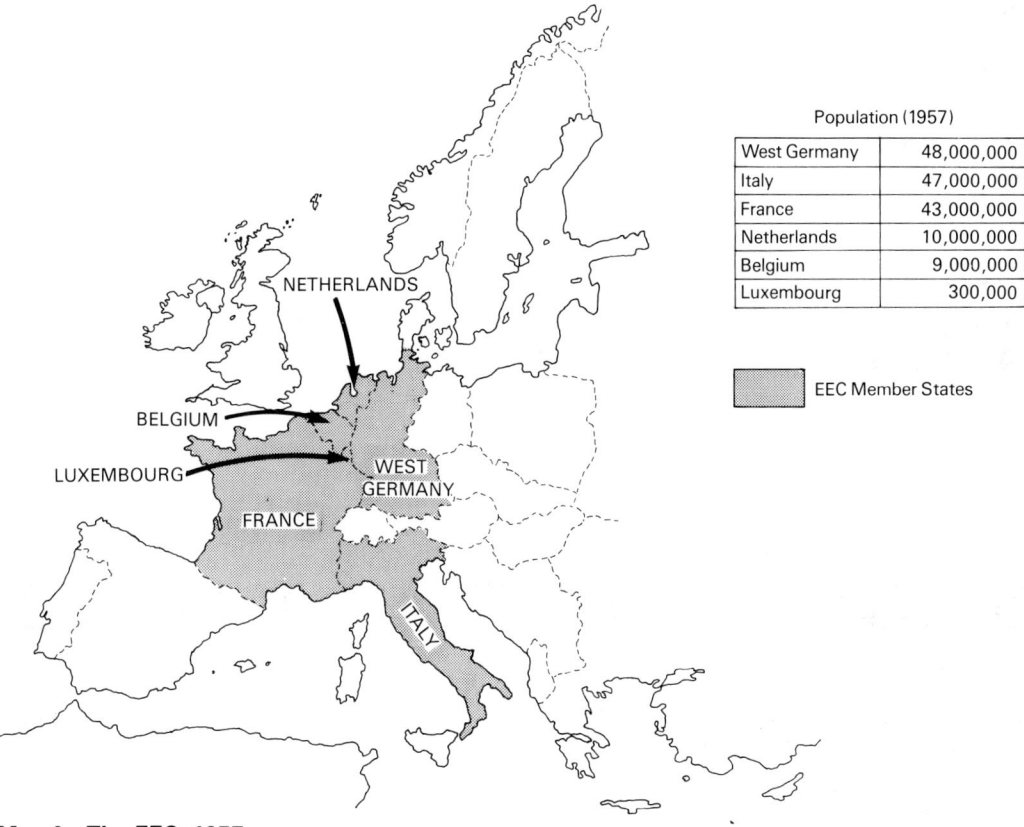

Population (1957)	
West Germany	48,000,000
Italy	47,000,000
France	43,000,000
Netherlands	10,000,000
Belgium	9,000,000
Luxembourg	300,000

EEC Member States

Map 6   The EEC, 1957

1 a Which six countries formed the ECSC in 1951?

b Suggest reasons why they decided to form the EEC in 1957.

c Would you expect the formation of the EEC to help or hinder Britain's trade with Europe? Give reasons for your answer.

Study continued

In the 1950s Britain had strong trading links with Commonwealth countries. For example, New Zealand exported butter to Britain and imported British manufactured goods. This trade helped to hold the Commonwealth together. British governments did not want Britain to become a full member of the EEC. Instead Britain applied for *associate* membership which might have given some of the advantages of full membership.

2 a What was the total population of the EEC in 1957 (Map 6)?

b What advantages may Britain have hoped to gain from associate membership?

c Suggest reasons why the government might not have wanted full membership.

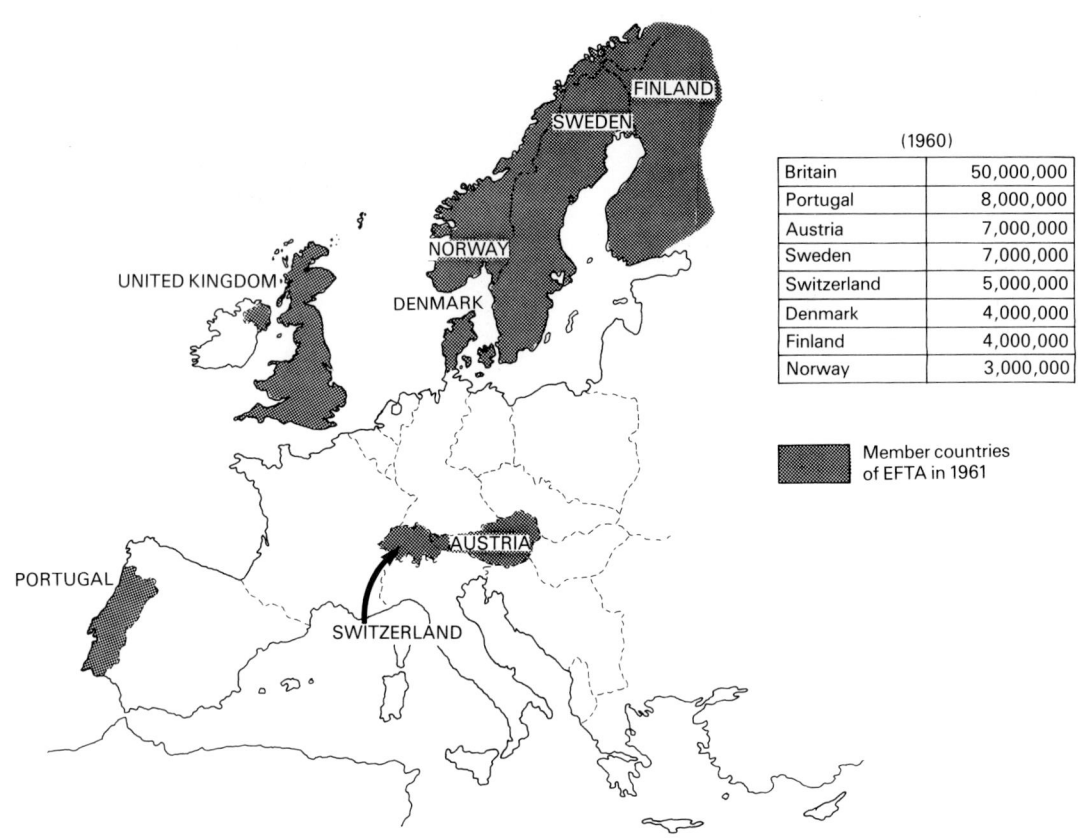

(1960)	
Britain	50,000,000
Portugal	8,000,000
Austria	7,000,000
Sweden	7,000,000
Switzerland	5,000,000
Denmark	4,000,000
Finland	4,000,000
Norway	3,000,000

Member countries of EFTA in 1961

Map 7   The European Free Trade Association, 1960

Britain's application for associate membership was refused because it seemed that the British did not wholeheartedly support the aims of the EEC.

In 1959 Britain and seven other countries set up the European Free Trade Association (EFTA). In spite of this, Britain applied for *full* membership of the EEC in 1961 and 1967.

3 a Which seven countries formed EFTA in 1959?

b What was the total population of EFTA's member states?

c Why may Britain have applied for full membership of the EEC even though it belonged to EFTA?

In 1973 Britain joined the EEC as a full member. In 1975 this decision was confirmed by a referendum, in which every citizen had the right to vote.

4 a Suggest reasons why the majority of voters were in favour of remaining a full member of the EEC.

b Why may opponents of membership have believed it would harm Britain?

c As a result of the referendum, Britain decided to remain a full member of the EEC. Why was this decision so important?

Summing up

Britain's trade can now only be kept in balance by the earnings of banks and insurance companies, and by exports of North Sea oil. Oil exports have provided Britain with money to invest overseas. When the oil eventually runs out the interest on these investments will be essential to help to balance the country's trade with the rest of the world.

Recall

1 Explain these terms in your own words: invisible exports; bounties; dumping; imperial preference.
2 Rewrite the list below, matching dates and events correctly.

1931	For the first time in 200 years, Britain imported more manufactured goods than it exported.
1932	Britain helped to form EFTA.
1959	The Ottawa Conference agreed to imperial preference.
1985	Britain ceased to be a free trade country.

3 How and why did Britain's share of world trade change between 1880 and 1985?

Diagram 3

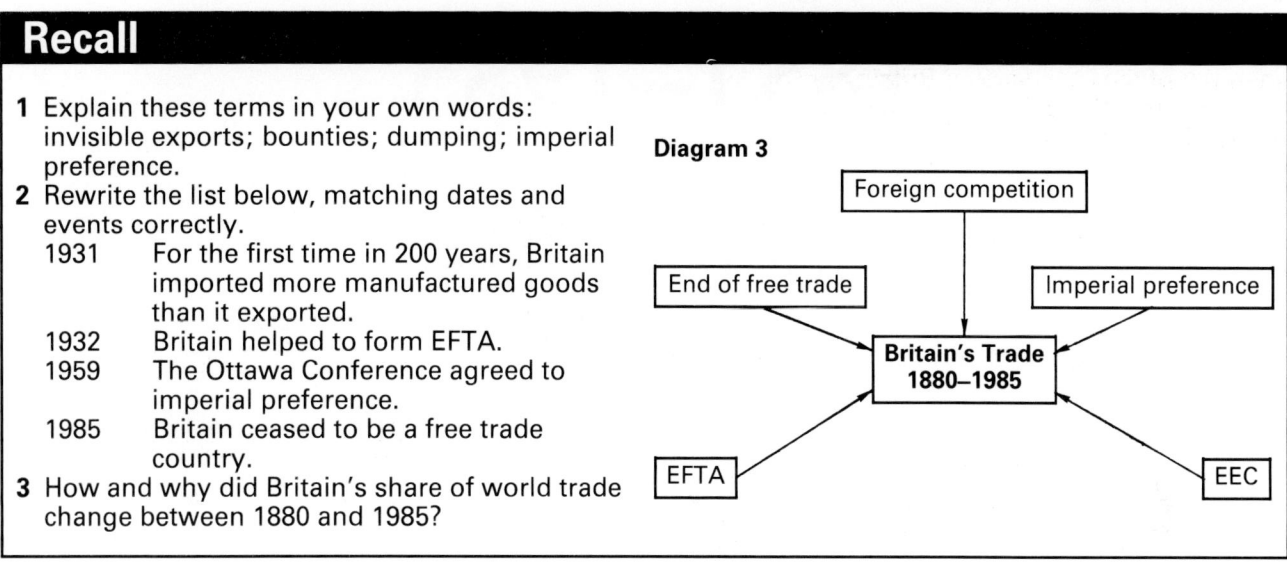

16
The Traditional Industries 1851–1985

Part One
Coal 1851–1985

THE PATTERN OF DEMAND 1851–1939

Between 1851 and 1913 the demand for British coal grew. After 1913 the demand for British coal fell.

During World War I (1914–18) Britain exported no coal, and after 1919 coal owners found that many of their old overseas customers were buying from Germany and Poland. So the export trade was halved. Other coal-users also needed less. Modern steamships burned oil, which was clean and easy to load, instead of coal, and in 1938, modern gasworks used less than half as much coal as in 1913 to produce a unit of gas.

Diagram 1

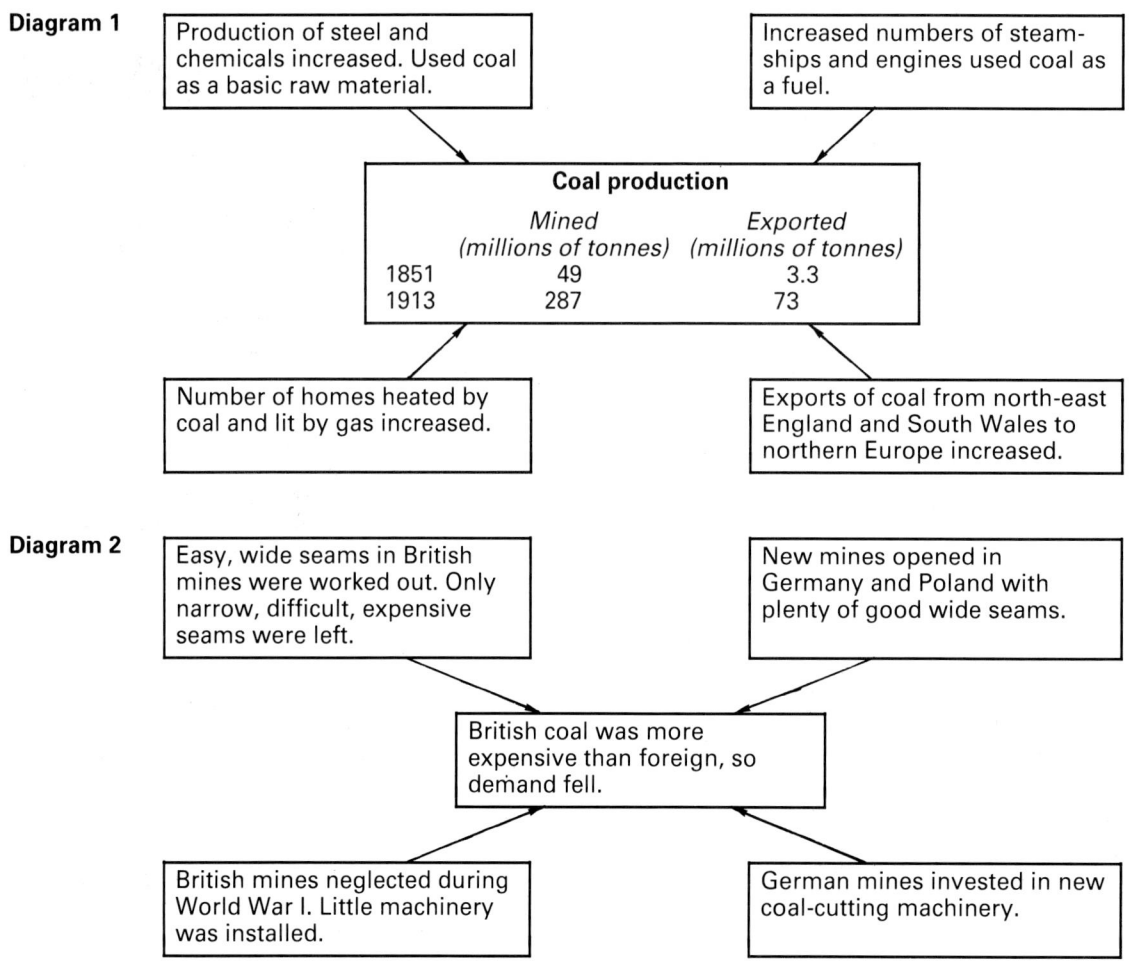

Production of steel and chemicals increased. Used coal as a basic raw material.

Increased numbers of steam-ships and engines used coal as a fuel.

Coal production

	Mined (millions of tonnes)	Exported (millions of tonnes)
1851	49	3.3
1913	287	73

Number of homes heated by coal and lit by gas increased.

Exports of coal from north-east England and South Wales to northern Europe increased.

Diagram 2

Easy, wide seams in British mines were worked out. Only narrow, difficult, expensive seams were left.

New mines opened in Germany and Poland with plenty of good wide seams.

British coal was more expensive than foreign, so demand fell.

British mines neglected during World War I. Little machinery was installed.

German mines invested in new coal-cutting machinery.

Study

This study aims to help you:

Ch understand why the demand for British coal changed between 1851 and 1939.

1 Why did the amount of coal mined in Britain incease between 1851 and 1913 (Diagram 1)?
2 How did the situation of the British coal industry during World War I lead to a fall in the demand for coal when the war ended (Diagram 2)?

3 By 1920 it was cheaper for Britain to buy some types of coal from Germany and Poland than to buy British coal. Explain why.

BETWEEN THE WARS 1919–39

The 1919 commission

During World War I the government took control of the mines. In 1919 they appointed a commission under Lord Sankey to enquire into the industry. A majority of the commissioners recommended that the mines should be nationalised and brought up to date. The government did not take their advice. In 1921 they handed the mines back to their original owners, who could not afford to modernise them.

The 1921 lockout

Many mine owners could not make a profit. Some sold their pits, or joined with other owners to form combines. In 1921, to cut the cost of coal, they reduced miners' pay. The miners refused to work for less so the owners locked them out. Railwaymen and transport workers promised to strike in support of the miners, but at the last moment they changed their minds. The miners could not win on their own. After being locked out for more than two months they accepted a pay cut and went back to work.

Illustration 1   A Kent miner working a seam about a metre thick in 1935.

The 1925 subsidy

In 1925 the owners asked the miners to accept another cut in pay. The miners refused. The owners threatened to lock them out. The Trades Union Congress (TUC) promised to help the miners, and ordered trade unionists not to move coal from the pits to the factories. This alarmed the government. To prevent the lockout they paid the owners a subsidy on condition that they did not cut miners' pay until a royal commission had investigated the industry.

Study

Your aim in this study is to use the information on pages 166–7:

Em to consider the disputes in the coal industry, 1921–1925, from the points of view of the people involved.

1 a Why may the Sankey Commission have decided that the mines should be nationalised in 1921?
  b Why may the government have ignored the Commission and handed the mines back to their original owners?
2 a Why may the owners have believed that miners would be better off in the long run if they accepted a pay cut in 1921?
  b Suggest reasons why the miners abandoned their strike and accepted the pay cut.
3 a What may the owners have hoped to achieve when they threatened to lock out the miners in 1925?
  b Why, do you think, was the government alarmed when the TUC told trade unionists not to move coal from the mines to the factories?
  c Suggest reasons why many miners in 1925 thought they had been badly treated since the end of World War I.

The General Strike 1926

Chronology	
March	*The Royal Commission* recommended a pay cut. *The owners* said miners must work longer hours for less pay.
April	*The Miners' Union* secretary, A. J. Cook, said, 'Not a penny off the pay, not a minute on the day.' The owners locked the miners out.
3 May	The TUC called a General Strike of transport workers, printers, electricians, builders and gas workers to support the miners. Volunteers from the public kept the country going (Illustration 2).
12 May	All the unions, except the miners', called the strike off.
November	The miners called off the strike and agreed to accept lower wages. The owners ended the lockout.
1927	The Trades Disputes Act made general strikes illegal.

It was ten years before the miners' union was strong enough to put in another wage claim.

Illustration 2   Volunteers unloading milk churns during the General Strike.

Study

In this study you will:

Ev consider what Sources 1A and 1B can tell us about the mine owners' attitude to the miners during and after the 1926 General Strike.

Refer also to the Chronology table on this page.

Source 1A

There was the manager standing there. 'Come on you, come on you.' And a gang of lads they would take. They knew everything. To those that had been militant, 'You're not to come, get off, nothing for you' . . . I knew families that never did get back after the '26 strike.

A Nottinghamshire miner, describing what happened when men at his pit returned to work in November 1926.

Source 1B

Why did the miners' lock-out last so long? The intransigence [refusal to compromise] of the miners certainly did not encourage them to go back to work. But even more important was the fact that the government . . . seemed uninterested in putting pressure on the mine owners to offer terms that would make . . . [a] speedy return to work more likely. The owners were even more unreasonable . . . They were determined not only to drive the miners back on the worst terms possible but to destroy the [Miners' Union] too.

Patrick Renshaw, *The General Strike* (1975).

1 Give two or more reasons why the miners were worse off after the General Strike than they were before.

2 Does Source 1A prove that mine managers victimised miners who took part in the strike? Give reasons for your answer.

3 a For how long were the miners locked out by the owners?

   b In Source 1B Patrick Renshaw says *why* the lockout lasted so long. Do you think that he is:

   giving an opinion based on very little evidence;

   making a considered judgment based on reliable evidence?

Give reasons for your answer.

Study

Increased mechanisation

Your aim in this study is:

S to compare mechanisation in British and German pits from 1929 to 1939.

Source 2A Percentage of coal cut by machine

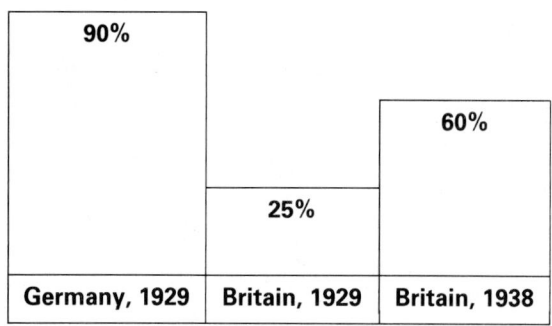

Germany, 1929	Britain, 1929	Britain, 1938
90%	25%	60%

Source 2B The Coal Mines Act 1930

The government promised to pay owners a subsidy to modernise their pits.

Source 2C

It was all hand got, pick and shovel, sledge and wedge . . . There were no machines at all. A man and a boy could fill about five or six tons of coal in a shift . . . It was graft. We used to go home too tired to eat our food.

A British miner talking about his work.

Source 2D

A coal-cutting machine at Ashington colliery in the mid 1930s.

1 Consider:
  a the headings under which you might compare conditions in British and German mines;
  b the best way to arrange your information;
  c any other information in the sources that you think you should include.
2 Write an essay comparing mechanisation in British and German pits, 1929–39.

1939–1985

Bevin boys

When war broke out the number of miners fell. Some were called up to serve in the armed forces, and others left the mines to get better paid jobs in new war industries. In 1942 the amount of coal produced fell to 204 million tonnes. This was not enough. The government had to increase the number of miners. So Ernest Bevin, the Minister of Labour, increased miners' pay, and sent men conscripted to serve in the army to work in the pits instead. In all there were 22,000 of these 'Bevin boys'.

Coal is nationalised

By the end of the war Britain's mines were in a bad state. They needed new machinery and equipment to bring them up to date. The privately owned mining companies had no money to spare. In 1946 the Labour government decided to nationalise them, and set up the National Coal Board (NCB) to manage the mines (see Source 3A).

The NCB made a bad start. In 1947 there was a very cold winter, and coal stocks ran out. But the Board spent millions of pounds on new machinery to re-equip the pits. By 1950 the output of coal was beginning to rise. Within a few years the mines were producing enough coal for the country's needs.

Study

In this study you will:

Ch consider change and continuity in the coal industry after nationalisation in 1947.

Source 3A

The coal industry was nationalised in 1947.

Source 3B

A Coal Board poster.

Source 3C

We suddenly had enough capital [from the NCB] to do things which we needed to do and should have done many years before. We mechanised everything we could lay our hands on, and we had very full co-operation from the union.

Philip Weekes, manager of a mine in South Wales in 1947.

Source 3D

The first day the men bathed . . . They were singing and shouting. They issued us with carbolic soap. And the smell was great. And I went home nice and clean . . . Because before that I used to have a bath in front of the fire in the old tin bath.

William Young, a miner, talking about the pit-head bath installed by the NCB.

Source 3E

We all assembled . . . The manager came to a point in the colliery and he said, 'This is your colliery' . . . Nothing was further from the truth. We still had to work for our living. The manager was the same manager, he would still make the decisions, good or bad.

Dick Brown, a South Wales miner, talking about 1 January 1947.

1 In what ways did the situation in the mines remain unchanged after nationalisation?
2 What changes did the NCB bring about in the pits when the mines were nationalised in January 1947?
3 What impression did the NCB's propaganda (Sources 3A and 3B) give in 1947 of miners' prospects for the future? Give reasons for your answer.

The decline of the coal industry

Diagram 3

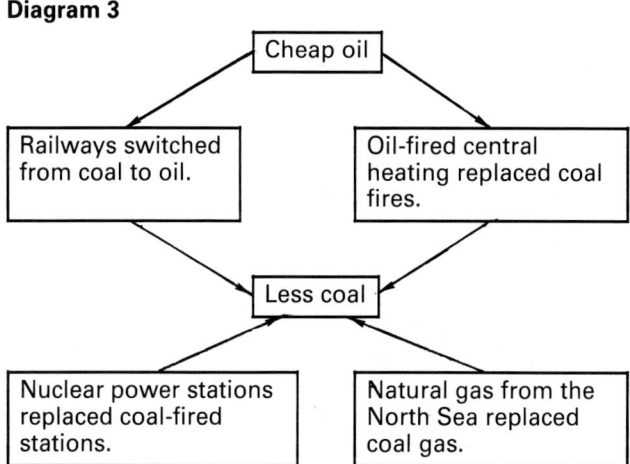

After 1960 the demand for coal began to fall. The NCB, under Lord Robens, their chairman from 1961 to 1971, closed down pits where coal was expensive to mine, put new machinery into others, and persuaded miners to accept lower pay increases than other workers.

Miners' strikes

At first the miners co-operated with the NCB, but in 1972 and 1974 under the leadership of Joe Gormley, President of the National Union of Mineworkers (NUM), they went on strike for higher pay. Without coal, power stations could not produce enough electricity to keep industry working, and eventually the miners won their extra pay.

The plan for coal

In 1973 the price of oil suddenly increased. This made coal more competitive and in 1974 the NCB, the government and the NUM agreed on a *plan for coal*: output would be increased by opening new mines and re-equipping old ones. Then North Sea oil began to come ashore, and demand for coal fell again. As a result the Board wanted to close down more pits. The NUM opposed this because most people living in pit villages depend on the mines for their living. When a mine closes the villagers have to leave to look for work, and the village slowly dies.

The 1984 strike

In 1984 the NUM called a strike to prevent the Board from closing down so-called 'uneconomic' pits. But some miners refused to strike and the coal they produced, together with stocks and imports, was enough to keep the coal-fired power stations going. So the strike failed, and the Board went ahead with its plan to close uneconomic pits.

In the long term the future for the coal industry is bright. Britain still has huge reserves of coal. The country will need them when North Sea oil runs out.

Study

During the 1950s there was a good relationship between the NCB and the NUM. Your aim in this study is to consider:

Ca why changes in demand for coal helped to cause disagreements between the NCB and the NUM;

the results of these disagreements.

1 a Why did the demand for coal:
   fall between 1961 and 1971;
   rise in 1973?
   b Why will the demand for coal probably rise after the year 2000?
2 a How did the NCB deal with:
   the fall in demand for coal 1961–71;
   the rise in demand by 1973;
   the fall in demand by the early 1980s?
   b What demands did the leaders of the NUM make when the union went on strike in 1974 and 1984?

3 a Suggest reasons why the leaders of the NUM thought that they could lead a successful strike in *i* 1974; *ii* 1984?
   b Why was:
   the 1974 strike successful;
   the 1984 strike unsuccessful?

Study

Your aim in this study is to:

Em work out some of the effects that pit closures 1985–6 had on mining communities in South Wales.

Table 1   South Wales pit closures, 1984–8

Number of pits		Miners employed	
1984	1988	1984	1988
26	11	c. 21,000	c. 10,000

Source 4A

There are 33 unemployed for every job offered in this part of Glamorgan. Only three or four men get on the morning buses into the Bridgend factory estates, and they sit hemmed in by the wives and daughters of their former pitmates who are, increasingly, the breadwinners of Garw.

Brian James, reporting on conditions in the village of Garw, *The Times*, 23 December 1986.

Table 2

Jobs lost	New developments
16 Welsh pits closed.	*Small industries* (e.g. electronics and furniture).
43,000 miners made redundant.	*Tourist attractions* (e.g. a Rhondda Heritage Park).

Source 4B

Had a few months sitting about on £48 a week dole, watching my payment for 17 years of my life slipping away. Thought the only thing worth investing in was myself. I am working all hours, but with £5,000 in stock and a lot more in tools, if this goes, I'm in trouble.

Ray Bennett, an ex-miner who used his redundancy pay to set up a tyre workshop. Reported in *The Times*, 23 December 1986.

This imaginary family might have lived in a South Wales mining village in 1985.

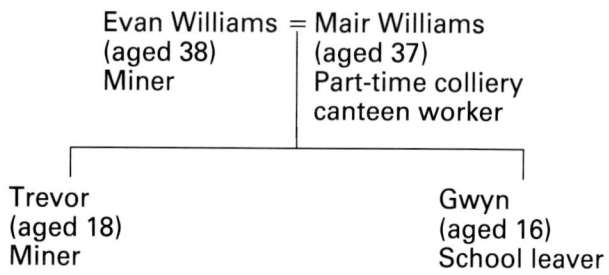

When the 1984 strike began, Evan Williams had worked as a machine operator at the local colliery for twenty two years. When the pit closed he was given £20,000 redundancy pay.

1 a Using the sources above, and your imagination, make brief notes on the way in which you think the life of each member of the family may have changed as a result of the closure of the colliery in 1985.
   b Ask one person to read his or her notes to the class. What do the rest of you think?
2 What reasons can you suggest to explain why the 1984 miners' strike was strongly supported in South Wales?
3 Write an essay on *Changes in a South Wales mining community: 1984 and after.*

—————— Part Two ——————

Iron and Steel

BESSEMER, SIEMENS AND GILCHRIST THOMAS

Henry Bessemer

Between 1851 and 1880 the British iron and steel industry continued to develop, due mostly to the work of Henry Bessemer (1813–98). He was the son of a French refugee, and made his living as an inventor. During the Crimean War (1854–6) he invented a new gun, but as it was made of iron, it quickly wore out. He wanted to make his gun of steel, which is purer and tougher, but steel was very expensive. So Bessemer tried to find a cheap and reliable way to convert iron into steel.

Study

Your aim in this study is to use various sources to:

Ch consider change and continuity in the steel industry in the second part of the nineteenth century.

Remember what you have learned about Henry Cort and the puddling process.

Table 3

1856	*Henry Bessemer* invented a *converter* which changed molten iron into mild steel by blowing hot air through it to remove impurities.
1857	*Robert Mushet*, an ironmaster, improved Bessemer's process by adding manganese.
	As a result of Bessemer's and Mushet's work, the price of steel fell from £60 a tonne to £13 a tonne.
1866	*William Siemens*, an engineer, developed the *open-hearth* process which made steel by running molten iron into shallow troughs and blasting it with a mixture of hot air and coal gas.
	Siemen's open hearth took longer than Bessemer's converter, but produced better steel.

Source 5A

A Bessemer steel plant at Ebbw Vale, 1860.

Source 5B

Iron puddlers at work, making a cylinder for HMS *Agincourt*.

Source 5C

In one compact mass we had as much metal as could be produced by two puddlers and their two assistants working arduously for hours with an expenditure of much fuel. We had obtained a pure . . . 10 inch [25 cm] ingot as the result of thirty minutes blowing, wholly unaccompanied by skilled labour or the employment of fuel.

Henry Bessemer, *Autobiography* (1897).

1 a How did the process shown in Source 5A remove impurities from iron?
   b How did the process shown in Source 5B remove impurities from iron?
2 Why could manufacturers who changed to using the process shown in Source 5A afford to reduce the price of steel?
3 a What advantage did Siemens's open hearth process have over the process shown in Source 5A?
   b Why may many steel makers have continued to use the process shown in Source 5A after the open hearth process was introduced in 1866?

Illustration 3 Ironworkers preparing moulds for molten iron in this Kirkaldy foundry, photographed in 1907.

Steel replaces iron

At first, engineers were reluctant to use steel because it was still more expensive than iron. So Mushet sent a length of steel rail to the Midland Railway Company at Derby for them to test. They laid it at a busy crossing where iron rails lasted about six months. The steel rail lasted for more than ten years. Railway managers realised that steel rails were more economical than iron and from 1870 onwards, railway companies gradually replaced iron rails. Shipbuilders and civil engineers also began to use steel because it was stronger and lighter than iron. Steel production increased from about 250,000 tonnes in 1870 to 6,400,000 tonnes in 1910.

New mills on the coast

Most British iron ore could not be used to make steel in the converter or the open hearth because it contained too much phosphorous. This made the steel brittle. So British manufacturers had to import ore from Sweden or Spain. To cut transport costs they set up steel mills on the coast near coalfields in north-east England, along the Clyde estuary in Scotland, and on the coast of South Wales.

Gilchrist Thomas and phosphoric iron

Sidney Gilchrist Thomas was a London police court clerk. He had studied metallurgy in evening classes, and had a cousin working as a chemist in a South Wales ironworks. In 1879, with the help of his cousin, Gilchrist Thomas found a way to remove phosphorous from iron by lining furnaces with a kind of limestone. This produced iron suitable for converters and open hearths.

British manufacturers did not seem interested in Gilchrist Thomas's discovery.

Germany had huge reserves of phosphoric iron. German steel makers soon began to use Gilchrist Thomas's discovery, setting up modern works producing cheaper steel than the British.

Study

This study asks you to:

Em consider some of the decisions that a steel manufacturer might have had to make between 1855 and 1879.

In pairs

In 1857 a steel manufacturer is looking for a site in Britain to build a mill incorporating a Bessemer converter.

1 Why might he think it was a good time to invest his money in making steel?
2 a List the following items in their order of importance to the manufacturer when looking for a site. A nearby:
   coalfield;
   supply of skilled iron and steel workers;
   harbour;
   established railway network;
   deposit of iron ore.
  b Why might he have decided that the first item on his list was the most important, and the last was the least important?
3 In 1879 he considers the advantages and disadvantages of the Gilchrist Thomas process and decides against using it. Why may he have reached this decision?
4 Ask one person to read his or her answers to the class. Do the rest of you agree?

WORLD WAR I – AND AFTER

During World War I (1914–18), huge quantities of steel were needed to make guns, ships, tanks and shells. Steelworks were enlarged, and production increased by a third. But the works were out of date. An American manager visiting Britain noticed:

'A great many very antiquated ironworks . . . in operation. There are furnaces which in the United States would have been done away with years ago . . . Those furnaces are much too small. The outputs are really ridiculous'.

In 1917 Charles G. Atha, General Manager of the Frodingham Iron & Steel Company visited the USA. When he came back he told a Board of Trade Committee:

'The work to be done to reconstruct our industry on modern lines is enormous as the final aim must be nothing short of a complete replacement of the great majority of existing plants by much larger and more efficient units, and learning to manage and operate such plants in accordance with modern practice and methods'.

At the end of the war a government enquiry recommended a 'radical reconstruction' of the industry, with 'new units for cheap production'. But most firms were too small to afford to re-equip, and would not combine with their rivals. So they went on working with old equipment.

Workers had to use all their skill to make high quality steel with out-dated equipment. It was also very dangerous. A worker remembered that sometimes men standing with their backs to the furnaces caught fire. It was so hot 'you didn't even know if your clothes were on fire until someone else told you, or came to put you out'.

British steel was much more expensive than European steel:

1931 Bar steel prices per tonne
British: £5
Belgian: £3

Nobody wanted to buy British steel. By 1932 nearly half the men in iron and steel making plants were out of work, and many steel workers thought that the government should nationalise the steel industry.

ATTEMPTS TO MODERNISE

The 1932 deal

In 1932 the government made a deal with the iron and steel makers. *The government* put a duty of thirty three per cent on steel imports. *The manufacturers* set up the Iron and Steel Federation to modernise the industry. The federation closed some small ironworks, allowed some mills to be extended, and encouraged manufacturers to build some large new works.

For example, a Scottish company, Stewarts and Lloyds, built a huge new works at Corby in Northamptonshire, where there was plenty of cheap iron ore. The factory was designed by Americans, and was very profitable.

The industry grows

With the help of import duties, the steel industry prospered after 1932. The growing car industry used large quantities of steel, and so did the armaments industry when Britain began to re-arm after 1936. During the war, furnaces and mills were run as hard as possible and there was no time to maintain them. By the end of the war many were worn out.

Study

The Ebbw Vale works

In 1935 Richard Thomas & Co wanted to build a mill to make steel sheets for the car industry. There were two possible sites—Northamptonshire and Ebbw Vale. In this study you will use the sources below to understand:

K why Ebbw Vale was chosen as the site and why the mill never made a great profit.

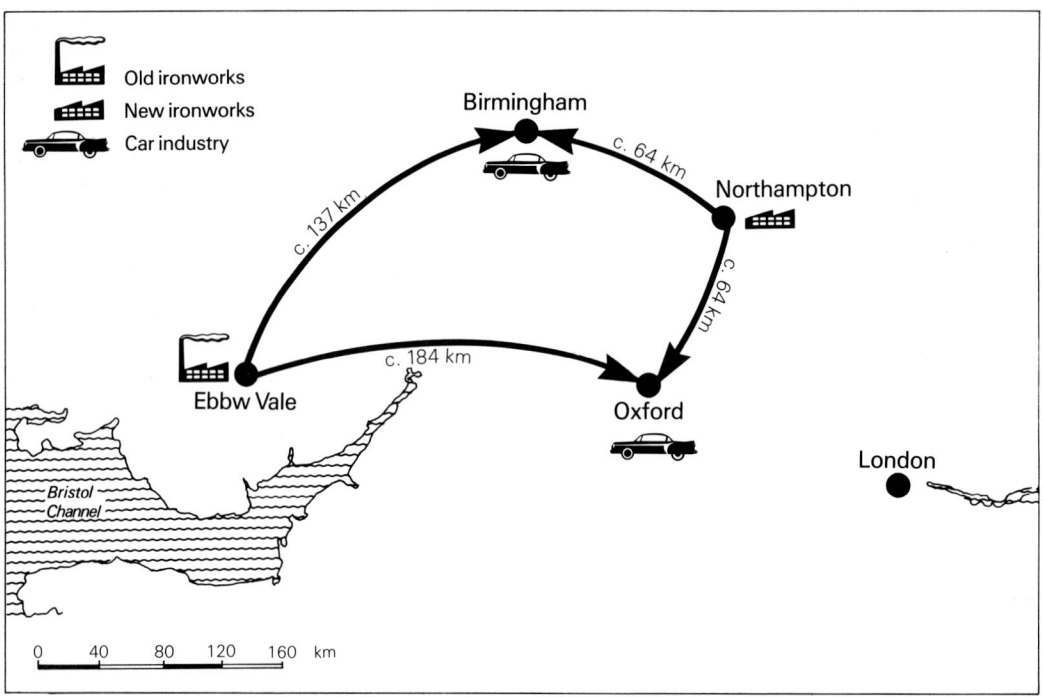

Map 1 The car industry, Ebbw Vale

Table 4 1929 production costs

(shillings per ton of pig iron)	
Ebbw Vale	72
Northamptonshire	55

Source 6A

It would be absurd and against national interests to build modern works in South Wales. Northamptonshire and Lincolnshire are undoubtedly the natural centres for the economic production of British steel.

Sir William Firth, Chairman of Richard Thomas & Co, reported in *The Times*, 1936.

Source 6B

I have helped quietly and out of the limelight to do my bit in pushing [it] along.

Stanley Baldwin, the Prime Minister, speaking after the decision to build the new mill at Ebbw Vale had been announced.

1 Do you think a new mill would have been more likely to be profitable in Ebbw Vale or in Northamptonshire?

2 Why, do you think, was the new mill built at Ebbw Vale?

3 Which three points listed below do you think account for the fact that the Ebbw Vale mill never made much profit?
The new factory was expensive to build.
In 1932 the government put an import duty of thirty three per cent on all steel imports.
The Iron and Steel Federation closed some works, but allowed others to be extended.
Iron ore and finished steel had to be transported long distances to and from Ebbw Vale.
From 1936 Britain began to build up stocks of armaments.
Give reasons for your answers.

THE POST-WAR STEEL INDUSTRY

Table 5   Changes in ownership 1949–67

1945	The new Labour government believed that the industry needed to be re-organised, and decided to nationalise it.
1949	Steel industry nationalised. Put under the control of the Iron and Steel Corporation.
1953	New Conservative government de-nationalised the industry. Set up the Iron and Steel Board to control it.
1967	New Labour government re-nationalised the industry.

Port Talbot, 1951

Between 1945 and 1964 the demand for steel increased, and the industry made large profits. Sheet steel, used for tin cans, cars, refrigerators and washing machines was particularly scarce. So in 1951 a new steel plant was opened at Port Talbot in South Wales. The new works produced eight times as much steel as older mills. But its output per man was only half that of older American factories. In 1967, 16,000 men worked at Port Talbot. A similar plant in the USA employed 5,000.

Llanwern and Ravenscraig

In 1958 Richard Thomas and Baldwin decided to build a strip mill at Llanwern in South Wales to produce three million tonnes a year. But the government insisted that two mills should be built, one in South Wales and the other at Ravenscraig in Scotland, each producing 1.5 million tonnes. This meant that neither was really profitable.

Llanwern needed fewer workers than older mills but trade union officials insisted that just as many men were employed. The equipment was very expensive, and management could not afford to let it lie idle. They did not dare risk a strike, and gave way to the unions. So the mill was over-manned. A foreman said, 'Where you would normally put one on a job, you would have to try and slide two onto a job . . . making the job cost twice as much'. In 1967 steel output per man in South Wales was only half as much as in the USA.

Illustration 4   Port Talbot steelworks.

Illustration 5 Llanwern steelworks.

Study

In this study you will:

Ca consider why the British steel industry continued to decline between 1960 and 1980.

Table 6

Date	Event	Comment
1960	The BOS process was coming into use abroad, e.g. Japan and the USA.	BOS steel plants could: 1 produce as much steel in thirty minutes as an open hearth made in twelve hours 2 cut the price of their steel by thirty per cent.
1965	Eighty per cent of British mills still used open hearth furnaces.	
1967	The Labour government: 1 re-nationalised British steel; 2 set up the British Steel Corporation (BSC).	Between 1950 and 1960 profits in the British steel industry fell from £50 million to £23 million a year.
1973	BSC announced plans to spend £3,000 million on new steel mills.	The new mills were planned to produce thirty six million tonnes of steel a year by 1980.
1974	Oil prices quadrupled. BSC closed plants and dismissed workers.	World trade slumped. Demand for steel fell. Steel production costs rose. Competition for markets increased—only the most efficient plants could survive.
1980	British steel production down to twelve million tonnes. Unions went on strike against further dismissals.	Strike failed.
1983	Only 70,000 steel workers compared with 250,000 in 1950. Only the most modern plants, e.g. Llanwern and Port Talbot, still open.	

Table 7   New steel plants 1974

Japan	New steel plants each produced six million tonnes a year.
Britain	No plant, even the newest, produced more than three million tonnes a year.

Table 8   Steel production (million tonnes)

	Britain	Japan
1970	28	33
1980	12	111

1 a What evidence is there to suggest that the *demand* for British steel fell between 1950 and 1967?
  b What changes took place in the ownership and organisation of the steel industry in 1967?
2 a When BSC announced its modernisation programme in 1973, how many tonnes of steel did it aim to produce by 1980?
  b By how many tonnes a year did BSC fall short of this aim?
3 What long term and short term reasons can you suggest to explain why BSC failed to reach the production target it set in 1973?

—— Part Three ——
Shipbuilding

1851–1914

Wood to iron: south to north

In 1851 ships were built in almost every port in Britain. Most shipyards were small and built wooden sailing ships. The biggest yards were along the banks of the Thames. But more steam-powered, iron ships were being built. So shipyards opened near ironworks and coalfields along the Clyde and the Tyne. By 1870 Clyde shipyards were making three quarters of all the iron ships launched in Britain. Meanwhile the yards on the Thames were closing down. By 1912 they had all gone.

Specialisation

British shipyards were the most up to date and efficient in the world. In 1913 the average output of British shipyard workers was twice that of Americans, and four times that of Germans. British ships were built by gangs of specialised craftsmen, who were hired to do their job and dismissed when it was finished. There were shipwrights, platers, riveters, engineers, blacksmiths, joiners, caulkers, drillers, electricians and, said one shipyard worker, 'many more small trades'.

Demarcation disputes

This system of using specialised craftsmen sometimes led to 'demarcation disputes' in which two trades claimed the right to do the same job, but on the whole it worked well. In 1907 Tyne shipworkers took only eighteen months to build the *Mauretania*, one of the largest passenger liners in the world, and British yards were building at least sixty per cent of the world's ships.

Study

In this study you will:
Ev assess the value of an old photograph as evidence of conditions in the shipbuilding industry.

Source 7A

Cammell Laird shipyard.

Source 7B

You'd be walking on two planks, about 60 or 70 feet up. They used to put this staging right round the ship, and you had to stand on that. The ends of these planks were put through wooden uprights, tied with what they call grass rope. Secure so they shouldn't slide. But if somebody wanted a bit of rope it was nothing for them to take a knife and cut if off.

A riveter talking about his work about 1900.

1 What clues can you find in Sources 7A and 7B that would help us to find out:
   when the photograph was taken;
   where the photograph was taken?
2 How might you follow up these clues?
3 Is an old photograph of any use to historians if we do not know when and where it was taken? Give reasons for your answer.

1914–1939

Shipyards in wartime

During World War I, shipyards had to work hard to replace merchant ships sunk by German submarines and to build warships for the Navy. The Admiralty took control of all shipyards, allocated work to them, and fixed prices. There was a serious shortage of workers. For the first time women were allowed to work in the yards, doing such jobs as heating rivets and painting, while unskilled labourers had to do work which had previously been done by craftsmen. But after the war craftsmen insisted on having their jobs back.

Boom and slump

In 1919 and 1920 shipbuilding boomed. Ship-owners all over the world replaced ships which had been sunk in the war, and brought their fleets up to date. In 1920 more ships than ever before were launched from British yards, and new shipyards were built in Germany, Holland and Scandinavia. Then came the slump.

In 1930 British shipbuilders formed a new company—National Shipbuilders Security Ltd, which bought up out-of-date yards and closed them down. In Jarrow most people depended on the shipyard for a living, so when the company closed it down in 1933, they made almost all the men in the town unemployed. By 1937 the size of the shipbuilding industry had been reduced by about a third.

Diagram 4

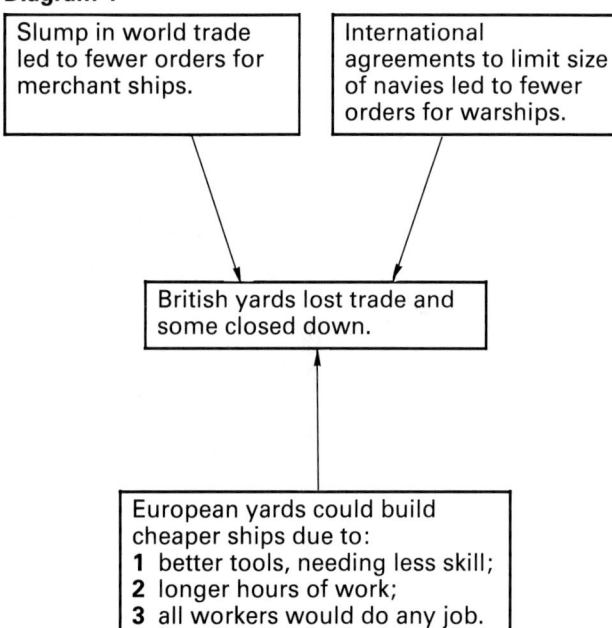

| Slump in world trade led to fewer orders for merchant ships. | International agreements to limit size of navies led to fewer orders for warships. |

British yards lost trade and some closed down.

European yards could build cheaper ships due to:
1 better tools, needing less skill;
2 longer hours of work;
3 all workers would do any job.

Illustration 6 Riveting the deck plates on the *Tuscania* at Fairfield's shipyard in Glasgow in 1920.

Study

In this study you will:

S consider the similarities and differences between the British and German shipbuilding industries, 1914–39.

1 a Copy the heading and sentences below.
Shipbuilding in Britain and Germany, 1914–39
Between 1914 and 1939 both Britain and Germany had important shipbuilding industries. The industries were similar because . . .
b List the ways in which the shipbuilding industries in the two countries were similar.
2 a Copy the words below.
The industries in the two countries differed because . . .
b List the ways in which the shipbuilding industries in Britain and Germany differed.
3 During the 1930s there was mass unemployment in both Britain and Germany. Which country do you think had the higher proportion of unemployed shipyard workers? Give reasons for your answer.

Study

Jarrow is a town in Tyne and Wear. In this study you will use the sources below to find out:
Ev why men from Jarrow marched to London in 1936; what happened as a result.

Source 8A

The Jarrow marchers reach Harrogate.

Source 8B

If [marching is] generally adopted . . . it may bring us . . . into grave public confusion and danger.

Hensley Henson, Bishop of Durham, in a letter to *The Times*, October 1936.

Source 8C

Two hundred men were chosen out of the many hundreds who volunteered and on Monday, 5 October they set out on the high road for London, nearly three hundred miles away. Their objective was to reach the capital by the time the new King Edward opened Parliament . . .

Their slight bodies were covered with dark clothing-club suits and each wore a roll of mackintosh across the chest and over the shoulder like a bandolier. . . . They marched gravely in step to the sound of mouth organs and with the diminutive Ellen Wilkinson at their head.

Ronald Blythe, *The Age of Illusion* (1963).

Source 8D

I ask leave to present to this honourable House the petition of the people of Jarrow . . . During the last fifteen years Jarrow has passed through a period of industrial depression unparalleled . . . Its shipyard is closed and its steelworks have been denied the right to re-open. Where formerly 8,000 persons, many of them skilled workmen were employed, only a hundred are now employed on a temporary scheme. The town cannot be left derelict.

Ellen Wilkinson, MP for Jarrow, in a speech to the House of Commons, 2 November 1936.

Source 8E

[In Jarrow] in 1934, 67.8 per cent of insured workers, mostly shipyard men, were out of a job and in September 1935, 72.9 per cent. Led by Ellen Wilkinson, their fiery little MP, 200 Jarrow men made a 'hunger march' to London to draw attention to the town's plight, and this helped towards the founding of new industries in the area and elsewhere.

R.J. Unstead, *Britain in the Twentieth Century* (1966).

1 What do you think the men of Jarrow hoped to achieve by marching to London?
2 Do you think the information in Source 8C is reliable? Give reasons for your answer.
3 Do you think the information in Source 8D is reliable? Give reasons for your answer.
4 What did the marchers achieve? Explain your answer.

Study: Library work

The aim of this study is to:

K use library books to find out more about the Cunard passenger liners.

Source 9A

The *Queen Mary*.

Source 9B

The *Queen Elizabeth*.

The photographs above show two famous passenger liners built by Cunard in the 1930s.

1 List the sections of your school or local library where you might find out more about the *Queen Mary* and the *Queen Elizabeth* (N.B.—not the *Queen Elizabeth II*.)

2 Write brief notes about each ship on:
the reasons why it was built;
where the money to build it came from;
the passengers' accommodation.

3 Using the information in your notes, write an essay on *Two great passenger liners*.

1939–1985

British shipbuilding revives

During and immediately after World War II, British shipyards were very busy. Shipowners had to replace vessels sunk or worn out during the war. German and Japanese yards had been destroyed, so there was not much competition, and by 1950 Britain was making half the ships in the world.

The decline of British shipbuilding

After 1950 British yards gradually became less competitive. This was because:

1 They were very slow to introduce new, cheaper methods. They still concentrated on building individually designed ships for each customer.
2 They were slow to bring in new machines.
3 When they did unions quarrelled with management and each other over which union was to operate new machines, and how many men should work them.

Meanwhile in Germany and Japan new yards were being built.

1 They used the latest machinery.
2 They built all their ships to the same design. They were very much cheaper than British ships.
3 Their workers used new machines without complaint.

By 1956 both Germany and Japan were building more ships than Britain. By 1963 tankers built in Britain cost £10 a tonne more than those built in Japan, and even British shipowners were having ships built abroad.

Government action

In 1966 a government committee enquired into the British shipbuilding industry. They recommended that the government should make grants to the industry, provided that small, inefficient yards closed down, and the number of unions was reduced. The government agreed, but still British yards could not compete. In 1977 the industry was nationalised, and huge sums were spent to bring it up to date. But yards continued to close, and in 1984 Britain only built about three per cent of the world's ships.

Study

In this study you will explore:

Ca the reasons why the British shipbuilding industry declined rapidly between 1960 and 1984.

You will need to refer to the sources below, and the information above.

Source 10A

It was . . . the trade unions. Their attitudes towards progress were really lamentable . . . The Swedes invented a small portable hand-welding machine . . . In Sweden four machines were worked by one man, ditto in Germany, ditto in France. In Britain one man to one machine and that took a long time, because the fact that it was automatic was objected to.

A British manager.

Source 10B

If they had been given better job security, sick pay, pensions, better working conditions, and that was possible with the vast profits they made, then in my opinion they could have won the co-operation of the workers. But they felt that gaffers wore bowler hats, and had the divine right to rule.

A trade union official.

Source 10C

Everything was very easy . . . We could more or less . . . ask what we liked for our ships . . . The problem was that . . . we weren't worried about keeping costs down . . . with the net result that we . . . became very inefficient.

A shipyard owner, talking about the 1950s.

Sources 10A, 10B and 10C give three men's opinions on why the British shipbuilding industry declined between 1950 and 1984.

1 a Whom does each speaker blame for the industry's decline?
  b Do you think that each speaker's opinion is based on reliable evidence? Give reasons for your answer.
2 What kind of evidence might you look for if you wanted to *check* whether or not each speaker's opinion is reliable?
3 What reasons would *you* give to explain why the British shipbuilding industry declined rapidly between 1950 and 1984?

— Part Four —

Cotton

1851–1914

New rivals: new markets

In 1851 Lancashire was the centre of the world's cotton industry. Most Lancashire cotton was exported. At first, much went to Europe and the USA, but European and American manufacturers began to establish their own mills. So British manufacturers began to export to Asia and Australasia. By 1914 most of their output was exported to India and China. The industry was proud and prosperous. In 1912 a writer described it as, 'the best organised and most finely managed industry in Great Britain, if not in the world'.

Table 9　Percentage of British cotton exports going to India

1815	0.5%
1850	23%
1860	30%

Study

In this study you will use the maps below to:

K understand why Australia and India were important to the Lancashire cotton industry in the second half of the nineteenth century.

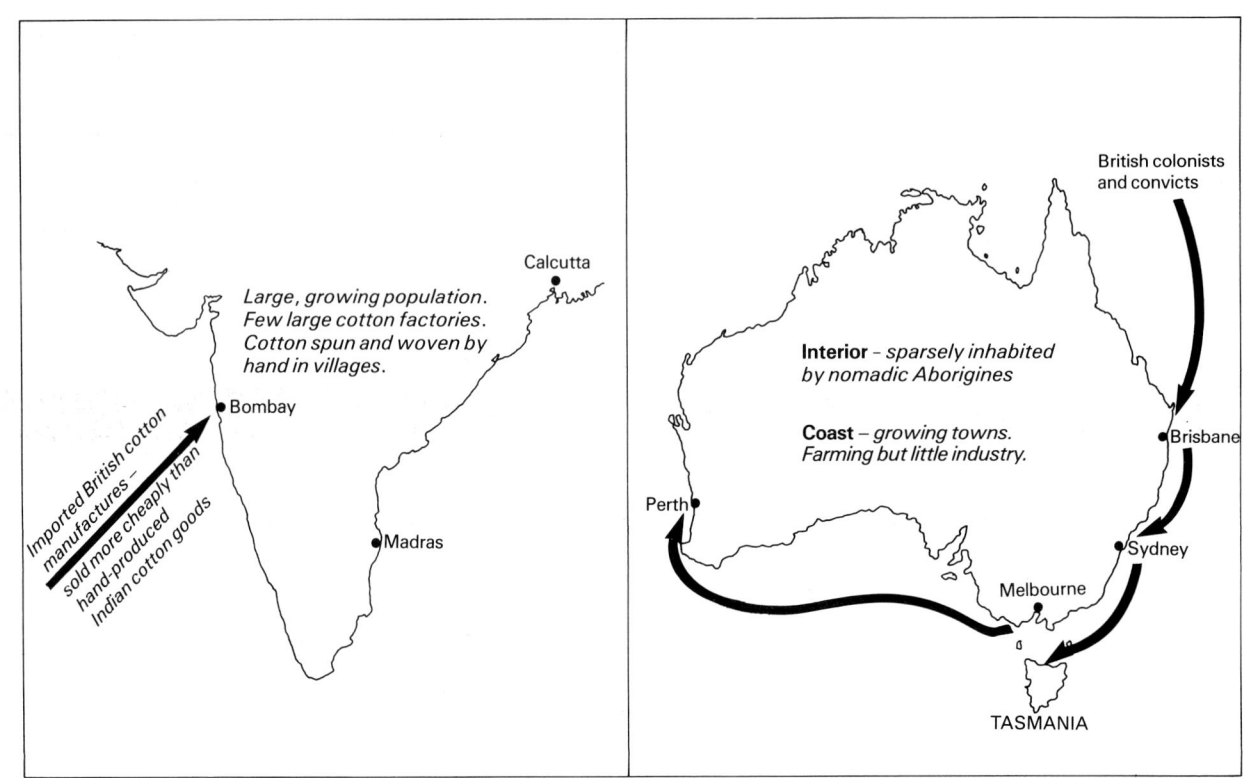

Map 2　Britain's cotton trade with India

Map 3　Britain's cotton trade with Australia

1 Why was there a growing demand in Australia after 1850 for Lancashire cotton goods?

2 Why was India important to the Lancashire cotton industry 1861–65?

3 Why, after 1865, did the demand for:
raw Indian cotton fall in Lancashire;
manufactured Lancashire goods rise in India?

1914–39

The impact of World War I

During the war, textile workers were busy making ammunition and khaki cloth for uniforms. As soon as the war ended the mills went back to making towels, sheets and cloth for garment-making. At first they sold all they produced. But in 1920 trade suddenly slackened, the price of cotton cloth fell, and British manufacturers could not make a profit.

Japanese competition

Meanwhile Japanese manufacturers were setting up cotton mills equipped with automatic looms and ring-spinning machines. These were more efficient than Lancashire power looms and spinning mules. Japanese manufacturers ran their mills for two shifts a day and used electric power. Lancashire mills only worked one shift and used coal. So Japanese cotton was much cheaper than British.

British exports decline

Lancashire mill-owners could not cope with this crisis. Their mills were small and out of date. Lancashire weavers worked four power looms. In foreign mills weavers each ran forty automatic looms. Lancashire cotton could not compete. Exports fell, workers were dismissed and some mills closed. In 1930 the Home Secretary told mill-owners, 'Lancashire must choose between losing her trade or changing her methods'. But the owners felt helpless. One said afterwards, 'We were struggling desperately . . . from an appalling depression. There just wasn't the sort of money around . . . to indulge in massive capital expenditure'.

Within a few years Japan took over most of the Chinese cotton trade, and sold cotton strongly in Africa and South America. To make matters worse, as part of a campaign to persuade the British to leave India, Mahatma Gandhi, the Indian leader, persuaded his followers not to buy British cotton. British exports to India fell by seventy five per cent.

Table 10   The decline of the cotton industry 1912–38

	Yarn (million lb)		Cloth (million sq yd)		Employees ('000)
	Total produced	Total exported	Total produced	Total exported	
1912	1,982	244	8,050	6,913	621.5
1930	1,047	137	3,500	2,472	564.1
1938	1,070	123	3,126	1,494	393

Study

Your aim in this study is to examine:

K the reasons why the Japanese cotton industry 1919–39 was more efficient than the British;

Ca the effect that Japanese competition had on overseas markets for British goods.

1 a Copy the table opposite.
  b Complete your table by making notes comparing the British and Japanese industries under these headings: shifts worked; power used; weavers per loom.
2 Why did the manufacturing methods used in the two countries mean that British cotton goods were dearer than Japanese?
3 Was the greater efficiency of the Japanese the main reason or one of several reasons for the rapid fall in British cotton exports, 1930–38?

Cotton Manufacture 1919–39	
Britain	**Japan**
Small and out-dated factories	Large and up-to-date factories

1939–1985

Date	Britain	Abroad
1939–45 World War II	Some mills made munitions. Others made fabric for balloons, parachutes and uniforms.	Japan took over British markets in the Far East.
1945–50 Post-war period.	*1946 Government Report* urging millowners to modernise was ignored. High demand for cotton meant mills had plenty of work, took on workers and made good profits.	Japan lost markets to Britain and America. American mills produced cheap cloth. 6.3 looms could do the work of 15 British looms.
1950–60 Britain loses trade.	Mill owners failed to modernise. *1959 Cotton Industry Act:* 1 Compensated firms that destroyed old machines. 2 Gave grants for new machines to be installed.	Japan re-established its cotton industry. Hong Kong, India and Pakistan built new mills. It was cheaper to export their cloth to Britain than to buy British.
1960–70 Decline of British cotton.	1964 Courtaulds built a huge factory at Skelmersdale (Illustration 7) to make synthetic fibre.	Overseas factories produced and exported cloth cheaply. Their factories were modern and workers in some countries only had low wages.
1970–80	Only highly specialised mills stayed in business.	
Between 1945 and 1985 over a thousand mills closed. 'There's no cotton about now,' said one worker in 1984.		

Illustration 7   Courtauld's mill in Skelmersdale.

———— Part Five ————
The Toolmakers

Study: Library work

A toolmaker is a craftsman who designs machines to make tools and parts for other machines. See what you can find out about two important toolmakers, Henry Maudslay and Joseph Whitworth, who worked in the middle of the nineteenth century.

Source 11

This museum exhibit shows two toolmakers working at a wooden lathe.

1 List the sections in your school or local library where you might find information about Henry Maudslay and Joseph Whitworth.
2 Answer the following questions in brief notes.
   a Why, by the end of the eighteenth century, did toolmakers need more advanced lathes than the one shown in Source 11?
   b Give examples to show how the work of Maudslay and Whitworth helped toolmakers to provide nineteenth-century inventors with the machine parts they needed.
   c Without the work of toolmakers such as Maudslay and Whitworth, Britain could never have become a great industrial country. Explain why not.
3 With the help of your notes, write an essay on: 'Maudslay and Whitworth—two important toolmakers'.

Recall

1 What was: the open hearth process (1866); the depression (1929–36); the *Queen Mary* (1933); a Bevin boy (1939–45); the plan for coal (1974)?
2 What were the terms of: the 1927 Trades Disputes Act; the 1959 Cotton Industry Act?
3 In what ways where British and Japanese manufacturing industries *i* similar and *ii* different at the beginning of the twentieth century? How had their positions as manufacturing nations changed by 1980?

Diagram 5

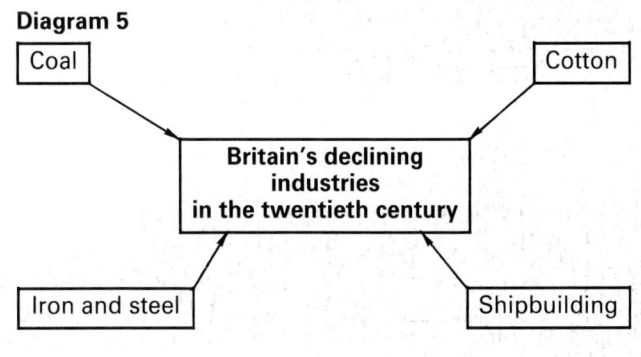

17
The New Industries

—— Part One ——
Chemicals

BEGINNINGS

The British chemical industry came into existence to help cloth manufacturers. In the middle of the eighteenth century the amount of cloth produced in Britain was increasing. All the cloth had to be bleached. It was soaked alternately in sour milk and solutions of ashes, and dried in the sun. This was a slow process, and cloth manufacturers wanted to speed it up. Cloth also had to be thoroughly washed, so manufacturers also needed cheap soap.

The first chemical works

Chronology	
1746	John Roebuck set up a factory at Prestonpans in Scotland to manufacture sulphuric acid.
1790	Nicholas Leblanc, a French chemist, discovered how to make cheap soda using sulphuric acid and salt. Factories were set up at St Helens and Widnes.
1798	Charles Tennant opened a factory at St Rollux in Glasgow to make chlorine bleaching powder. He made fifty two tonnes in the first year.
1825	St Rollux works produced 9,250 tonnes of bleach.
1840	St Rollux, the biggest chemical works in the world, also produced sulphate of ammonia.
1850	St Rollux produced superphosphates.

GERMANY TAKES THE LEAD

Coal tar dyes

In the middle of the nineteenth century, chemists were experimenting with chemicals extracted from coal tar, and in 1856 William Henry Perkin (1838–1907) accidentally discovered how to extract dyes from tar. British firms were not interested, but German manufacturers set up factories to produce the new dyes.

British methods

Most British chemical works were badly designed and poorly equipped. As a result they could not compete with German firms, and Britain had to import most of the chemicals needed for dyes, medicines and photography from Germany.

The only really efficient chemical factory in Britain was Brunner Mond's works at Northwich in Cheshire. This had been set up by Ludwig Mond. He was born in Germany, and had settled in Britain in 1864.

THE BRITISH INDUSTRY REVIVES

The impact of war

In 1914 German scientists discovered how to extract nitrogen from the air to help make fertilisers and explosives. This gave Germany an advantage in the war, as Britain used imported nitre from Chile to make chemicals. During the war the British government had to set up special factories to make chemicals for munitions.

The Billingham factory

At the end of the war, British chemists went to Germany and explored a derelict chemical factory. They managed to work out how the process for extracting nitrogen worked. When they came back to England, Brunner Mond took over the process and built a factory at Billingham on Teeside to manufacture cheap fertilisers to export to the colonies.

Study

In this study your aim is to cross-reference a number of different sources to work out:

Ca why manufacturing chemicals became one of Britain's most important industries between 1746 and 1850.

You will also need to refer to the chronology table on page 188.

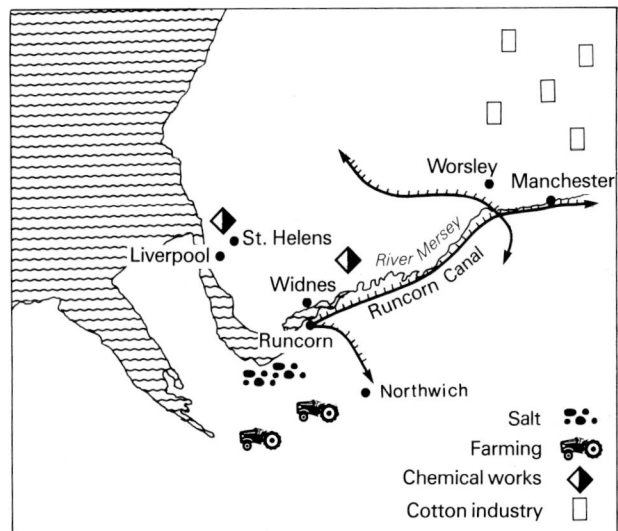

Map 1 The chemical industry, St Helens

Chemicals used in cloth-making
Sulphuric acid can be used to make bleach. It also produces washing soda—an important ingredient in soap.
Salt can be mixed with sulphuric acid to make soda.
Chlorine can be used to make a dry bleaching powder.

Source 1

Between 1780 and 1850 exports of cotton cloth increased more than a hundred fold. The old methods of bleaching, shown here, could not have coped with the increase.

1 Why were cloth manufacturers willing to buy the sulphuric acid that John Roebuck manufactured?
2 Why was St Helens a good place for a Le blanc factory to be set up?
3 Give reasons why by 1840 Britain was one of the world's leading chemical manufacturing countries.

ICI is formed

In 1925 a huge new combine of chemical firms—IG Farben—was set up in Germany. In 1926, to compete with Farben, Brunner Mond, the biggest British firm, combined with three of its rivals to form Imperial Chemical Industries (ICI), which produced nearly half the chemicals made in Britain.

ICI made a deal with major German and American firms, by which ICI agreed not to export to Europe and the USA, and in return was given a free hand in the British Empire and most of South America and Asia. This gave ICI a secure market, and its management was able to invest millions of pounds in their factories to keep them up to date. They paid workers well, and set up a system of consultative committees to keep them in touch with management. This meant that their employees worked hard and purposefully. So, during the thirties, when many British industries were contracting, the chemical industry continued to grow.

1939–85

When World War II broke out, the chemical industry was ready. Between 1936 and 1939, seven new explosives factories had been built. During the war the amount spent on chemical research more than doubled and many important discoveries, including plastics, new medicines and insecticides were made. By the end of the war many factories were out of date. They still used coal as their main raw material. American factories were beginning to use oil. In 1950 a number of British chemists visited the USA, and found that American factories were better equipped than British, and that American workers were three times as productive as British. An ICI manager tried to explain why British factories had fallen behind. He said:

'Partly it was resting on the laurels of success during the war . . . A hell of a lot had gone well, and I suspect there was a sense of saying, "Now you've won, when do we celebrate?" But of course it wasn't a time for celebrating. It was a time for working even harder.'

After 1950 the chemical industry began to re-equip. It was hard-hit when the price of oil quadrupled in 1974, but has continued to be one of the most profitable and successful in the country. By 1980 it was producing nearly twice as much as in 1964, even though the number of workers in the industry had fallen by twenty five per cent.

Study

In this study you will consider a piece of propaganda produced by ICI when it was trying to build up the company two years after it was founded. You will also need to remember what you have read about the formation of ICI on page 189.

Your aim is:

Ev to decide what this propaganda can and cannot tell us about ICI.

Source 2

THE BRIDGE

This cartoon appeared in the ICI company magazine issued to their workers in 1932.

Artists who draw propaganda cartoons use pictures to put across an idea or a message.

1 Which people was the message in the cartoon intended for? Give reasons for your answer.
2 What was the artist trying to tell them about ICI's new labour programme?
3 The directors of ICI won support for the ideas put forward in the cartoon, and the company prospered in the 1930s. Does this prove that ICI's success was based on the skilful use of propaganda? Give reasons for your answer.

Study

In this study you will:

K look at the effect that the oil crisis of 1974 had on the British chemical industry and the reasons why the industry was able to survive the crisis.

Use the information in the sources below and in the sections headed **1939–1985** on page 192.

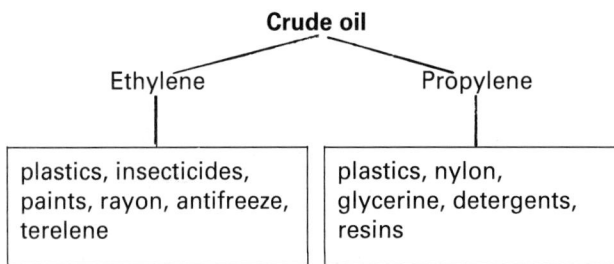

Map 2   British oil in the late 1970s

In 1974 when the price of oil quadrupled Britain's chemical industry depended on imported oil. The first oil from the North Sea came ashore in 1975.

Source 3A   Oil products

Crude oil

Ethylene

Propylene

| plastics, insecticides, paints, rayon, antifreeze, terelene | plastics, nylon, glycerine, detergents, resins |

Note: chemical products, for example plastics and artificial fibres, can be produced more cheaply than natural materials such as iron, wood, cotton and wool. By 1973 chemical products were used to make a wide range of goods. The quantity of plastics produced from petrochemicals has declined since 1973, but the amount of fertilisers and insecticides has increased.

Source 3B

By 1973 virtually the whole of the chemical industry throughout the world was dependent on oil to make its products. It had become totally enslaved to oil. It was oil, oil, oil, and when the price went up fourfold that was very nasty indeed. I don't think we could really believe it . . . Then the realisation of what it would do to costs and prices. That's when the market turned sour.

A manager in the British chemical industry giving an interview in 1984.

1 Why did the cost of producing chemicals rise sharply in 1974?
2 Why, do you think, was the manager of the British chemical firm (Source 3B) worried when he heard about the rise in oil prices?
3 Suggest reasons why the British chemical industry was able to survive the oil crisis of 1974?

——————— Part Two ———————
The Motor Industry

BEGINNINGS TO 1939

Growth and protection

Before 1914 British cars were built in small workshops. Most firms made a few cars a week, and took a pride in the attention they gave them. Cars were expensive—about £300 each—so only rich people could afford them.

During the war, car firms manufactured munitions, armoured cars and tanks. To protect them from imports, the government put a duty of thirty three per cent on imported cars. This duty was left in place after the war.

Mass production

In 1911 the American manufacturer, Henry Ford, set up a large factory at Trafford Park in Manchester to produce his Model T car. This sold for £135 because it was produced on a production line, which was cheaper than building individual cars in a workshop.

Between 1919 and 1939 the British car industry grew. Industrialists such as William Morris and Herbert Austin set up factories in Oxford, Birmingham and Coventry. Compared with American plants, many were badly equipped, so productivity was poor. In 1930 each American car worker produced an average of eight cars a year. A British worker only produced 1.5.

In 1931 the Ford Motor Company opened an American-style production line at Dagenham in Essex. British companies also built production lines and the number of cars produced steadily increased. In 1938 British manufacturers produced 200,000 cars.

1939–1985

Unions and overmanning

During World War II (1939–45) car factories manufactured tanks, aeroplanes and aero engines. They were short of labour, and manufacturers asked the unions to help to bring in more workers and increase production. This strengthened the unions. After the war they used their power to prevent employers cutting the number of workers on production lines. Within a few years British factories were overmanned. British manufacturers only made small profits and could not afford to build new plants or do the research necessary to produce new models.

Location of industry

When the war ended, car manufacturers built the same models as before the war. Most were exported. The only competition came from the USA, because most car plants in Europe had been destroyed. By 1960 car exports were falling, but British factories were still busy making cars for the home market, which had been neglected since the war. New factories had to be built. The government insisted that they should be placed in areas such as Merseyside and Scotland, where industries like steel-making and shipbuilding were declining. This caused problems. Standard-Triumph designed a new car called the Herald. One of their managers said, 'the Herald was made in pieces. Some in Liverpool. Some in Birmingham. Some in other places. It wasn't really a successful body construction at all'. On the continent, cars were produced from beginning to end in one factory.

Foreign competition

Most cars built in Britain after the war had been designed for British conditions, and were not suitable for rougher continental roads. To make matters worse, cars were produced as quickly as possible, and were not properly inspected. So British cars got a bad reputation abroad.

Within a few years, France and Germany rebuilt their motor industry. Then the Japanese also built car factories. These foreign works became more efficient than British plants.

Table 1   Cars produced per employee, per year

	1955	1965	1973
Japan	1.2	7.4	12.2
USA	11.1	13.9	14.9
Germany	3.9	7.1	7.3
France	3.6	6.1	6.8
UK	4.2	5.8	5.1
Italy	3.0	7.5	6.8

Study

Use the primary sources below to help you:

Em understand what it was like to work on a car assembly line.

Source 4A

The post-war Rover production line.

Source 4B

. . . we could work any hours we liked. So I worked all the hours I could. I had £7.17 10d wages, and I was only a boy of 17. £2 was a week's wages for a bus driver.

A Coventry car worker.

Source 4C

I work on a small conveyor which goes around in a circle. We call it a 'merry-go-round'. I make up zigzag springs for front seats. Every couple of feet on the conveyor there is a form for the pieces that make up the seat springs. As that form goes by me, I clip several springs together, using a clip gun. I then put the pieces back on the form, and it goes on around to where other men clip more pieces together . . . The only operation I do is work the clip gun. It takes just a couple of seconds to shoot six or eight clips onto the spring, and I do it as I walk a few steps. Then I start right over again.

A worker, quoted in C. Walker and R. Guest, *The Man on the Assembly Line* (1952).

Source 4D

The conveyor belt is our master. If the management in the factory decide to increase the speed by 10 per cent, a thousand hands work 10 per cent faster.

William Ferrie, a car worker, 1934.

1 Why might a young man of seventeen have thought he was lucky to be given a job on an assembly line?
2 a Why may he have disliked the job by the time he was twenty five?
  b Suggest reasons why he may have stayed on the job even though he disliked it.
3 Why may he have feared that he would not be able to keep his job after he reached the age of forty five?

Illustration 1   Coachbuilders making the bodies of Austin cars in the late 1920s.

To try to compete with foreign companies, rival British companies merged. This failed. Some were taken over by foreign companies. Eventually there was only one large-scale British manufacturer left—British Leyland, and this lost so much money that it had to be taken over by the government. They invested huge sums of money to install up-to-date production lines, and sacked 70,000 workers to enable it to compete with foreign companies. In order to avoid the costs of developing new models themselves, British Leyland makes some cars designed by the Japanese firm, Honda.

Study

In this study you will be investigating:
Ca the reasons why the British car industry declined after 1945.

In pairs

1 Re-write the following points in order of importance as causes of the decline of the British car industry.
   a After 1945, the trade unions used their powerful position to keep plants over-manned.
   b During the 1960s the government insisted that car firms built new factories in areas where older industries were declining.
   c Cars made for export were designed for British roads.
   d British cars were not inspected thoroughly.
   e By the mid-1950s the French, German and Japanese car industries had recovered from World War II and were more efficient than the British.
   f British Leyland was nationalised.

2 Write brief notes on why you chose the *most* and the *least* important points on your list.

3 Ask one person to read his or her list to the class and say why the first and last points were given these placings. Do the rest of you agree?

---- Part Three ----
The Aircraft Industry

EARLY GROWTH

The effects of World War I

Before World War I, most aircraft were built in small workshops. The only large factory was the Royal Aircraft Factory at Farnborough. During the war the industry grew. By 1918 about fifty companies with 350,000 workers were making planes for the Air Force. The British aircraft industry was the biggest in the world.

Between the wars

At the end of the war the Air Force needed fewer planes. Most companies went out of business, but the government realised that Britain needed aircraft designers and manufacturers to keep the Air Force up to date. So they selected sixteen companies and sent them occasional orders for sample aircraft.

1935–85

The pre-war years

In 1935 Britain began to re-arm, and aircraft firms had to employ teams of draughtsmen and engineers to design fighters and bombers. When the designs had been approved, factories were set up to produce the new aircraft. By 1939 aircraft manufacturers were making 700 warplanes a month.

The impact of war

During World War II, the government and aircraft manufacturers worked closely together. Manufacturers were given all the designers, engineers, production workers and materials they needed. By 1943 1,700,000 men and women were working in aircraft factories. It was the biggest industry in the country. Most workers were not there from choice. One said, 'They were sent here by the Ministry of Labour whether they wanted to or not. Some wanted to leave. They couldn't go. They were stuck here'. They worked long hours. 'You did twelve hour shifts, eight to eight . . . and then doing fire-watching in between, staying a night at the factory. It was more or less work and sleep all the while.'

Illustration 2   Two Lucas employees working on a gun turret for an RAF plane.

Study: Library work

In this study your aim is:
K to find out more about Hurricanes and Spitfires—two famous types of planes flown by the RAF in World War II.

1 List the sections in your school or local library where you might find information about these planes.
2 Find out:
   the name of the designer of each plane;
   how the planes played an important part in the Battle of Britain.
3 Use this information and the information under the heading 'The impact of war' to write a paragraph on
   either Aircraft design 1935–45;
   or Aircraft factories and their importance 1939–45.

Great improvements were made in the design of aircraft. The most important was the invention of the jet engine by Sir Frank Whittle.

Nationalised airlines

When the war ended the government set up two nationalised airlines—the British Overseas Airways Corporation and British European Airways—and encouraged manufacturers to produce new airliners to equip them. Many of their designs were unsuitable, but two—the turbo-prop Vickers Viscount and the jet-propelled de Havilland Comet—were more advanced than any foreign aircraft, and sold all over the world.

Viscount and Comet sales were so good that British aircraft manufacturers hoped that they would be able to build up a flourishing industry. They were very pleased when the American airline, Pan Am, showed an interest in the Comet.

Study

In this study you will consider the role of one individual in the growth of the aircraft industry. Geoffrey de Havilland was a famous aircraft designer and manufacturer. Your aim is to use the sources below to work out:

K what he was like and why he was successful.

Source 5A   de Havilland's career

1882	Born, son of Rev. Charles de Havilland. Educated at schools in Rugby and Oxford.
1900–3	Course in mechanical engineering at Crystal Palace engineering school.
1903–8	Worked for various vehicle firms as an engine designer.
1908	Set up his own firm to design and build aircraft.
1910	First plane flew. de Havilland was taken on by the Army Aircraft Factory.
1913	Joined the Aircraft Manufacturing Company (Airco) 'as a designer and pilot of aeroplanes'.
1914–18	Designed fighters and bombers for the Air Force. By the end of the war, 3,877 DH aircraft were in service with the RAF. In 1913 Airco made a profit of £10,000 and in 1918, a profit of £177,000.
1920	Airco taken over by BSA, who closed down the aircraft building business. de Havilland set up the de Havilland Aircraft Co Ltd to design and build passenger aircraft.
1925	Brought out the 'Moths', a series of fast, light aircraft.
1941–5	Built Mosquitos—fast, light bombers.
1945 onwards	Built Comets, Chipmunk trainers, Vampire and Venom fighters.
1960	de Havilland combined with Hawker Siddely.

Source 5B

[He] would fly all his own aeroplanes himself first, always . . . And he would come down with various comments on the behaviour of the aeroplane and we would then immediately start to cut bits and pieces off and make them a bit shorter or longer . . . He would put a designer—perhaps a young man—in charge of a project and not interfere.

C. Martin Sharp, *DH: A History of de Havilland* (1982).

Source 5C

He was the same to all at all levels, whether talking to an air marshal or to a labourer . . . He made you feel completely relaxed, and that he was genuinely interested in what you had to say.

R. M. Clarkson, in the de Havilland Memorial Lecture (1966).

1 When people suggested ways of improving aircraft, de Havilland always considered their ideas from the point of view of the pilot who would be flying the plane or the engineer who would be making it. This shows he was practical. What else do Sources 5B and 5C tell us about his character?

2 Do you think the information about de Havilland in Sources 5B and 5C is reliable? Give reasons for your answer.

3 After World War I, de Havilland's was one of the sixteen companies to which the government gave occasional orders for sample aircraft. Suggest reasons why the government gave the de Havilland Company this work.

Study

In this study you will:

Ca consider the history of the de Havilland Comet, and

Em how it was viewed by builders and buyers of jet airliners.

Remember what you have learned about nationalised airlines (page 196).

Background information

Between 1945 and 1980 the number of people travelling by air increased. Businessmen used airliners to carry them rapidly from one country to another and tourists flew on cheap package holidays. Many countries invested large sums of money in setting up or expanding airlines.

Source 6

A Comet 1.

October 1952	Pan Am ordered three Comets, promising to buy more if they were successful.
10 January 1954	BOAC Comet 1 GALYP Rome–London crashed in sea off Elba. Crew and passengers all killed.
8 April 1954	BOAC Comet 1 GALYY Rome–Cairo crashed in sea near Naples.
12 April 1954	Comet's certificate of airworthiness withdrawn. All Comets grounded.
14 November 1954	Court of inquiry found that the Comet crashes were caused by metal fatigue.
October 1955	Pan Am ordered twenty American Boeing 707 airliners.
4 October 1958	Modified Comet 4 went into service, but sales were disappointing.
By 1986	Boeing had built half the world's jet airliners.

1 Why did the directors of Pan Am in 1952 think that the Comet was a good aircraft to buy for their airline?

2 Suggest reasons why the Pan Am directors decided to buy Boeings rather than Comets in 1955.

3 Later, Sir Arnold Hall, managing director of Hawker Siddely said, 'The Comet failures did affect the future history of jet transport aircraft in Britain.' Suggest reasons why Sir Arnold said that the history of the jet aircraft industry in Britain would have been different if there had been no Comet failures.

Mergers and joint ventures

It became very expensive to design and build new aeroplanes. This affected buyers and builders.

Buyers

Only the government and the two nationalised airlines could afford to buy new aircraft. To encourage them to order planes, manufacturers concealed the real cost. An Air Ministry Official said:

'There was a terrible tendency to announce the cost of one prototype and say "This is going to be, say, fifty million", ignoring the fact that to develop the aircraft properly you are going to have at least six prototypes just to get through all the testing that was needed'.

On several occasions the government cancelled contracts when they realised how much they were going to have to pay. This annoyed some of the manufacturers.

Builders

Aircraft companies could not afford to develop aeroplanes on their own, so they merged or co-operated in joint ventures such as the Anglo-French Concorde (see Illustration 3) and the European Airbus.

Illustration 3   Concorde.

Chronology: Concorde	
1962	British and French governments signed an agreement for joint development and manufacture of supersonic airliners. (British Aircraft Corporation and Sud Aviation were the two companies involved)
1967	First prototype rolled out at Toulouse.
1968	Second prototype rolled out at Filton.
1969	Maiden flights of both prototypes.
1973	First standard production Concorde flew.
1975	Certificate of airworthiness granted.
1976	Concordes entered service with British Airways and Air France.

NB: Concorde will never recover research, development and building costs—about £1,000,000,000.

Chronology: Airbus	
1977	Aviation industries of France, Germany, Britain, Holland and Spain formed Airbus Industrie with the help of government loans and grants to build a European 'Airbus'. British Aerospace invested fifty million dollars, and spent 250 million dollars on its share of the Airbus. BA made the wings for the Airbus.
1986	Airbus Industrie was the second biggest aircraft seller after Boeing.
1987	The British aircraft industry, which employed about 190,000 people, spent most of its time making parts of aircraft which were assembled in other countries.

Study

In this study you will:

K discuss some of the risks involved in the government's decision to help set up Airbus Industrie in 1977.

Use the information on mergers and joint ventures on page 197.

In pairs

1 What risks did the government have to consider when it was deciding whether or not Britain should joint Airbus Industrie?

2 What reasons may it have had for deciding it would support the company?

3 Consider the development of Airbus Industrie between 1977 and 1986. Was the British government of 1977 justified in joining the company? Give reasons for your answer.

4 Ask one person to read his or her answers to the class. What do the rest of you think?

—— Part Four ——
Electronics

RADIOS AND RADAR

The British electronics industry began when radio broadcasts became popular after 1925. Manufacturers set up factories to produce radio sets. Most of the work consisted of fitting components together to form completed receivers.

By 1939 British scientists had developed a system based on radio waves for tracking aeroplanes. This system was called radar.

JAPANESE COMPETITION

By 1948 Bell Laboratories in the USA had developed transistors, which did the same job as glass valves. Japanese scientists realised that transistors made it possible to manufacture small, light, radio and television sets. So they paid Bell Laboratories for the right to develop and manufacture transistors.

Japanese firms set up large-scale automated

Study

In this study your aim is to explore:

Em why electronics manufacturers should set up factories in Lancashire in the 1920s, and how work in an electronics factory differed from that in a cotton mill.

Source 7A

Women at work in Ferranti's radio factory in Lancashire.

Source 7B

Spinners at work in a Lancashire mill in the 1930s.

Source 7C

You had trays at either side of you, and you had to pick a grid up, and cathodes, heaters and these, and put them on top of each other. They were so fragile that it was really surprising how we didn't damage them, but it was a skill that came naturally to you, being in the mill.

Ethel Tillotson, an ex-cotton mill worker, assembled radio valves for Philips, at their Lancashire factory.

1 In what ways was Ethel Tillotson's work in an electronics factory different from her work in a cotton mill?
2 In what ways was the work similar?
3 Suggest reasons why Philips decided to set up a factory in Lancashire.

Study

In this study you will use various sources to:
K consider the growth of the electronics industry 1939–55.

Source 8

After the war the BBC began to establish a nationwide television service in addition to its radio network.

Table 2 Money spent on electronics by armed forces	
1939	£5 million
1944	£123 million

Table 3 Number of TVs made	
1946	6,000
1955	2 million

Table 4 Workers employed in electronics	
1943	98,000
1945	80,000 (mostly making radios)
1955	180,000

1 a By how much did government spending on radio and radar increase between 1939 and 1945?
  b Why did spending increase so rapidly in this period?
2 Why did the number of workers employed in electronics factories:
  fall between 1943 and 1945;
  rise between 1945 and 1955?
3 In what ways may the demand for radio and radar during World War II have helped the television manufacturing industry to develop rapidly between 1945 and 1955?

factories which produced huge numbers of cheap, reliable radio and television sets. British firms could not compete. Some were forced to close down. Others were kept going by manufacturing military equipment for the Ministry of Defence, who did not want to have to rely on foreign manufacturers. Later Japanese firms set up factories in Britain to manufacture television sets and other electronic equipment.

Study

In this study you will consider:
Ca why Japanese-owned electronics firms were welcome in South Wales in the 1980s.
Remember what you have learned about the decline of the South Wales coal industry in the 1980s.

Source 9

Hitachi Welsh aid

Up to 200 new jobs are to be created in South Wales by the Japanese electronics giant Hitachi after its decision to invest £7 million in a new factory there to produce microwave ovens.

The new plant will be at Hirwaun near Merthyr Tydfil where Hitachi already has a factory producing televisions, video and hi-fi equipment and employing 850 staff.

A spokesman for the company said that Wales had been chosen for the new project in competition with other locations in France and West Germany because of the excellent industrial relations in the region. The plant is to be the sole producer of microwave ovens outside Japan.

Hitachi said that a single-union, no strike agreement with the electricians union, the EEPTU, had been an important deciding factor in bringing the project to Britain. The Welsh Development Agency is to build an 85,000 sq ft factory on the four-acre site and production is scheduled to begin in December.

Some 100 jobs are to be created by the end of the year and a further 100 by the end of 1988. The news of the jobs comes hard on the heels of Hitachi's announcement that it is to create 120 new jobs at its existing South Wales plant.

News item from *The Guardian*, 12 January 1987.

1 a A union that agrees not to strike gives up one way of protecting its members' rights. Why may the electricians have given up the right to strike at the Hirwaun factory?
  b What reasons may Hitachi have had, apart from the non-strike agreement, for deciding to set up a factory at Hirwaun?
2 The Welsh Development Board tries to create employment in Wales. What kinds of work may it have hoped to create when it agreed to help Hitachi to set up their factory? Give reasons for your answer.
3 Would you expect the Ministry of Defence to give any contracts to the Hitachi factory at Hirwaun? Give reasons for your answer.

COMPUTERS AND MICROCHIPS

Computers

Chronology:	
1948	Scientists at Manchester University produced the first electronic computer with a memory.
1951	Ferranti produced the first production model for business use.
	An American company, IBM, bought permission to use some of the ideas developed at Manchester. IBM was a large company with plenty of money to spend on research. It was able to develop business computers which sold well all over the world, including Britain.
1968	To help the British computer industry to compete, the government persuaded the main computer firms to merge into one company, International Computers Ltd (ICL). It was hoped that ICL would be big enough to produce computers to compete on the world market.

Microchips

In 1957 a scientist working at the government radar establishment at Malvern suggested a way to graft a number of electronic circuits onto a piece, or 'chip', of silicon. The British government would not grant any money to follow up the idea, but the American Air Force gave an American company, Texas Instruments, $2 million to investigate the process. With the help of this money, Texas Instruments produced the first commercial microchips. The USA soon became the world's leading 'chip' manufacturing country.

Electronics today

Today the electronics industry in Britain consists of:
1 factories owned by large firms, such as ICL and overseas companies;
2 small firms producing specialist computers, using mostly imported components;
3 small firms producing 'software'—the 'programs' which enable computers to carry out their tasks.

The computer industry is 'high risk'. Many new firms go bankrupt within a year or two. Only a few survive and grow.

Study

During the 1970s and 1980s the computer industry became concentrated in two regions of Britain. Your aim in this study is to use the maps below to:

Ca work out why certain areas proved more attractive than others to the computer industry.

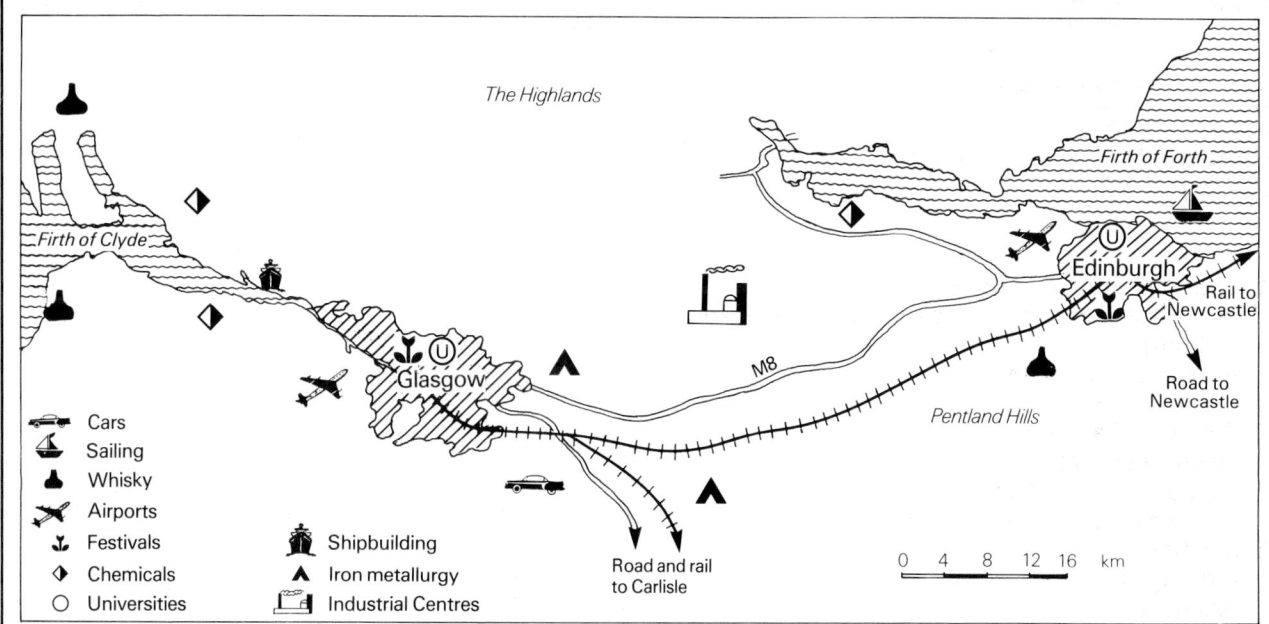

Map 3   Central Scotland

Study continued

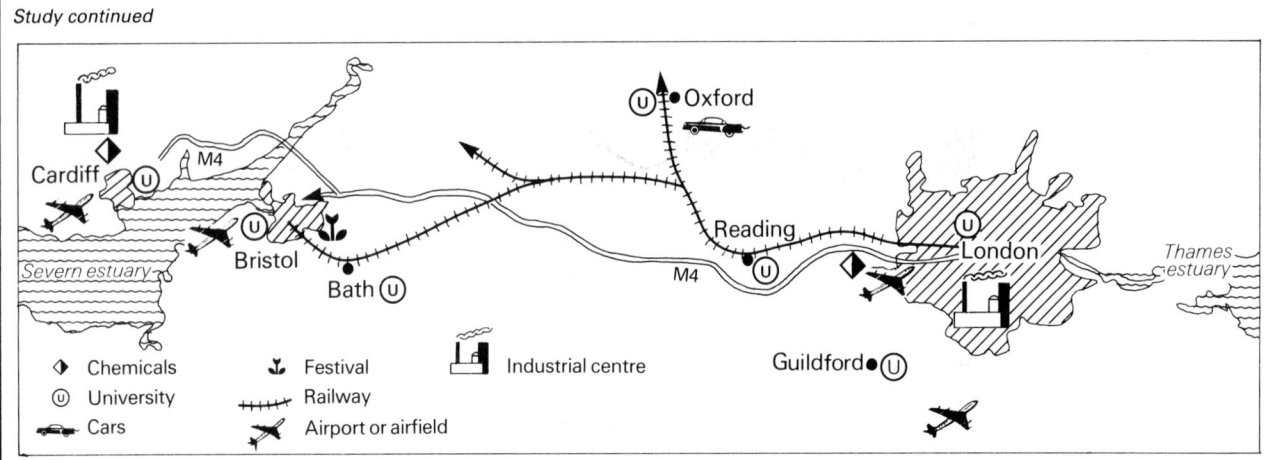

Map 4   London–Cardiff corridor

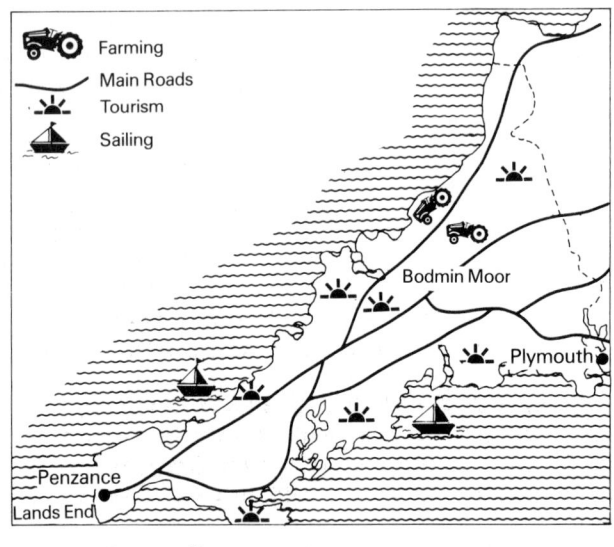

Map 5   Cornwall

Computer industry's needs

Factory sites must have:
good links with British and overseas markets;
access to research centres.
Surrounding areas must offer:
good housing and pleasant surroundings;
good leisure facilities to attract staff.
Workforce must be well-educated and highly trained.

1 Most computer firms are to be found either in central Scotland between Glasgow and Edinburgh (Map 3) or in southern England between London and Cardiff (Map 4).
   Choose one of these regions and make notes to show why it has attracted the computer industry under these headings: factory site; surrounding area; workforce.
2 Under the same headings, make notes showing why Cornwall (Map 5) has failed to attract the computer industry.

Recall

1 What was manufactured at: Farnborough; St Rollux; Trafford Park?
2 Why do we remember these manufacturers: Geoffrey de Havilland; Ludwig Mond; William Morris; William Perkin?

3 Give examples to show how World War I (1914–18) and World War II (1939–45) helped the chemical and electronics industries to develop. Why do you think ICI remained under British control while large sections of the electronics industry are owned by foreign companies?

18
Developments in Towns 1851–1980

Part One

The New Corporations

POWER IN THE TOWNS

In 1843 Sheffield was given a mayor and corporation. But they had to share running the town with several other bodies.

Organisation	Responsibilities
Police commissioners	Cleaning, lighting and policing town centre.
Town trustees	Street improvements.
Highway boards	Repairing main roads.
Poor law guardians	Dealing with the poor.
Private companies	Provided gas and water.

So town councillors had little prestige and power.

BIRMINGHAM UNDER CHAMBERLAIN

The new men

The situation changed in the 1860s when

'a few Birmingham men made the discovery that perhaps a strong and able Town Council might do almost as much to improve the conditions of life in the town as Parliament itself . . . They spoke of sweeping away streets in which it was not possible to live a healthy and decent life; of making the town cleaner, sweeter and brighter; of providing gardens, parks and museums; they insisted that the great monopolies like the gas and water supply should be in the hands of the corporation; that good water should be supplied without stint at the lowest possible prices; that the profits of the gas supply should relieve the pressure of the rates'.

H. W. Crosskey, Birmingham Unitarian Minister, writing in 1877.

Chamberlain's policies

In 1873 Joseph Chamberlain (1836–1914), a prosperous Unitarian businessman, became Lord Mayor of Birmingham. Under his control the Council set to work. This table shows their most important reforms.

Chronology	
1874	They took over Birmingham's two private gas companies. In the first year the council-owned gas works made a profit of £34,000. Later the council used part of the gas committee's profits to build an art gallery.
1875	The Artisans' Dwellings Act allowed councils to buy up and redevelop slum property. Birmingham Corporation bought twenty hectares of slums and rebuilt them. The Public Health Act allowed councils to organise new drainage and sanitation schemes. Birmingham Corporation helped to set up a District Drainage Board to provide sewage disposal for Birmingham and the surrounding area.
1876	Birmingham Corporation took over the company supplying Birmingham's water.

In 1876 Chamberlain resigned as mayor, and became an MP. He wrote:

'I think I have now almost completed my municipal programme . . . The town will be parked, paved, assized, marketed, gas-and-watered and improved—all as a result of three years active work'.

Later Birmingham Corporation set up and controlled the city's tramway system.

MUNICIPAL SOCIALISM

Other town councils did much the same as Birmingham. Some people called it municipal socialism, though Chamberlain and his fellow councillors were all Liberals.

Gradually, Parliament gave town councils more to do. By 1914 they controlled: education; police; parks; public health; lighting; libraries; local roads; rubbish disposal.

Study

In this study you will:

Ev see what you can *infer* about Birmingham Corporation in the 1870s by studying pictures of the city's buildings.

Source 1A

The Gullet was part of the slums pulled down after the Artisans' Dwellings Act.

Source 1B

Corporation Street was build on the site of the Gullet.

Source 1C

Birmingham Council House was completed in 1879. The dome and columns were copied from ancient Roman buildings. The Romans were famous for building well-designed towns where people could live civilised lives.

1 What do Sources 1A, 1B and 1C tell us about Birmingham Corporation's building programme, 1873–79?
2 What do you notice about:
   the size of the Council House;
   the style in which it is built?
3 Suggest reasons why the Council chose this design for their new Council House.

Part Two

The Growth and Development of Towns

SUBURBS

The first suburbs

In the middle of the nineteenth century, factory workers walked to work, so their houses were packed together close to the factories. They never got away from the smell and noise of the works. But factory owners and managers had horses and carriages to travel to and from work, so they built large houses at a distance from the factory. Soon there were large areas of such houses. These became known as suburbs. Every manufacturing town had at least one. For example, Birmingham had Edgbaston and London had several, including Paddington and Kensington. All suburbs had space, sunlight and fresh air.

Study

The sources below show two kinds of suburban houses built in the late nineteenth century. Your aim is:

S to work out the similarities and differences between them.

Source 2A

Back-to-back houses.

Source 2B

Victorian suburban houses.

Source 2C

There would be five or six rooms and a scullery . . . The front room, which might contain a pianola, would only be used on special occasions. There would be no bathroom, but in the kitchen a galvanised iron bath would serve both for laundering and for the regular bath-nights of the members of the family. A mangle would be the only labour-saving device in the kitchen. If the father had chosen well, the house would have a small garden at the back, and here he would grow such vegetables as could survive the soot of London's millions of coal fires.

Cecil Roberts, *Life in Edwardian England* (1969).
(Houses of this kind were built for clerks and skilled manual workers. They cost about 12s 6d a week to rent.)

1 What similarities can you see in the houses shown in Sources 2A and 2B?
2 What differences can you see?
3 Which house do you think fits the description in Source 2C? Give reasons for your answer.

Study: Library work

In this study you will use your library to:
K find out what you can about Sir Titus Salt, George Cadbury and William and James Lever, industrialists who built suburb-like communities for their workers.

1 List the sections in your school or local library where you might find information about these men and the communities they built.
2 Make brief notes on:
   a the names of the communities they built;
   b the layout and buildings of one of these communities;
   c the reasons why Salt, Cadbury and the Lever brothers built communities for their workers.

Suburban spread

As hours of work decreased and cheap transport became available workers could afford time and money to travel to work. So towns spread, with inner suburbs of terraced houses for the less well-to-do, and outer suburbs of detached and semi-detached houses for the better paid.

Growing towns engulfed nearby villages and spread over farm land. Most suburbs were unplanned. Builders bought land, built houses and laid out streets as they pleased. Shops, churches and chapels also had to be built, and water, sewerage and gas connected. In some suburbs small factories were set up, but most of the people travelled to work in the centre of the town. In 1881, 270 million passengers were carried on London trams, buses and trains. In 1901 the number was 847 million.

GARDEN CITIES

In 1902 Ebenezer Howard, a London reporter, published *Garden Cities of Tomorrow*. He said that existing towns should not be allowed to grow and spread indefinitely. Instead, to accommodate the growing population, new 'garden cities' should be built about thirty miles from the original towns, with belts of farm land in between. He thought that each garden city should contain about 30,000 people with enough factories to employ them, and with spacious parks, boulevards and arcades. He wanted 'to raise the standard of health and comfort of all true workers of whatever grade . . . by a healthy . . . combination of town and country life'. (E. Howard, *Garden Cities of Tomorrow* (1902).)

Study

In this study you will:
Ev work out what Source 3 can tell us about garden cities at the beginning of the twentieth century. You may need to refer to the information on garden cities on this page.

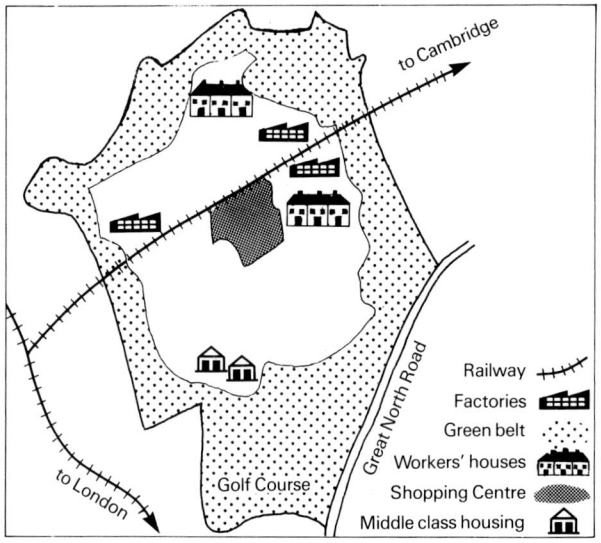

Map 1   Letchworth

Source 3

All the essentials of that town, from the factory sites to the plots for the cottages and villas had been planned from the beginning . . . determining the size and contour of the town before a brick was laid; providing streets, gas and water . . . allocating sufficient garden space to the poorest houses, as well as to the best houses on the estate; reserving open spaces . . . assigning a distinct position to factories . . . while around all this a belt of open land had been reserved, so that the inhabitants would always be within reach of the real country.

Report of the Garden City Association (1907) on the building of Letchworth.

1 What evidence is there to suggest that there was a movement to support the building of garden cities at the beginning of the twentieth century?
2 What evidence is there to suggest that the architects who designed Letchworth:
   had taken advantage of the fact that they did not have to build on to an existing town;
   expected both rich and poor people to live in Letchworth;
   had tried to carry out the aims put forward in *Garden Cities of Tomorrow*?
3 What other primary sources might you look for if you wanted to find out more about garden cities in the early twentieth century?

INTER-WAR HOUSING

Council housing

In 1890 the Housing of the Working Classes Act allowed local authorities to build houses for working people at public expense. Few were built before World War I. At the end of the war Lloyd George, the prime minister, declared that Britain must be made 'a fit country for heroes to live in'. The government decided that new houses were needed. So they encouraged councils to build houses for working people.

In 1919 the Housing and Town Planning Act:
1 ordered local authorities to draw up plans to deal with their housing needs;
2 offered government funds to help to build workers' houses.

In 1924 the new Labour government passed another Housing Act promising long term subsidies to local authorities who built low cost rented accommodation.

By 1939 more than one million 'council' houses had been built.

Private housing

At the same time private builders erected estates of detached and semi-detached houses for sale round most towns and cities in the south and west. In all, about three million private houses were built between 1919 and 1939. So most towns were surrounded by a belt of new suburbs.

The slums

Though there were good houses on the outskirts of towns, there were still slums in the centres. Many cities planned to pull them down and re-house the people in modern homes, and some cleared their worst slums. But the outbreak of World War II in 1939 put a stop to these ideas.

Study

Your aim is to use the sources below to work out:

K what planners had in mind when they designed inter-war council estates;

Ca how these estates may have influenced the ideas of later planners.

Source 4A

Council estates were on the outskirts of towns—a long way from where people worked.

Source 4B

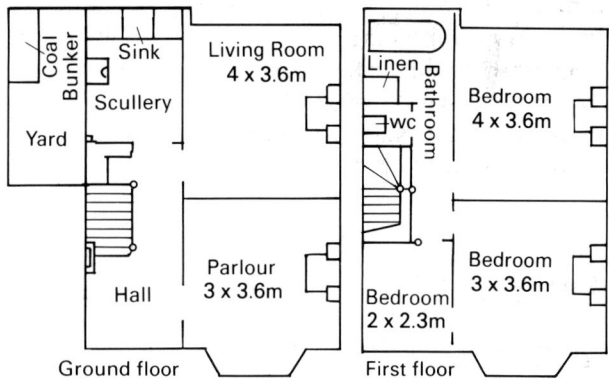

Source 4C

... low density [no more than thirty houses were built to a hectare] with blocks of houses arranged along streets following geometric layouts; dwellings set back behind front gardens ... green spaces to complement garden space, and with a deadening similarity of house styles and materials over vast areas.

Gorden E. Cherry, *Urban Change and Planning* (1972), describing a typical council estate.

1 a Why did all the houses on a large council estate look similar?
  b What reasons may the planners have had for making them look similar?
2 Suggest reasons why many planners thought that they had provided working-class people with good homes in a pleasant environment?
3 What drawbacks of inter-war council estates may later planners have tried to avoid?

TOWN HOUSING SINCE 1945

Post-war replacement

During World War II (1939–45) air raids destroyed or damaged about 750,000 houses in towns and cities. Public opinion polls showed that people thought that replacing these houses was the most important job facing the new Labour government. So Parliament passed two Housing Acts in 1946 and 1949. They granted local authorities money to build houses to rent, but gave nothing to private builders. Between 1945 and 1950, 806,000 new houses were built. Three quarters of them were council houses. Some were small, temporary, prefabricated dwellings, but most were slightly larger versions of pre-war council houses.

Clearing the slums

By 1950 the houses destroyed in the war had been replaced. But many people were still badly housed. The 1951 census showed that a third of the houses in England and Wales had no bath, and seventy per cent had been built before World War I. Many were nineteenth-century working-class houses, which were out of date and falling into disrepair.

In 1951 a Conservative government was elected. They encouraged private builders as well as local authorities and the number of houses built increased. In 1968 it reached 413,700 in a single year. The increasing number of new houses enabled local authorities to begin clearing their slums.

At the same time, architects and planners changed their ideas about the kind of homes they ought to build. Instead of semi-detached houses with separate gardens, they decided to put up blocks of high-rise flats. By 1960 these blocks could be constructed easily and quickly from prefabricated kits which were bolted together on site. So most town councils built tower blocks to house people cleared from nineteenth-century slums. The new flats were modern and convenient. Politicians and planners liked them.

The new slums

Tower blocks have always been unpopular with many of the people living in them. The flats have modern kitchens, bathrooms and toilets, but they are expensive to heat and often suffer from condensation. Lifts frequently break down, and in many blocks the shared stairs, passages and landings are neglected and vandalised. They can be lonely. In a

Study

In this study you will see:

Ch how the lives of three generations of a family were affected by changes in housing in the twentieth century.

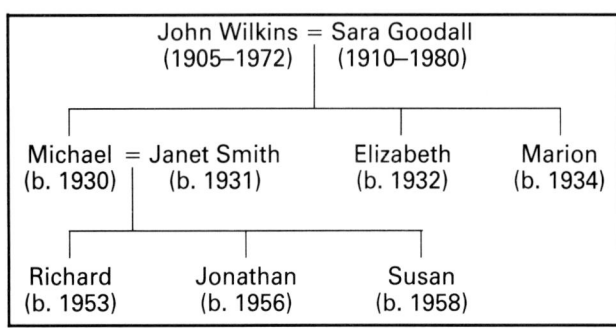

```
            John Wilkins = Sara Goodall
            (1905–1972)  |  (1910–1980)
                         |
        ┌────────────────┼──────────────────┐
  Michael = Janet Smith     Elizabeth      Marion
  (b. 1930) | (b. 1931)     (b. 1932)     (b. 1934)
            |
     ┌──────┴───────┬──────────────┐
  Richard      Jonathan        Susan
  (b. 1953)    (b. 1956)      (b. 1958)
```

1 John Wilkins and Sara Goodall grew up in Borough Street, a street of small, nineteenth-century terraced houses in a Midlands city. Their parents rented the houses from private landlords. John and Sara married in 1929 and lived with Sara's parents. Sara shopped in the nearby city centre. John could walk to his work in ten minutes. In 1931 they moved to a house on a newly-built council estate on the outskirts of the city, about three miles from John's work.

a In what way was the ownership of their new house different from that of the houses in which they grew up?

b In what ways may they have found the council estate *i* more convenient, *ii* less convenient than Borough Street?

Michael Wilkins and Janet Smith grew up on the council estate. They married in 1950, and in 1961 the council allotted them a flat on the twelfth floor of a tower block on a redeveloped site half a mile from the city centre where Michael worked as a salesman.

c In what way was their living accommodation similar to the houses in which they grew up? In what ways was it different?

In 1982 the council held a meeting with the residents in the tower block to discuss problems which had arisen, and to see if they could solve them.

d What complaints might residents have made?

e What suggestions might have been put forward to solve their problems?

street, people can see their neighbours passing and can easily go out and chat to them if they wish. In a tower block people rarely see their neighbours, and so feel isolated. Mothers with small children often find life in tower blocks particularly difficult, because there is nowhere safe for children to play.

In 1968 a gas explosion destroyed one corner of a tower block at Ronan Point in east London. People wondered if the blocks were safe. Checks proved that many were made of inferior materials and were carelessly assembled. Some needed so much money spending on them that it was cheaper to blow them up and build new houses to replace them. Most new council homes were in two or three storey 'low-rise' blocks, which are much more popular than towers.

In 1980 council tenants were given the right to buy their houses. Many tenants in new or up-dated semi-detached houses want to buy them. Few tenants in tower blocks are interested.

POST-WAR TOWN PLANNING

Planning laws

Until World War II towns had grown without any overall plan. Somehow the growth of towns had to be limited. So after the war the government passed two Acts. The 1946 New Towns Act allowed 'designated' New Towns to be planned and built by development corporations; and the 1947 Town and Country Planning Act gave county councils control over all building within their boundaries. Towns were to be surrounded by a 'green belt' of farmland that must never be built on.

New Towns

Since Parliament passed the New Towns Act, thirty four new towns have been 'designated' (see Map 2).

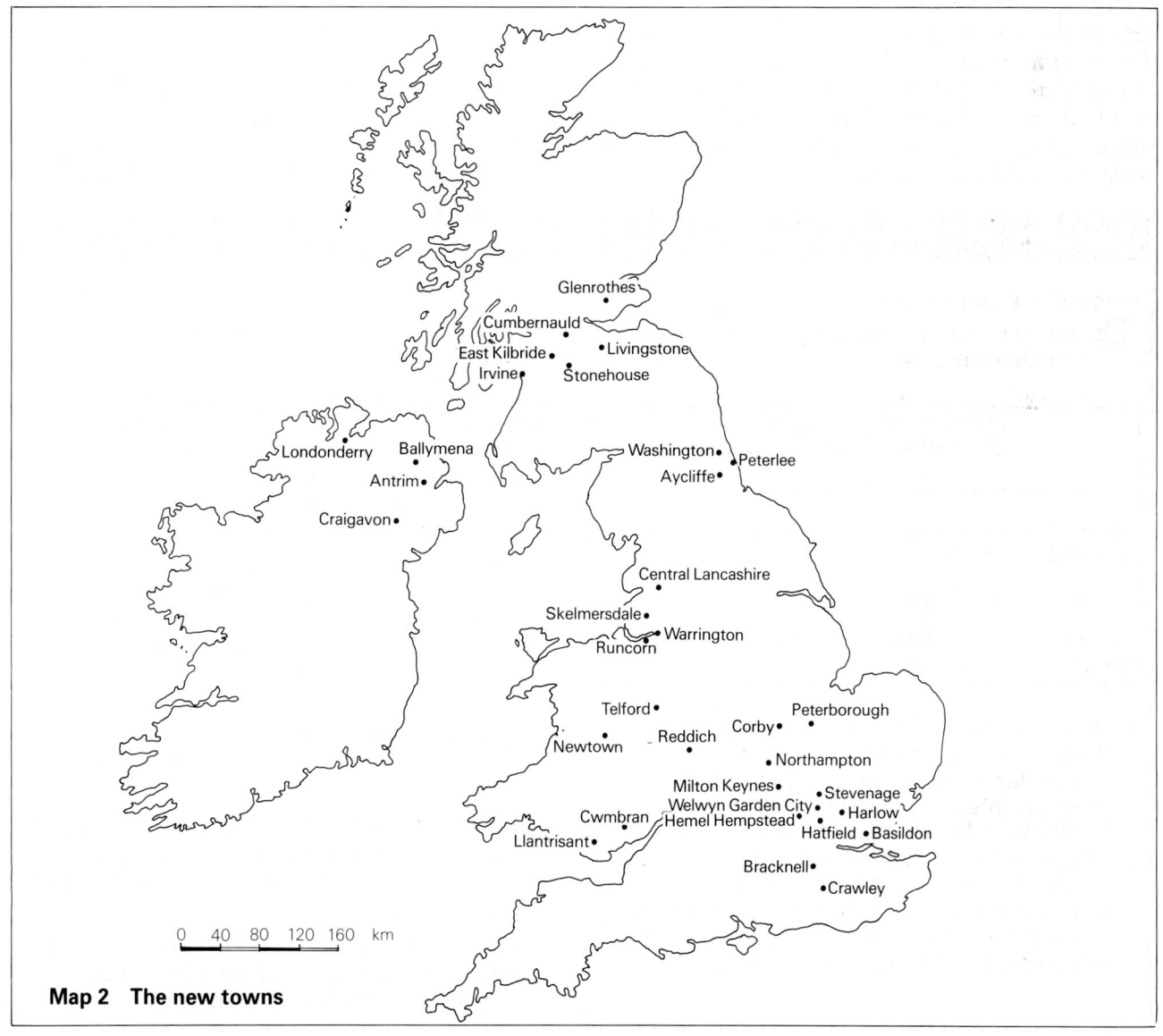

Map 2   The new towns

Study

In this study you will use the sources below to:

Ca discover more about the New Towns that were built after World War II.

Source 5A

The towns [are] throwing their ever-lengthening tentacles of brick and mortar over the country . . . In fifty years time there will, in southern England, be neither town nor country, but only a single dispersed suburb, sprawling unendingly from Watford to the coast.

C. E. M. Joad, *The People's Claim* (1938).

Source 5B

[New Towns should be] roughly round in shape, would have a radius of about a mile, which would enable all its industrial workers to be within walking or cycling distance of their work, of the town centre, and of the open country, and [would also enable] an extensive rural community to have easy access to the markets and social attractions of the town.

F. J. Osborn, *New Towns after the War* (1942).

Source 5C

Cumbernauld. The houses were laid out so that they all have a view of the surrounding hills.

Features of Cumbernauld

Location	Central Scotland.
Origin	Completely new settlement.
Shape and site	Roughly circular on hilly ground. More compact than some new towns.
Traffic	Street system separates traffic and pedestrians. No traffic lights and no right turns.

1 An octopus has tentacles. What did C. E. M. Joad (Source 5A) mean when he said that towns were 'throwing their ever-lengthening tentacles of brick and mortar over the countryside'?

2 Why did the planners in the 1940s think that by making towns roughly circular they would:
protect the British countryside;
help people who lived in the countryside to lead fuller lives?

3 **a** In what ways is Cumbernauld typical of new towns built after World War II?

   b What features of Cumbernauld would you NOT expect to find in all new towns? Give reasons for your answers.

Some, such as Northampton, are existing towns which have been extended. Others, such as Stevenage, are new settlements built from scratch in open country. Each town was planned and built by a development corporation.

Planners tried out fresh ideas in the new towns. Many designed traffic-free shopping centres. Since 1980, Milton Keynes has become famous for building energy-efficient houses, which cost very little to heat. Planners in other towns and cities have copied many ideas from the new towns.

Many people moved to new towns to take advantage of the good housing. Industries have been slower to move in, so instead of working in the town where they live, residents have to travel long distances to work. So some new towns have become extra suburbs of existing towns—not what their founders intended.

Towns and traffic

Between 1939 and 1960 the number of cars in Britain increased from less than two million to about six million. Many car owners wanted to travel to and from work in their cars. The number of lorries and vans was also increasing. Britain's towns could not cope with all these vehicles. Traffic slowed to a crawl, and often came to a complete standstill. In 1960 the Minister of Transport asked Professor Colin Buchanan to study the problems and suggest solutions.

The Buchanan Report

Professor Buchanan's report was published in 1963. He recommended that most traffic should be funnelled through towns on urban motorways, and

Study

Your aim in this study is to:

Ev interpret the photo below in the light of towns and traffic and the Buchanan Report.

Source 6

An underpass in Newcastle-upon-Tyne.

1 What can you see in the photograph that suggests it was taken after 1963? Give reasons for your answer.

2 What else can you see in the photograph that would help you to check the date when it was taken?

3 Suggest reasons why there are no pedestrians in the photograph.

that existing streets should be reserved for pedestrians and traffic with business in the area.

As a result, many small towns made inner ring roads to keep traffic out of the town centre, while some large towns pulled down thousands of houses, factories and offices to make urban motorways. Some had to replan whole sections of the town. As a rule they tended to replace houses and small shops by office blocks and multiple stores, whose tenants could afford high rents and rates.

The flow of traffic speeded up, but it was difficult for pedestrians to make their way around the new city centres.

Present problems

In 1987 there were still plenty of problems in Britain's towns. Few people lived in town centres, which were lonely places after the office workers and shop workers had gone home. Further out, Victorian suburbs were beginning to decay. Many houses there had been built for large families with several servants, and were too big for modern families. Prosperous middle-class people moved to modern convenient houses in the outer suburbs, and the Victorian houses were divided into flats and bedsits. These were occupied by people who could not afford to buy houses of their own. They could not get council accommodation because the government reduced the amount of money spent on housing, and there was a serious shortage of council property.

The problems were worse in some parts of the country than others. People tended to move into the south and east, because they believed they had a better chance of work there. In some south-eastern towns there was nowhere for them to live except bed and breakfast hotels, while there was room to spare in northern towns.

Recall

1 Explain these terms in your own words: slum; municipal socialism; suburb; garden city; low density; high rise.
2 In what ways were these men similar: Sir Titus Salt; George Cadbury; the Lever Brothers?
3 **Parliament and housing**
1875   Artisans' Dwelling Act
1890   Housing and the Working Class Act
1946   New Towns Act
1947   Town and Country Planning Act
1949   Housing Act (Labour Government)
1951   Housing Act (Conservative Government)
a Why did many people live in sub-standard or overcrowded houses in *i* the early 1870s, *ii* the early 1950s?
b How did governments in the 1870s and 1950s try to improve housing conditions?
c Do you think their efforts were successful? Give reasons for your answer.

19
Transport and Communications

RAILWAYS 1851–1914

Extending the network

In 1851 there was a good network of main railway lines except in Wales, Cornwall and northern Scotland. But there were very few suburban lines. Between 1851 and 1914 the gaps were filled in (see Chronology).

Suburban and rural lines

At the same time many branch and suburban lines were built. By 1914 there were about 37,000 km of railways in Britain. The largest settlement in mainland Britain without a railway within five kilometres was Painswick in Gloucestershire (population 2,638).

Chronology	
By 1859	The network reached Cornwall (Illustration 1) and South Wales.
1874	The Highland Railway reached Thurso in the far north of Scotland.
1886	Severn Tunnel opened to link South Wales industrial towns with London.
By 1890	The Tay and Forth bridges improved access to eastern Scotland.
1899	The Great Central Railway from Sheffield to London—the last main line to be built—was opened.

Illustration 1   Royal Albert Bridge at Saltash, designed by Brunel, was completed in 1859. It linked Cornwall and Devon by rail.

Speed, comfort and safety

Speed

After 1851 larger, faster engines reduced journey times.

Table 1 Journey times from London

	Fastest coach	Rail 1854	Rail 1914
Birmingham	11 h	3 h	2 h
Manchester	18 h	5 h 30 min.	3 h 30 min.
Newcastle	30 h	7 h 25 min.	5 h 20 min.
Plymouth	22 h	7 h 10 min.	4 h 7 min.
Edinburgh	43 h	10 h 50 min.	8 h 15 min.

Comfort

At the same time trains were made more comfortable and convenient. In 1850 passengers travelled in unheated, enclosed compartments lit by oil lamps. First and second class passengers had padded seats, but third class passengers sat on wooden benches. Gradually conditions improved. By 1900 all passengers travelled in heated coaches with padded seats. Most long distance trains had corridor coaches and some had restaurant cars. A few even had sleeping cars.

Safety

In 1851 railway travel was quite dangerous. Only the tender of the engine and the guard's van had brakes. The rest of the train had none. Signalling was also inadequate. As a rule, signals were left at 'danger' for a few minutes after a train had passed, and then reset at 'safe'. Bad brakes and poor signalling led to many accidents. So the government intervened (see the Chronology table on page 215). By 1914 passenger rail travel was safe, comfortable and speedy. But freight was often delayed. Coal

Study

Your aim in this study is to:

Ev see what you can learn from the painting below about railway travel in 1859.

Source 1

Passengers on a London–Brighton train in the 1850s.

1 Do you think the passengers are travelling in a first, second or third class compartment? Give reasons for your answer.
2 What do you think the artist was trying to show about rail travel at the time? Give reasons for your answer.

3 Why are we unable to form a complete picture of travelling conditions on a London to Brighton train in the 1850s by studying the painting?

trains had to be fitted in between passenger traffic and sometimes on the Midland Railway goods engine drivers spent an entire eight hour shift waiting for a signal to change to allow their trains onto the main line.

Organisation

Date	Number of companies
1851	180 (Many were small companies with only one or two short routes.)
1866	366
1914	106 (The Midland, the Great Western, the London and North Western and the North Eastern controlled fifty three per cent of the network between them.)

Chronology	
1871	The Board of Trade was given the right to inquire into every railway accident.
1871–89	Board of Trade inspectors urged companies to improve brakes and signalling, but progress was slow because companies did not want to spend the necessary money.
1889	Following an accident in Armagh in which 80 people were killed: **1** all trains had to be fitted with continuous automatic brakes; **2** no trains were to be allowed to enter a section of line until the signalman knew it was clear.

Study

In this study you will explore:

Ev how easy it is to form wrong ideas about the past, and how new evidence may help to give a more accurate picture.

Source 2A

If you look at a map of this country you see it covered with railways, and your first impression is that there is a most easy and most uninterrupted transit from one extremity to the other. Examine it more closely and you will find that this is not a uniform system of railways, all under one management . . . and is altogether a far more complicated affair than at first sight it appears.

Edward Cardwell, President of the Board of Trade, 1854.

Source 2B

. . . arrives 3 minutes earlier on Tuesdays and the third Saturday of the month.
Stops to set down first class passengers only.
Carriages detached—the Train does not stop.

Extracts from *Bradshaw's Railway Guide*, c. 1900. This book gave train timetables and other information needed by rail travellers.

1 Why might you think, from looking at Map 1, that it was easy to travel from one end of Britain to the other at that time?

2 Why may a passenger travelling by rail from Plymouth to Aberdeen in 1854 have found his journey more difficult than he expected?

3 Why can historians never be sure that they know exactly what life was like in the past?

Map 1 The railway system in the 1850s

WORLD WAR I AND AFTER

The war years

When World War I broke out in 1914 the government took over the railways and used them for such tasks as moving troops and munitions to the Channel ports, bringing back the wounded, and carrying steam coal for the fleet from mines in South Wales to northern Scotland. They converted railway workshops into munitions factories, and allowed railwaymen to join the armed forces. As a result, track fell into disrepair and rolling stock wore out. So journey times increased and breakdowns were frequent.

The Railway Act 1921

By the end of the war the railways needed millions of pounds spending on them. The government realised that small companies could not afford this. So in 1921 they passed the Railway Act. This set up four new companies to run the railways. These were the London, Midland and Scottish; the Great Western; the Southern; and the London and North Eastern. The Southern electrified the whole of its London suburban network, but the other companies had little money to spend on everyday improvements. Instead they spent their money on a few prestige express passenger trains such as the *Flying Scotsman*, the *Bristolian* and the *Cheltenham Flier*. On average trains ran slower in 1930 than in 1914.

Freight

After the war, the railways lost goods traffic. This was partly because by law railway companies were 'common carriers'. This meant that they had to accept everything they were asked to carry. To cover this they had a very complicated system of charges and routes. In addition, many railway goods wagons belonged to private firms. Most were small, four-wheeled trucks with manual brakes. At the top of a hill goods trains had to stop, and the guard had to walk along the train and pin down the brakes on each wagon. At the bottom of the hill all the brakes had to be released. So railway goods traffic was slow and unreliable, and could not compete with vans and lorries.

The four railway companies were all losing money, so they began to close down some of the loss-making branch lines.

World War II

When World War II broke out, the government again took control of the railways. The number of

Illustration 2   A World War II railway poster.

Study

In this study you will:

K work out why railway companies were constantly short of money between 1914 and 1945.

You will need to refer to the section World War I and after.

1 Why did the railways need a great deal spending on them by the end of World War I (1914–18)?
2 Why did the way in which the railway companies spent their money after 1921:
   make a few journeys much faster;
   make many journeys slower?
3 Suggest reasons why railways companies were:
   still losing money at the beginning of World War II in 1939;
   unlikely to make a profit after the war.

passengers increased. This was partly due to a shortage of petrol which prevented people from travelling by car, and partly to the armed forces who were given warrants to travel by train. For the first time railway companies tried to discourage people travelling by rail (Illustration 2).

By the end of the war, parts of the railway system had been damaged in air raids, the coaches were delapidated, the engines were worn out, the track was in poor condition, and only inferior coal was available for the locomotives. After the war, improvements were very slow to come.

Nationalisation

In 1947, the Labour government nationalised the railways and set up the British Transport Commission to control all rail, road and water transport. Since then development of the railways has been controlled by the government.

Chronology	
1955	The government approved a modernisation plan involving: **1** replacing steam engines with diesels or electrics; **2** installing new colour light signals; **3** replacing old goods wagons by modern stock. They hoped these improvements would enable the railways to make a profit.
1961	Dr Richard Beeching, Chairman of the British Transport Commission, was ordered to recommend how to make the railways pay.
1963	Dr Beeching recommended the closure of many branch lines. The network was reduced to 18,000 km.
1966	A new, fast electric service was introduced between London and Manchester.
1974	The new service was extended to Glasgow. The number of passengers using trains on the route doubled.
1975 onwards	New diesel electric 125 express services (Illustration 3) were brought in on main lines, resulting in faster services. But though individual lines made a profit, the network as a whole lost money.

Table 2   Journey times from London (hs/mins)

	1951	1971	1981	1986
Aberdeen	11.55	9.37	7.26	7.21
Birmingham	2.19	1.34	1.31	1.33
Glasgow	8.35	5.59	5.08	5.10
Manchester	3.45	2.31	2.28	2.33
Penzance	6.55	6.00	5.06	4.52

Social Trends, 1987.

Study

The changes that governments made to the railways between 1955 and 1975 affected millions of people and caused a great deal of discussion. In this study you will:

Em consider the changes from the point of view of some people whose lives might have been affected by them.

Use the information in the Chronology table on this page.

In pairs

1 Each question below is divided into parts *i* and *ii*. Decide which part each of you will take.
2 Look at the year you are dealing with. What change did the government make to British Rail in that year and what may the person or persons you are considering have thought about it?
Give reasons for your answer.
   a 1955
      i A steam engine driver.
      ii A railway apprentice who hopes to make working on the railway his career.
   b 1963
      i An elderly couple who cannot afford a car and who have retired to a village linked by a branch line to the town five miles away.
      ii The owner of a small bus company in a rural area.
   c 1975
      i A businessman who believes that the government should not subsidise businesses that do not pay.
      ii A member of the public who wants to keep as much traffic off the road as possible.
3 Ask two people to read their answers to the class. What do the rest of you think?

Illustration 3   An InterCity 125.

UNDERGROUND RAILWAYS

By 1855 more than 270,000 people travelled into central London to work, and the streets were jammed with horse buses, cabs, carts and carriages. A traveller from Brighton complained that it took him longer to travel from London Bridge station to his office in the Strand, a distance of 3.5 km, than from Brighton to London, a distance of 85 km.

In 1859 a company was set up to build an underground railway between Paddington and Farringdon Street in the City to carry some of these commuters. They made the railway by digging out a trench wide enough for both sets of rails, and then roofing it in. This was very expensive.

In 1863 the Metropolitan Railway, as it was called, was opened. It was the first underground railway in the world. The trains were drawn by steam engines, fitted with condensers to consume the smoke and steam. In spite of this a passenger wrote that on a journey on the railway he 'was coughing and spluttering like a boy with his first cigar'.

Nevertheless, the Metropolitan Railway carried ten million passengers in its first year and made a profit. So it was extended and copied.

London is the only city in Britain with a network of underground railways. In 1986, 1,900 million passenger journeys were made on the London Underground. If all these passengers had to travel above ground the streets would be jammed solid.

TRAMS

Trams are passenger vehicles which run along rails set in the road surface. The first trams were horse drawn. In some towns horses were replaced by steam engines, but eventually all Britain's trams were powered by electricity.

Trams were only used in large towns. It cost so much to lay the rails and put up the power lines that they had to carry a large number of passengers to make the expenditure worth while.

Each electric tram could carry sixty or more passengers. So a frequent service could move hundreds of people an hour. Tram fares were cheap. Most passengers were working people. They used trams to travel to and from work—trams enabled them to live several miles from their workplace and to travel to local parks, museums, shops, football matches, etc. in their time off.

The decline of the tram

As motor traffic increased, trams became a nuisance. Other traffic had to dodge round them. This

Chronology	
1875	Most London railway terminuses linked by the Circle underground line.
1884	The Circle line was completed.
1890	The Monument to Stockwell line was opened. This was the first 'tube', made by tunnelling underground. The trains were powered by electricity.
1892	A London-wide network of tubes was approved, and has been growing ever since.
1896	The Glasgow Underground was opened.
1913	All the underground railway companies in London were combined into one company.
1933	The London Passenger Transport Board was set up to control passenger transport in London.

Chronology	
1860	Horse trams first introduced in London and Birkenhead.
1860–80	Horse tram services set up in Birmingham, Glasgow, Portsmouth, Plymouth, Leeds, Middlesborough and Hull.
1870	The Tramway Act gave local authorities the right to take over private tram companies in their areas.
1877	Steam trams introduced in Glasgow.
1889	Bradford set up an electric tram system.
1924	Maximum mileage of tramlines— 4,225 km with 14,000 tramcars reached.

Illustration 4   A train on the Metropolitan line in 1863.

caused delays, and could be dangerous for passengers getting on and off. Maintenance work on the track and overhead wires also disrupted traffic. Motor buses could carry almost as many passengers, and fitted in better with the rest of the traffic. So gradually trams were scrapped and replaced by buses. By 1960 almost all the British trams had gone, though many continental cities still have them.

BUSES

Horse buses

George Shillibeer started the first regular bus service in Britain in London in 1829. His bus was a large box-like vehicle with seats inside along each side. The driver sat on a box seat at the front and the conductor stood on a step by the side of the door at the

Study

In this study you will use various sources to:

K find out what you can about London's public transport, 1851–1900, and the passengers who travelled on it.

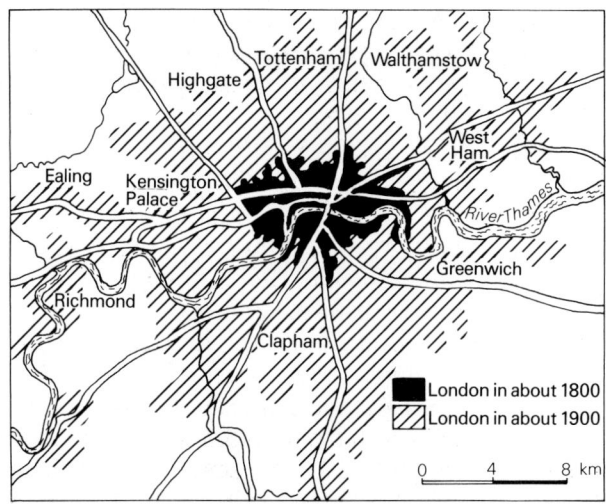

Map 2   The growth of London, 1800–1900

Table 3   Population of London

1841	2.23 million
1861	3.22 million
1881	4.77 million
1901	6.58 million

Source 3A

I have seen . . . such carriages filled inside, I might venture to say although I never was in one, to almost suffocation—and, the outside packed with individuals to an extent that was truly dangerous; and drawn too, by two miserable animals that were scarcely able to drag the carriage even if it were empty. The drivers paid no regard to the passengers nor to the poor animals, which were compelled to move onward by merciless lashings.

Colonel Sibthorp MP (1847) describing conditions on horse buses.

Source 3B

A journey from King's Cross to Baker Street is a form of mild torture which no person would undergo if he could conveniently help it.

The Times, 1884, reporting on London's underground railways.

Source 3C

Trams were obviously much more in place in the working-class areas than when they run up to the 'good residential' districts. Their . . . shape, their extraordinary noisiness, which makes two or three together sound like a small fairground . . . their wonderful double necklace of lights at night—all make them . . . working-class vehicles.

Richard Hoggart, *The Uses of Literacy* (1957).

1 Why, do you think, did more passengers travel on public transport in 1900 than in 1850?
2 What three kinds of public transport could Londoners use?
3 What social class or classes do you think most passengers on London's public transport belonged to? Give reasons for your answer.

Illustration 5 A London 'knifeboard' horse bus in the 1890s.

back and took the fares. Shillibeer's bus was popular. Soon there were several regular bus services in London. They too became very popular.

In about 1860 'knife-board' buses came into service. In addition to the seats inside they had two long seats mounted back to back along the roof, reached by a flight of steps at the back. By 1890 they were being replaced by buses with seats facing the front on either side of a central gangway. These held more passengers than knife-board buses. London relied more on buses than trams for public transport. By 1905 there were 3,484 horse buses (Illustration 5) on the streets of London, run by about sixty separate companies.

Motor buses

The first motor buses appeared on the roads in 1900. In 1902 there were twenty eight in London. In 1905 there were 241. The first regular country motor bus service was run by the Great Western Railway Company from Helston to the Lizard in Cornwall. It was started in 1903.

At first motor buses were no faster than horse buses, and less reliable. But gradually they improved, and by 1925 they had entirely replaced horse buses and were beginning to replace trams as well. By 1960 most towns relied on them for almost all their public transport.

At the same time a network of long distance motor coaches was established. Coaches were slower than trains, but cheaper. In 1961 a quarter of all travel was by bus or coach, compared with fifteen per cent by train. Then the growth of the motorway network, and the Beeching cuts of the railways encouraged more people to travel by coach. Long distance coaches became more and more luxurious, with television sets and built-in toilets.

Nationalisation and deregulation

The Transport Commission, set up in 1947, took over a number of independent companies and combined them to form the National Bus Company. This nationalised company ran about a third of the country's bus services. In 1986 the government denationalised the National Bus Company, and abolished many of the regulations controlling bus and coach services. They hoped that this would encourage bus companies to compete, and so bring down fares and improve services.

Study

Between 1945 and 1973 the number of foreign tourists visiting Britain increased, and more British people went on holidays. Tourism became one of Britain's most important industries.
In this study you will consider:

Em why many tourists in Britain preferred to travel by coach rather than train.

1 In pairs: The following is a list of reasons why tourists might have chosen to travel by coach. Rewrite them in order of importance.
  a New motorways speeded up long distance coach travel.
  b The 'Beeching cuts' of 1963 made it more difficult to reach remote country districts by rail.
  c Coaches became more comfortable, with reclining seats and air conditioning.
  d Coach travel was cheaper than rail travel.

  e Many places of interest to tourists, for example historic houses, provided facilities for coach travellers.
  f Coaches could adapt their schedules and stopping places to suit their customers more easily than trains could.
2 Ask one person to read the first and last item on his or her list to the class, and say why the items were given these placings. Do the rest of you agree?

SHIPS

Clippers

In the middle of the nineteenth century, steamships often had to fill their boilers with sea water. This corroded the pipes. So engine designers could not use high pressure steam in case it blew holes in them. Low pressure engines are inefficient, and on very long voyages steamships could not compete with well-designed sailing ships.

The best designed sailing ships were clippers, which originated in the USA. They could sail more than 500 km a day, and specialised in the China tea trade. Every year clippers loaded up in China with the new season's crop and raced to London. The first cargo landed sold at a higher price than the rest, so clipper crews tried hard to be first back. These races became famous. The most exciting was in 1866. The *Ariel* beat the *Teeping* by ten minutes in a voyage lasting ninety nine days.

Cutty Sark (Illustration 6) is the most famous clipper.

Chronology: Cutty Sark	
1869	Built in Dumbarton.
1870–77	Involved in the tea trade. Carried 600,000 kg of tea from Shanghai to Britain. Voyage took an average of 115 days.
1883–95	Worked in the Australian wool trade. Carried 5,000 bales of wool from New South Wales to London. Voyage took between seventy and eighty days.
1895	Sold to Portuguese shipowners. Used for general cargo work.
1922	Brought back to Britain and refitted. Now on display in dry dock at Greenwich.

Illustration 6 The *Cutty Sark* under sail.

New steamships

Cutty Sark was sold in 1895 because sailing ships could no longer compete against new, more efficient steamships.

Condensers

By 1860 engineers had perfected a device to condense exhaust steam back into water to use again. Ships no longer had to re-fill their boilers with sea water. The pipes did not corrode, and there was less danger of leaks and explosions. Engineers could now install efficient high pressure steam engines in ships. By 1890 there were plenty of new, powerful steamships which carried cargo faster and cheaper than sailing ships.

Turbines

In 1884 Charles Parsons, a young British engineer, patented a steam turbine which was much smoother and more efficient than piston engines. In 1896 he built *Turbinia*, a small turbine-driven boat. In 1897 he went to Spithead where a naval display was taking place and sailed *Turbinia* into the middle of it. The navy's fastest destroyers tried to catch him, but *Turbinia* was too fast for them.

In 1901 two Clyde steamers were fitted with turbines. Within six years Cunard fitted them into their three latest passenger liners. As soon as one of them, the *Mauretania*, went into service, it captured the 'Blue Ribband' for the fastest crossing of the Atlantic and kept it for twenty two years.

Transatlantic liners

Ocean liners carried passengers quickly and comfortably all over the world. The route across the Atlantic was the most important, and steamship companies competed to offer the best service. Three ships were needed to operate an efficient weekly service. Every Saturday one of them sailed from Britain. Six days later it reached New York, remained there for five days and then sailed back to Britain.

In 1907 the managers of the White Star Line decided to build three luxury liners, bigger than any of their rivals. The first, the *Olympic*, made its maiden voyage in 1911. It was described as 'a floating palace'. It accommodated 2,400 passengers on seven decks, with a swimming pool, a gymnasium, lounges and restaurants. The 700 first class passengers had spacious cabins and plenty of room to wander around. The thousand third class passengers had much less space.

Study

In this study you will:

S examine the similarities and differences between two famous passenger ships.

Source 4A

The *Great Britain* was launched in 1843. Its propeller was driven by a piston engine. It took a fortnight to cross the Atlantic.

1 In what ways were the *Great Britain* and the *Mauretania* similar?
2 In what ways did they differ?

Source 4B

The *Mauretania* was launched in 1907. Its propellers were driven by steam turbines and it took four or five days to cross the Atlantic.

3 Why, do you think, were the engineers on board the *Great Britain* and the *Mauretania* important members of the crew?

During World War I, one transatlantic liner, the *Lusitania*, was torpedoed on a voyage from New York. Several others were used as troopships. After the war they went back into passenger service. Bigger, faster boats were built until in 1939, Cunard had two ships, the *Queen Mary* and the *Queen Elizabeth*, which were so fast that the two of them could maintain a weekly service on their own. But before the *Queen Elizabeth* could go into service, World War II broke out and both ships were commandeered for use as troopships. After the war liners were busier than ever. In 1957 one million people sailed across the Atlantic.

In October 1958 an American jet airliner flew from New York to Paris in less than seven hours. Steamships could not compete. By 1970 only four per cent of people crossing the Atlantic went by sea, and ocean liners were either scrapped or used for holiday cruises.

Cargo ships

Steam turbines were also installed in cargo ships, which made them faster and more reliable. But most still carried a mixture of different cargoes which were packed down into the holds, and then man-handled out by dockers. Since World War II all this has changed. Many cargo ships are now designed to carry metal containers which also fit onto lorries and railway trucks. These containers are filled in the factories, and are loaded on and off the ships by huge cranes. Other ships are bulk carriers which carry cargoes such as oil or grain which are pumped in and out of them by machine.

Most container ships and bulk carriers are very large. Eighteenth- and nineteenth-century docks are too small for them. So new deep water docks have been built. For example, London docks, admired by Defoe, are now derelict, while a new container port at Felixstowe in Suffolk flourishes.

Study

The liners built by Cunard and the White Star Line seemed the safest and most luxurious ships ever to cross the North Atlantic. Everyone was amazed and horrified when the *Titanic* (Source 5), the *Olympic*'s sister ship, sank on its maiden voyage.

In this study you will:

Ca consider some of the reasons for this disaster;

Em and look at the disaster from the perspective of some passengers, a crew member and a journalist.

Remember what you learned about transatlantic liners on pages 221–2.

Source 5

The *Titanic* on her maiden voyage.

In April 1912 the *Titanic* set out from Southampton, bound for New York. The voyage was expected to take between four and five days. Passengers in the most expensive cabins had paid $4,000 to make the crossing—four times as much as the average American family earned in a year. The ship was full, and the first class passengers knew that many of their friends would be on board.

1 Why may so many wealthy people have decided to cross the Atlantic on the *Titanic* in April 1912?

■

Four days after leaving Southampton the *Titanic* was sailing at full speed across a calm sea when the duty officer received a wireless message warning that there were several huge icebergs in his path. The duty officer did not tell anyone and the *Titanic* sailed on.

2 Why may the duty officer have decided to ignore the warning?

■

The *Titanic* hit an iceberg and sank rapidly. There were only enough lifeboats for about half the passengers and crew, and 1,500 people were drowned. Three days after the disaster a leading article in *The Times* criticised 'the mad competition' between shipping companies operating luxury liners on the transatlantic crossing.

3 a Suggest reasons why the writer of the article called the competition between shipping companies 'mad'?
  b What may he have hoped to achieve by criticising the shipping companies?

AIR TRAVEL

The pioneers

In 1903 in the USA the Wright brothers flew the first powered heavier-than-air machine. At the same time, engineers were building airships, or steerable balloons which were lighter than air. In 1908 a British airship flew over London at a speed of twenty-five miles an hour.

In 1909 Louis Bleriot flew across the Channel from Calais to Dover. Years later he remembered how he climbed into his plane at 4.35 a.m.

'In an instant I am in the air, my engine making 1,200 revolutions—almost its highest speed—in order that I may get quickly over the telegraph wires along the edge of the cliff. As soon as I am over the cliff I reduce my speed. There is now no need to force my engine. I begin my flight, steady and sure towards the coast of England . . . I am making over 40 mph . . . Ten minutes go. I turn my head to see whether I am proceeding in the right direction . . . There is nothing to be seen . . . I am lost. [Ten minutes passed] Then I saw the cliffs of Dover.'

Bleriot landed in a nearby field. His flight of thirty-one miles had taken forty minutes—an average speed of 46 mph. Bleriot made flying popular in Britain and aviators toured the country giving flying displays. Planes were improving all the time.

Passenger air services

In 1919 the first daily commercial air service in the world was set up between London and Paris. The flight took up to two and a half hours, depending on the weather. It did not make a profit.

Passenger flights could be very uncomfortable, but in time, larger, more stable and more comfortable aircraft were built, the number of passengers increased and the airline business expanded.

Chronology	
1924	Imperial Airways set up with a government subsidy.
1929	Established a regular service to India. Flight took six days.
1934	Established a regular service to Australia. Flight took twelve days.
1934	First regular inter-continental air mail service set up (Illustration 7).
1935	British Airways, a rival company, was set up.
1939	Imperial Airways and Pan American set up the first regular transatlantic service.
1939	Imperial Airways and British Airways combined, with the help of government subsidies, to form the British Overseas Airways Corporation (BOAC).

Illustration 7 Air mail being loaded aboard an Imperial Airways plane at Croydon in 1934.

Study: Library work

Your aim in this study is to:

K find out what you can about Alcock and Brown, and Keith and Ross Smith who were pioneer airmen.

1 List the sections in your school or local library where you might find information about them and their work.
2 With the help of this information, make brief notes showing why these men are famous and how they obtained money to help them to carry on their work.
3 Use the information on pages 224–5 to write an essay on one of the following topics:
1919—an important year in aviation history.
The ways in which money was found to develop long-distance flights between 1919 and 1939.
How the work of Alcock and Brown and Keith and Ross Smith was carried on between 1924 and 1939.

Study

World War I

World War I (1914–18) was the first war in which aircraft were used. Your aim is to use the sources below to:

K consider the effect that aircraft had on that war.

Source 6A

Zeppelins were the main type of lighter-than-air craft used in World War I.

Source 6B

Zeppelins were big, slow and easy to shoot down. So both sides developed 'bombers'—heavier-than-air craft which could carry a load of bombs over long distances.

Source 6C

. . . a British aviator vol-planed down to his own line with a wing damaged by shrapnel . . . He jerked out his story . . . He had seen . . . new batteries going into position. He had seen, far away, still more German regiments.

From a report in *The Times*, 5 March 1915, reporting the German attack which launched the First Battle of Ypres in Belgium.

Source 6E

I left Furnes . . . under orders to . . . look for Zeppelins and attack the Berchem St Agathe Airship Shed with six 20 lb bombs.

The Berchem St Agathe shed was part of a Zeppelin base. From a report by Flt Sub Lt R. A. J. Warneford, 7 June 1915.

Source 6D

Breithaupt had reserved his bombs until he was well over . . . the city. . . . He dropped his first high-explosive at Exeter Street . . . killing one person and injuring two more. Immediately . . . the searchlights of the London defences swung towards L 15 [a Zeppelin], and the guns . . . began to fire at her.

K. Poolman, *Zeppelins over England* (1960).

1 Give an example of:
   a lighter than air machine used in World War I;
   a heavier than air machine used in World War I.
2 In what ways could aircraft be destroyed?
3 In what ways were soldiers and civilians affected by the use of aircraft in World War I?

During World War II better, faster aircraft were developed. After the war, passenger aircraft had pressurised cabins which enabled them to fly 'above the weather', and turbine engines, which gave smoother and speedier travel. So air travel expanded.

Chronology	
1946	The Civil Aviation Act set up two nationalised airlines, British European Airways (BEA) and BOAC.
1948	The Vickers *Viscount*, a turbo-prop airliner, went into service.
1950	British scheduled airlines carried 1,156,000 passengers.
1952	BOAC set up the first jet airline service, using *Comets*.
1970	First jumbo jet, carrying up to 500 passengers, went into service.
1971	British scheduled airlines carried 14,462,000 passengers.
1972	BOAC and BEA combined to form British Airways.
1976	Anglo-French supersonic Concorde airliner went into service.
1987	British Airways sold to private investors.

Table 4 Trips from the UK to Europe (thousands)

	Air flights	Sea voyages
1971	4,192	3,090
1981	6,869	7,090
1985	9,236	7,355

Table 5 Domestic public transport (billion passenger km)

	Air	Bus/Coach	Rail
1961	1	67	39
1971	2	51	36
1981	3	42	34
1986	4	41	37

(Information from *Social Trends 1988*.)

Air travel is now taken for granted by businessmen and holidaymakers. The increasing size and number of aircraft has meant that huge new airports have had to be built, often miles from the city they serve. This means that even on quite long journeys, the time taken on the flight is less than that spent getting to and from the airport.

Study

In this study your aims are:

Ch to see what the sources below tell us about changes in commercial air travel between the 1920s and the 1980s;

Ev to decide whether or not you think these sources are reliable.

Source 7A

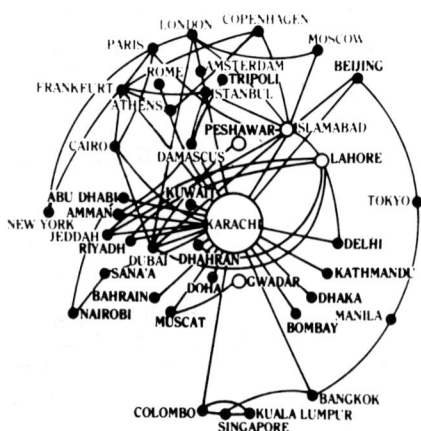

Part of a 1987 advertisement for Pakistan International Airlines.

Source 7B

[Passengers suffer from] air-sickness, drumming in the ears, head-ache and other forms of discomfort . . . The problems of passenger air travel are grouped thus: ventilation, heating, odours, noise and vibration, sickness in the air and general comfort.

From a report in *The Times*, November 1922.

Source 7C

We used to go to a cooked meat shop in Croydon and buy ham, tongue and a bit of veal and ham pie; then we'd go back to Croydon Airport and boil a few potatoes for potato salad.

A stewardess working on one of the first commercial airlines in the 1920s.

1 In the 1920s, the commercial airlines flying to and from London were owned by Europeans. What evidence is there that by 1987 Asian airlines were flying passenger services to London?
2 Why may more people have enjoyed travelling by air in 1987 than in the 1920s?
3 Do you think the information in *i* Source 7A; *ii* Source 7B; *iii* Source 7C is reliable? Give reasons for your answers.

—————— Part Two ——————

Private Transport

BICYCLES

The first practical bicycle, the 'ordinary' or 'penny-farthing', was developed in about 1870. It was very heavy, had solid tyres, and was difficult to control. So there were very few cyclists. But by 1890 safer and lighter bicycles were developed and cycling grew steadily more popular (see Diagram 1).

Cycling clubs were set up, and adventurous young cyclists set out on long trips.

Diagram 1

Cheaper than a horse to buy and keep. → Increasing number of cyclists. ← Enabled townspeople to explore the countryside.

Provided a quick and healthy way to get to work and visit friends. → Increasing number of cyclists. ← Easily available as factories were set up, especially in Coventry, Oxford and Nottingham.

Study

Use the information in the sources below to find out:

Ca why cycling was popular with women in the 1890s, but became less popular with them in the early years of the twentieth century.

Source 8A

Cyclists as a cartoonist saw them in *The Sketch* in 1896.

Source 8B

HEALTH SUGGESTIONS

YOU NEED EXERCISE—there are several

REASONS WHY

IF IN POOR HEALTH, you can regain good health through the judicious use of the Bicycle. "G. & J." Tyres reduce excessive vibration, and make the exercise safe.

IF IN GOOD HEALTH, Bicycle riding will keep you so. In your children the Bicycle lays the foundation of a healthy and useful life. A good intellect reaches its highest excellence only in a healthy body.

IF YOU ARE BEAUTIFUL, Bicycle riding will preserve your beauty. Exercise means health. There is no real beauty without Good Health.

IF YOU ARE NOT A BEAUTY, you may at least make yourself more attractive. The Bicycle brightens the eye, puts a flush of health on the cheek, takes you out to Nature, to the pure fresh air. They are yours; enjoy them—do it "luxuriously" on a Bicycle fitted with "G. & J." Tyres.

YOU ARE A WOMAN, and to you the Bicycle affords a most pleasant means of obtaining exercise, which you, of all, most need. Riding any Bicycle is exercise—riding a Bicycle fitted with "G. & J." Tyres is "comfortable and luxurious exercise."

For comfortable riding have "G. & J." Tyres.

Gormully & Jeffery Mfg. Co.,

COVENTRY.

Chicago. Boston. Washington. New York. Brooklyn. Detroit.

Ad advertisement from the *Lady Cyclist* in 1895.

> *Study continued*

Source 8C

Cycling was considered such a dangerous pastime that the members of the earliest cycling clubs telegraphed home news of their safe arrival at the farthest point of their journey.

Flora Thompson, *Lark Rise to Candleford* (1945).

1 Why, do you think, were many women attracted to cycling in the 1890s?
2 Some people in the 1890s thought cycling was unsuitable for women. Why may they have thought this?

Source 8D

. . . the quiet English roads were a cyclist's paradise . . . You had the road to yourself . . . The arrival of the motor killed all the old cycling as I knew it.

J. Platts-Betts, a champion racing cyclist, in a BBC interview.

3 Cycling was most popular between 1900 and 1905. After this fewer women took up cycling. What do you think caused this change?

Study: Library work

Your aim in this study is to:

K find out what you can about J. K. Starley and John Dunlop, two inventors who helped to popularise cycling.

1 List the sections in your school or public library where you might find information about these men and their work.
2 Find the information you need to write brief notes on:
the invention which J. K. Starley patented in 1885;
the invention which John Dunlop patented in 1888.

3 With the help of your notes and the information on pages 227–8 write an essay on one of the following topics:
why bicycles were more popular in 1890 than in 1870;
why many young people between 1885 and 1905 wanted to own a bicycle;
why the period 1885–1905 might be described as 'The glorious days of cycling'.

MOTOR CARS

Early cars

Motor cars were developed in Germany in 1885 and 1886 by Daimler and Benz. A few were imported into Britain in 1888. They were noisy, unreliable and uncomfortable. What was more, they were forbidden to travel faster than 4 mph (6.5 kph) on British roads, and a man carrying a red flag had to walk in front of them to warn people that they were coming. Cars did not sell well in Britain.

In 1896 Parliament changed the law to allow cars to travel at 12 mph (20 kph). The *Illustrated London News* said:

'Horseless carriages promise to be a great institution for ladies with plenty of pluck to go about alone and steer themselves, but not enough vital force to propel a bicycle.'

But the *Daily Mail* thought:

'the motor carriage will never displace the smart trotting pony'.

The growth of motoring 1900–39

Between 1900 and 1914 motoring developed rapidly in Britain. In 1909 the government set up the Road Fund, financed by a tax on petrol and licence duty on cars. The fund was spent on improving roads. The first job was to spray them with tar to bind the surface together and prevent dust from rising.

After World War I, motor manufacturers tried to produce cheap, reliable cars which the middle class and the skilled working class could afford. In 1924

Study

In this study you will:

K consider what sources 9A, 9B and 9C tell us about some of the first motorists.

Source 9A

Daimlers cost about £300 to buy in Britain. Many working class people took more than three years to earn this amount.

Source 9B

Motoring costume in about 1900.

Source 9C

Last Saturday His Majesty drove from Sandringham to Newmarket and back on his 12 h.p. Daimler . . . Hitherto he has always had a special train. The roads were extremely dusty, but His Majesty expresses himself as delighted with the drive. At Downham great crowds collected to see him pass down the High Street, which he did at a right royal speed of between 20 and 30 miles per hour.

From *Autocar*, a magazine for motorists published in April 1901.

1 Why may motorists have found it necessary to wear the kind of clothes shown in Source 9B?
2 Why, do you think, did only a few people own cars before 1900?
3 What are we told in Source 9C to suggest that by 1901:
   motorists did not keep to the 12 mph speed limit;
   it was becoming fashionable to own a car;
   people wanted to know more about cars?

William Morris, afterwards Lord Nuffield, said:

'Until the worker goes to his factory by car, I shall not believe that we have touched more than a fringe of the home market'.

Cars steadily fell in price and their number increased (see Chronology). Between 1930 and 1939 more by-passes were built and roads widened. In addition, houses to accommodate commuting motorists were built along main roads on the outskirts of towns and cities. This was known as 'ribbon development'.

Chronology	
1922	315,000 cars on the road.
1925	'Bull nosed' Morris Cowley produced, costing less than £200.
1929	Austin 7, costing £130, produced.
1930	Over one million cars on the road.
1935	Ford 8, costing £100 produced.
As the number of cars increased the country's roads were adapted to accommodate them.	
1920	First filling station opened.
1926	First roundabouts installed.
1929	First traffic lights installed.
1930	The Kingston By-pass, the first large scale by-pass, opened.

Study

In this study you will consider the reasons why:

Ca the number of car owners increased after 1922 and the appearance of towns changed when the number of car owners increased.

You will need to refer to the section on the growth of motoring on page 228.

1 William Morris was a car manufacturer. Why did he want workers to be able to drive to work in their own cars?
2 How did Morris and other car manufacturers make it possible for more workers to own cars between 1922 and 1939?
3 In what ways did the appearance of towns change as the number of workers owning cars increased?

Post-war motoring

During World War II, no cars were made and no petrol was available for ordinary motorists. So the number of cars on the road fell. After the war as petrol supplies increased and car production started up again the numbers of cars grew.

In 1984 there was approximately one car for every three people in Britain, and private cars made up eighty three per cent of the traffic on the roads. The total distance travelled by car also increased. To make room for cars towns and cities were re-planned (see Chapter 18) and a nationwide network of motorways was built.

Study

Use the sources below to:

Ca work out why a motorway network was built in Britain during the second half of the twentieth century.

Source 10

A stretch of the M4.

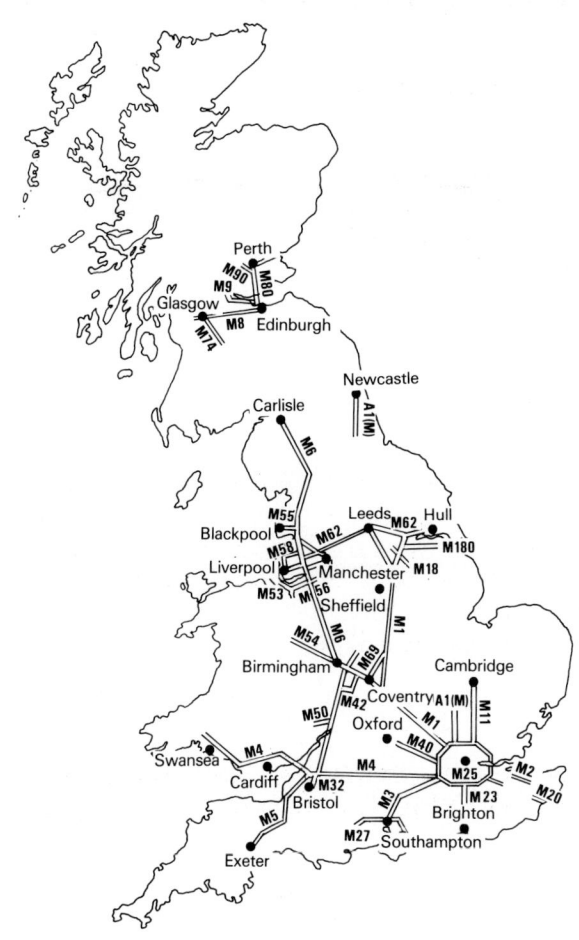

Map 3 The motorway network, 1987

Table 6   Number of cars on the road (millions)

1950	2.3
1961	6.3
1971	12.1
1981	15.3
1985	16.9

Social Trends 1987 (Central Statistical Office).

Table 7   Distances travelled (billion passenger km)

	Public transport	Car*
1961	107	142
1971	89	284
1981	79	380
1985	82	432

* Includes motor cycles and taxis.
Social Trends 1987

1 a How many more cars used Britain's roads in 1985 than in 1950?
  b Did the distances travelled by car increase or decrease between 1961 and 1985?
2 Why, do you think, was the network of motorways shown in Map 3 laid down between 1950 and 1985?
3 a Why can motorists travel faster on motorways than on most other types of road?
  b Why are motorists sometimes not able to travel as quickly as intended on motorways?

Study

In this study you will discuss:
K the advantages and disadvantages of cars.

Some advantages and disadvantages of cars are listed below. You can probably think of others.

Advantages
Enable users to travel when they like.
Give comfortable transport to anywhere in the country.

Disadvantages
Pollute the atmosphere.
Cause traffic jams.
Kill over 5,000 people a year.
Use huge quantities of oil products.
Cost huge sums in road building and maintenance.

In pairs

1 What do you think is the car's greatest advantage? Give reasons for your answer.
2 What do you think is the car's greatest disadvantage? Give reasons for your answer.
3 Give an example of a change that might lead to a decrease in the number of cars on the road in your lifetime.
4 Ask one person to read his or her answers to the class. What do the rest of you think?

—— Part Three ——
Postal Services

Study

In this study you will use the information in the sources below to:

S compare the work done by telegraph boys and telephone operators in the first half of the twentieth century;

Ch see how the importance of their work changed.

Source 11A

Town post offices employed 'telegraph boys' to deliver telegrams. At first they went on foot. Then they were given bicycles. Finally, after World War II, they used motor cycles. The inland telegram system was abolished in 1982.

Source 11C

When I went to work at seventeen shillings a week as a telephonist at the new Central Exchange, some people seemed to think it rather saucy . . . to be a switchboard girl. I don't know whether this was because our job required us to speak to a great number of strange men, but as a matter of fact we were strictly supervised. When we started at the Central Exchange it had only two hundred subscribers, but so great was the public interest that within three months the number had increased to three thousand.

A telephone operator describing her work at the Central Exchange in 1902.

Source 11D   Percentage of homes with phones

1973	45
1979	67
1984	78
1985	81

Source 11B

Until 1927, every call was connected in the exchange by operators using plugs and sockets. Until 1958, all long distance and overseas calls had to be made through an operator. By 1980 it was possible to dial calls direct to most parts of the world.

1 **a** In what way was the work done by telegraph boys and telephone operators similar?

 b In what ways was their work different?

2 Suggest reasons why telegraph boys were redundant after 1982.

3 **a** What evidence is there to suggest that job opportunities for telephone operators increased rapidly between 1902 and 1927?

 b What kind of evidence might you look for to check if employment of telephone operators increased in this period?

 c Between 1958 and 1985 the percentage of homes in Britain with phones increased, but the number of people employed as telephone operators fell. Explain why.

LETTER POST

On Saturday morning, 21 March 1857, Madeleine Smith, a young Glasgow woman, posted a letter to her lover Emile, who lived in another part of the city. The letter was delivered later the same day. But Emile was away for the weekend at Bridge of Allan, thirty miles away. So a friend posted it on to Bridge of Allan post office, where Emile collected it the next day. People took an efficient postal service for granted. In many towns there were six deliveries a day.

Since 1900 the frequency of collections and deliveries has decreased.

TELEGRAPH

The only means of sending messages in the second half of the nineteenth century was the telegraph. Most post offices could send and receive telegraph messages, and by the end of the century there was a world-wide network of cables. As soon as a post-office received a message it was written down, put in an envelope and delivered by hand.

TELEPHONES

The development of telephones lessened the need for speedy deliveries of letters and telegrams.

Chronology	
1876	Alexander Graham Bell invented the telephone in the USA.
1879	The first telephone exchange was set up in London by the National Telephone Company.
1902	The Post Office opened seven telephone exchanges in London.
1912	The Post Office took over all telephone exchanges in Britain, except those in Hull.
1927	First automatic telephone exchange opened at Holborn in London.
1939	3,235,000 telephones in Britain.

After World War II the number of subscribers continued to increase. British Telecom, a separate organisation independent of the Post Office, was set up to run the telephone system and in 1985 it was sold to private investors.

Part Four

Radio and Television

WIRELESS TELEGRAPHY

At the end of the nineteenth century, inventors were experimenting with 'wireless telegraphy'—using radio waves to send messages through the air. In December 1901 Guglielmo Marconi (Illustration 8) and his assistants sent a wireless message across the Atlantic from Cornwall to Newfoundland. He said afterwards:

'Shortly before midday I placed the single earphone to my ear and started listening . . . at 12.30 . . . I heard, faintly but distinctly pip-pip-pip . . . The electric waves sent out into space from Poldhu had traversed the Atlantic . . . It was an epoch in history. I now felt for the first time absolutely certain that the day would come when mankind would be able to send messages . . . between the farthermost ends of the earth.'

Illustration 8 Marconi with his wireless receiver.

Study

Jules Verne (1828–1905) was a famous writer. Several of his books were what we would now call science fiction. In this study you will consider:

K what these books tell us about their author and the times in which he lived

Remember what you have already learned about transport and communications.

Books by Jules Verne:
Five Weeks in a Balloon (1862) (an air journey across Africa).
From the Earth to the Moon (1865) (a space voyage).
Twenty Thousand Leagues under the Sea (1869) (an under-sea adventure in a submarine).
Around the World in Eighty Days (1874) (a journey by boat and rail).

Source 12A

'The world has got smaller, since one can travel over it ten times more rapidly than a hundred years ago . . .'
   'In as few as eighty days,' said Phileas Fogg.
   'Yes, indeed,' added John Sullivan, 'in eighty days, now that the section of the Great Indian Peninsula Railway between Rothal and Allahabad has been opened'.

(*Around the World in Eighty Days*).
(Phileas Fogg makes a bet that he will go round the world and meet his friends again in eighty days.)

Source 12B

Suez

Rowan, Chief of Police, Scotland Yard, London. Am shadowing bank thief, Phileas Fogg. Send without delay warrant for arrest Bombay.
Detective Fix

(*Around the World in Eighty Days*)
(Detective Fix mistakenly thinks that Phileas Fogg is on the run after robbing a bank.)

1 What form of transport that became widely used during Jules Verne's lifetime helped to give him the idea of writing *Around the World in Eighty Days*?

2 a What forms of transport which were not widely used, or which had not been invented during his lifetime, play an important part in three of his other novels?

   b What incident that happened in real life in 1910 was similar to an incident in the novel he published in 1874?

3 What do Jules Verne's novels tell us about their author and transport and communications during his lifetime?

At first all wireless messages were sent in morse code. Marconi set up a company to send telegrams by radio, which was cheaper than cable, and a few ships installed radios to keep in touch with each other and with the shore. Two events made radio famous. In 1909 the liner *Republic* collided with an Italian passenger boat off the coast of North America in a fog. The radio operator sent out a distress signal. Ships in the area came to their help and saved all the passengers. The *Daily News* reported, 'The immense value of the invention of Signor Marconi to the cause of humanity was demonstrated in this remarkable manner'.

Then in 1910 Dr Crippen murdered his wife in London and, together with his mistress, boarded a liner bound for Canada. The captain recognised Crippen, who was travelling under a false name. He radioed to Liverpool, and the message was passed on to Scotland Yard. A detective was booked onto a fast ship to Canada and was waiting for Crippen when he landed. One reporter called radio 'the invisible bloodhound' which had 'followed the scent across the high seas'.

PUBLIC BROADCASTING

Radio

By 1922 speech and music could be transmitted by radio. In October the British Broadcasting Company was set up by the Post Office and a number of radio manufacturers to broadcast to the public. Its chairman, Sir William Noble, said:

'Each evening there will be given a brief synopsis of the world's news . . . Then the Meteorological Department of the Air Ministry is supplying us with two weather reports . . . In addition there will be concerts, instrumental and vocal, and it may be that later we shall arrange for speeches written by popular people to be broadcast'.

In 1927 the company was replaced by the British Broadcasting Corporation. The number of radios steadily increased. Owners had to pay an annual

Table 9

1922	35,000
1924	1.3 million
1927	2.5 million
1929	3 million
1939	9 million
1949	12 million

licence fee, which went to the BBC to pay for broadcasts. By 1939 the BBC provided news, light entertainment, music, plays, talks and documentaries in people's homes at the touch of a button.

Study

Your aim in this study is:

K to see why between 1927 and 1945 the radio, or 'wireless' was an important feature in many homes.

You will need the information on Radio on page 234.

Source 13A

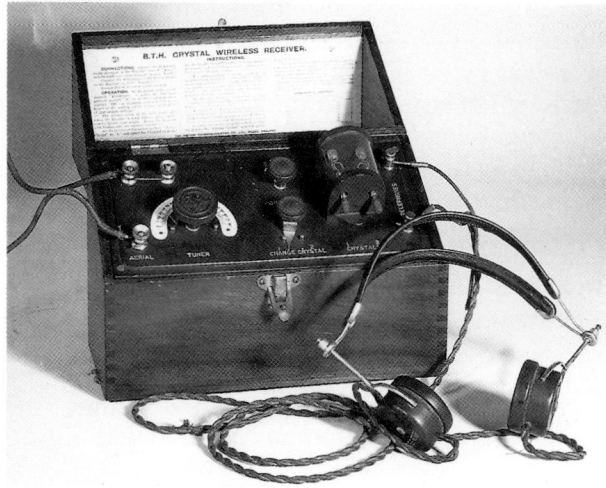

A crystal set with headphones.

Source 13B

A valve set in a family sitting room.

Source 13C

> **LONDON**
> 877 Kc., 342 M.)
> 10.15.—Daily Service.
> 10.30.—Time, Weather and Shipping.
> 10.45.—Bath Pump Room Orchestra, from Bath.
> 11.45.—Organ Recital by Albert Taylor, from Belfast.
> 12.15.—Parker-Crook Trio; A. Langford (soprano).
>
> 1.15.—City of Birmingham Orchestra, from the Town Hall.
>
> 2.0.—Time Signal from Greenwich. Imperial Hotel Orchestra, directed by Russell Smythe, relayed from Blackpool.
>
> 3.0.—The Band of the Royal Marines, Plymouth Division, conducted by Captain F. J. Ricketts; Foster Manley (bass); from Plymouth.
>
> 4.0.—The West Country Gazetteer. First number, Dorset.
> 4.45.—B.B.C. Northern Ireland Orchestra, from Belfast.
>
> 5.15.—Children's Hour: Meet Mickey Mouse (No 5), Mickey's Nightmare.
>
> 6.0.—Time Signal, First News, Weather Forecast.
> 6.30.—The Wallsend Shipyard Prize Band, conducted by J. C. Welsh.
>
> 7.0.—Brass Band (continued).
> 7.15.—Victor Olof Sextet.
> 7.55.—Anona Winn and her Winners.
>
> 8.15. — The Royal Philharmonic Society's Concerts; The London Philharmonic Orchestra, conducted by Sir Hamilton Harty; Ethel Bartlett and Rae Robertson (two pianos); relayed from Queen's Hall, London.
>
> 9.10.—During the Interval.
> 9.25.—Philaharmonic Society's Concert (continued).
>
> 10.15.—Time Signal, News Summary, and Weather.
> 10.25.—The Casani Club Orchestra, directed by Charles Kunz.
>
> 11.0.—Dance Band (continued). (Time Signal at 11.30.)
> 12.0.—Close Down.

The *Radio Times*, 21 November 1935.

1 Why may many families who were not prepared to license a crystal set have been willing to license a set with valves?

2 Which programmes broadcast on Thursday, November 21 1935 might these members of a family have listened to:
the mother who was at home all day and who enjoyed orchestral music and programmes of educational interest;
the son and daughter aged five and six who were at school from 9 am to 4.30 pm;
the father, who was interested in current events and who was away from home from 8.30 am until 6.30 pm?

3 World War II broke out in 1939. In that year about nine million wireless licences were issued.
a About how many people would you estimate listened to the wireless daily in 1939? Give reasons for your answer.
b In the early years of the war there was a danger that German troops would invade Britain. Many British towns were bombed and food and clothing were rationed. How may BBC programmes have helped families to support the war effort?

Television

Television originated in the mid 1920s.

Chronology	
1926	John Logie Baird transmitted the first television picture.
1936	The BBC began regular transmissions in the London area.
1939	Transmissions stopped on outbreak of war.
1946	Transmissions began again.
1953	Coronation of Queen Elizabeth II televised.
1954	ITV set up.
1967	Colour transmissions began.

Table 10 Number of licences (millions)

1939	0.012
1949	0.25
1959	10.0
1969	15.9
1979	18.8
1985	19.8

Since 1979, ninety seven per cent of all households have owned at least one television set. In 1986 the average viewer spent twenty eight hours a week watching television, and the average listener spent about eight and a half hours listening to the radio.

The growth of radio and television resulted in a decline in the number of visits people made to theatres, cinemas and live sporting occasions.

Study

Before the twentieth century, most people learned what was happening elsewhere from what they were told, or from what they read. The invention of moving films enabled them to *see* what was happening. Until 1950 most films were shown at cinemas.

In this study you will:

Ca consider some changes that resulted when TV became more popular than the cinema;

Ev think how today's films may help historians in the future.

Source 14A

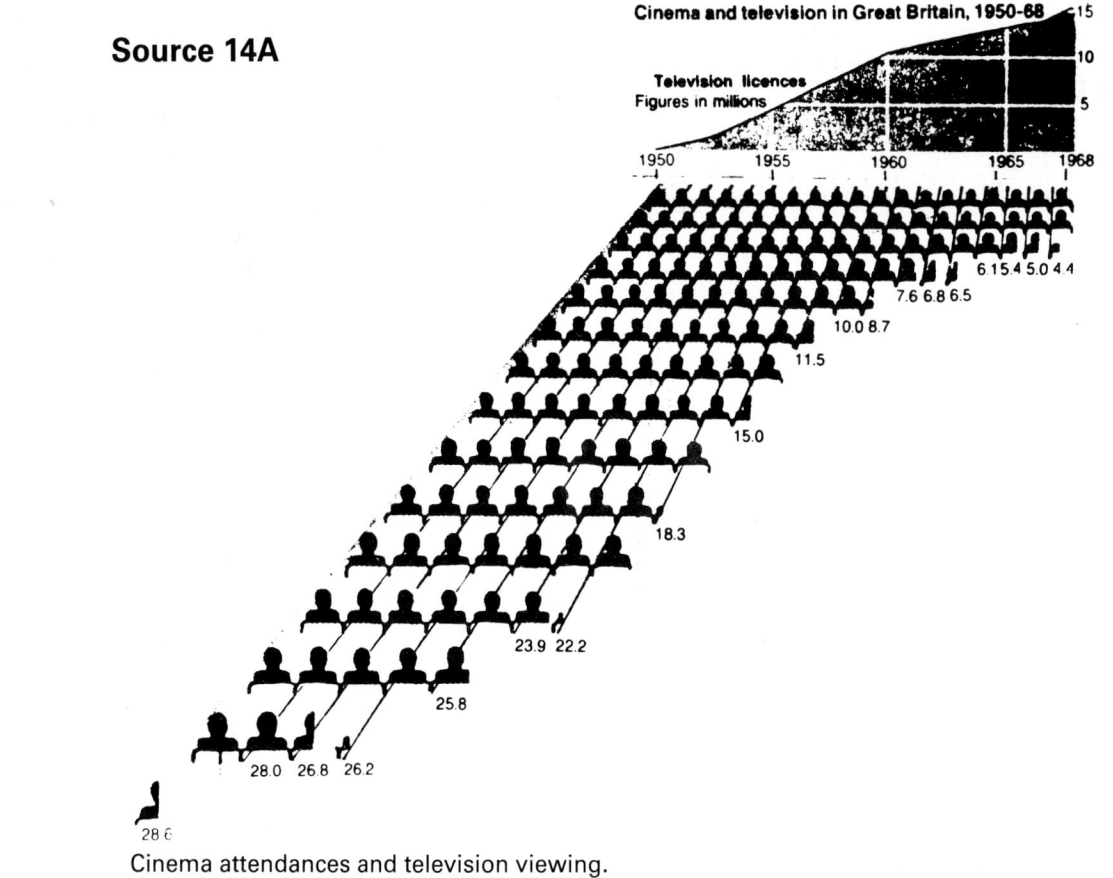

Cinema and television in Great Britain, 1950-68

Television licences
Figures in millions

Cinema attendances and television viewing.

Source 14B

Buzz Aldrin walks on the moon, 1969. Neil Armstrong is reflected in his visor.

Source 14C

A scene from the American soap opera, *Dallas*.

1 To see a film in 1950, most people had to go to the cinema. What evidence is there that by 1968 most people watched films in their own homes?
2 In 1950 people watched newsreels showing them events that had happened during the previous week. Why, do you think, had most cinemas stopped showing newsreels by 1968?

3 Choose *i* a news programme and *ii* an item of entertainment that you have recently seen on TV or at the cinema.
  a What would they tell a historian living a hundred years from now about life in Britain today?
  b Does the fact that the historian will be able to see events happening mean that he or she will not need to read written accounts of them? Give reasons for your answers.

—— Part Five ——

Newspapers

NINETEENTH-CENTURY PAPERS

In the middle of the nineteenth century, newspapers were dull and expensive. They had to pay three taxes. Paper was taxed, advertisements were taxed and a duty was levied on every newspaper sold.

Most working-class people could not read, so editors took it for granted that their readers were middle-class people who were interested in politics. Much of the space was filled with long extracts from speeches. For human interest editors relied on accounts of sensational law cases.

By 1890 circumstances had changed.

Diagram 1   Changing circumstances

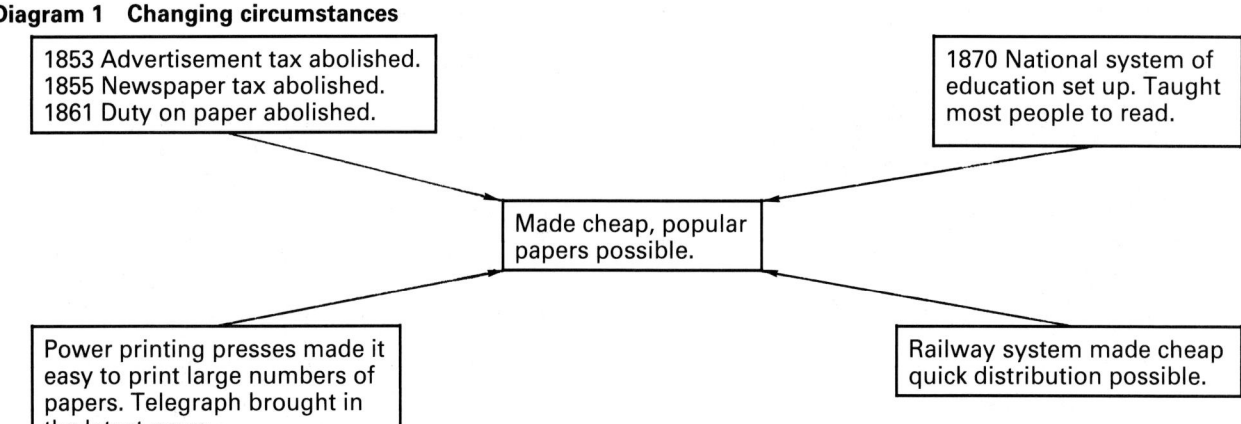

1853 Advertisement tax abolished.	1870 National system of
1855 Newspaper tax abolished.	education set up. Taught
1861 Duty on paper abolished.	most people to read.

Made cheap, popular papers possible.

Power printing presses made it easy to print large numbers of papers. Telegraph brought in the latest news.

Railway system made cheap quick distribution possible.

THE POPULAR PRESS

In 1895 Alfred Harmsworth set up the *Daily Mail*, the first cheap, mass circulation daily paper in Britain. It cost a halfpenny. Other papers cost a penny. Harmsworth tried to make it exciting. He said, 'Each day we must have a feature . . . something different . . . a surprise.' If there was no exciting news, he made it up. The articles were written in short, snappy sentences. Lord Salisbury said it was 'A paper written by office boys for office boys', but it made Harmsworth a fortune and earned him a peerage.

Before the days of radio, people relied on papers for news and if an important item came in in the middle of the day, editors printed a special edition and got it onto the streets as quickly as possible.

Radio and television have altered the job of newspapers. Now people read them either for entertainment or for comments on the news. After 1945 the number of newspapers fell. Production costs were very high, and even papers with a circulation of over a million could not pay. But since 1980 new methods of production have been developed which are much cheaper, and new papers have been founded to take advantage of them.

Table 11   Readership (not sales) of daily papers (millions)

	1971	1986
The Sun	8.5	11.4
Daily Mirror	13.8	8.9
Daily Express	9.7	4.5
Daily Mail	4.8	4.7
The Star	—	4.3
The Daily Telegraph	3.6	2.9
The Guardian	1.1	1.5
The Times	1.1	1.2
The Financial Times	0.7	0.7

Social Trends 1988.

Study

All the sources below come from the *Daily Mirror*, 21 January 1936. Your aim is to:

Ev use the evidence in them to find out more about the paper and the kind of people who read it.

Source 15A

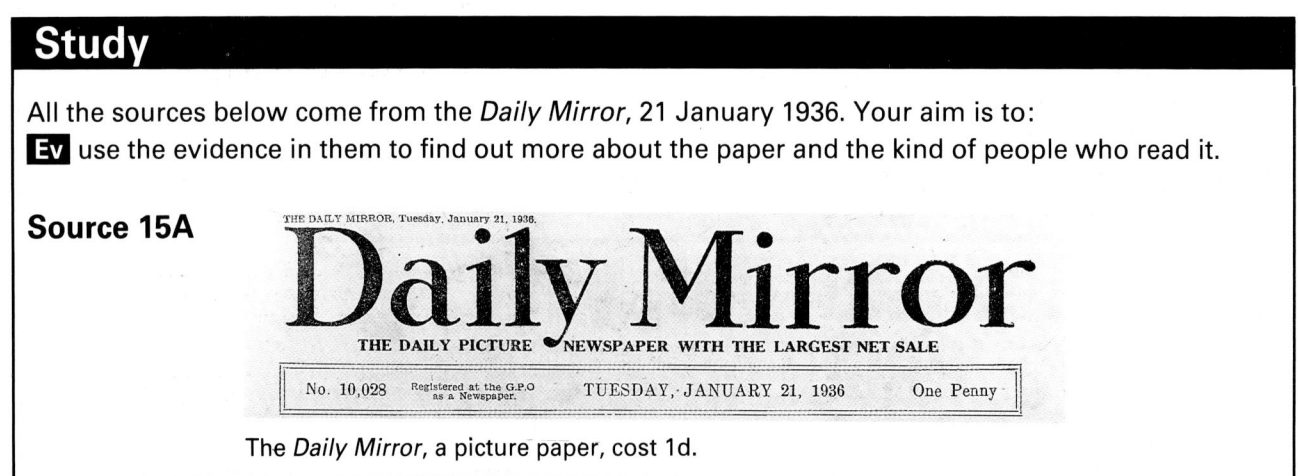

THE DAILY MIRROR, Tuesday, January 21, 1936.

Daily Mirror

THE DAILY PICTURE NEWSPAPER WITH THE LARGEST NET SALE

No. 10,028   Registered at the G.P.O as a Newspaper.   TUESDAY, JANUARY 21, 1936   One Penny

The *Daily Mirror*, a picture paper, cost 1d.

Source 15B

An advertisement from the *Daily Mirror*.

Source 15C

A *Daily Mirror* headline.

Source 15D

'I know you, Saint,' Murdoch said raspingly. His big hands rolled his glass between them as if they were playing with the idea of crushing it to fragments with a single savage contraction, and the hard implacable lights were smouldering under the surface of his eyes.

From *Saint Overboard*, serialised in the *Daily Mirror*.

1 What evidence is there to suggest that the *Daily Mirror* was:
a popular newspaper;
aimed at readers who did not have high incomes;
designed to encourage readers to go on buying it?

2 What do Sources 15C and 15D suggest about the interests of *Daily Mirror* readers? Give reasons for your answer.
3 What evidence is there to suggest that the *Daily Mirror* did not depend on the price readers paid for it to make a profit?

Recall

1 What form of transport was: the *Cutty Sark*; the *Titanic*; the Zeppelin; the Daimler?
2 Rewrite the list below, matching dates and events correctly:
1863 The British Transport Commission was set up.
1926 Concorde went into service.
1884 The first TV pictures were transmitted.
1947 The Metropolitan underground railway was opened.
1976 The steam turbine was patented.

Discussion

Do you agree or disagree with this statement?
The fact that transport and communications have improved means that people today can form an accurate picture of what is going on in the world. Give reasons for your answer.
Ask one person to give his or her answer to the class. Do the rest of you agree?

Diagram 2

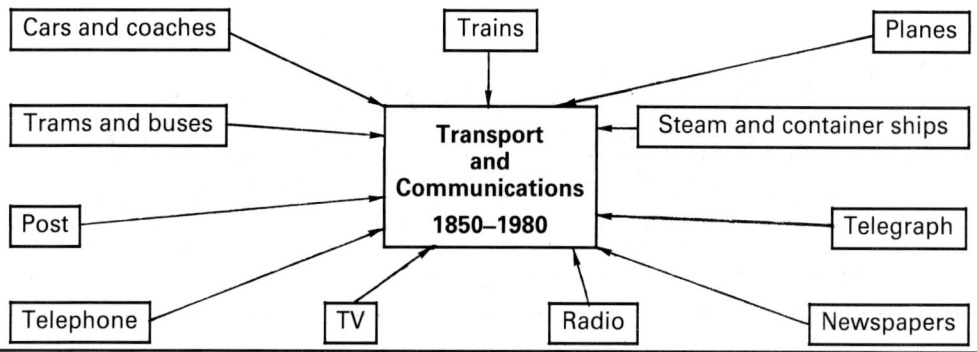

20
Social Security

———— Part One ————
The Victorian Poor

BOOTH AND ROWNTREE

The two surveys

In 1885 the *Pall Mall Gazette* published an article claiming that one in four Londoners lived in poverty. Charles Booth, a wealthy shipowner, thought the paper was exaggerating. He decided to do a thorough survey himself. It took him seventeen years, but soon he realised that the *Gazette* had underestimated the number of poor people. He reckoned that about thirty per cent of Londoners were poor. He defined poor people as those who were, at best, 'living under a struggle to obtain the necessaries of life and make both ends meet.' Ten years later Seebohm Rowntree did a similar survey in York. He found that about twenty nine per cent of the inhabitants were poor. He explained what being on the poverty line meant:

> [They must never] spend a penny on a railway fare or omnibus. They must never go into the country unless they walk. They must never purchase a halfpenny newspaper or spend a penny to buy a ticket for a popular concert. They must write no letters to absent children, for they cannot afford to pay the postage. They must never contribute anything to their church or chapel, or give any help to a neighbour which costs them money. They cannot save, nor can they join a sick club or Trade Union, because they cannot pay the necessary subscriptions. The children must have no pocket money for dolls, marbles or sweets. The father must smoke no tobacco and must drink no beer. The mother must never buy any pretty clothes for herself or her children . . . Finally the wage-earner must never be absent from his work for a single day.

(B. S. Rowntree, *Poverty: A Study of Town Life* (1901).)

Illustration 1 Workers' houses in White Hind Alley, Bankside, London, photographed in 1896.

Study

Most respectable people took it for granted that the poor were badly off because they were lazy or because they spent their income on drinking and gambling.

In this study you will use the sources below to:

Ca consider the reasons for poverty in the late nineteenth century.

Source 1A Causes of poverty

85% of poverty was caused by: 1 **death or illness;** 2 **low pay;** 3 **unemployment;** 4 **large family size: e.g. large numbers of children or elderly relatives to look after.**	*Only 15% was caused by* **drink or idleness or gambling.**

Based on figures in Booth's *Life and Labour of the People*.

Source 1B

In little rooms, no more than eight feet square [2.4 m], would be found living father, mother and several children . . . Fifteen rooms out of twenty were filthy to the last degree . . . Not a room would be free from vermin, and in many life at night was unbearable . . . for bugs and fleas . . . The little yard at the back was only sufficient for dust-bin and closet and water-tap serving for six or seven families. The water would be drawn from cisterns which were receptacles for refuse and perhaps occasionally a dead cat.

C. Booth, *Life and Labour of the People* (Vol. 2, 1891).

Source 1C

Many a man takes to beer, not from love of beer . . .

William Booth, founder of the Salvation Army.

Source 1D

. . . bread, margarine, tea and sugar.

Charles Booth's description of the diet of one poor family he knew. He said that the family was also given 'charitable soup' two or three times a week by the local church.

Source 1E

If they did not like the houses they could leave them, and let someone come in who would pay seven shillings instead of six shillings, the present rental. We were told of numbers who had been made ill by the drains.

C. Booth, *Life and Labour of the People*, giving a landlord's reply to tenants who had complained of a blocked lavatory.

1 Which of the causes of poverty given in Source 1A **a** can; **b** cannot be supported by Sources 1B, 1C, 1D and 1E? Explain your answers.
2 Suggest reasons why some men became drunkards.
3 **a** Does the evidence in the sources prove that the reasons Booth gave for poverty at the end of the nineteenth century were correct? Give reasons for your answer.
   b Consider what you are told about Booth on page 240. Would you expect his account of the reasons for poverty to be biased? Give reasons for your answer.

Study

In this study you will use the information in the sources below to:

Em find out what life was like for poor women in the second half of the nineteenth century;

Ev decide whether or not the sources are reliable.

Source 2A

I have not done any work for about three months. I cannot get anything to do. I have two girls, one fourteen years the other not sixteen—both delicate. The youngest was working but lost her place through sickness, so I have only one working now at a very small pay, and it takes it to pay the debt I fell into through idleness [unemployment]. I have got notice from the factor to leave my house and I really don't know what to do. I cannot get work, having no trade . . . None of my friends can help me, they are too poor. As I write this I have neither fire or meat in the house.

Undated letter in Strathclyde regional archives, written by a widowed washerwoman to a local charity in Glasgow in about 1908.

Study continued

Source 2B

Many outworkers were very badly paid. Women working at home were paid threepence for making all the button holes and sewing the buttons on a dozen shirts.

Source 2C

On Sundays she generally obtains a moderately good dinner, but on other days the food consists mainly of bread with a little butter or dripping, a plain pudding, and vegetables for dinner or supper and weak tea. She may obtain a little bacon at dinner once, twice, or thrice a week; but more commonly she does not obtain it.

Dr E. Smith, *Food of the Lower Labouring Classes* (1863), describing the kind of diet eaten by many poor women.

1 Why, do you think, did women take jobs as outworkers for shirt manufacturers when the pay was so low?
2 A family of three needed a minimum of 10s 6d a week to cover the rent, food, heat and lighting. There were 12d (pence) to a shilling. How many shirts would a widow with two children have to take in to support herself and her family?
3 a Do you think Source 2B gives an exaggerated picture of the poverty in which outworkers lived? Give reasons for your answer.
  b Do you think that the information in *i* Source 2C and *ii* Source 2A is reliable? Give reasons for your answers.

Part Two

The Relief of Poverty

PRIVATE CHARITIES

The Salvation Army

Voluntary organisations tried to help the poor. In 1878 William Booth, a missionary in the East End of London, founded the Salvation Army. As well as preaching, the Army set up shelters where poor people could get food and a night's shelter for four pence. Some people lived in the shelters, but most only used them occasionally.

Dr Barnardo

One night Charles Booth found several poor children outside a light, warm hall where a prayer meeting was being held. They shouted 'Let's come in , Guv'nor, we won't make no noise; we'll behive our-

selves'. Booth said they ought to be at home in bed. A girl of about eight answered, ' 'Garn, we're ahrt wiv ahr blokes; that's my bloke.' 'Yus', said the other girl, 'and that's mine'. They pointed to two boys about their own size. At this there was a general shout of laughter, and then came a plaintive plea from the first child, 'Give us a penny will you, Guv'nor?'

Thomas Barnardo, a London doctor training to be a missionary, discovered that many children wandering London's streets were homeless orphans. In 1867 he founded a mission for destitute children in London, and three years later he opened the first *Dr Barnardo's Home* for orphaned children. He fed and clothed the children, and trained them to do useful work. When they left most took jobs as servants or labourers. Many were sent to Canada to work on farms.

Study

Your aim is:

Ev to see how much you can *infer* about Dr Barnardo's Homes and the boys admitted to them by studying the photograph on the right.

Source 3

Boys admitted to Dr Barnardo's home in about 1880.

1 Why might the boys have had their photograph taken?
2 Suggest reasons why there are no girls in the photograph.
3 **a** What impression does the photograph give of the kind of boys who were admitted to Dr Barnardo's Homes? Give reasons for your answer.
   b How might you check to see whether or not your impression is correct?

GOVERNMENT ACTION

Reasons for action

In 1906 the government began to take action to help the poor. There were several reasons for this (see Diagram 1).

Diagram 1

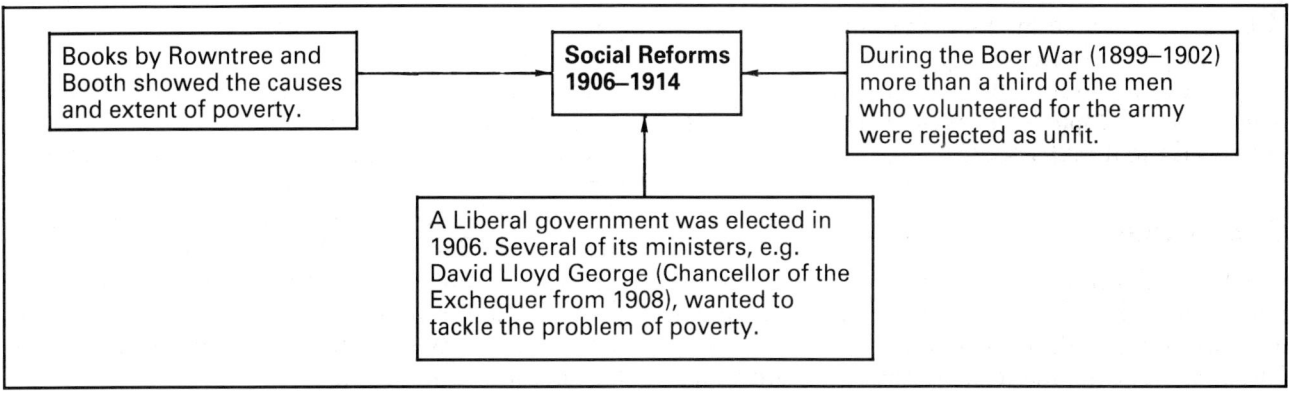

Books by Rowntree and Booth showed the causes and extent of poverty. → **Social Reforms 1906–1914** ← During the Boer War (1899–1902) more than a third of the men who volunteered for the army were rejected as unfit.

A Liberal government was elected in 1906. Several of its ministers, e.g. David Lloyd George (Chancellor of the Exchequer from 1908), wanted to tackle the problem of poverty.

The Liberal reforms 1906–11

Chronology	
1906	Local authorities were allowed to provide free school meals for poor children.
1907	Medical inspection of school children began.
1908	Hours worked by children before and after school were regulated. The Old Age Pensions Act gave five shillings a week to all those over seventy with an income of less than ten shillings a week.
1909	Trade boards set up to fix minimum wages in some trades.

THE PHILANTHROPIC HIGHWAYMAN.

Mr. Lloyd-George. *"I'LL MAKE 'EM PITY THE AGED POOR!"*

Illustration 2 A cartoon published in *Punch* in 1909.

Study

In this study you will consider:

Em why some people thought that the Liberals were spending too much money on reforms, and why others supported them.

Remember what you have learned about poverty and wealth in Britain, and about the Liberal reforms 1906–9.

In the House of Lords debate on old age pensions Lord Rosebery, a wealthy racehorse owner said, 'a scheme so prodigal [wasteful] of expenditure might be dealing a blow at the Empire which could be almost mortal'.

1 Lord Rosebery opposed old age pensions. Why may he have thought that the Empire would have been strengthened if taxpayers' money was spent on improving the health and education of poor children, but weakened if it was spent on pensions?

■

Flora Thompson, who lived in a small village, described the scene in the post office when old people first went to draw their pensions: '. . . tears of gratitude would run down the cheeks of some, and they would say, as they picked up their money, "God bless you, miss!"'

2 a Why, do you think, did old people cry when they drew their first pension money?

b By 1909 most working class men had the vote. Would you expect them to support or oppose the Liberals? Give reasons for your answer.

■

During one speech in the 1910 election campaign Lloyd George held up a copy of Rowntree's book and said: 'Four spectres haunt the poor—old age, accident, sickness and unemployment . . . We are going to drive hunger from the hearth. We mean to banish the workhouse from the horizon of every workman in the land.'

3 Many middle-class voters supported Lloyd George, even though they knew it meant they would have to pay higher taxes. Suggest why they may have supported the Liberals.

In 1909 Lloyd George demanded extra taxes in his budget to pay for pensions (see Illustration 2). The House of Lords rejected it, and there had to be a general election. The Liberals were re-elected. In 1911 they passed the National Insurance Act. This had two parts.

Part One brought in a compulsory health insurance scheme based on one in use in Germany. Workers paid four pence a week, employers paid three pence a week and the state paid two pence. All the money collected went into a fund used to provide sick pay for workers and give doctors fees to look after them.

Part Two set up an unemployment insurance scheme. At first it only applied to seven industries with 2.25 million workers, but in 1920 it was extended to all workers.

Part Three

Workers, Women and Politics

WORKERS AND THE VOTE: 1867–1928

In the middle of the nineteenth century very few working men had the vote, and it was almost impossible for a worker to get into Parliament (see Chapter 12). Gradually the situation changed.

Chronology	
1858	The property qualification for MPs was abolished.
1867	Most working men who lived in towns were given the vote.
1872	Voting by secret ballot prevented employers bribing or threatening workers at elections.
1884	Most country working men were given the vote.
1918	All men over twenty one got the vote.

WOMEN'S RIGHTS

Education

Girls were usually given a more limited education than boys because they were expected to look after their families and leave business matters to men. Some women set out to change this situation.

Chronology	
1848	Queen's College training college for women teachers set up.
1850	Frances Buss set up North London Collegiate School.
1858	Dorothea Beale appointed head of Cheltenham Ladies' College. (Miss Buss and Miss Beale had both attended Queen's College. Their schools gave girls a sound academic education.)
1871	Girls' Public Day School Trust set up to establish more such schools.
1873	Girton College opened at Cambridge University.
1876	Newnham College opened at Cambridge.
1879	Lady Margaret Hall and Somerville College opened at Oxford. (Women students at Oxford and Cambridge could attend lectures and sit exams, but were not given degrees. At new universities women were given degrees.)
1910	Local authorities made a grammar school education equally available to boys and girls.
1920	Oxford University allowed women to take degrees.
1948	Cambridge University allowed women to take degrees.

Study

Personal and professional

People's jokes tell us a great deal about their attitude to those they are making fun of. In this study you will consider what the sources below show us about:

Ch changes in the kind of work done by women in the medical profession;

Em changes in people's attitude.

Chronology	
1865	Elizabeth Garrett Anderson qualified as a doctor.
1870	She was appointed to a London hospital.
1882	Married women allowed to own property.
1920	Legal profession and accountancy opened to women.

In the nineteenth century most nurses were women, but until Florence Nightingale's reforms in the 1850s very few were highly trained or qualified. It was even harder for women who wanted to be doctors, as hospitals were unwilling to train them.

Source 4A

OUR PRETTY DOCTOR.

Dr. Arabella. " WELL, MY GOOD FRIENDS, WHAT CAN I DO FOR YOU ? "

Bill. " WELL, MISS, IT'S ALL ALONG O' ME AND MY MATES BEIN' OUT O' WORK, YER SEE, AND WANTIN' TO TURN AN HONEST PENNY HANYWAYS WE CAN ; SO, 'AVIN' 'EARD TELL AS YOU WAS A RISIN' YOUNG MEDICAL PRACTITIONER, WE THOUGHT AS P'RAPS YOU WOULDN'T MIND JUST A RECOMMENDIN' OF HUS AS NURSES.' "

A cartoon published in *Punch* in 1870.

Source 4B

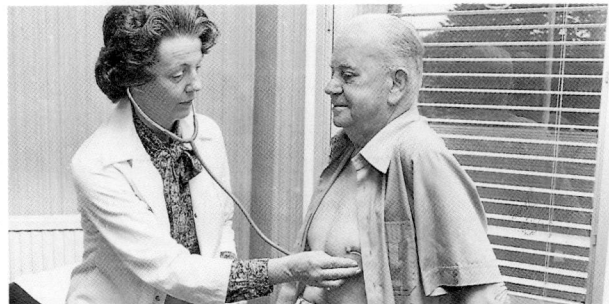

A doctor and patient.

1 Is the cartoonist (Source 4A) making fun of Dr Arabella or of Bill and his friends? Give reasons for your answer.
2 Do you think that many people living in 1870 would have thought the cartoon was funny? Give reasons for your answer.
3 Would there be any point in publishing the cartoon in *Punch* today? Give reasons for your answer.

Study: Library work

In this study you will:
K find out about the Suffragettes and Suffragists.

Chronology	
1869	Women ratepayers allowed to vote in municipal borough elections.
1870	Women ratepayers allowed to vote for and sit on school boards.
1888	Women ratepayers allowed to vote in county and county borough elections.

More men were gradually given the vote during the nineteenth century, but no women could vote in parliamentary elections. This meant they were powerless to alter laws which enabled men to dominate them. Two movements were formed to campaign for votes for women. The Suffragists, led by Millicent Fawcett, believed in peacefully persuading people to accept their ideas. The Suffragettes, led by Emmeline Pankhurst, used violence to further their aims.

1 List the sections in your school or public library where you might find information about the Suffragists and Suffragettes.
2 a Find and write down the answers to these questions about Source 5.
  b How do the initials on her sash reveal that the woman is a Suffragette?
  c Which Act of Parliament led the artist to draw this poster?
3 In which year were:
women over the age of thirty given the vote;
women over the age of twenty-one given the vote?

Source 5

A suffragette poster.

4 While you have been looking up these answers you have probably read a good deal of other interesting information about women in the earlier twentieth century or the Suffragette movement that you would like to follow up.
  a Make up the title of an essay that you would like to write.
  b List the main points you would like to make in your essay and make sure that you have the necessary information.
  c Write your essay.

THE GROWTH OF THE LABOUR PARTY

Beginnings

At first most workers voted Liberal, but many thought they ought to have their own party. They were influenced by socialists such as Karl Marx, whose book *Das Kapital* was published in 1867. Socialists believed that the main sources of national wealth such as coal mines, railways and agricultural land ought to be owned by the workers and run for their benefit.

Illustration 3 Keir Hardie upset MPs by wearing informal clothes in the House of Commons.

Chronology	
1889	A group of workers in Scotland founded the Scottish Labour party to put forward socialist ideas.
1893	Three Labour MPs, including Keir Hardie (1856–1915), a Scottish miner, were elected to Parliament. Hardie helped to form the Independent Labour Party (ILP).
1895	At a general election the ILP put forward twenty eight candidates. They were all defeated.
1899	The trade unions called a special conference to devise ways to get Labour MPs elected.
1900	The conference set up the Labour Party. Keir Hardie (Illustration 3) was chairman. Ramsay MacDonald (1866–1937) was secretary. Two Labour MPs were elected.
1906	Twenty nine Labour MPs elected.
1910	Forty two Labour MPs elected.

The Osborne Judgement (1910)

When the Labour Party was founded, MPs had no salary, so the unions used some of their funds to pay Labour MPs and help with election expenses. Some union members were Liberals or Conservatives. They thought that unions ought not to use their funds to support the Labour Party. W. V. Osborne, a Liberal member of the Society of Railway Servants, thought the payments were illegal. In 1908 he took the union to court. In December 1910 the House of Lords declared that Osborne was right, and ordered the Railway Servants to stop paying money to the Labour Party.

The Osborne Judgement, as it was called, meant that trade unions could not use funds to support a political party. Sixteen Labour MPs who relied on money from unions for their living were suddenly left penniless.

Chronology	
1910	The unions asked for the law to be changed. The Liberal Government, which needed the vote of Labour MPs to stay in power, agreed to help.
1911	The House of Commons voted to pay MPs a salary of £400 a year. Labour MPs no longer had to rely on grants from unions for a living.
1913	Parliament passed the Trade Union Act. This allowed unions to fund political parties so long as their members agreed. This ensured that the Labour Party had enough money to keep going.

Study

When the ILP was set up in 1893 many people thought it would soon break up.
Your aim in this study is to :

Ca decide why the Labour Party succeeded in establishing itself between 1893 and 1910.

Use the information on page 248.

a Keir Hardie, the founder of the ILP, was a miner who understood working class people.
b The ILP believed in gradual reform, not revolution.
c The 1899 TUC supported the ILP.
d In 1910 the House of Lords supported W. V. Osborne.
e The Liberal Government of 1910 needed the support of Labour MPs, so it passed Acts to help the Labour Party get the funds it needed.
f Reforms in the voting system between 1858 and 1918 made it possible for workers to vote for the party they supported and to become MPs.

In pairs

1 a Re-write the opposite list, leaving out any items on it that did NOT help the growth of the Labour Party.
  b Give your reasons for thinking that the item or items you left out did not help the growth of the Labour Party.
2 Which item on your re-written list do you think was *i* the most important, *ii* the least important in helping the Labour Party to establish itself? Give reasons for your answer.
3 Ask one person to give his or her answers to the class. Do the rest of you agree?

WELFARE AND POLITICS 1914–39

Post-war unemployment

During and immediately after World War I, hardly anyone was out of work and the insurance system set up by the Liberal Government worked well. So in 1920 unemployment insurance was extended to cover about twelve million workers. But then unemployment increased.

Table 1

1920	858,000
1921	2,170,000
1922	1,400,000
1923	1,200,000

The insurance scheme's funds were not big enough to support so many unemployed, so in 1921 it borrowed £30 million from the government to pay to unemployed workers who had drawn all the money they were entitled to from the scheme. This extra money was known as 'dole'.

Poor Law reform 1928

Some unemployed workers asked Poor Law guardians for help. Some Boards of Guardians paid them allowances. The Poplar Board in east London was one of the most generous. Most of its members were Labour supporters. The government thought that Poor Law Boards ought not to pay these allowances, so in 1928 they abolished the system of elected Poor Law Boards, and put public assistance committees (PAC) of county councils in charge of payments to the poor.

The first Labour governments, 1923 and 1929

Unemployment benefited the Labour Party. Workers, who had been promised 'a land fit for heroes to live in' after the war, turned against the Liberal and Conservative politicians who were running the country, and voted Labour instead.

At a general election in 1923, 191 Labour MPs were elected, and Ramsay MacDonald, the Labour leader, became Prime Minister. He had to rely on the support of the Liberals to stay in power. In September 1924 the Liberals voted with the Conservatives and defeated the government. There was another general election. This time the Conservatives won easily.

At a general election in 1929 the Labour Party won 288 seats, which was more than either of the other two parties. So Labour once again formed a government with Ramsay MacDonald as Prime Minister.

Study

In this study you will:

Ev consider two posters published by the Labour Party in 1923.

You will need to refer to the information on pages 248–9.

Source 6A   **Source 6B**

YESTERDAY-THE TRENCHES TO-DAY-UNEMPLOYED

Two Labour posters.

1 What points do you think the artist was trying to make about the men in the posters?

2 Why, do you think, did the Labour Party publish these posters?

3 Do you think the posters are biased? Give reasons for your answer.

The economic crisis, 1929

In 1929 there was a world-wide slump (see page 159). Factory owners reduced production and sacked many workers. So unemployment rose.

Economists and politicians could not agree how to solve this problem. Some economists, such as Maynard Keynes, thought the government ought to borrow money and spend it on unemployment benefit and on work such as making roads and building hospitals. This would create new jobs, reduce unemployment, and eventually increase the amount of money paid in taxes. But many bankers and economists believed that the government ought to 'balance its budget'—reduce the amount it spent until it matched the amount of taxes coming in, even

Illustration 4 Ramsay Macdonald, in formal dress, after resigning from the Cabinet in 1937.

if it meant cutting unemployment benefit. They thought that this would make the country more prosperous in the long run.

In 1931 international bankers threatened to withdraw their money from Britain if the government did not balance its budget. Philip Snowden, the Chancellor of the Exchequer, said that he would need to cut unemployment benefit by ten per cent. Only half the ministers, including Ramsay MacDonald, would agree and the Labour Government had to resign.

The National Government, 1931

In place of the Labour Government MacDonald (Illustration 4) set up a National Government, with Labour, Liberal and Conservative ministers. Most Labour MPs opposed the new government but the electorate thought MacDonald was right. At a general election in 1931 they elected 521 supporters of the National Government, and only fifty two Labour MPs.

The means test

The National Government reduced unemployment benefit by ten per cent. They also transferred responsibility for paying the dole to the PACs and

---

Study: Library work

In this study you will:

K find out more about the Wall Street Crash.

Wall Street is the financial centre of New York, and the 'Wall Street Crash' began the economic crisis of 1929.
1 List the sections of your school or public library where you might find information on the Wall Street Crash.
2 Find out the answers to these questions:
   What crashed at Wall Street in 1929?
   What caused the 'Crash'?
   Why did the Wall Street Crash trigger a world-wide economic crisis?

Study

In this study you will:

K discover how well you understand the unemployment figures for the 1920s and 1930s, and the different ways in which people thought the problem should be tackled.

You will need the information in Table 2 below and on pages 249–51.

Table 2   Unemployment figures

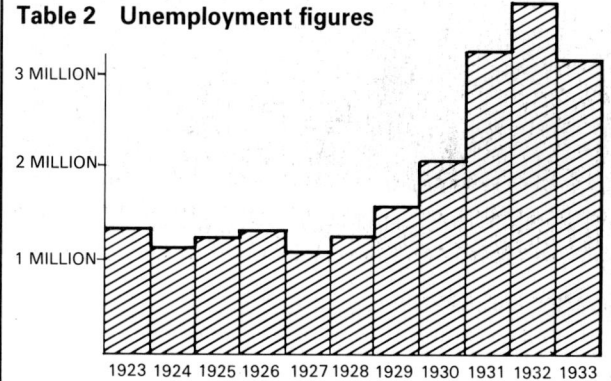

1 a Why was there severe unemployment in the years after 1929?
  b In what way or ways did the unemployment figures for 1929–31 differ from those for 1926–28?
2 a How would Maynard Keynes's solution to the problems caused by the crisis of 1929 have benefited the unemployed?
  b Why were some bankers and economists prepared to make the unemployed worse off?
3 a Which party formed the government in 1929?
  b Why, do you think, did many Labour supporters feel that Ramsay MacDonald betrayed them in 1931?

introduced a means test on payments. This meant that families could not get any dole until they had spent all their savings and were destitute. Officials demanded details of all their savings, and even took account of a few shillings earned by a boy or girl on a paper round. If one of the family was seen wearing new clothes, the officials would ask how they got them.

The government discovered that not all PACs paid the same amounts of dole. So in 1934 they passed an Act setting up the Unemployment Assistance Board (UAB) which gradually took over from the PACs. The UABs fixed the following weekly rates of relief for 1936–7:

single man—fifteen shillings;
married couple—twenty four shillings;
each child—from three to six shillings according to age.

At the end of 1937 the average wage of an adult male was about seventy shillings a week, and Seebohm Rowntree calculated that the minimum amount needed by a man, woman and three children to keep going was fifty-three shillings a week, made up as shown in Table 3.

Table 3

	20s	6d
Food		
Rent	9	6
Clothing	8	0
Fuel & light	4	4
Household goods	1	8
Miscellaneous	9	0

In 1938 the Pilgrim Trust did a survey of unemployed families and discovered that forty four per cent of them were living on or below the 'bare subsistence level' laid down by the British Medical Association.

WELFARE AND POLITICS 1939–1980

The impact of war

When World War II broke out, workers were needed to make munitions and take the place of those who had joined the forces. So unemployment disappeared. In 1940 the government was re-organised. Members of the Labour Party were given several important ministries. They insisted that the whole Assistance system should be re-organised (see the Chronology table).

Chronology	
1940	PACs were abolished. Their work was taken over by the UAB, now known as the Assistance Board.
1941	The household means test was abolished. In assessing how much money an individual needed only his or her income was considered and not the income of other members of the household.

The Beveridge Report 1942

In 1941 the government asked Sir William Beveridge, an expert on unemployment insurance, to draw up an insurance scheme to cover the whole population. In 1942 he published his report (see Diagram 2). Beveridge wanted the flat rate benefits to be enough to live on. He thought that most people would also take out private insurance to give them extra money. He believed his plan would conquer the five 'giants' of want, sickness, squalor, ignorance and idleness.

Diagram 2

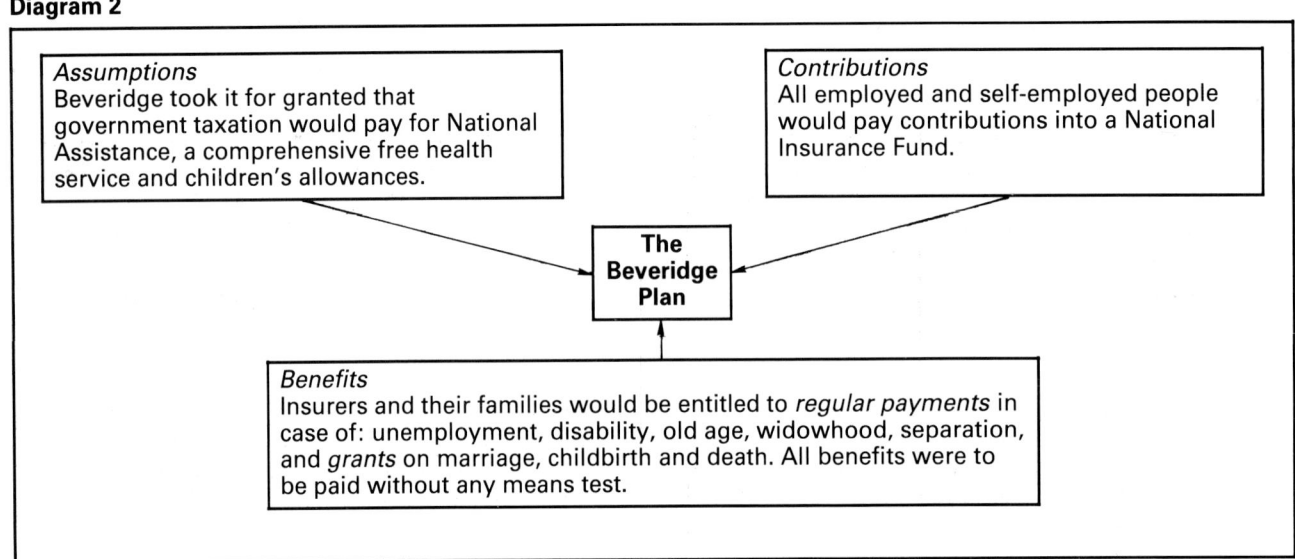

Assumptions
Beveridge took it for granted that government taxation would pay for National Assistance, a comprehensive free health service and children's allowances.

Contributions
All employed and self-employed people would pay contributions into a National Insurance Fund.

The Beveridge Plan

Benefits
Insurers and their families would be entitled to *regular payments* in case of: unemployment, disability, old age, widowhood, separation, and *grants* on marriage, childbirth and death. All benefits were to be paid without any means test.

Study

In this study you will:

Ev consider the nature and reliability of the sources below.

Source 7A

Police clash with demonstrators against the means test in Bristol in 1933.

Source 7B

[The means test] stimulated petty tyranny and insolence on the part of the Labour exchange clerks and managers. The weekly visit to the exchange would bring the sudden curt announcement by the clerk: 'They've knocked you off the dole'.

Walter Greenwood, *Love on the Dole* (1933) a novel.

Source 7C

One little collier boy fifteen years of age went home to his parents the other day and proudly announced that he had an increase of three shillings a week. The following week the Board reduced the allowance of his unemployed father.

Aneurin Bevan, a Labour MP, writing in the *Daily Express*, 23 April 1937.

1 Consider each Source. Is it primary or secondary? Give reasons for your answer.
2 Do you think the information given in *i* Source 7B, *ii* Source 7C, is reliable? Give reasons for your answers.

3 What reasons may *i* Walter Greenwood (Source 7B), *ii* Aneurin Bevan (Source 7C) have had for writing about the effects of the means test?
4 How do Sources 7B and 7C add to our understanding of Source 7A?

Table 4

(£ millions)	1970	1975	1980	1985	1986
Pensions	1,818	4,898	8,816	16,677	17,739
Unemployment insurance	158	473	653	1,618	1,704
Other benefits and administration	1,951	4,380	9,939	22,919	25,025
Total	3,927	9,751	19,408	41,214	44,468

Social Trends 1988.

The Welfare State

Nothing was done to put Beveridge's plans into operation during the war, but early in 1945 the government passed the Family Allowances Act, which granted five shillings a week to mothers for every child except the first. In July 1945 there was a general election and a Labour Government was returned to power with a large majority. They re-formed the welfare system much as Beveridge had recommended.

Pensions and National Insurance

1946 The National Insurance Act

This set up an insurance scheme for the whole population. Insured people contributed twenty per cent of the cost, employers paid thirty per cent and the government paid the rest. All insured people received benefits when they were unemployed or off sick. Pensions were paid to the old and to widows and orphans. Funeral grants, maternity benefits and industrial injury benefits were also paid.

1948 The National Assistance Act

The benefits under the Insurance Act were not enough to live on, so the government set up the National Assistance Board to pay extra money to those in need. In 1966 the NAB was taken over by the Ministry of Social Security, which in 1968 became the Department of Health and Social Security.

1973 The Social Security Act

This stopped payment of unemployment benefit to people who were out of work for more than a year. Long-term unemployed had to apply to the DHSS for benefit. The amount they got depended on their means.

The DHSS administered a number of allowances for those in need. The amount of money spent on pensions and other benefits increased enormously (see Table 4).

The Health Service

1946 The National Health Service Act

This set up a free health service, financed out of taxation, available to every citizen. Every kind of medical, optical and dental treatment was available without charge. The service came into operation in July 1948. In the first year:
  8.5 million dental patients were treated;
  5.25 million pairs of glasses were dispensed;
  187 million prescriptions were dispensed.
The service cost £400 million.

The price of health

Ministers knew that to begin with the Health Service would be very expensive, because some items, such as dentistry and optical services had never been freely available before. So millions of people needed treatment. Most experts believed that after a year or two the cost would level out, or even fall. But it did not. The cost of the Health Service continued to rise. In 1980 it was £11,897 million; in 1985, £17,560 million (see Diagram 3).

Diagram 3

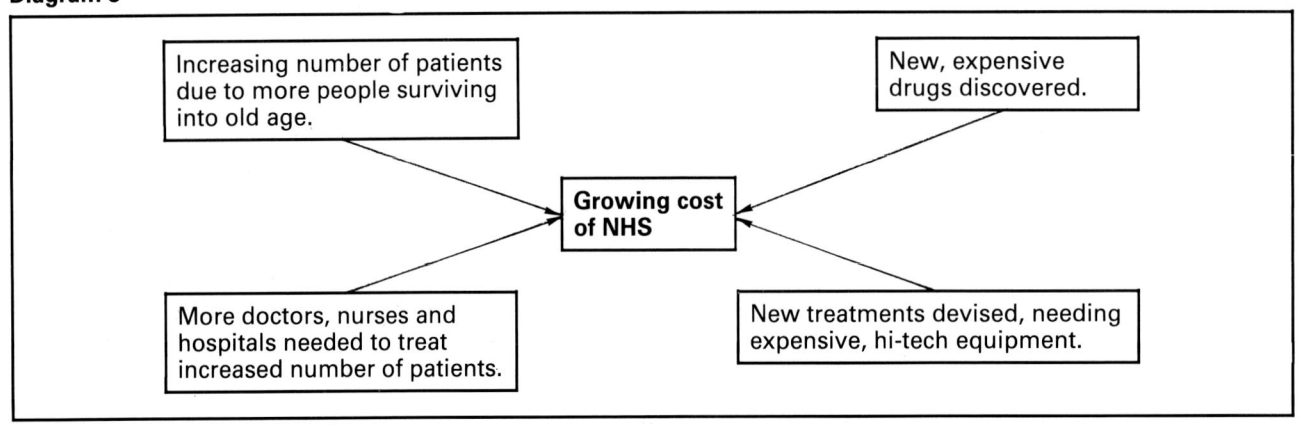

Study

In this study your aim is:

S to compare two views of the Beveridge Plan.

Background: World War II 1939–45

The Allies (Britain; USA; Russia) *v.* The Axis (Germany; Italy; Japan).

1942 was a turning point in the war. By the middle of the year the Axis powers controlled most of Europe and were advancing into Russia. In the Far East, the Japanese captured many American and British bases. But then the war began to turn in the Allies' favour.

October 1942:   The German and Italian forces were defeated at El Alamein in Egypt.

December 1942:   The Beveridge Report was published.

February 1943:   The German Sixth Army surrendered at Stalingrad in Russia.

Source 8A

A *Daily Express* cartoon by Sir David Low, published in 1946.

Source 8B

The way of the Beveridge Report is the road to moral ruin in the nation . . . It is the way of sleep.

A letter to *The Times*, 1942.

1 a How are Britain and its people shown in Source 8A?

b How does the cartoonist suggest that: the British people have come through hard times; Parliament has the power to decide whether or not people's lives will be easier in future?

2 a What is similar about the way in which Source 8A and Source 8B describe the Beveridge Plan?

b Why, do you think, do they describe it in this way?

3 Do you think that the cartoonist (Source 8A) and the correspondent to *The Times* (Source 8B) held the same views on the Beveridge Plan? Give reasons for your answer.

In 1951 the government decided to make patients pay a charge for prescriptions and spectacles. Aneurin Bevan, the Minister of Health, resigned from the government in protest. By 1985 considerable charges had been put on prescriptions, dental treatment and spectacles. Yet the cost of the service has continued to increase.

Waiting lists

When the NHS started there were not enough hospitals, nurses or doctors to deal with all the non-urgent cases, such as those needing hospital dental treatment, hernia operations and many orthopaedic operations. Long waiting lists built up. New hospitals were built, but the waiting lists remained. Hospital authorities said this was because they could not afford to employ enough nurses to staff the new buildings.

Many NHS hospitals had 'private' wards for patients who preferred to pay for their treatment. There was also a growing number of private hospitals. Private wards and hospitals did not have waiting lists. So some people who could afford to pay were treated at once. Others had to wait.

Study

In this study you will:

Ch consider change and continuity in the National Health Service, 1948–86.

Use the information on pages 252–6.

1 a In what way did the people who set up the National Health Service expect its cost to change once the system was established?
  b How did the cost of the service change between 1948 and 1985?
2 In 1948 the service was free, financed out of taxation and available to every citizen.
  a How did this situation change in 1951?
  b In what way did the situation remain unchanged?
3 a In what way did hospital services for non-urgent cases remain unchanged between 1948 and 1986?
  b In what way did private provision for fee-paying patients change between 1948 and 1986?

Recall

1 Explain these terms in your own words: the destitute poor; women's suffrage; subsistence level; the Welfare State.
2 What contribution did each of these men make to social welfare in Britain between 1850 and 1950? Charles Booth; Dr Barnardo; William Beveridge; Lloyd George; Aneurin Bevan.

3 Study Diagram 4 and make a similar one showing the causes of unemployment, 1880–1980. What did the Beveridge Report of 1942 suggest should be done to prevent unemployment and help the unemployed?

Diagram 4

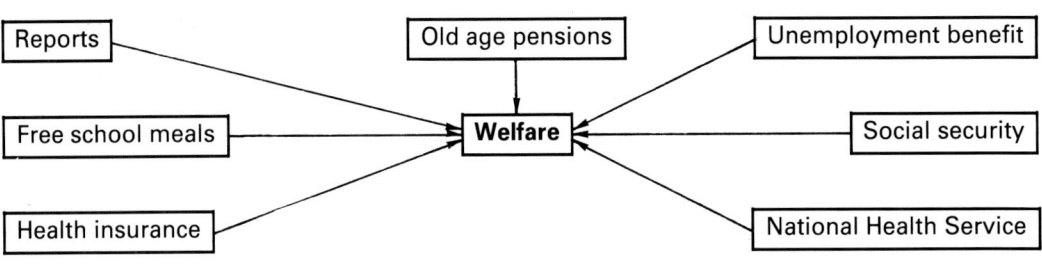

21
Local Study

Your aim in this study is to use the information in the maps below to:

Ch trace the development of part of Birmingham
in the nineteenth century;

Ev think of ways in which you could find out more about life and work in
nineteenth-century Birmingham.

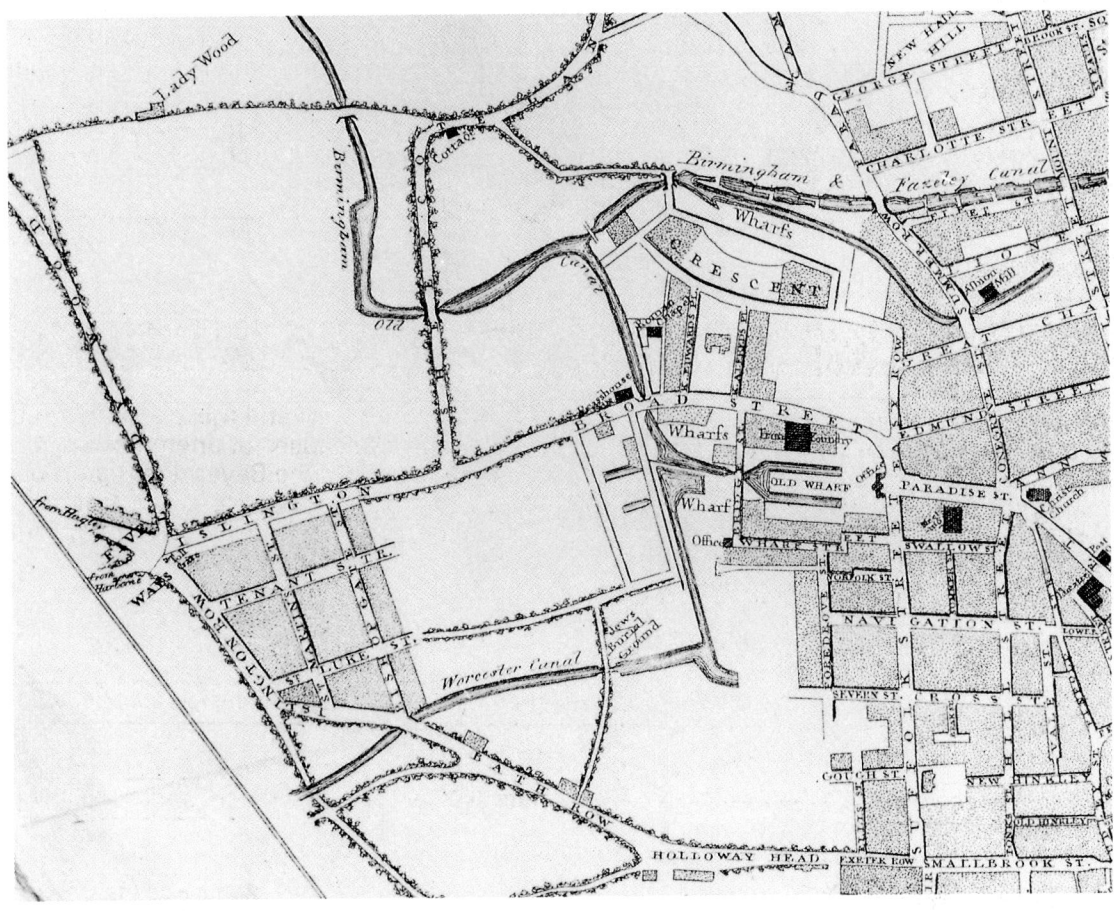

Map 1   1808

Look at Map 1

1 List the industrial buildings that you can see
marked on the map.
2 Why was this a good area in which to set up
industries?
3 Find Birmingham Old Canal and the Worcester
Canal. Do you think the area to the east or to the
west of these canals was the first to be
industrialised? Give reasons for your answer.

257

Map 2   1864

Compare Maps 1 and 2

4 Give three examples of new industries that were set up in the district between 1808 and 1864.

5 What evidence is there to suggest that the population of the district increased between 1808 and 1865?

6 In what ways did the district remain unchanged between 1808 and 1864?

Map 3 1890

Compare Maps 2 and 3

7 How did the system of communications in the area change between 1864 and 1890?
8 Do you think that this was still an important industrial district of Birmingham in 1890? Give reasons for your answer.

Further studies

9 You may find that iron work on nineteenth-century buildings in *your* locality is stamped with the name of a Birmingham manufacturer. How might your local museum help you to find out more about goods made in Birmingham in the nineteenth century?
10 How might books on the following topics help you to find out more about life and work in nineteenth-century Birmingham: costume; architecture; transport and communications; iron and steel?

Field study

Your aim in this study is:

k to find out what your locality was like in the nineteenth century;

Ch to work out what has changed and what has remained the same since that time.

1 General survey

You will need maps of your area:
   as it is today;
   as shown in the 1890 Ordnance Survey;
   as it was in the early nineteenth century.
List five or more ways in which the area **a** changed and **b** remained the same between 1800 and 1890 and between 1890 and the present.

2 Street study

You will need:
   street directories from the late nineteenth and early twentieth centuries;
   any other information you can find about the area you have chosen to study, e.g. old photographs, newspaper advertisements.
Your local library and public record office are the best places to look for these sources. Choose two streets in the area you are studying and list this information about them at two different periods of time:
   names of owners of shops or business premises;
   names of families occupying houses;
   use to which buildings were put, e.g. shops, workshops, houses.
a In what ways did the area change within the period you are studying, e.g. changes in ownership and use of buildings; change of character from industrial to residential?
b In what ways did it remain unchanged, e.g. schools and churches still in use; families remaining in the area; character still the same?

3 Visit to the area

You will need:
   clipboard, drawing paper and pencil.
a With the help of your teacher, identify and sketch two or more nineteenth-century buildings.
b How are the buildings used today?

4 In class

Compare your sketches with pictures in books of architectural drawings and old photographs.
a Has the appearance of the buildings changed? If so, how, e.g. modern replacement windows; new shopfronts?
b What are the buildings used for today, e.g. large terraced houses turned into flats; churches used as social centres?

5 Summing up

What conclusions can you draw about change and continuity in the area in the nineteenth and twentieth centuries?

Index

Page numbers in **bold** refer to illustrations